The German Classics

The German Classics

Paul Heyse
Joseph Victor Von Scheffel
Marie Von Ebner-Eschenbach
Heinrich Seidel

Volume 13

Masterpieces of German Literature
Translated into English

Patrons' Edition
in
Twenty volumes

Ross & Perry Inc.
Washington, D.C.

Copyright 1914, The German Publication Society
Reprinted by Ross & Perry, Inc. 2002
© Ross & Perry, Inc. 2002 on new material. All rights reserved.

Protected under the Berne Convention.

Printed in The United States of America

Ross & Perry, Inc. Publishers
216 G St., N.E.,
Washington, D.C. 20002
Telephone (202) 675-8300
Facsimile (202) 675-8400
info@RossPerry.com

SAN 253-8555

Library of Congress Control Number: 2002102655

http://www.rossperry.com

ISBN 1-931839-65-4

CONTRIBUTORS AND TRANSLATORS

VOLUME XIII

Special Writers

CAMILLO VON KLENZE, Ph.D., Professor of German Literature, Brown University:
The Life of Paul Heyse.

MAX WINKLER, Ph.D., Professor of the German Language and Literature, University of Michigan:
The Life of Joseph Victor von Scheffel.

JOHN PRESTON HOSKINS, Ph.D., Professor of Germanic Languages and Literatures, Princeton University:
The Life of Marie von Ebner-Eschenbach.

ARNOLD WERNER-SPANHOOFD, Ph.D., Head of the Modern Language Department, Washington, D. C., High Schools:
The Life of Heinrich Seidel.

Translators

ARNOLD WERNER-SPANHOOFED, Ph.D., Head of the Modern Language Department, Washington, D. C., High Schools:
Leberecht Hühnchen.

C. L. TOWNSEND, Assistant Professor of German, Trinity College:
The Spell of Rothenburg.

ALFRED REMY, A. M., Professor of Modern Languages, Brooklyn Commercial High School:
Nino and Maso.

JULIA FRANKLIN:
The District Doctor.

EPHRAIM EMERTON, Ph.D.:
Margaretha; Parting; Old Heidelberg.

A. I. DU P. COLEMAN, A.M., Professor of English Literature, College of the City of New York:
Krambambuli; In the Rhaetian Alps.

MARY WILSON:
L'Arrabiata; "Blind."

SOFIE DELFFS:
Ekkehard.

MRS. ANNIS LEE WISTER:
Aphorisms.

CONTENTS OF VOLUME XIII

PAUL HEYSE

JOSEPH VICTOR VON SCHEFFEL

MARIE VON EBNER-ESCHENBACH

HEINRICH SEIDEL

ILLUSTRATIONS — VOLUME XIII

EDITOR'S NOTE

INSTEAD of selections from German painting that might serve as artistic parallels to the authors represented here, this volume brings, for illustration, views of towns and places which in one way or another may be considered typical of the life work of the writers grouped here together. Thus it may be said that Munich and Italy formed the background of Paul Heyse's literary career; that Scheffel was the poet of the picturesque hills and dales between Heidelberg and Lake Constance; that the historic sites and the scenic beauty of the Austrian landscape live in Marie von Ebner-Eschenbach's stories. As for Heinrich Seidel, his humble and contented bourgeois characters are clearly an outgrowth of the life in old fashioned North German towns.

KUNO FRANCKE,

THE LIFE OF PAUL HEYSE

By CAMILLO VON KLENZE, Ph.D.

Professor of German Literature, Brown University

 AUL HEYSE, a conspicuous figure in the literary life of modern Germany, is a master of that peculiar type of narrative art which the Germans call *Novelle,* and which, though it has points in common with the American short-story, differs from it in some essentials. Nothing is farther removed from the truth than the statement, repeatedly made of late years, that the German *Novelle* owes its existence to the example of Poe. Both the *Novelle* and Poe's short-stories, to be sure, differ in principle from the novel (German *Roman*). The latter paints with epic breadth a wealth of detail, both of characterization and of action, which enriches the picture. We need but think of the episodes, sub-plots, disquisitions, descriptions, etc., in *Tom Jones, Vanity Fair, Mill on the Floss, Wilhelm Meister.* The short-story and the *Novelle* pivot the entire plot upon one striking event or scene, eliminating descriptive episodes and details not essential to the central thought. And yet, in spite of this identity of general purpose, there is an important difference between the short-story of the Poe type and the *Novellen* of a Heyse or a C. F. Meyer. Poe was a lyricist. In his *Essay on Hawthorne* (1842), in which Poe the artist subtly reveals himself, we read that to him that form of literary art in which "the highest genius could be most advantageously employed is a rhymed poem, not to exceed in length what might be perused in an hour." Significantly he continues that "next to the lyric

the short prose narrative, requiring from half an hour to one or two hours for its perusal, is most adapted to fulfil the demands of a high genius.'' And these tenets are borne out by his literary productions. To him the ultimate purpose of both the lyric and the short-story was the creation of a unified mood. For this end brevity was an essential, as a break in the reading meant a break in the mood. Because of his genius, Poe exercised a determining influence upon this form of American art, and not only for good. While American writers of short-stories since Poe's time have pursued other objects than the creation of a unified mood, yet his demand for brevity as an essential law has been obeyed almost unanimously. In many cases this has resulted in flimsiness of material and superficiality of treatment, which have led even advocates of the short-story into classifying it as an inferior form of art.

In the German *Novelle*, brevity is a secondary consideration. There are, to be sure, some *Novellen* which both in form and content correspond to Poe's tales, like Tieck's *Love's Lure* and Storm's *A Green Leaf;* but a very important type — and of this Heyse is one of the greatest exponents — has in common with Poe's short-stories only the pivoting of the action on the central point. Such a *Novelle* may, as in the case of C. F. Meyer's *The Saint*, require two hundred pages for the motivation and depiction of the action. In Poe's *The Fall of the House of Usher*, the effect of mysterious gloom would be very much weakened by an interruption. Where Poe aims at the creation of a unified mood, be it '' terror, passion, or horror,'' this type of German *Novelle* depicts a series of actions culminating in a turning-point through which every character of the story is vitally affected. An excellent example is the aforementioned *The Saint*, by C. F. Meyer. Here the various and diversified incidents of the first half of the story are all focused on the pivotal point, the seduction of Becket's daughter by the king, from which moment the lives of all take a different turn.

These German *Novellen* have much in common with the drama, as Poe's short-stories have with the lyric; while the novel (German *Roman*) may be called a prose epic.

As a distinct art-form, the *Novelle* rose for the first time toward the close of the eighteenth century, when Goethe in his *Conversations of German Immigrants* created a modern *Decamerone*, composed of character-sketches, anecdotes, tales, and at least one true *Novelle* (the story of Ferdinand). From this time on, we have a virtually uninterrupted flow of brief narrative fiction which often, as in the case of Kleist and some of the romanticists, is of a very high order. But before Heyse, few, if any, of the writers of fiction had a clear conception of the peculiar character of the *Novelle*. Heyse, who gave to the world a wealth of *Novellen*, the charm of which has been felt by many nations, was the first to work consistently upon a clearly defined principle.

The better to understand the peculiar character of Heyse's work, it will be advisable to glance for a moment at his life. Paul Heyse was born in Berlin in 1833. His father, a professor at the University there, was a philologist of excellent repute. His mother, connected with some of the most distinguished Jewish families of Europe, like the Mendelssohns and the Rothschilds, was a representative of transplanted oriental aristocracy. In his memoirs Heyse speaks of her as passionate and imaginative. This parentage explains, at least in part, the often surprising combination in his art of rich sensuousness and rationalistic restraint. Even in his most impassioned moments he never loses himself in romantic vagaries. On the other hand, he lacks that Promethean quality, that titanic striving after the Infinite, which is the fascinating gift of the gods to the Germanic peoples.

Young Heyse's home-life was peculiarly adapted to foster the artistic instincts of the precocious child. Scholars, artists, and literary men frequented the house and created an intellectual and artistic environment which left an indelible impress upon his temperament. His sympathy with every phase of the fine arts was deepened by an intimacy formed in his youth with the historian of art Kugler, whose daughter he afterward married.

His choice of a profession, Romance Philology, in the pursuit of which he went for a time to Bonn and worked under Dietz, the founder of that science in Germany, was to bear good fruits later. His Provençal studies are reflected in his *Novellen* of Troubadour life; his study of Spanish made him intimately acquainted with Cervantes, whose art enriched his own; and his Italian studies furnished him with the " sesame " into that enchanted land of the " racconteurs " — of Boccaccio, Bandello — and others, who were in large measure to determine the character of his narrative style. His translations of Spanish popular poetry, in collaboration with Geibel, and of the Italian poets Giusti and Leopardi rank his work among those masterly translations like Schlegel's Shakespeare, Gildemeister's Dante, Schack's Firdusi which have naturalized many foreign poets in Germany.

The pursuit of his Romance studies took him early in life to Italy. This was the first of innumerable pilgrimages to the home of Michelangelo, Palladio, Titian, and Raphael, of Leopardi and Giusti, which extended throughout his life and made Italy a veritable home to him. He thus belongs to that large group of literary artists, among whom are Goethe, Stendhal, and the Brownings, to whom Italy was a passion and the source of noblest inspiration. Heyse's Italy is a land of color and of grace, of picturesqueness and of splendid elemental passions — an Italy from which are eliminated all problems arising from the sordid struggles in industrial life, from the vulgar brutality and base lust which inform the admirable tales of the modern Italian " naturalistic " writer Verga.

Even in these early days he attracted the attention of a wide circle in Berlin by publishing lyrics, dramas, and tales in verse and prose, distinguished by a remarkable sense of form and imaginative glow. In consequence, King Max of Bavaria in 1854 called him, at a salary of one thousand five hundred florins a year, to his court at Munich. He was thus, by a kindly turn of fortune, transferred to an environment ideally suited to his temperament. But little more than a generation before, the art-loving King Louis I. had made of Munich — heretofore but an insignificant provincial capital — the home of painters and of sculptors. He had adorned his city with buildings suggestive of Romanesque power, Greek dignity, Italian elegance. It was the ambition of his successor, Max, to supplement this work by associating with his person scholars and literary men of reputation and of promise. In this coterie the most conspicuous figure was the poet Geibel — to whom indeed Heyse owed his call — whose graceful verse had made him for the time the most beloved poet of Germany. Soon after Heyse, Schack came to Munich: versatile historian, scholar, poet, and above all the Maecenas who bequeathed the Schack-gallery to the Bavarian capital. His presence greatly contributed to the intellectual and artistic life of the city. The Munich group consciously upheld the ideal of beauty as the ultimate aim of art in protest against the " realism " immaturely and inartistically practised and defended by the " Young Germans," the literary school that had long held sway. This change from the rationalistic Prussian capital to the milder atmosphere of the South German city, together with the assured salary, at once raised Heyse above the plane of sordid materialistic struggles, and deepened the mellowness of his artistic personality. From now on to the day of his death, April 2nd, 1914, Munich remained his home, even though, with characteristic manliness, he severed his connection with the court (in 1868), when Max's successor, the unfortunate King Louis II., insulted Heyse's friend Geibel.

The astonishing fecundity of imagination which had characterized him since early youth continued during the following decades. The finish, originality, and charm of his work brought him fame throughout all German-speaking countries. This literary success, combined with unusual graciousness of manner, a distinguished personality, and exceptional physical beauty made him for awhile the cynosure of all eyes. Since Goethe, there had not been in Germany such a favorite of the gods. Yet these apparently flawless years were not free from grief and conflict. Tragic family bereavements—to them we owe some of his finest lyrics—darkened his path. And the soul of the artist began to canker in an atmosphere that was steadily growing more hostile to his literary tenets. Realism, vanquished when represented by the "Young Germans," now reappeared with formidable vitality, when championed by such giants as Zola and Ibsen. From 1880 to 1900 it became the fashion to pass Heyse by. Today, a maturer criticism acknowledges the great value of his contribution, and when in 1910 he received the Nobel Prize, public opinion rejoiced in the payment of a just debt. And now the villa in Munich, in which the venerable poet passed the last years of a singularly rich life and to which once flocked distinguished men from all parts of Germany, has again become an object of pride and reverence.

Nor do we feel today that Heyse's depiction of life is antagonistic to realism. Nothing is more foreign to him than the phantastic or the unreal. All his best works deal with problems of actual—in many cases contemporaneous—life. Only, in contradistinction to the "naturalistic" school, he, like his acknowledged master Goethe, pitches his world in a somewhat higher key than that of the actual, by eliminating all mention of the sordid and the squalid. This appears both in his choice of characters and in the setting of the stories. No slums, no filth, no abject poverty ever meet the eye. He never treats of the mob—ugly, filthy, offensive, rebellious. Heyse's world is untouched by industrialism and socialism. The only rabble which he depicts at all—and then with scathing contempt—is the rabble in kid-gloves which, as in his *Incurable,* puts base constructions upon unconventional acts.

In an age which discovered the artistic value of ugliness, Heyse, for better and for worse, remained a priest at the altar of beauty to the end. His staunch fidelity to his ideals proved at once a source of strength and of weakness. Of weakness, because it made him unfair in his judgments of a generation which, through its Flauberts, its Ibsens, its Hauptmanns, its Gjorkis, has vastly enlarged the horizon of art and sharpened the methods of portraying life; of strength, because we are bound to do homage to an artist to whom nature and man remain essentially things of beauty, at a time when for some of us science seems to have shorn life of all loveliness. How keenly Heyse felt the discord between himself and the world is strikingly symbolized in his story, *The Centaur*. Here, the creature of an unrealistic and myth-making age, awakened from the slumber of centuries, suddenly appears in a modern village, is first laughed at, then brutally driven back into the woods by an unintelligent mob.

In examining Heyse's choice of characters, we are at first surprised to find that this aristocrat of the soul and of the intellect feels irresistibly drawn to simple folk — fishermen, peasants, vintagers — until we discover, that of the upper classes also he prefers those with whom impulse rather than reason controls action. One of his most delightful figures, the peasant heroine of *Fenice,* regrets that at a critical moment of her life she followed the wise counselings of reason rather than the call of passion. But passion and instinct with Heyse, however violent, are never offensive, since all his characters, whether nobleman or peasant, move in a plane above the vulgar. Even when, as in *The Unpardonable Word,* the story turns upon an act of moral vulgarity (here on the part of a young gentlewoman), it is but the temporary aberration of an innately refined soul. Hence the difference in principle between the rôle which instinct plays in Heyse's world and in that of Zola.

When force of instinct is coupled with picturesqueness

and physical beauty, it becomes irresistible to him. Consequently his profound sympathy for Renaissance Italy, for the society that could produce a Benvenuto Cellini, whose very crimes were picturesque, and whose brutality contained an element of uplift. Through his Renaissance stories (like *Nino and Maso*) Heyse associates himself with a large number of narrators of the nineteenth century who felt the same attraction: from Tieck with his *Vittoria Accorombona*, Stendhal with his *Chroniques Italiennes*, Halm with his powerful *The House on Verona Bridge*, to C. F. Meyer with his *The Temptation of Pescara*, and Hewlett with his *Little Novels of Italy*.

His vigorous personalities he places in a fascinating environment. Very few, even among contemporary writers, have shown a finer sense for the " soul of cities " or the sorcery of landscape. When we turn the pages of Heyse's volumes, we move in a world of ineffable loveliness or grandeur: the Tyrolese Alps, slumberous Rothenburg, turretted Sienna, Provençal France, the Lake of Garda.

His style is a fit instrument for the transmission of his visions. Its perfect clarity and unimpeded flow have led some of his admirers into calling it " elegant "—which must not, however, be taken to mean " fine writing," but must be understood in Heyse's own definition of the term (in *Kleopatra*) as implying absolute unobtrusiveness. This quality of style is everywhere apparent in his works : lyrics, dramas, novels, and *Novellen* — giving them all a distinctive character. His lyrics, indeed, with their almost Petrarchian finish, seem more closely allied to Romance than to German poetry, of which the peculiar note is naïve simplicity, dewy freshness, and spontaneity. His dramas, too, please rather by the perfection of their form than by dramatic sweep, though some of them, like *Hans Lange,* are fine dramatic portrayals of those simple characters conspicuous for innate nobility with which his *Novellen* have made us familiar. His long novels (*Romane*), of

PAUL HEYSE

which the best known is *Children of the World,* while
charmingly written and abounding in interesting episodes,
are somewhat lacking in epic flow and breadth, are in fact
rather a collection of detached situations.

In all these fields he has been successful, but his lasting importance lies in his *Novellen.* He looms large in
the history of the German *Novelle* which — all unknown to
English criticism — has, through its Kleist, its Storm, its
Heyse, its Keller, its Meyer, its Schnitzler, its Saar, and
others, furnished an important contribution to the world's
literature of the nineteenth century. By his famous definition of the *Novelle* as a short tale " with a silhouette,"
Heyse emphasized the necessity of concentration and elimi-
nation. He further insists upon the extraordinary event
with its turning point from which the hero's life takes a
different course. A careful perusal of Heyse's many
Novellen reveals the perfect consistency with which he
has followed these tenets. The main event with its turning-
point is in every one apparent, and often most originally
worked out. Admirable is the self-restraint and tact with
which an exuberant imagination is controlled. Never do
descriptions of the beauty of nature or of human beings
blur the " silhouette " of the story. The two tales before
us are good illustrations of this artistry. Rothenburg with
its charmed seclusion and the fierce towers of gleaming
Siena are not enlarged upon for their own sake, but serve
merely as appropriate motivation — in the one case for the
young wife's naïve instinctiveness, in the other for the passions, violent but not base, of Renaissance Italians. In other
Novellen he displays the same discreetness, as, for instance,
when he describes the Mountains of Meran in *Incurable,*
or the azure Bay of Naples in *L'Arrabiata,* or the lawless
grandeur of the Appenine in *Fenice,* or the sensuous melancholy of the Roman Campagna in *Villa Falconieri,* or the
sunny beauty of Provençe in his Troubadour stories.

Unerring certainty of touch also determines his use of
monologue, his distribution of direct and indirect speech,

etc., making of every one of his many *Novellen* a finished product, a perfectly consistent reflection of Heyse's conception of the inherent law of this form of fiction.

Because of his extraordinary fertility, Heyse did not succeed, like some sparer writers, such as C. F. Meyer, in producing only masterpieces. Of the large bulk of his *Novellen* some twenty will continue to charm readers capable of appreciating fine narrative art. Among them might be mentioned *L'Arrabiata, The Unpardonable Word, Fenice, Cousin Gabriel, The Prodigal Son, The Broiderer of Treviso, Incurable,* as especially happy products of his genius.

The nineteenth century is apt to be one-sidedly judged as the age merely of science and practical invention, of industrialism and commercialism penetrating all phases of life, as the age of Darwin and of Helmholtz, of Morse, Marconi, and Siemens, of Röntgen and Pasteur, of Rockefeller and Ballin. Let us not forget that it was also the age of Ruskin, and Morris, and Walter Pater; of the Parnassiens in France; of Goethe in his old age protesting against the inroads of industrialism, of Jacob Burckhardt, the master-interpreter of the Renaissance spirit, of Böcklin, the painter of tranced visions. In these ranks fights Heyse, the disciple of Goethe, sworn enemy of vulgarity and ugliness.

PAUL HEYSE

" BLIND "* (1852)

TRANSLATED BY MARY WILSON

CHAPTER I

T a window which opened over a little flower-
garden stood the blind daughter of the village
sexton, and sought revival from the wind as
it blew over her hot face. The delicate, half-
grown figure shook, and the small, cold hands
lay clasped upon the window-sill. The sun had already set
and Indian jassamines began to spread their odors.

Farther back in the room sat a blind boy, on a stool before
the old spinet, playing restless melodies. He might be about
fifteen; scarcely a year older than the girl. No one who
saw and heard him, as he lifted up his large open eyes, or
bent his head toward the window, could have guessed him
to be so afflicted — there was so much security, nay, vehe-
mence, in his movements.

He broke off suddenly, in the midst of a sacred song that
had been running wild beneath his fingers.

" Did you sigh, Marlene? " he asked, without turning his
head.

" Not I, Clement; what should I sigh for? I only started
when the wind burst in so suddenly."

" But sigh you did! Do you think I do not hear you when
I play? When you shiver, I feel it even here."

" Yes, it is cold now."

* Permission Bernhard Tauchnitz, Leipzig.

"You don't deceive me! If you were cold, you would not be standing there at the window. And I know what makes you sigh and tremble; you are afraid because the doctor is to come tomorrow and pierce our eyes with needles. Yet he told us how quickly it is done, and that it is only like the sting of a gnat. You used to be so brave and patient. When I was little, and used to cry when I was hurt, were not you always held up as a pattern to me by my mother, though you are only a girl? And now you cannot find your courage, and do not in the least think of all the joy that is to come after."

She shook her head. "Can you believe me to be afraid of so short a pain? And yet I am oppressed by foolish childish fancies, from which I cannot see my way. From that day when the strange doctor for whom the baron sent, came down from the castle house to see your father, and your mother called us in to him from the garden — from that hour there has been a weight upon me which will not go. You were so glad, you took no notice; but when your father knelt down, and began to return thanks to God for this great mercy, my heart was dumb within me, and I could not join. I tried to find a reason for being thankful, but I could feel none."

She said this very quietly, and her voice was steady. He struck a few gentle chords. Between the hoarse jarring tones peculiar to such old instruments, sounded the distant song of returning field laborers — contrasting, as did that life, in its plenitude of light and power, with the dream-life of these two blind children.

The boy appeared to feel it; he rose hastily, and went to the window with unerring step — for he knew that room and everything it contained — and, tossing back his fine fair curls, he said:

"You are strange, Marlene; our fathers and mothers and all the village wish us luck, and should it not be joy? — before they promised this, I did not mind. We are blind, they say; I never knew what it was we wanted. When visitors used to come and see my mother, and we heard them pity us, and say: 'Ah, those poor children!' I used to get so angry. What right have they to pity us? I thought. Still, I always knew that we are not like other people. They often spoke of things I did not understand, but yet which must be lovely; now that we are to know these too, curiosity has taken hold of me, and will not let me rest night or day.''

'' I was quite content before,'' said Marlene, sadly. '' I was happy, and could have been happy all my life—now it will be different. Do you never hear people complain of care and trouble? and what did we know of care?''

'' That was because we did not know the world; and I want to know it, at whatever risk. I, too, have been contented to grope about with you, and to be left in idleness— but not forever. I will have no advantage over those who have to work. Sometimes, when my father used to teach us history, and tell us of all the heroes and their doings, I would ask him if any of these men were blind also? But every man who had done anything to speak of could see. The like thoughts would keep tormenting me for days. Then, when I was at my music, or was allowed to play the organ in your father's place, I would forget my grievances. Again, I often thought, 'Am I eternally to play this organ, and walk these few hundred steps about this village here forever? and beyond this village never to be heard of by one living soul, or spoken of when I am dead?' You see, since that doctor has been up there at the castle, I have had a hope of growing up to be a man like other men—and to be able to go out into the wide world, and go where I please, and have nobody to mind.''

'' Not even me, Clement?''

She spoke without complaint or reproach, but the boy broke out passionately:

'' How can you talk such stuff, which you know I can't abide? Do you think I would go away and leave you all alone, or steal from home in secret? Do you think I could do that?''

"I know how it is. When the village-lads begin their wanderings, or go away to town, nobody ever may go with them, not even their own sisters; and here, while they are children still, the boys run away to the forest with their like and tease the girls whenever they come near them. Till now they let you stay with me, and we learned and played together; you were blind, as I was — what should you have done with other boys? But when you see, and wish to stay with me, they will mock you, and hoot after you, as they do to all who do not hold to them; and then you will go away, for ever so long a time, perhaps — and I — how shall I ever learn to do without you?"

The last words were spoken with an effort, and then her terrors overcame her, and she sobbed aloud.

Clement drew her toward him, and stroked her cheeks, and said with earnest tenderness: "You must not cry; I am not going to leave you — never — rather remain blind and forget the rest. I will not leave you if it makes you cry so. Come now, be calm; do be happy! — you must not heat yourself, the doctor said; it is not good for the eyes, dear darling Marlene!"

He took her in his arms, and clasped her close, and kissed her cheek — a thing he had never done before. Just then he heard his mother calling to him from the vicarage close by; and leading the still weeping girl to a rocking chair by the wall, and seating her upon it, he hurried out.

Shortly after, a venerable pair might be seen walking down the hill, from the castle toward the village. The vicar, a tall and stately form, with all the power and majesty of an apostle; and the sexton, a simple slight-built man, with humble gait and hair already white. Both had been invited to pass the afternoon with the lord of the manor and the doctor, whom he had sent for from the adjacent town, for the purpose of examining the children's eyes and attempting an operation. The doctor had repeatedly assured the two delighted fathers that he had every reasonable hope of a perfect cure; and he had requested them to hold themselves in readiness for the morrow.

It was the mother's business to prepare what was needful in the vicarage. The children were not to be parted on the day appointed to restore to both the light, of which, together, they had been so long deprived.

When the two fathers reached their homes (they were opposite neighbors), the vicar gave his old friend's hand a squeeze, and said, with glistening eyes: "God be with us and them!"—and then they parted. The sexton went into his house, where all was quiet, for the servant-girl was in the garden. He went into his room, rejoicing in the stillness that made him feel alone with his God. But when he crossed the threshold he was startled by his child. She had risen from her chair, holding her handkerchief to her eyes, her bosom heaving, as if in spasms, her cheeks and lips dead white. He sought to comfort her; begging her to be composed, and anxiously inquiring what had happened. Tears were her only answer—tears which, even to herself, she could not have explained.

CHAPTER II

THE children had been laid in two small rooms with a northern aspect, in the upper story of the vicarage. In default of shutters, the windows had been carefully hung with shawls, making soft twilight of the brightest noonday. The vicar's quiet extensive orchard, while it gave the walls abundant shade, kept off the din of village life beyond.

The doctor had enjoined extreme precaution, for the girl especially. As far as depended upon himself, the operation had proved successful. In solitude and silence, Nature must be left to do the rest. The young girl's temperament was so excitable as to require the utmost care, and most attentive watching.

At the decisive hour Marlene had not flinched; and when her mother had burst into tears on first hearing the doctor's step on the threshold, she had gone up to her to comfort her.

The doctor began the operation with the boy. Though

somewhat agitated, he had seated himself bravely, and borne it well. At first he would not suffer himself to be held during the operation, and only yielded to Marlene's entreaties. When, for a second, the doctor removed his hand from his unveiled eyes, he had raised a cry of surprise and delight.

Marlene started; then she too proceeded to undergo the short ordeal without a murmur. Tears gushed from her eyes, and she shook from head to foot, hastily tying on the bandage. The doctor helped them to carry her into the adjoining room, for her knees knocked together, and she could hardly stand. There, stretched on her little couch, she had a long alternation of sleep and faintness; while the boy declared himself to be quite well, and only his father's serious orders induced him to go to bed. To go to sleep was not so easy. Confused visions of forms and colors — colors for the first time — flitted across his brain; mysterious forms that had as yet been nothing to him, and were now to be so much, if those were right who wished him happiness. He asked a thousand questions while his father and mother sat by his bedside — riddles not yet expounded by the deepest science. For what can science tell us, after all, of the hidden springs of life? His father entreated him to be patient; with God's help, ere long, he would be able to resolve these doubts himself; at present, quiet was the one thing needful — especially to Marlene, whom he must not wake by talking. This silenced him, and listening at the wall, he whispered a petition that the door between them might be left ajar, in order that he might hear whether she slept or if she was in pain. When his mother had done his bidding, he lay quite still, and listened to the breathing of his little sleeping friend; and the quiet rhythm as it rose and fell, sang him like a lullaby to sleep.

Thus they lay for hours. The village was much more still than usual. Those who had to pass the vicarage with carts, took every possible precaution against noise. Even the village-children, warned, most likely, by their teachers, in place of running riot on coming out of school as usual, went quietly by in couples to their remotest playgrounds, whispering as they passed, and looking up at the house with wistful eyes. The birds alone among the branches did not hush their song. But when did a bird's voice ever vex or weary child of man, be he ever so sorely in need of rest?

Only by the bells of the homebound flocks were the children at last awakened. The boy's first question was for Marlene, and whether she had been asking for him? He called to her in a suppressed tone, and asked her how she felt? That heavy sleep has not restored her, and her eyes are burning under the slight handkerchief that binds them. But she does violence to her sensations, and forces herself to answer that she feels much better, and to talk cheerfully to Clement, who now gives utterance to all the wildest speculations of his fancy.

Late, when the moon stands high above the woods, a shy small childish hand is heard to knock at the vicarage door. The little village-girls have brought a garland for Marlene; woven from their choicest garden-flowers, and a bunch of them for Clement. When they are brought, the boy's whole countenance lightens up. The perfume and the cooling dew refresh him. "Give them my kindest thanks," he begs; "they are such kind good girls! I am not well yet, but when I have my sight I shall always be on their side and help them against the boys." When the wreath was brought to Marlene, she pushed it gently from her with her small pale hands. "I cannot have it here," she said; "it makes me faint, dear mother, to have these flowers so near — give these to Clement too."

Again she sank into a sort of feverish slumber; only the healing approach of day brought something like repose. And the doctor, who came in the morning very early, was able to pronounce her out of danger, which indeed was more than he had hoped for. He sat long by the boy's bedside, listening to his strange questions with a smile, benevolently admonishing him to patience; and, filled with the most sanguine hopes, he left them.

But to be admonished to quiet and patience after one has had a glimpse of the promised land! In each interval of his duties, his father had to go upstairs to that little room and talk. And the door was left ajar, so that Marlene too might hear these charming stories. Legends of godly men and women, to whom the Lord had sent most heavy trials, and then withdrawn them. The story of poor Henry, and of that pious little maiden who would have sacrificed herself in her humility; and how God had guided all to the most blissful consummation; and as many of such edifying histories as the worthy pastor could find to unfold.

And when on the good man's lips, story would unconsciously turn to prayer; or his wife would raise her clear voice in a hymn of thanksgiving, Clement would fold his hands and join — but he would so soon break in with fresh inquiries, as to prove his mind to have been far more present with the story than with the song.

Marlene asked no questions; she was kind and cheerful to every one, and no one guessed the thoughts and questions that were working in her mind.

They recovered visibly from day to day; and on the fourth, the doctor allowed them to get up. He himself supported the young girl, as, all weak and trembling, she crept toward the door, where the boy stood joyously holding out a searching hand for hers, and then holding hers fast, he bid her lean on him, which she did in her usual confiding way.

They paced up and down — he with the perceptions of locality peculiar to the blind, guiding her carefully past the chairs and cupboards that stood against the walls. "How do you feel now?" he asked her. "Well;" she answered again — and always.

"Come," he said; "lean heavier on me; you are so weak. It would do you good to breathe the air, and the scent of the flowery meadows; it is so close and heavy here. Only the doctor says it might be dangerous; our eyes might get sore again, and even blind, if we were to see the light too soon. Ah! now I know the difference between light and darkness! No sound in music is so sweet as that feeling of space about the eyes. It did hurt me rather, I must confess; yet I could have gazed forever at those bright colors — the pain was so beautiful (you will soon feel it also). But it will be many a long day before we are allowed to enjoy that pleasure. At first, I know I shall do nothing but look all day long. One thing I should like to know, Marlene; they tell us each thing has its color — now what is the color of your face and mine? I should so like to know — bright or dark? Would not it be disagreeable if they should not be bright and fair? I wonder whether I shall recognize you with my eyes? Now when I only feel with the tip of this little finger, I could distinguish you from every other human being in the world.

"But then! — ah! then we shall have to begin again. We must learn to know each other by sight. Now, I know that your cheeks and hair are soft to touch — will they be soft to look at? I do so long to know, and have so long to wait!"

In this way he would run on, talking unceasingly. How silently she walked by his side, he never noticed. Many of his words sank deep into her heart. It had never yet occurred to her that she should see herself as others saw her — she could hardly fancy that could be. She had heard of mirrors, but she never had been able to understand them. She now imagined that when a seeing person's eyes are opened, his own image must stand before him.

Now as she lay in bed, her mother believing her to be asleep, the words recurred to her again: "It would be awful if we should find our faces dark!" She had heard of ugliness and beauty; she knew that ugly people were generally much pitied, and often less loved. "If I should be ugly," she said to herself, "and he were to care less for me! He used to play with my hair and call it silk — he will never do that now if he finds me ugly. And he? — if *he* should happen to be ugly, I never would let him feel it—never! I should love him just the same. Yet, no; *he* cannot be ugly — not he. I know he is not.'' Thus she brooded long, lost in care and curiosity. The weather was hot and close. From the garden the nightingale was heard complaining, while fitful gusts of west wind came rattling at the window-panes. She was all alone in her room. Her mother, who till now had slept beside her, had had her bed removed, to lessen the heat within that narrow space. It was unnecessary to watch her now, they thought, as all feverish symptoms were supposed to have disappeared. This night, however, they did return again, and kept her tossing restlessly until long after midnight. Then sleep, though sleep dull and broken, had taken pity on her, and come to close her weary eyelids.

Meanwhile the storm that had been encircling the horizon half the night, threatening and growling, had arisen with might, gathered itself just above the wood, and paused — even the wind had ceased. Now a heavy crash of thunder breaks over the young girl's slumbers. She starts up, half dreaming still — what it is she feels or wants, she hardly knows; impelled by some vague terror, she rises to her feet. Her pillows seem to burn her. Standing by her bed, she listens to the pattering rain without; but it does not cool her fevered brow. She tries to collect her thoughts — to remember what had passed. She can recall nothing but those melancholy fancies with which she had fallen asleep. A strange resolution forms and ripens in her mind. She will go to Clement; he too is alone — what is to prevent her resolving all her doubts at once, by one look at him and at herself? Possessed by this idea, the doctor's injunctions are all forgotten. Just as she had left her couch, with groping, trembling hands, she finds the door which stands half open; feeling for the bed, she steals on tiptoe to the sleeper's side; holding her breath, bending forward where he lies, she tears the bandage from her eyes.

But how terrified she is to find that all is as dark as ever.

She had forgotten that it was night, and that she had been told night makes all men blind. She had believed it was the light streaming from a seeing eye that lighted up itself and other objects round it. She can distinguish nothing, although she feels the boy's soft breath upon her eyelids. In distress, almost in despair, she is about to leave the room, when a sudden flash of lightning flames through the now less carefully darkened panes; a second, and then a third — the whole atmosphere seems to surge with lurid light. Thunder and rain increase their roar. But she stands motionless, her rapt gaze fastened on the curly head before her, resting so peacefully upon its pillows. Then the picture begins to fade — the water gushes from her eyes; seized with unutterable terror, she takes refuge in her room, and hastily replacing the bandage, she throws herself upon her bed. She knows — she feels irrevocably — her eyes have looked and seen for the first time — and for the last!

Chapter III

Weeks have passed — the young powers of these eyes are to be tried for the first time by the light of day. The doctor, who, from the adjacent town where he lived, had hitherto directed the children's simple treatment, had come over on a clouded day to be present, and with his patients to enjoy the first fruits of his skill.

Green wreaths in lieu of curtains had been hung about the windows, and both rooms festively adorned with flowers and foliage. The baron himself, and from the village the nearer friends of both the families, had assembled to wish parents and children joy, and to rejoice in the happy wonder of the cure.

When Clement, scarlet with delight, was placed before Marlene, and took her hand, in shy terror she had half hidden herself in a corner behind some foliage. He had begged to be allowed to see her first — both bandages had been loosened at the same moment. A cry of speechless rapture had sounded from the boy's lips; he remained rigid on the same spot, a beatified smile upon his lips, turning his flashing eyes on every side. He has forgotten that Marlene was to be placed before him; he had yet to learn what the human form is like, and she did nothing to recall it to him. She stood motionless. Only her long lashes quivered over her large clear brown passive eyes. No suspicions were awakened yet. " Those unknown wonders of sight are strange to her," they said. But when the boy broke out into this sudden rapture, and they said to him, " This is Marlene," and in his old way he had felt for her cheek with his hand, and stroked it, saying, " Your face is bright;" then her tears gushed out. She hastily shook her head and said, almost inaudibly — " It is all dark; it is just as it always was! "

The horror of that first moment who shall describe? The agitated doctor drew her toward the window and proceeded to examine her eyes; the pupils were not to be distinguished from seeing ones, save by their lifeless melancholy fixedness. " The nerve is dead! " he said; " some sudden shock, through a sudden, vivid light must have destroyed it." The sexton's wife turned white and fell fainting in her husband's arms. Clement could hardly gather what was passing — his mind was filled with the new life given him. But Marlene lay bathed in tears and returned no answer to the doctor's questions. Nothing was ever learned from her; she could not tell how it had happened, she said; she begged to be forgiven for her childish weeping. She could bear all that was appointed for her, for had she not always been in the same situation.

Clement was beside himself when the extent of her misfortune was made known to him. " You shall see too! " he cried, running to her; I do not care to see if you do not! It cannot be so hopeless yet. Ah, now I know what it is you lose! Seeing would be nothing; it is that everybody else has eyes, that look so kindly on us — and so shall you see them look on you! Only have patience and do

THE MARIENPLATZ, MUNICH

not cry!'' And then he turned to the doctor and with tears implored him to cure Marlene. Large tears stood in the good doctor's eyes; he could scarcely so far compose himself as to bid the boy first be careful of himself; meanwhile he would see what could be done; he was forced to leave him a ray of hope to spare him dangerous agitation.

From the disconsolate parents, however, he did not withhold the truth.

The boy's grief had been some comfort to Marlene. As she was sitting by the window, in a low voice she called him to her: '' You must not be so grieved,'' she said; '' it is the will of God. Rejoice, as I rejoice, that you are cured. You know I never cared so much; I could have been contented as it was. If only father and mother would not mind!—but they will get used to it again and so will you. If you will only love me just as well now that I am to remain as I was, we may still be very happy.''

But he was not so easily to be comforted, and the doctor had to insist on their being parted. Clement was taken into the larger room, where the villagers came pressing round him, shaking hands with him by turns, with cordial words and wishes. The crowd half stunned him, and he only kept repeating: '' Marlene is still blind; she will never see! have you heard?'' he would say, and burst into tears afresh.

It was high time to tie the bandage on again, and lead him to a cool, quiet room—there he lay exhausted with joy and grief and weeping. His father came to him and spoke tenderly and piously; which did not much avail him. He cried even in his sleep and appeared to be disturbed by distressing dreams.

On the following day, however, wonder, joy, and curiosity asserted their rights again; sorrow for Marlene only appeared to touch him nearly when he had her before his eyes. The first thing in the morning he had been to see her, and with affectionate anxiety to inquire whether she felt no change—no more hopeful symptom? Then he became absorbed in the variegated world that was expanding before his eyes. When he returned to Marlene, it was only to describe some new wonder to her, although sometimes, in his fullest flow of narrative, he would stop suddenly, reminded by a look at the poor little friend beside him, how painful to her his joy must be. But in reality, she did not find it painful. For herself she wanted nothing — listening to the enthusiasm of his delight was joy enough for her. Only when by-and-by he came more rarely, believing to afflict her by his visits, or remained silent, because all he could have said appeared as nothing to what he did not dare to say — only then she began to feel uneasy. Hitherto, by day, she had hardly ever been without him, but now she often sat alone. Her mother would come to keep her company; but her mother, once so lively, in losing her dearest hope, had also lost her cheerfulness.

She could find nothing to say to her child save words of comfort, which her own sighs belied, and which therefore could not reach her heart. How much of what the young girl now was suffering had she not foreseen with terror! And yet the feeling of what she had lost came upon her with pangs of unknown bitterness.

She would now again sit spinning in her father's garden, and when Clement came, these poor blind eyes of hers would light up strangely. He was always kind, and would sit beside her, stroking her hair and cheek as he had done of old. Once she entreated him not to be so silent — she felt no touch of envy when he told her what the world was like, and what it daily taught him; but when he left her to herself, she felt so lonely! Never, by word or look, did she remind him of that evening when he had promised he would never leave her — such hopes as these she had long resigned. And since he had nothing to conceal from her, he appeared to love her twice as well.

In the fulness of his heart, he would sit for hours telling her of the sun and moon and stars; of all the trees and flowers; and especially how their parents looked and they themselves. To her very heart's core she felt a thrill of joy

when he innocently told her that she was fairer far than all
the village maidens; he described her as tall and slender,
with delicately-chiseled features and dark eyebrows. He
had also seen himself, he said, in the glass; but he was not
nearly so good-looking, but he needs no beauty and it is
indifferent to him how he looks if he but become a smart
fellow. Men in general were not, by a great deal, so handsome as women. All this was more than she could quite
comprehend; only so much she did: her own looks pleased
him, and more than this her heart did not desire.

They did not again return to this topic; but on the
beauties of nature he was perfectly inexhaustible. When
he was gone she would recall his words and feel a kind of
jealousy of a world that robbed her of him. In secret this
hostile feeling grew and strengthened — growing stronger
even than the pleasure she had felt in his happiness. Above
all, she began to hate the sun; for the sun, he told her, was
brighter than all created things besides. In her dim conceptions, brightness and beauty were the same; and never
did she feel so disheartened as when, toward evening, he
sat beside her, intoxicated with delight, watching the
sun go down. Of herself he had never spoken in such
words — and did this sight so cause him to forget her that
he did not even see the tears that started to her eyes — tears
of vexation, and of a curious kind of jealous grievance?

Her heart grew heavier still, when, with the doctor's
sanction, the vicar began the education of his son. Before
his eyes had been couched, the greater part of his day had
been spent in practising his music. Bible teaching, something of history and mathematics, and a trifle of Latin was
all that formerly had been considered needful and possible.
In all those lessons, not extending beyond the most conventional acquirements, Marlene had taken a part.

Now that the boy manifested a very decided taste for
natural history, his time was filled up in earnest; preparing
him for one of the higher classes of a school in the neighboring town. With a firm unwearying will, and his natural

disposition aiding, he labored through all that had been omitted in his education, and soon attained the level of his years. For many an hour together he would sit in the sexton's garden with his book; but there was now no question of their former chat. Marlene felt her twofold loss — her lessons and her friend.

Chapter IV

THE autumn came and with it a few days' pause in the lad's studies. The vicar resolved to take his son, before the winter, on an excursion among the mountains; to show him the hills and dales and give him a deeper insight into a world that already had seemed so fair, even upon the meagre plains around their village.

When the boy first heard of it he said: "Marlene, I suppose, will go with us?" They attempted to dissuade him, but he refused to go without her. "What if she cannot see?" he said; "the mountain-air is strengthening, and she has been so pale and weak, and she falls into such gloomy moods when I am away."

They did his bidding therefore; the young girl was lifted into the carriage beside Clement and his parents, and one short day's journey brought them to the foot of the mountain-chain. Here commenced their wanderings on foot. Patiently the boy conducted his little friend, now more reserved than ever. He often felt a wish to climb some solitary peak that promised a fresh expanse of view, but he insisted upon supporting her himself and would not give up the charge, often as his parents would have relieved him of it.

Only when they had reached a height, or were resting in some shady spot, would he leave the young girl's side; seeking his own path among the most perilous rocks, he would go collecting stones or plants not to be found below. Then when he returned to the resting party he had always something to bring Marlene — some berries, a sweet-scented flower, or some soft bird's-nest blown from the trees by the wind.

She would accept them with gentle thanks; she appeared to be more contented than at home, and she really was so, for all day long she breathed the same air with him. But, her foolish jealousies went with her. She felt angry at the mountains, whose autumn glory, as she believed, endeared the world still more to him and estranged him more from her.

At last the vicar's wife was struck by her strange ways. She would occasionally consult her husband about the child, who was as dear to both as if she had been their own. Her obstinate dejection was attributed by both to the disappointment of her hopes of sight; and yet the young girl felt no pain in losing that which had only been promised to her, or depicted to her fancy — it was all in the loss of what she had already known; of what had been her own.

On the second evening of their journey they halted at a solitary inn, celebrated from its situation close to a waterfall. Their wanderings had been long and the women were very weary. As soon as they reached the house, the vicar took in his wife before going on farther to the cleft, from whence they already heard the roaring of the water. Marlene was also quite exhausted, yet she would persist in following Clement, who felt no want of rest. They climbed the remaining steps, and louder and nearer sounded the tumult of the waters. Midway up the narrow path Marlene's remaining strength gave way. "Let me sit down here," she said, "while you go on, and fetch me when you have looked long enough." He offered to lead her home before going farther, but she was already seated, so he left her and went on, following the sound; touched at once and charmed with the solitude and majesty of the spot.

Seated upon a stone, the young girl began to long for his return. "He will never come!" she thought. A chill crept over her and the dull distant thunder of the falls gave her a shudder.

" Why does he not come? " she said; " he will have forgotten me in his delight, as he always does. If I could only
find the way back to the house that I might get warm
again! " And so she sat uneasy and listened to every distant sound. Now she thought she heard him calling to her;
trembling, she rose — what was she to do? Involuntarily
she tried a step, but her foot slipped and she staggered and
fell. Fortunately the stones on the path were all overgrown
with moss. Still the fall terrified her, and losing all self-
command, she screamed for help; but her voice was unable
to reach across the chasm to Clement, who was standing
on the edge, in the very midst of the uproar, and the house
was too far off. A sharp pain cut to her heart, as she lay
among the stones, helpless and deserted. Tears of desperation started to her eyes as she rose with difficulty. What
she most dearly loved seemed hateful to her now — her
heart was too full of bitterness even to feel that an all-seeing
God was nigh. Thus Clement found her; when for her sake
he had torn himself with an effort from the spell of so
magnificent a scene.

" I am coming! " he called to her from a distance. " It
is lucky that you did not come with us — the place was so
narrow, one false step would have been enough to kill you.
The water falls so far, deep down, and roars and rushes,
and rises again in clouds of spray, it makes one giddy.
Only feel how it has powdered me with fine, watery vapor.
But how is this? You are cold as ice, and your lips are
trembling. Come, it was very wrong of me to leave you
sitting out so late in the cold! God forbid that it should
make you ill! "

She suffered herself to be led back in perverse silence.
The vicar's wife was much alarmed at seeing the child's
sweet countenance so distorted and disturbed. They prepared some warm drink for her in haste, and made her go
to bed without being able to learn more than that she felt
unwell.

And in truth she did feel ill — so ill that she wished to

die. Life that had already proved itself so adverse had also become odious to her. She lay there, giving full vent to her impious rancorous thoughts, wilfully destroying the last links that bound her to her fellow-creatures. "I will go up there tomorrow," she said to herself, in her dark brooding. "He himself shall take me to the spot where one false step may kill me. My death will not kill him. Why should he have to bear my burden longer?—he has only borne it out of pity."

This guilty thought wound itself closer and closer round her heart. What had become of her natural disposition, so tender and transparent, during those last few months of inward struggle? She even dwelt without remorse on the consequences of her crime. "They will get used to it, as they have got used to my being blind; he will not always have the picture of my misery before his eyes, to spoil his pleasure in this beautiful world of his!" This last reflection invariably came to strengthen her resolves when a doubt would arise to combat them.

The vicar and his wife were in the adjoining room, separated from hers by a thin partition. Clement still lingered out of doors, under the trees; he could not part from the stars and mountains, or shut out the distant music of the waters.

"It distresses me to see how Marlene pines and falls away," said the vicar's wife. "If the slightest causes agitate her so, she will be soon worn out. If you would only talk to her and tell her not to make herself so miserable about a misfortune that cannot be repaired."

"I am afraid it would be useless," returned the vicar. "If her education, her father's and mother's tenderness, and her daily intercourse with ourselves, have not spoken to her heart, no human words can do so. If she had learned to submit herself to the will of God, she would bear a dispensation that has left her so much to be thankful for with gratitude, and not with murmurings."

"But He has taken much away from her!"

"He has, but not all — not for ever, at least. That is my hope, my prayer. Now she seems to have lost the faculty of loving; of holding all things as nothing, compared to the love of God and of His creatures. And this faculty only returns to us when we return to God. As she now is, she does not wish to return to Him — her grievances and her discontent are still too dear to her; but the tone of her mind is too healthy to harbor these sad companions long. Sometime, when her heart is feeling most forlorn, God will take possession of it again, and love and charity will resume their former places, and then there will be light within her, even though it be dark before her eyes."

"God grant it! yet the thought of her future life distresses me."

"She is not lost yet if she does nothing to lose herself. And even if all those who now love and cherish her should be taken from her, charity never dies. And if she take heed to the guiding of the Lord and the ways it pleaseth Him to lead her, she may yet learn to bless the blindness that from her infancy has separated her from the shadow and given her the reality and truth."

Clement interrupted their discourse. "You cannot think how lovely it is tonight!" he cried from the threshold where he stood. "I would gladly give one eye if I could give it to Marlene, that she might see the splendor of the stars. I hope the noise of the waterfall may not prevent her sleeping. I can never forgive myself for having left her to sit out there in the cold."

"Dear boy, speak lower," said his mother; "she is asleep close by. The best thing you can do, I think, would be to go to sleep yourself." And the boy whispered his goodnight.

When his mother went to Marlene's room, she found her quiet and apparently asleep — that troubled look had given place to an expression of peace and gentleness.

The tempest was overpast, and had destroyed no vital part. Even remorse and shame were hardly felt. So absolute was the victory of that joyful peace that had been preached in the room beside her. Slowly, and by side-paths, does the principle of evil steal over us and assume its sway — good asserts its victory at once.

CHAPTER V

NEXT morning her friends noticed with astonishment the change that had come over her. The vicar's wife could only explain it by supposing Marlene to have overheard their conversation of the night before. " So much the better," said the vicar. " If she has heard it, I have nothing more to say."

After this, the young girl's gentle tenderness toward Clement and his parents was touching to behold. She only wished to be considered as belonging to them. Any proof of their affection she received with glad surprise; as more than she expected or deserved. She did not talk much, but what she said was gay and animated. In her whole manner there was a softness, an abnegation of herself, that seemed meant for a mute apology. In their wanderings she again took Clement's arm, but she often begged to be allowed to sit down and rest. Not that she was tired; she only wished to give the boy his freedom to climb about whenever he saw anything to tempt him. And when he came back to tell her what he had seen, she would welcome him with a smile. Her jealousy was gone, now that she desired nothing for herself but the pleasure of seeing him pleased.

Thus strengthened and raised to better feelings, she came to the end of her excursion — and the strengthening had come when it was needed. She found her mother laid low by a dangerous disease, which carried off the delicate woman in a couple of days. And after the first few weeks of mourning, she found that her sadly altered life exacted duties of her for which before she hardly would have been fitted. The household occupied her late and early. She found her way, in spite of her infirmity, into every nook

and corner of their small home; and though there were
many things she was unable to do herself, she showed both
cleverness and foresight in her arrangements and in her
watchful care that her afflicted father should want for
nothing.

She soon acquired a remarkable degree of firmness and
quiet dignity. Where formerly repeated admonitions had
been necessary, she ruled the men and maids with a gentle
word. And if ever any serious instance did occur, of neglect or real ill-will, one earnest look of those large blind
eyes would melt the coarsest nature.

Since she had understood that she had to be cheerful for
her father's sake — that the molding of their daily life was
entirely in her hands, she had much less time to feel the
pain of Clement's absence; and when he was sent to school
in town, she was able to bid him a more composed farewell
than any of the others. For some weeks, it is true, she
went about the house as though she were in a dream — as
though she had been severed from her happier self. But
she soon grew gay again, jesting with her father to win him
to a laugh, and singing to herself her favorite songs. When
the vicar's wife would come with letters, and read the news
and messages from Clement, her heart would beat quick
in secret; and that night, perhaps, she would lay awake for a
longer time than usual; but in the morning she would rise
serene as ever.

When Clement came home for the holidays his first steps
were to the sexton's house — and his step Marlene knew —
ever so far off. She stood still and listened whether it was
for her he asked, then with her slim hands she hastily
smoothed back her hair that still hung in its heavy plaits
upon her slender neck, then rose and left her work, and by
the time he had crossed the threshold there was not a trace
of agitation on her features. Gaily she offered him her
hand, and begged him to come in and sit down beside her and
tell her what he had been doing. There he would often forget the hours and his mother would come after him, for she

began to grudge any of his time she lost. He very rarely stayed all his holidays in the village; he would go rambling about the mountains, absorbed by his growing love of nature and of its history.

And so the years rolled on in monotonous rotation. The old were fading gradually and the young growing fast in bloom and strength.

Once when Clement came home at Easter and saw Marlene as, rising from her spinning-wheel, she came to meet him, he was struck with the progress of her loveliness since autumn. " You are quite a grown-up young lady now," he said; " and I too have done with boyhood — only feel my beard, how it has grown over my winter studies. She blushed a little as he took her hand and passed it across his chin to make her feel the down upon it. And he had more to talk of than he used to have. The master with whom he boarded had daughters, and these daughters had young lady friends. She made him describe them to her to the least details. " I don't care for those girls," he said; " they are so silly and vain, and talk so much. There is only one, Cecilia, whom I don't dislike, because she does not chatter and make those faces the others do to beautify themselves — and what are they all to me? The other evening when I came home and went into my room I found a bunch of flowers on the table; I let it lie, and did not even put it in water, though I was sorry for the flowers — but it provoked me, and next day there was such a whispering and tittering amongst the girls! — I felt so cross I would not speak a word to them. Why can't they let me alone? — I have no time for their nonsense."

When he talked so Marlene would hang upon his lips and, treasuring up his words, would interweave them with an endless web of her own strange fancies. She might, perhaps, have been in danger of wasting her youth in fruitless reveries, but she was saved from this by serious sorrows and cares that were very real. Her father, who had long fulfilled with difficulty the duties of his place, was now struck with paralysis, and lay entirely helpless for one whole year, when his sufferings were put an end to by a second stroke. She never left him for an hour. Even in the holidays which brought Clement she would not spare the time to talk to him, save when he would come to spend ten minutes in the sick-room.

Thus concentrating her life she grew more self-denying. She complained to no one, and would have needed no one, had not her blindness prevented her doing everything herself. Her misfortune had been a secret discipline to her and had taught many a humble household virtue that those who see neglect. She kept everything committed to her care in the most scrupulous order. Her neatness was exaggerated, for she had no eyes to see when she had done enough.

Clement was deeply moved when he first saw her trying to wash and dress her helpless father, and carefully combing his thin gray hair. If in that sick-room her cheek grew somewhat paler there was a deeper radiance in her large dark eyes and, to her natural distinction, those lowly labors were, in fact, a foil.

The old man died. His successor came to take possession of the house and at the vicarage Marlene found a kind and hospitable home.

Clement only heard this by letters rarely written and still more rarely answered. He had gone to a more distant university and was no longer able to spend all his holidays at home. Now and then he would inclose a few lines to Marlene, in which, contrary to his former custom, he would address her as a child, in a joking tone, that made his father serious and silent and his mother shake her head. Marlene would have these notes read aloud to her and, listening to them gravely, would carefully keep them. When her father died Clement wrote her a short agitated letter, neither attempting to console her nor expressing any sorrow; containing only a few earnest entreaties to be careful of her health, to be calm, and to let him know exactly how she was and what she felt. It was then winter, and this was his last letter to Marlene.

At Easter he had been expected, but he did not come; he only wrote that he had found an opportunity, too good to be lost, of accompanying one of the professors on a botanical tour. His father had been satisfied and Marlene was at last successful in soothing his impatient mother.

He came unannounced at Whitsuntide, on foot, with glowing cheeks, unwearied by a long march before break of day — a fine-grown young man. He stepped into the silent house where his mother was alone and busy, for it was the eve of a great holiday. Surprised, with a cry of joy, she threw herself upon his neck. " You! " she exclaimed, as soon as she had recovered herself, drawing back to gaze upon him, the long absent one, with all her love for him in her eyes. " You forgetful boy, are you come at last? You can find the way back, I see, to your old father and mother! I began to think you only meant to return to us as a full-fledged professor, and who knows whether my old eyes would have yet beheld you here on earth? But I must not scold you now that you are my own good boy, and are come to bring us a pleasanter Whitsuntide than I have known for years — me, your father, and all of us! "

" Mother," he said, " I cannot tell you how glad I am to be at home again. I could not hold out any longer. I don't know how it happened. I had not resolved to come — I only felt I must. One fine morning, instead of going up to college, I found myself without the gates, walking for very life — such journeys in a day as I never took before, though I was always a good pedestrian. Where is my father, and Marlene? "

" Don't you hear him? " said his mother; " he is upstairs in his study." And in fact they heard the old man's heavy tread walking up and down. " It is just as it used to be — that has been his Saturday's walk all these twenty years I have known him. Marlene is with the laborers in the hay-field — I sent her away that I might be left to do my work

in peace. When she is in the house she would always have
me sitting idle in the corner with my hands before me. She
must needs do everything herself. We have new men just
now and I am glad that she should look after them a little
until they get accustomed to their work. Won't she be
surprised to find you here? Now come, we must go upstairs to father and let him have a look at you. It will be
midday directly. Come along — he won't be angry at your
disturbing him.''

She led her son after her, still keeping hold of his hand
while she slipped up the narrow staircase before him; then
softly opening the door, with a sign to Clement, she pushed
him forward while she stepped back. '' Here he is at last! ''
she said; '' there you have him! '' '' Whom? '' cried the
old man somewhat ill-humored and as if he had been started
from deep meditations; and then he saw his son's bright
face beside him radiant in the morning sunshine. He held
out his hand: '' Clement! '' he cried, between surprise and
joy, '' you here! '' '' I was homesick, father,'' said his
son, with a warm grasp of the proffered hand. '' I have
come to stay over the holidays, if there be room for me now
that you have Marlene here.'' '' How you talk! '' eagerly
broke in his mother; '' if I had seven sons, I know I should
find room for them. But I will leave you to your father
now; I have to go about the kitchen, and I must rifle our
vegetable-beds, for in town, I doubt not, they have been
spoiling you.''

And with that she went, leaving father and son still
standing silently face to face. '' I have disturbed you,''
at length said Clement; '' you are in the middle of your
sermon.''

'' You can't disturb a man who has already disturbed
himself. I have been going about all the morning, turning
over my text in my mind, but Grace was not with me — the
seed would not spring up. I have had strange ideas; mis-
givings I could not master.''

He went to the little window that looked upon the church.

The way thither was through the churchyard. It lay peacefully before them, with its flowers and its many crosses glittering in the noonday sun. '' Come hither, Clement,'' said the old vicar gently; '' come and stand here beside me. Do you see that grave to the left, with the primroses and monthly roses? It is one you never saw before. Do you know who it is sleeps there? It is my dear old friend; our Marlene's father.''

He left his son standing at the window and began pacing up and down the room again; in their silence they only heard his even tread crunching the sand upon the wooden floor. '' No one ever knew him as I did,'' he said, drawing a deep breath—'' Nobody lost so much, in losing him; for he was to no one else what he was to me. What did he know of the world and the wisdom of this world, which is foolishness in the sight of God! What science he possessed was revealed to him—by scripture or by suffering. I know he is blessed now, for he was already blessed on earth.''

After a pause he went on: '' Whom have I now to put me to shame, when I have been puffed up?—to save me, when my faith is wavering—to unravel the vexed thoughts that by turns accuse and excuse each other! This world is growing so terribly wise! What I hear is more than I can understand—what I read my soul rejects, lest it should lead it to perdition. Many there be who lift up their voices, and dream they have the gift of tongues; and behold, it is naught but idle lip-work, and the scorners listen and rejoice. Ah! my dear old friend, would I were safe, where you are now!''

Clement turned to look at him. He had never so heard his father speak, in the anguish of his soul. He went up to him, trying to find the right words to say. '' Don't, my son,'' said his father, deprecatingly, '' there is nothing you can say to me, that saints have not said better. Do you know, one day, shortly after his death, I had fallen asleep, here in this very room; night had come with a tempest that awoke me; my heart was heavy, even unto death, when suddenly I saw him — a great light was shining round him, but he appeared in the clothes he usually wore, just as if he were alive. He did not speak, but remained standing at the foot of my bed, calmly looking down upon me. At first it agitated me terribly, I was not worthy of the grace vouchsafed me; of beholding a sainted face. Only the day after, I felt the peace it had left behind. He did not come again until last night. I had been reading one of those books, written to seduce man from God, and from the word of God, and had gone to bed in grief and anger, when soon after twelve o'clock I woke up again, and saw him standing as before, holding an open Bible in his hand, printed in golden letters. He pointed to them with his finger; but so great a radiance was streaming from the pages that I strained my dazzled eyes in vain; I could not read a line. I sat up, and bent nearer to him. He stood still, with a look of love and pity in his face; which presently changed to anxiety when he saw that I was trying to read, and could not. Then, blinded by the brightness, my eyes ran over — became obscured entirely and he vanished slowly, leaving me in tears.''

He went to the window again, and Clement saw him shudder. ''Father!'' he said, and took his hand as it hung down limply by his side — he found it cold and damp — ''dear father, you distress me! You are ill — you should send for a doctor.''

''A doctor?'' cried his father, almost violently, drawing himself up to his full height — '' I am well, and that is the worst of it. My soul feels, longs for, approaching death, while my body is still obstinately rebellious.''

'' These dreams are destroying you, father.''

'' Dreams! I tell you, I was as wide awake as I am now.''

'' I do not doubt it, father; you were awake, and that is just what makes me so uneasy. It is fever that gives you those waking dreams, the very memory of which distresses you enough to quicken your pulse and make you ill. I need not be a doctor to know that last night you were in a fever, as you are now.''

" To know! and what do you think you know, poor mortal that you are! Oh, admirable wisdom! Grace-giving science!—but after all, whom do I accuse? What do I deserve?—for babbling of God's most precious mysteries, and baring my aching heart as a mark for scorners. Are these the fruits of all your studies? What grapes do you hope to gather from thorns like these? I know you well, poor vain creatures that you are, who would set up new gods for others, while in your hearts you worship no gods but yourselves; I tell you, your days are numbered." His bald brow was flushed crimson as he turned to go, without one look at Clement, who stood shocked and silent, his eyes fixed on the floor. Suddenly he felt his father's hand upon his shoulder.

" Speak truth, my son; do you really hold to those of whose opinions I have read with horror? Are you among those bright votaries of matter who jest at miracles; to whom the Spirit is as a fable which nature tells, and man listens to? Have neither your youth nor the seed of gratitude, sown by the Lord in your heart, been able to choke these weeds? Answer, Clement!"

" Father," said the young man after some consideration, " how shall I answer you? I used my most strenuous efforts in the solution of these questions—I have heard them answered in so many different ways by men I love and honor. Some of my dearest friends profess the opinions you condemn: I listen and learn, and have not yet ventured to decide."

" He who is not with me, is against me, saith the Lord—"

" How could I be against Him? How could I strive against the Spirit? Who does deny the Spirit even among those who would bind it to the laws of matter? Are not its miracles the same, even if they be no more than nature's fairest blossoms? Is a noble image to be scorned for only being of stone?"

" You talk as they all do; you intoxicate yourselves with your own cloudy metaphors — you are so deafened with the sound of your empty words that the small voice within you speaks unheard — and is it thus you come to celebrate our Whitsuntide?"

"I came because I love you—"

There was silence again between them. The old vicar's lips parted more than once, as if to speak, and firmly closed again. They heard Marlene's voice below, and Clement left the window at which he had been sorrowfully standing to listen. "It is Marlene," his father said: "Have you forgotten her? Does not — when your profane associates vie with each other in their madness to deny the Spirit its free Sonship of God — does not the image of the playfellow of your youth appear then before your soul? Does she not remind you of the wonders the Spirit, when severed from the outward senses, can work out of itself alone, that is out of God, through His grace in a humble breast that is firm in faith?"

Clement kept back the answer that was on his lips. They heard the blind girl's light step upon the stairs. The door opened, and she stood on the threshold with blushing cheeks. "Clement!" she cried, turning her gentle brown eyes to the spot where he actually stood. He went up to her and took the hand she held out waiting for him. "How glad you have made your parents! Welcome, welcome! a thousand welcomes! but why are you so silent?" she added.

"Yes, dear Marlene," he said, "I am here again. I wanted so much to see you all again; and how well you look! You have grown taller."

"The spring has set me up again — this winter was very hard to bear — but your parents are so good to me, Clement. Good morning, father dear," she said, turning to him — "it was so early when we went out to the field that I could not come up to shake hands then"—and she held out hers to him.

"Go downstairs now, dear child, and take Clement with you. You can show him your garden—you have a little while to yourselves yet before dinner; and you, Clement,

THE KÜNSTLERHAUS, MUNICH

think over what I have been saying to you." And then the young people went away.

" What is the matter with your father? " asked the young girl, when they had got downstairs; " his. tone sounded rather strange, and so does yours. Have you had any angry words together? "

" I found him very much excited; his blood appears to be in a disordered state. Has he been complaining of late? "

" Not to me. He sometimes appears to be ill at ease, and will not speak for hours together, so as even to surprise mother. Was he severe on you just now? "

" We had a discussion upon very serious subjects. He questioned me, and I could not conceal my convictions."

Marlene grew pensive, but her countenance brightened when they got into the fresh air.

" Is it not pleasant here? " she asked, stretching out both hands.

" Indeed I hardly know the place," he said; " what have you done to this neglected little spot? As far back as I can remember there never was anything here but a few fruit-trees, and the hollyhocks and asters, and now it is all covered with roses."

" Yes," she said; " your mother never used to care much about the garden, but she now likes it too. The bailiff's son learned gardening in the town, and he made me a present of some rose-trees, and planted them for me — by degrees I got the others, and now I am quite rich. The finest are not in flower yet."

" And can you take care of them all yourself? "

" Do you wonder at that, because I cannot see? " she said, merrily, " but all the same, I understand them very well, and I know what is good for them — I can tell by the scent which of them are fading, and which are opening, and whether they are in want of water — they seem to speak to me. Only I cannot gather one for you; I tear my hands so with the thorns."

" Let me gather one for you," he said, and broke off a

monthly rose. She took it. " But you have broken off too
many buds," she said. " I will keep this one to put in
water, and there is the full-blown rose for you."

They walked up and down the neatly-kept path, until
they were called to dinner. Clement felt embarrassed with
his father, but Marlene, generally so modest in the part she
took in conversation, now found a thousand things to ask
and say. And thus the vicar forgot the painful feeling
left by that first meeting with his son, and the old footing
of cordiality was soon resumed.

In the course of the next few days, however, they could
not fail to find occasion to revive their quarrel. His father
inquired about the present state of theology at the university, and soon the conversation turned to general subjects.
The farther Clement retreated, the hotter grew his father
in pursuit. Often an anxious, and sometimes an angry look
from his mother, would come to support him in his resolution to avoid all plain speaking on this subject; but whenever he broke off, or uttered a phrase that to him meant
nothing, the awkward silence fell upon his spirits, and
chilled him to the heart. Marlene alone was always able
to recover the proper tone. But he saw that she too was
grieved, and therefore he avoided her when she was alone.
He knew that she would question him, and from her he
could have concealed nothing. A shadow came over him
now whenever he saw her. Was it the memory of that
childish promise he had long since broken? Was it the
feeling that in the schism of opinions that threatened to
estrange him from his parents she silently stepped to their
side?

And yet he felt his inclination for her more irresistibly
than ever; it was a thing he couldn't longer disown and
against which he painfully struggled. He was too much
absorbed in his science and in his visions of the future, not
to struggle with the positiveness of an aspiring nature
against everything that might cling to his steps, or eventu-
ally chance to clog them.

"I have to be a traveler," he then said; "a traveler on foot; my bundle must be light." He felt strangely burdened when he thought of binding himself to a wife who would have a claim to a share of his life; and a blind one too, whom he would feel it wrong ever to leave. Here in her native village, where everything wore the simple aspect she had known from childhood, she was secure from the embarrassments which a residence in a town must inevitably have produced; and so he persuaded himself that he should do her a wrong also by drawing closer to her. That he could be causing pain to her by his renunciation was more than he could trust himself to believe.

His decision became more firm. On the last day of his stay, after he had embraced his parents, and heard that Marlene was in the garden, he left a farewell message for her, and with a beating heart he took the road to the village, and then turned down a path across the fields to reach the woods. But the vicarage garden also opened to these fields, and the nearest way to them would have been through its small wicket gate. It was a long way round he had preferred, but at the last, he could not make up his mind to go farther on his narrow way through the young corn, without, at least, once looking back.

Thus he stood still in the serene sunshine, looking toward the hamlet with its cottages and houses; behind the hedge that bounded his father's garden he caught sight of the young girl's slender figure. Her face was turned his way, but she had no perception of his presence.

His tears sprang quick and hot, but he struggled and overcame them; then, leaping wildly over banks and ditches, he reached the hedge; she started. "Farewell, Marlene!" he said with a clear voice. "I am going. I may be away for a year;" and he passed his hand over her hair and forehead.

"Good-by! You are going?" she said; "one thing I should like to ask of you; write oftener;—do! Your mother needs it, and sometimes send me a little message."

" I will," he said in an absent way — and again he went.

" Clement! " she called after him. He heard, but he did not look back. " It is well that he did not hear me," she murmured; " what could I have found to say to him? "

Chapter VI

AFTER this Clement never made a stay of any length in his father's house. Each time he came he found him harsher and more intolerant. His mother was tender and loving as before, but more reserved; Marlene was calm, but mute whenever the men became earnest in discussion. At such times she would rather avoid being present.

On a bright day toward the end of autumn we find Clement again in the small room where, as a boy, he had spent those weeks of convalescence. One of his friends and fellow-students had accompanied him home. They had gone through their course at the university, and had just returned from a longer tour than usual, during which Wolf had fallen ill, and had desired to come hither to recover in the quiet of village life. Clement could not but acquiesce, though of all the young men he knew, Wolf was the one, he thought, least likely to please his father. But, contrary to his expectations, the stranger prudently and cleverly contrived to adapt himself perfectly to the opinions of the old couple; especially winning the mother's goodwill by the cheerful interest he manifested in household matters. He gave her good advice, and even succeeded in curing her of some little ailment with a very simple remedy. He had been preparing himself to follow his uncle in his business as apothecary — an avocation far beneath that for which his natural talents and acquirements would have fitted him; but he was by nature indolent, and was quite contented to settle down, and eat his cake betimes.

Mentally, he never had had anything in common with Clement; and on first coming to the vicarage, he had felt himself in an atmosphere so oppressive and uncongenial, that he would have left it, after the most superficial recovery, had not the blind girl, from the first moment he saw her, appeared to him as a riddle worth his reading.

She had avoided him as much as possible; the first time he had taken her hand she had withdrawn it, with unaccountable uneasiness, and had entirely lost the usual composure of her manner. Yet he would remain in her society for hours, studying her method of apprehending things, and with a playful kind of importunity which it was not easy to take amiss, taking note of her ways and means of communication with the outer world, and watching her senses in their mutual endeavor to supplement the missing one.

He could not understand why Clement appeared to care for her so little — and Clement would avoid her more than ever when he saw her in company with Wolf. He would turn pale then, and escape to the distant forest, where the villagers would often meet him, plunged in most disconsolate meditations.

One evening, when he was returning from a long discontented walk, where he had gone too far and lost himself, he met Wolf in a state of more than natural excitement. He had been paying a long visit to Marlene, who had fascinated him more than usual; he had then found his way to the village tavern, where he had drunk enough of the light wine of the country to make him glad of a cool walk among the fields in the fresh evening air.

" I say! " he called to Clement. " It may be a good while yet, before you will get rid of me; that little blind witch of yours is a pretty puzzle to me. She is cleverer than a dozen of our town ladies, who only use their eyes to ogle God and man — and then that delicious way she has of snubbing me is a masterpiece in itself."

" You may be glad if she ends by making you a little tamer," said Clement shortly.

" Tamer! that I shall never be — and that magnificent figure and lovely face of hers are not calculated to make a fellow tame. Don't believe I mean to harm her. Only you know, sometimes, I think if she were to be fond of one, there would be something peculiar in it. A woman who can't see — who can only feel, and feel as no other creature can — I say if such a woman were to fall upon a fellow's neck, I say, the feeling might prove especially pleasant to them both."

"And I say, you had better keep your thoughts to yourself."

"Why, where's the harm? Who would be harmed should I make her fall just a very little bit in love with me, to see how her nerves would carry her through the scrape? In general so much fire finds its safety valve in the eyes, but here — "

"I must beg you to refrain from making any such experiments," flared up Clement. "I tell you very seriously, that I do not choose to see or hear anything of the kind, and so you may act accordingly."

Wolf gave a sidelong look at him, and, taking hold of his arm, said with a laugh: "I do believe you really are in love with the girl, and want to try the experiment yourself. How long have you been so scrupulous? You used to hear me to the end, before now, when I have told you what I thought of women."

"Your education is no concern of mine. What have I to do with your unclean ideas? But when I find them soiling one so near and dear to me, one who is a thousand times too good for you to breathe the same air, that is what I can and will prevent."

"Oho!" said Wolf tranquilly — "too good you say? too good? It is you who are too good a fellow, Clement, far too good! so take yourself away, out of my air, good lad."

He clapped him on the back, and would have moved on. Clement stood still, and turned white. "You will be so good as to explain the meaning of those words," he said resolutely.

"No such fool; ask others if you wish to know — others may be fond of preaching to deaf ears; I am not."

" What others? What do you mean? Who is it dares to speak slightingly of her? I say who dares?" He held Wolf with an iron grasp.

" Foolish fellow, you are spoiling my walk," he growled, " with your stupid questions; let me go, will you?"

" You do not stir a step until you have given me satisfaction," cried Clement, getting furious.

" Don't I? Go to the bailiff's son if you are jealous! Poor devil! to coax him so, till he was ready to jump out of his skin for her, and then to throw him over! Fie! was it honest? He came to pour out his grievances to me, and I comforted him. She is just what all women are, says I, a coquette. It is my turn now, but we are up to a thing or two, you know, and may not be inclined to let our mouths be stopped, when we would warn other fellows from falling into the same snare."

" Retract those words!" shouted Clement, shaking Wolf's arm in a paroxysm of rage.

" Why retract? if they are true, and I can prove them? Go to! you are but a simpleton!"

" And you a scamp."

" Oho! I say, it is now your turn to retract."

" I won't retract."

" Then I suppose you know the consequences. You shall hear from me as soon as we get to town."

And having thus spoken, he turned in cold blood back to the village. Clement remained for a moment standing where he was.

" Villain!—miserable scoundrel!"—fell from his lips; his bosom heaved, a cruel pain had coiled itself about his heart, he flung himself flat upon the ground among the corn, and lay there long, recalling a thousand times each one of those words that had made him feel so furious.

When he came home at a very late hour, he was surprised to find the family still assembled. Wolf was missing. The vicar was pacing violently up and down the room. His wife and Marlene were seated with their work in their laps, much against their custom at so late an hour. On Clement's entrance the vicar stopped, and gravely turned to look at him.

"What have you been doing to your friend? Here he has packed up and gone, while we were all out walking, leaving a hasty message. When we came home, we only found the man who had come to fetch his things. Have you been quarreling? else why should he be in such a hurry?"

"We had high words together. I am glad to find that he is gone, and that I shall not have to sleep another night under the same roof with him."

And what were your angry words about?"

"I cannot tell you, father. I should have been glad to avoid a quarrel, but there are things to which no honest man can listen. I have long known him to be coarse, and careless in feeling, both with regard to himself and others, but I never saw him as he was today."

The vicar looked steadily at his son, and then in a low tone: "How do you mean to settle this quarrel between you?" he asked.

"As young men do," said Clement gravely.

"And do you know what Christians do, when they have been offended?"

"I know, but I cannot do the same; if he had only offended me, I might easily have forgiven him, but he has insulted one who is very dear to me."

"A woman, Clement?"

"A woman. Yes."

"And you love this woman?"

"I love her," murmured the young man.

"I thought so," burst out his father. "Yes! you have been corrupted in the town. You are become as the children of this world, who follow wanton wenches, fight for them, and make idols of them; but I tell you, while I live, I shall labor to win you back to God. I will smash your idols. Did the Lord vouchsafe to work a miracle for you, for you to deny him now? Far better have remained in darkness, with those gates closed forever, through which the devil and all his snares have entered in, and taken possession of your heart!"

The young man had some struggle to suppress his rising passion. "Who gave you the right, father, to suppose my inclinations to be so base?" he said. "Am I degraded, because I am forced to do what is needful in the world we live in, to crush the insolence of the base? There are divers ways of wrestling with the evil one; yours is the peaceful way, for you have the multitude to deal with. I have the individual to deal with, and I know the way I have to walk."

"It is a way you shall not go," hotly returned the father; "I say you shall not trample on God's commandments. He is no son of mine, who would do violence to his brother. I prohibit it with the authority of a parent and a priest. Beware of setting that authority at naught!"

"And so you spurn me from your home," said Clement, gloomily. A pause ensued. His mother, who had burst into tears, now rose, and rushed up to her son. "Mother," he said earnestly, "I must be a man. I cannot be untrue to myself." He went toward the door, with one look at Marlene, whose poor blind eyes were searching painfully; his mother followed him — she could not speak for sobbing. "Do not detain him, wife," said the vicar, "he is no child of ours, since he refuses to be God's; let him go whither he pleases; to us, he is as dead."

Marlene heard the door close and the vicar's wife fall heavily to the ground, with a cry that came from the depths of her mother's heart. She woke from the trance in which she had been sitting, went to the door, and with an immense exertion, she carried the insensible woman to her bed. The vicar stood at the window and never uttered a word; but his folded hands were trembling violently.

About a quarter of an hour later, a knock came to Clement's door. He opened it and saw Marlene. She entered quietly. The room was in disorder — she struck her foot against the trunk. "What are you going to do, Clement?" she asked painfully.

The stubbornness of his grief softened at once, and he took her hands and pressed them to his eyes which were wet with tears. " I must do it," he cried, " I have long felt that I have lost his love. Perhaps when I am gone, he may feel that I have never ceased to be his child."

She raised him up, and said: " Do not weep, or I shall never have strength to tell you what I have to say. Your mother would tell it to you if your father did not prevent her. And even he — I heard by his voice how difficult he found it to be so hard; yet hard he will remain — for I know him well — he believes that he is serving the Lord by being severe, and serving him best, in sacrificing his own heart."

"And you think the same?"

" No, I don't, Clement. I don't know much about the world, nor the laws of that opinion that forces a man to fight a duel; but I do know you enough to know that every one of your thoughts and actions — and therefore this duel also — is submitted to the severest test of self-examination. You may owe it to the world, and to her you love; only I think you owe your parents more than either. I do not know the person who has been insulted, and do not quite feel why it should make you so indignant, to be prevented doing this for her. Do not interrupt me. Do not suppose me to be influenced by the fear of losing any remnant of our friendship which you may have retained during the years that have parted us. I would be willing to let her have you all to herself, if she be able to make you happy, but not even for her sake should you do what you are about to do, were she dearer to you than either father or mother. From their house you must not go in anger, at the risk of its being closed to you forever. Your father is old, and will carry his principles with him to the grave. If he were to give way to you, he would sacrifice to you that which is the very pith and marrow of his life; and the sacrifice on your side would be merely the evanescent estimation in which you believe yourself to be held by strangers. If the woman whom you love could break with you because you are unwilling to embitter the last years of your father's life, that woman, I say, was never worthy of you." Her voice failed her; Clement threw himself on a chair and groaned violently.

She was still standing by the door, waiting to hear what he would say; and there was a strange look of tension about her brow — she seemed to be listening with her eyes. Suddenly he sprang to his feet, laid his two hands on her shoulders, and cried: " It was for you I would have done this, and now for your sake I will not do it;" and rushing past her, he ran downstairs.

She remained where she was. His last words had thrilled to her very marrow, and a sudden tide of gladness broke over that timid, doubting heart of hers. She sat down on the portmanteau trembling all over. " It was for you! for you! "— the words echoed in her ear. She half dreaded his return; if he should not mean what she thought! and how could he mean it? What was she to him?

She heard him coming upstairs at last; in her agitation she rose, and would have left the room, but he met her at the door, and taking her in his arms, he told her all.

" It was I who was blind," he cried, " and you who saw — who saw prophetically. Without your clear-sightedness where should I have been now? — An orphan forever, without a home; banished from the only hearts I love, and by my own miserable delusions. And now — now they are all my own again; mine and more than I ever believed to be mine — more than I could have trusted myself to possess."

She hung upon his neck in mute devotion; mute for very scorn of the poverty of language. The long repressed fervor of her affection had broken loose, and burned in her silent kiss.

Day dawned upon their happiness. Now he knew what she had so obstinately concealed, and what this very room had witnessed; where now, pledged to each other for life, with a grasp of each other's hands, they parted in the early morning.

In the course of the day a letter came from Wolf, written

the night before, from the nearest village. Clement might be at rest, he wrote; he retracted everything; he knew best that what he had said was nonsense. He had spoken in anger and in wine.

It had provoked him to see Clement going about so indifferent and cool, when, with a word, he might have taken possession of such a treasure — and when he saw that Clement really did mean to do so, he had reviled what had been denied to him.

He begged Clement not to think worse of him than he deserved, and to make his excuses to the young girl and to his parents; and not to break with him entirely, and forever.

When Clement read this to Marlene, she was touched: "I can be sorry for him now," she said; "though I always felt uneasy when he was here — and how much he might have spared us both, and spared himself! But I can think of him with charity now — we have so much to thank him for!"

L'ARRABIATA (1853)*

By PAUL HEYSE

TRANSLATED BY MARY WILSON

HE day had scarcely dawned. Over Vesuvius hung one broad gray stripe of mist; stretching across as far as Naples, and darkening all the small towns along the coast. The sea lay calm. But about the marina of the narrow creek that lies beneath the Sorrento cliffs, fishermen and their wives were at work already, with giant cables drawing their boats to land, and the nets that had been cast the night before. Others were rigging their craft — trimming the sails, and fetching out oars and masts from the great grated vaults that have been built deep into the rocks for shelter to the tackle over night. Nowhere an idle hand; even the very aged, who had long given up going to sea, fell into the long chain of those who were hauling in the nets. Here and there, on some flat housetop, an old woman stood and span; or busied herself about her grandchildren, whom their mother had left to help her husband.

"Do you see, Rachela? yonder is our Padre Curato;" said one to a little thing of ten, who brandished a small spindle by her side; "Antonino is to row him over to Capri. Madre Santissima! but the reverend signor's eyes are dull with sleep!" and she waved her hand to a benevolent looking little priest, who was settling himself in the boat, and spreading out upon the bench his carefully tucked-up skirts.

The men upon the quay had dropped their work to see their pastor off, who bowed and nodded kindly, right and left.

---

* Permission Bernhard Tauchnitz, Leipzig.

" What for must he go to Capri, granny? " asked the child. " Have the people there no priest of their own, that they must borrow ours? "

" Silly thing! " returned the granny. " Priests they have in plenty — and the most beautiful of churches, and a hermit too, which is more than we have. But there lives a great Signora, who once lived here in Sorrento; she was so very ill! Many's the time our Padre had to go and take the Most Holy to her, when they thought she could not live the night. But with the Blessed Virgin's help she did get strong and well — and was able to bathe every day in the sea. When she went away to settle in Capri she left a fine heap of ducats behind her for our church and for the poor; and she would not go, they say, until our Padre promised to go and see her over there, that she might confess to him as before. It is quite wonderful the store she lays by him! Indeed, and we have cause to bless ourselves for having a curato who has gifts enough for an archbishop; and is in such request with all the great folks. The Madonna be with him! " she cried, and waved her hand again as the boat was about to put from shore.

"Are we to have fair weather, my son? " inquired the little priest, with an anxious look toward Naples.

" The sun is not yet up " the young man answered. " When he comes, he will easily do for that small trifle of mist."

" Off with you, then! that we may arrive before the heat."

Antonino was just reaching for his long oar to shove away the boat when suddenly he paused and fixed his eyes upon the summit of the steep path that leads down from Sorrento to the water.

A tall and slender girlish figure had become visible upon the heights and was now hastily stepping down the stones, waving her pocket handkerchief.

She had a small bundle under her arm and her dress was mean and poor. Yet she had an almost distinguished,

if somewhat savage way of throwing back her head; and
the dark tress that wreathed it was like a diadem.

"What have we to wait for?" inquired the curato.

"There is some one coming who wants to go to Capri.
With your permission, Padre. We shall not go a whit the
slower. It is a slight young thing of about eighteen."

At that moment the young girl appeared from behind the
wall that bounds the winding path.

"Laurella!" cried the priest, "and what has she to do
in Capri?"

Antonino shrugged his shoulders. She came up with
hasty steps, her eyes fixed straight before her.

"Ha! l'Arrabiata! good morning!" shouted several
among the young boatmen. But for the curato's presence
they might have added more; the look of mute defiance
with which the young girl received their welcome seemed to
irritate the more mischievous among them.

"Good day, Laurella!" now said the priest; "how are
you? Are you coming with us to Capri?"

"If I may, Padre."

"Ask Antonino there, the boat is his. Every man is
master of his own, I say; as God is master of us all."

"There is half a carlin, if I may go for that?" said
Laurella, without looking at the young boatman.

"You need it more than I," he muttered, and pushed
aside some orange-baskets to make room: he was to sell
the oranges in Capri, for the little isle of rocks has never
been able to grow enough of this fruit for all its visitors.

"I do not choose to go for nothing," said the young girl,
with a slight frown of her dark eyebrows.

"Come, child," said the priest; "he is a good lad and
had rather not enrich himself with that little morsel of your
poverty. Come now and step in," and he stretched out his
hand to help her—"and sit you down by me. See now, he
has spread his jacket for you that you may sit the softer;
he has not done the same for me. Young folks are all alike;
for one little maiden of eighteen they will do more than for

ten of us reverend fathers. Nay, no excuse, Tonino. It is the Lord's own doing, that like and like should hold together.''

Meanwhile Laurella had stepped in and seated herself beside the Padre, first putting away Antonino's jacket without a word. The young fellow let it lie, and muttering between his teeth he gave one vigorous push against the pier and the little boat flew out into the open bay.

'' What are you carrying there in that little bundle?'' inquired the Padre, as they were floating on over a calm sea, now just beginning to be lighted up with the earliest rays of the rising sun.

'' Silk, thread, and a loaf, Padre. The silk is to be sold at Anacapri to a woman who makes ribbons and the thread to another.''

'' Self spun?''

'' Yes, sir.''

'' You once learned to weave ribbons yourself, if I remember right?''

'' I did, sir, only mother has been much worse and I cannot stay so long from home; and a loom to ourselves we are not rich enough to buy.''

'' Worse, is she? Ah! dear, dear! when I was with you last, at Easter, she was up.''

'' The spring is always her worst time; ever since those last great storms and the earthquakes she has been forced to keep her bed from pain.''

'' Pray, my child. Never grow slack of prayers and petitions that the Blessed Virgin may intercede for you; and be industrious and good that your prayers may find a hearing.''

After a pause: '' When you were coming toward the shore I heard them calling after you. ' Good morning, l'Arrabiata!' they said; what made them call you so? It is not a nice name for a young Christian maiden, who should be meek and mild.''

The young girl's brown face glowed all over, while her eyes flashed fire.

THE WITTELSBACH FOUNTAIN AT MUNICH

BY ADOLF HILDEBRAND

" They always mock me so because I do not dance and
sing, and stand about to chatter, as other girls do. I might
be left in peace, I think; I do *them* no harm."

" Nay, but you might be civil. Let others dance and
sing on whom this life sits lighter, but a kind word now and
then is seemly even from the most afflicted."

Her dark eyes fell and she drew her eyebrows closer
over them, as if she wanted to hide them beneath.

They went on a while in silence. The sun now stood
resplendent above the mountain chain; only the tip of
Mount Vesuvius towered beyond the group of clouds that
had gathered about its base. And on the Sorrento plains
the houses were gleaming white from the dark green of
their orange-gardens.

" Have you heard no more of that painter, Laurella? "
asked the curato; " that Neapolitan, who wished so much
to marry you? " She shook her head. " He came to make
a picture of you. Why would you not let him? "

" What did he want it for? There are handsomer girls
than I. Who knows what he would have done with it? He
might have bewitched me with it, or hurt my soul, or even
killed me, mother says."

" Never believe such sinful things! " said the little curato
very earnestly. "Are you not ever in God's keeping, without whose will not one hair of your head can fall; and is a
poor mortal with such an image in his hand to prevail
against the Lord? Besides, you might have seen that he
was fond of you; else why should he want to marry you? "

She said nothing.

"And wherefore did you refuse him? He was an honest
man, they say, and a comely; and he would have kept you
and your mother far better than you ever can yourself, for
all your spinning and silk winding."

" We are so poor! " she said passionately; " and mother
has been ill so long we should have become a burden to him;
and then I never should have done for a Signora. When
his friends came to see him he would only have been
ashamed of me."

"How can you say so? I tell you the man was good and kind. And beside he was willing to settle in Sorrento. It will not be so easy to find another, sent straight from Heaven to be the saving of you, as this man, indeed, appeared to be."

"I want no husband — I never shall," she said, very stubbornly, half to herself.

"Is this a vow, or do you mean to be a nun?"

She shook her head.

"The people are not so wrong who call you wilful, although the name they give you is not kind. Have you ever considered that you do not stand alone in the world, and that your stubbornness must make your sick mother's illness worse to bear — her life more bitter? And what sound reason can you have to give for rejecting an honest hand, stretched out to help you and your mother? Answer me, Laurella."

"I have a reason," she said, reluctantly, and speaking low; "but it is one I cannot give."

"Not give! not give to me? not to your confessor, whom you surely know to be your friend — or is he not?"

Laurella nodded.

"Then, child, unburden your heart. If your reason be a good one, I shall be the very first to uphold you in it. Only you are young and know so little of the world. A time may come when you may find cause to regret a chance of happiness, thrown away for some foolish fancy now."

Shyly she threw a furtive glance over to the other end of the boat, where the young boatman sat, rowing fast. His woolen cap was pulled deep down over his eyes; he was gazing for across the water, with averted head; lost, as it appeared, in his own meditations.

The priest observed her look and bent his ear down closer.

"You did not know my father?" she whispered, while a dark look gathered in her eyes.

"Your father, child! — why, your father died when you were hardly ten years old — what can your father (Heaven rest his soul in Paradise!) have to do with this perversity of yours?"

"You did not know him, Padre; you did not know that mother's illness was caused by him alone."

"And how?"

"By his ill treatment of her; he beat her and trampled upon her. I well remember the nights when he came home in his fits of frenzy—she never said a word and did everything he bid her. Yet he would beat her so, my heart felt like to break. I used to cover up my head and pretend to be asleep, but I cried all night. And then when he saw her lying on the floor, quite suddenly he would change and lift her up and kiss her till she screamed and said he smothered her. Mother forbade me ever to say a word of this; but it wore her out. And in all these long years since father died she has never been able to get well again. And if she should soon die, which God forbid! I know who it was that killed her."

The little curato's head wagged slowly to and fro; he seemed uncertain how far to acquiesce in the young girl's reasons. At length he said: "Forgive him, as your mother has forgiven! And turn your thoughts from such distressing pictures, Laurella; there may be better days in store for you, which will make you forget the past."

"Never shall I forget that!" she said, and shuddered; "and you must know, Padre, it is the reason why I have resolved to remain unmarried. I never will be subject to a man who may illtreat and then caress me. Were a man now to want to beat or kiss me I could defend myself; but mother could not—neither from his blows or kisses, because she loved him. Now I will never so love a man as to be made ill and wretched by him."

"You are but a child, and you talk like one who knows nothing at all of life. Are all men like that poor father of yours? Do all illtreat their wives and give vent to every whim and gust of passion? Have you never seen a good man yet, or known good wives who live in peace and harmony with their husbands?"

" But nobody ever knew how father was to mother — she would have died sooner than complained or told of him — and all because she loved him. If this be love — if love can close our lips when they should cry out for help; if it is to make us suffer without resistance, worse than even our worst enemy could make us suffer, then I say I never will be fond of mortal man.''

" I tell you you are childish; you know not what you are saying. When your time comes, you are not likely to be consulted by your heart, whether you choose to fall in love or not. Then nothing will avail you of all your present silly thoughts.'' After a pause: "And that painter — did you think he could have been cruel? ''

" He made those eyes I have seen my father make, when he begged my mother's pardon, and took her in his arms to make it up — I know those eyes. A man may make such eyes and yet find it in his heart to beat a wife who never did a thing to vex him! It made my flesh creep to see those eyes again.''

After this she would not say another word. The curato also remained silent. He bethought himself of more than one wise saying wherewith the maiden might have been admonished; but he refrained, in consideration of the young boatman who had been growing rather restless toward the close of this confession.

When, after two hours' rowing, they reached the little bay at Capri, Antonino took the Padre in his arms and carried him through the last few ripples of shallow water to set him reverently down upon his legs on dry land. But Laurella did not wait for him to wade back and fetch her. Gathering up her little petticoat, holding in one hand her wooden shoes and in the other her little bundle, with one splashing step or two she had reached the shore. " I have some time to stay at Capri,'' said the priest. " You need not wait — I may not perhaps return before tomorrow. When you get home, Laurella, remember me to your mother; I will come and see her within the week. You mean to go back before it gets dark? ''

" If I find an opportunity," answered the young girl, turning all her attention to her skirts.

" I also must return, you know," said Antonino, in a tone which he believed to be of great indifference — " I shall wait here till the Ave Maria — if you should not come, it is the same to me."

" You must come," interposed the little priest; " you never can leave your mother all alone at night. Is it far you have to go? "

" To a vineyard by Anacapri."

"And I to Capri, so now God bless you, child — and you, my son."

Laurella kissed his hand and let one farewell drop for the Padre and Antonino to divide between them. Antonino, however, appropriated no part of it to himself, he pulled off his cap exclusively to the Padre without even looking at Laurella. But after they had turned their backs he let his eyes travel but a short way with the Padre, as he went toiling over the deep bed of small loose stones; he soon sent them after the maiden, who, turning to the right, had begun to climb the heights, holding one hand above her eyes to protect them from the scorching sun. Just before the path disappeared behind high walls she stopped, as if to gather breath, and looked behind her. At her feet lay the marina; the rugged rocks rose high around her; the seat was shining in the rarest of its deep blue splendor. The scene was surely worth a moment's pause. But as chance would have it her eye, in glancing past Antonino's boat, met with Antonino's own, which had been following her as she climbed.

Each made a slight movement, as persons do who would excuse themselves for some mistake; and then, with her darkest look, the maiden went her way.

Hardly one hour had passed since noon and yet for the last two Antonino had been sitting waiting on the bench before the fisher's tavern. He must have been very much preoccupied with something, for he jumped up every moment to step out into the sunshine and look carefully up and down the roads, which, parting right and left, lead to the only two little towns upon the island. He did not altogether trust the weather, he then said to the hostess of the Osteria; to be sure, it was clear enough, but he did not quite like that tint of sea and sky. Just so it had looked, he said, before that last awful storm, when he had saved the English family with so great difficulty; surely she must remember it?

"No, indeed," she replied, "she didn't."

"Well, if the weather should happen to change before the night, she was to think of him," he said.

"Have you many fine folk over there?" she asked him after a while.

"They are only just beginning; as yet the season has been bad enough; those who came to bathe, came late."

"The spring came late. Have you not been earning more than we at Capri?"

"Not enough to give me maccaroni twice a week, if I had had nothing but the boat; only a letter now and then to take to Naples — or a gentleman to row out into the open sea, that he might fish. But you know I have an uncle who is rich — he owns more than one fine orange garden and — 'Tonino,' says he to me, 'while I live you shall not suffer want, and when I am gone you will find that I have taken care of you;' and so, with God's help, I got through the winter."

"Has he children, this uncle who is so rich?"

"No, he never married; he was long in foreign parts, and many a good piastre he has laid together. He is going to set up a great fishing business and set me over it to manage it.

"Why, then you are a made man, Tonino!"

The young boatman shrugged his shoulders. "Every man has his own burden," he said, starting up again to have another look at the weather, turning his eyes right and left, although he must have known that there can be no weather side but one.

"Let me fetch you another bottle," said the hostess; "your uncle can well afford to pay for it."

"Not more than one glass; it is a fiery wine you have in Capri, and my head is hot already."

"It does not heat the blood; you may drink as much of it as you like. And here is my husband coming, so you must sit awhile and talk to him."

And in fact, with his nets over his shoulder, and his red cap upon his curly head, down came the stately padrone of the Osteria. He had been taking a dish of fish to that great lady to set before the little curato. As soon as he caught sight of the young boatman he began waving him a most cordial welcome and came to sit beside him on the bench, chattering and asking questions. Just as his wife was bringing her second bottle of pure unadulterated Capri, they heard the crisp sand crunch and Laurella was seen approaching from the left hand road to Anacapri. She nodded slightly in salutation, then stopped and hesitated.

Antonino sprang from his seat. "I must go," he said; "it is a young Sorrento girl, who came over with the Signor curato in the morning. She has to get back to her sick mother before night."

"Well, well, time enough yet before night," observed the fisherman; "time enough to take a glass of wine. Wife, I say, another glass!"

"I thank you; I had rather not "—and Laurella kept her distance.

"Fill the glasses, wife; fill them both, I say; she only wants a little pressing."

"Don't," interposed the lad. "It is a wilful head of her own she has; a saint could not persuade her to what she does not choose." And taking a hasty leave, he ran down to the boat, loosened the rope and stood waiting for Laurella. Again she bent her head to the host and hostess, and slowly approaching the water, with lingering steps, she looked around on every side as if in hopes of seeing some other passenger. But the marina was deserted. The fishermen were asleep or rowing about the coast with rods or nets; a few women and children sat before their doors spinning or sleeping — such strangers as had come over in the morning were waiting for the cool of the evening to return. She had not much time to look about her; before she could prevent him Antonino had seized her in his arms and carried her to the boat, as if she had been an infant. He leapt in after her and with a stroke or two of his oar they were in deep water.

She had seated herself in the forepart of the boat, half turning her back to him, so that he could only see her profile. She wore a sterner look than ever, the low, straight brow was shaded by her hair; the rounded lips were firmly closed; only the delicate nostril occasionally gave a wilful quiver. After they had gone on a while in silence, she began to feel the scorching of the sun, and unloosening her bundle she threw the handkerchief over her head and began to make her dinner of the bread; for in Capri she had eaten nothing.

Antonino did not stand this long; he fetched out a couple of the oranges with which the baskets had been filled in the morning. "Here is something to eat with your bread, Laurella," he said; "don't think I kept them for you; they had rolled out of the basket, and I only found them when I brought the baskets back to the boat."

"Eat them yourself; bread is enough for me."

"They are refreshing in this heat and you have had to walk so far."

"They gave me a drink of water and that refreshed me."

"As you please," he said, and let them drop into the basket.

Silence again; the sea was smooth as a mirror. Not a ripple was heard against the prow. Even the white sea-birds that roost among those caves pursued their prey with soundless flight.

"You might take the oranges to your mother," again commenced Tonino.

"We have oranges at home and when they are gone I can go and buy some more."

"Nay, take these to her, and give them to her with my compliments."

"She does not know you."

"You could tell her who I am."

"I do not know you either."

It was not the first time that she had denied him thus. One Sunday of last year, when that painter had first come to Sorrento, Antonino had chanced to be playing Boccia with some other young fellows in the little piazza by the chief street. There, for the first time, had the painter caught sight of Laurella, who, with her pitcher on her head, had passed by without taking any notice of him. The Neapolitan, struck by her appearance, stood still and gazed after her, not heeding that he was standing in the very midst of the game, which, with two steps, he might have cleared. A very ungentle ball came knocking against his shins, as a reminder that this was not the spot to choose for meditation. He looked round, as if in expectation of some apology. But the young boatman who had thrown the ball stood silent among his friends in an attitude of so much defiance that the stranger had found it more advisable to go his ways and avoid discussion. Still, this little encounter had been spoken of, particularly at the time when the painter had been pressing his suit to Laurella openly. "I do not even know him," she had said indignantly when the painter asked her whether it was for the sake of that uncourteous lad she now refused him? But she had heard that piece of gossip and no doubt recognized Antonino on meeting him again.

And now they sat together in this boat, like two most deadly enemies, while their hearts were beating fit to kill them. Antonino's usually so good humored face was heated scarlet; he struck the oars so sharply that the foam flew over to where Laurella sat; while his lips trembled at times as if muttering angry words. She pretended not to notice, wearing her most unconscious look, bending over the edge of the boat, and letting the cool water pass between her fingers. Then she threw off her handkerchief again and began to smooth her hair as though she were alone. Only her eyebrows twitched and she held up her wet hands in vain attempts to cool her burning cheeks.

Now they were well out into the open sea. The island was far behind and the coast before them lay yet distant in the hot haze. Not a sail was within sight, far or near; not even a passing gull to break the stillness. Antonino looked all round, evidently ripening some hasty resolution. The color faded suddenly from his cheek and he dropped his oars. Laurella looked round involuntarily, in suspense but without fear.

" I must make an end of this," the young fellow burst forth. " It has lasted too long already. I only wonder that it has not killed me!—you say you do not know me? And all this time you must have seen me pass you like a madman, my whole heart full of what I had to tell you, and then you only made your crossest mouth and turned your back upon me."

" What had I to say to you? " she curtly said. " I may have seen that you were inclined to meddle with me, but I do not choose to be on people's wicked tongues for nothing. I do not mean to have you for a husband. Neither you nor any other."

" Nor any other? So will you not always say! You say so now, because you would not have that painter. Bah! you were but a child then. You will feel lonely enough yet some day; and then, wild as you are, you will take the next best who comes to hand."

" Who knows? Which of us can see the future? It may be that I shall change my mind yet. What is that to you? "

" What is it to me? " he flew out, starting to his feet, while the small boat leapt and danced; " what is it to me, you say? You know well enough! I tell you that man shall perish miserably to whom you shall prove kinder than you have been to me! "

"And to you, what did I ever promise? Am I to blame if you be mad? What right have you to me? "

"Ah! I know," he cried; "my right is written nowhere. It has not been put in Latin by any lawyer nor stamped with any seal. But this I feel; I have just the right to you I have to Heaven if I die an honest Christian. Do you think I could look on and see you go to church with another man and see the girls go by and shrug their shoulders at me? Ought I to bear this humiliation?"

" You can do as you please. I am not going to let myself be frightened by all those threats. I also mean to do as I please."

" You shall not say so long!" and his whole frame shook with passion. " I am not the man to let my whole life be spoiled by a stubborn wench like you! You are in my power here, remember, and may be made to do my bidding."

She could not repress a start, but her eyes flashed bravely on him.

" You may kill me, if you dare," she said slowly.

" I do nothing by halves," he said, and his voice sounded choked and hoarse. " There is room for us both in the sea; I cannot help thee, child,"—he spoke the last words dreamily, almost pitifully;—" but we must both go down together—both at once—and now!" he shouted, and suddenly snatched her in his arms. But at the same moment he drew back his right hand; the blood gushed out—she had bitten him fiercely.

" Ha! can I be made to do your bidding?" she cried, and thrust him from her with one sudden movement; " am I here in your power?" and she leapt into the sea and sank.

She rose again directly; her scanty skirts clung close; her long hair, loosened by the waves, hung heavy about her neck, she struck out valiantly and, without uttering a sound, she began to swim steadily from the boat toward the shore.

With senses maimed by sudden terror he stood, with outstretched neck, looking after her; his eyes fixed, as though they had just been witness to a miracle. Then, giving himself a shake, he pounced upon his oars and began rowing after her with all the strength he had, while all the time the bottom of the boat was reddening fast with the blood that kept streaming from his hand.

Rapidly as she swam, he was at her side in a moment. "For the love of our most Holy Virgin," he cried, "get into the boat! I have been a madman! God alone can tell what so suddenly darkened my brain. It came upon me like a flash of lightning and set me all on fire. I knew not what I did or said. I do not even ask you to forgive me, Laurella, only to come into the boat again so as to save your life!"

She swam on as though she had not heard him.

"You can never swim to land. I tell you, it is two miles off. Think upon your mother! If you should come to grief I should die of horror."

She measured the distance with her eye and then, without answering him one word, she swam up to the boat and laid her hands upon the edge; he rose to help her in. As the boat tilted over to one side with the young girl's weight, his jacket that was lying on the bench slipped into the water. Agile as she was, she swung herself on board without assistance and gained her former seat. As soon as he saw that she was safe, he took to his oars again while she began quietly wringing out her dripping clothes and shaking the water from her hair. As her eyes fell upon the bottom of the boat and saw the blood she gave a quick look at the hand which held the oar as if it had been unhurt.

"Take this," she said, and held out her pocket-handkerchief. He shook his head and went on rowing. After a time she rose and stepping up to him she bound the handkerchief firmly round the wound, which was very deep. Then, heedless of his endeavors to prevent her, she took an oar and seating herself opposite him she began to row with steady strokes, keeping her eyes from looking toward him —fixed upon the oar that was scarlet with his blood. Both were pale and silent; as they drew near land such fishermen as they met began shouting after Antonino and jibing at Laurella, but neither of them moved an eyelid or spoke one word.

The sun stood yet high over Procida when they landed at the Marina. Laurella shook out her skirt, now nearly dry, and jumped on shore. The old spinning woman who, in the morning, had seen them start, was again upon her terrace. She called down: " What is that upon your hand, Tonino? Jesus Christ!—the boat is full of blood!"

" It is nothing, Commare," the young fellow replied. " I tore my hand against a nail that was sticking out too far, it will be well tomorrow. It is only this confounded ready blood of mine that always makes a thing look worse than it really is."

" Let me come and bind it up, Comparello; stop one moment, I will go and fetch the herbs and come to you directly."

" Never trouble yourself, Commare. It has been dressed already, tomorrow morning it will be all over and forgotten. I have a healthy skin that heals directly."

"Addio!" said Laurella, turning to the path that goes winding up the cliffs. " Good night!" he answered, without looking at her; and then, taking his oars and baskets from the boat, and climbing up the small stone stairs, he went into his own hut.

Antonino was alone in his two little rooms and began to pace them up and down. Cooler than upon the dead calm sea, the breeze blew fresh through the small unglazed windows, which were only to be closed with wooden shutters. The solitude was soothing to him. He stopped before the little image of the Virgin, devoutly gazing upon the glory round the head (made of stars cut out in silver paper). But he did not want to pray. What reason had he to pray now that he had lost all he had ever hoped for?

And this day appeared to last forever. He did so long for night! for he was weary and more exhausted by the loss of blood than he would have cared to own. His hand was very sore; seating himself upon a little stool he untied the handkerchief that bound it, and the blood, so long repressed, gushed out again; all round the wound the hand was swollen high.

He washed it carefully, cooling it in the water; then he clearly saw the marks of Laurella's teeth.

" She was right," he said — " I was a brute and deserved no better. I will send her back the handkerchief by Giuseppe tomorrow, for never shall she set eyes on me again." And he washed the handkerchief with greatest care and spread it out in the sun to dry.

And having bound up his hand again as well as he could manage with his teeth and his left hand, he threw himself upon his bed and closed his eyes.

He was soon awakened from a sort of slumber by the rays of the bright moonlight and also by the pain of his hand; he had just risen for more cold water to soothe its throbbings when he heard the sound of some one at his door. " Who is there? " he cried, and went to open it. Laurella stood before him.

She came in without a question, took off the handkerchief she had tied over her head, and placed her little basket upon the table; then she drew a deep breath.

" You are come to fetch your handkerchief," he said, " you need not have taken that trouble. In the morning I would have asked Giuseppe to take it to you."

" It is not the handkerchief," she said quickly. " I have been up among the hills to gather herbs to stop the blood; see here." And she lifted the lid of her little basket.

" Too much trouble," he said, not in bitterness — " far too much trouble; I am better, much better; but if I were worse it would be no more than I deserve. Why did you come at such a time? If any one should see you? You know how they talk! Even when they don't know what they are saying."

" I care for no one's talk," she said, passionately; " I came to see your hand and put the herbs upon it; you cannot do it with your left."

" It is not worth while, I tell you."

"Let me see it then, if I am to believe you."

She took his hand that was not able to prevent her and unbound the linen. When she saw the swelling she shuddered and gave a cry—"Jesus Maria!"

"It is a little swollen," he said; "it will be over in four and twenty hours."

She shook her head. "It will certainly be a week before you can go to sea."

"More likely a day or two, and if not, what matters?"

She had fetched a basin and began carefully washing out the wound, which he suffered passively, like a child. She then laid on the healing leaves, which at once relieved the burning pain, and finally bound it up with the linen she had brought with her.

"I thank you," he said, when it was done; "and now, if you would do me one more kindness, forgive the madness that came over me; forget all I said and did. I cannot tell how it came to pass; certainly it was not your fault—not yours. And never shall you hear from me again one word to vex you."

She interrupted him: "It is I who have to beg your pardon. I should have spoken differently. I might have explained it better and not enraged you with my sullen ways. And now that bite!—"

"It was in self-defense—it was high time to bring me to my senses. As I said before, it is nothing at all to signify. Do not talk of being forgiven, you only did me good, and I thank you for it; and now go home to bed—here is your handkerchief; take it with you."

He held it to her, but yet she lingered; hesitated and appeared to have some inward struggle—at length she said: "You have lost your jacket and by my fault; and I know that all the money for the oranges was in it. I did not think of this till afterward. I cannot replace it now, we have not so much at home—or if we had it would be mother's—but this I have; this silver cross. That painter left it on the table the day he came for the last time—I have never looked at it all this while and do not care to keep it in my box; if you were to sell it? It must be worth a few piastres, mother said. It might make up the money you have lost; and if not quite, I could earn the rest by spinning at night when mother is asleep."

"Nothing will make me take it," he said shortly, pushing away the bright new cross which she had taken from her pocket.

"You must," she said; "how can you tell how long your hand may keep you from your work? There it lies, and nothing can make me so much as look at it again."

"Drop it in the sea, then."

"It is no present I want to make you, it is no more than is your due, it is only fair."

"Nothing from you can be due to me, and hereafter when we chance to meet, if you would do me a kindness, I beg you not to look my way. It would make me feel you were thinking of what I have done. And now good night, and let this be the last word said."

He laid the handkerchief in her basket and also the cross, and closed the lid. But when he looked into her face he started — great heavy drops were rolling down her cheeks; she let them flow unheeded.

"Maria Santissima!" he cried. "Are you ill? You are trembling from head to foot!"

"It is nothing," she said, "I must go home;" and with unsteady steps she was moving to the door when suddenly a passion of weeping overcame her, and leaning her brow against the wall she fell into a fit of bitter sobbing. Before he could go to her she turned upon him suddenly and fell upon his neck.

"I cannot bear it," she cried, clinging to him as a dying thing to life — "I cannot bear it, I cannot let you speak so kindly and bid me go with all this on my conscience. Beat me! trample on me, curse me! Or if it can be that you love me still, after all I have done to you, take me and keep me, and do with me as you please; only do not send me so away!" She could say no more for sobbing.

Speechless, he held her awhile in his arms. "If I can love you still!" he cried at last. "Holy mother of God! Do you think that all my best heart's blood has gone from me through that little wound? Don't you hear it hammering now as though it would burst my breast and go to you? But if you say this to try me or because you pity me, then go and I can even forget this — you are not to think you owe me this, because you know what I am suffering for you."

"No!" she said very resolutely, looking up from his shoulder into his face with her tearful eyes; "it is because I love you; and let me tell you, it was because I always feared to love you that I was so cross. I will be so different now — I never could bear again to pass you in the street without one look! And lest you should ever feel a doubt, I will kiss you, that you may say 'she kissed me;' and Laurella kisses no man but him whom she intends to marry."

She kissed him thrice, and escaping from his arms said: "And now good night, *amor mio, cara vita mia!* Lie down to sleep and let your hand get well. Do not come with me; I am afraid of no man, save you alone."

And so she slipped out and soon disappeared in the shadow of the wall.

He remained standing by the window, gazing far out over the calm sea, while all the stars in Heaven appeared to flit before his eyes.

The next time the little curato sat in his confessional he sat smiling to himself: Laurella had just risen from her knees after a very long confession.

"Who would have thought," he said musingly, "that the Lord would so soon have taken pity upon that wayward little heart? And I had been reproaching myself for not having adjured more sternly that ill demon of perversity. Our eyes are but shortsighted to see the ways of Heaven!

"Well, may God bless her, I say! and let me live to go to sea with Laurella's eldest born, rowing me in his father's place! Ah! well, indeed! L'Arrabiata!"

NINO AND MASO* (1881)

A Tale Drawn from a Sienese Chronicle

By Paul Heyse

TRANSLATED BY ALFRED REMY, A. M.

BOUT this time — the chronicler is referring to the beginning of the fifteenth century — there occurred in our city a strange and moving incident which well deserves mention in this place among the more important public events and political squabbles and is surely worth rescuing from oblivion, since in its day it excited the minds of the people and occupied them for many months quite as much as did warlike events and great public calamities and visitations. For not only were the two persons concerned in this sad story known and beloved, each for his own sake, in the whole city of Siena, but the firm and indissoluble bond of friendship which united them from their boyhood up to the time of their early death invested them in the eyes of their contemporaries with a peculiar radiance and an almost supernatural glory, as if they had been beings of another age. And as in ancient times poets had celebrated Damon and Pythias or Orestes and Pylades in song and story, so the people boasted of possessing among their fellow-citizens a pair of friends who in their devotion to each other did not rank below those heroes celebrated by the bards, but even surpassed them because joined in death.

They were the children of neighbors, but had grown up in quite different ranks of society. Antonino del Garbo was

---

* By permission of the author, and J. G. Cotta, publisher, Stuttgart.

the son of one of the most respected and wealthy citizens of Siena, who for some years had even held the office of *gonfaloniere* until a serious wound received in the wars with Florence compelled him to renounce all public affairs and honors. From that time on he lived solely for the education of his only son, whom he personally instructed in the rudiments of all the sciences, while at the same time he had been trained by the most skilful masters in gymnastic exercises and the fine arts. As Nino was not only a bright and at the same time a serious boy, but had also inherited the beauty of his mother, a Calandrini, and felt an ambition to become as proficient in all the arts of chivalry as his father was reputed to be, he developed into a perfect model of a young man, from whom his native city might well expect at some future day the most distinguished services.

Now in the adjoining house, which, to be sure, could not rival the *Casa del Garbo* either in external splendor or family wealth, there lived a modest goldsmith, Master Buonfigli by name, who at the early death of his wife had been left with two children, Tommaso or Maso, and Lisabetta. The girl, who was very charming, grew up in the care and custody of an old relative, who was called by the household Aunt Brigida; while the son at an early age was obliged to lend a helping hand in his father's workshop, and, for the rest, might pick up his education by himself as best he could. As nature had endowed him, not indeed with personal beauty, but with a pair of observant eyes and attentive ears, he succeeded in this astonishingly well, so that no one would ever have guessed how short a time he had sat on a school bench. The honest goldsmith lacked the necessary funds to keep expensive masters for his son, like his aristocratic neighbor, even if he had felt like dispensing with the boy's services as his assistant at the smelting-furnace and the chasing-table; for his artistic trade, although he was thoroughly master of it, yielded him only just enough to enable him to maintain his house on a

respectable footing and earn a decent living for himself
and his family. It was in fact his misfortune that his professional conscience was too sensitive and hypercritical,
and that he would not let a piece of work go out of his
hands until it could pass the most minute inspection;
thus it was that even the slightest mistake on the part
of one of his assistants would cause him to re-melt the
whole and begin anew, and, this being the case, it is no
wonder that he did not greatly prosper. However, such a
state of affairs did not particularly worry either him or
his son, who, it is true, had not inherited the scrupulous
disposition of his father, but, instead, possessed a happy,
light heart which made him welcome each day with new
joy and new hope, however little of all his fantastic dreams
met with realization. What contributed to this state of
mind was, above all, the happiness that he enjoyed in the
passionate love for his neighbor, young Nino del Garbo. It
seemed as if he tacitly regarded as his own legitimate
property whatever belonged to this boy so richly favored
by fortune, and in this attitude he was confirmed by an
answering affection on the part of the serious, reticent lad;
for not a day passed that these two, when the lessons were
over and the day's business done, did not meet, generally on
the walls that surrounded the city or outside the gates
in the beautiful valleys filled with bushes and trees. It
seemed then as though they were discussing the salvation
of the world, as their conversation never came to an end.
They avoided the other boys of their own age and their
fathers did not interfere with this inclination, as each had
carefully studied the son of the other to ascertain whether
he were really a fit companion for his own child; and both
fathers found this exclusive companionship less dangerous
than association with a crowd of good-for-nothing, quarrel-
some comrades.

After the boys had come to be young men, the scoffers —
who had given them all sorts of nicknames, such as '' The
two turtle-doves,'' '' The loving couple,'' '' The right hand

and the left hand ''—prophesied that their inseparable companionship would now come to an end, since the women would interpose, who, as is well known, have always cast the apple of discord among the men, or at least so exclusively captivate the mind and thoughts of a young fellow that no room remains for a third person, even though he were the least jealous of boon-companions and bosom-friends.

To their great astonishment, however, these wiseacres were doomed to see that their prophecies were not fulfilled. Neither Nino nor Maso seemed to be aware of the fact that they had been placed by the young women and maidens of the city upon the list of those of whom fond homage or even more serious wooing was expected. Even more than in the case of the handsome Nino, who was regarded as a young philosopher and whimsical ascetic, this indifference caused surprise when seen in his light-hearted friend, whose glance by no means avoided the beautiful eyes that were turned in his direction, but rather viewed with undisguised pleasure whatever was lovely and charming in the world. It must be admitted, however, that he seemed to make no distinction between an ornament of sparkling jewels, a blooming pomegranate-tree, and a woman possessed of beauty and youth. His interest in humanity, as something which he found more important and pleasurable than all other beautiful works from the hand of the Creator, seemed to begin only with his friend and to end with him; while of the fair sex there appeared to exist for him only one individual, little Lisabetta, and, as she was several years younger than he, he guarded her as the apple of his eye and with almost motherly care and jealousy.

Now it happened at last that Nino's father considered that the time had arrived to send his son to Bologna for some years to study law at the university. This first separation of the two friends caused them such great sorrow as is usually experienced only by two lovers who must part from each other; but both were too proud and bashful to permit any one to be a witness of their grief. The night before Nino's departure they spent without sleep in Maso's scantily furnished room. In the early morning when the young student, accompanied by his family and many friends, rode out of the city, Maso was nowhere to be seen among those who were waving farewell. He was sitting in his shop diligently at work on the skilfully ornamented hilt of a dagger which he had promised to send on after his friend.

But at the end of a month, when he had finished it, he disappeared one day from the city. No one knew what had become of him. He had left a note for his father in which he stated that he would return at the end of a week. Later it was learned that he had walked the long distance to Bologna for the sole purpose of passing a single day with Nino. His father, who loved him above everything, did not reproach him; only little Lisabetta pouted because he had brought her nothing from Nino but a greeting.

The other pretty maidens, who had had hopes of entering now upon Nino's heritage and appropriating to themselves the unattached heart of the solitary young fellow, found themselves disappointed. The hours which he had formerly spent with his friend he devoted to zealous practice on the lute, upon which instrument he soon became a great master. He himself also composed the most beautiful lays and love songs, which one could hear him singing on many a balmy night in the little garden behind his house, nor did he fail to instruct his sister in this art. Yet not one of the fair ladies of the city, who at a casual meeting on the street or at church were not chary of encouraging glances, could boast that he had ever practised his art at night under her window.

Moreover, he soon found himself in a situation where he no longer felt any inclination for playing and singing. His father, old Master Buonfigli, died suddenly, leaving to his son the care of his house, and his young sister who was not yet fifteen. Henceforth the smile vanished from the bright, good-natured face of the orphaned son, and with an energy of which he had scarcely been thought capable he assumed the reins of the household government. Up to that time he had pursued his art with indifference, though not without skill; now he began to devote himself to it body and soul, as he had firmly resolved to get together a substantial dowry for little Lisabetta — a matter that had never troubled his father.

Since he now sat over his skilful work from morning till night, and after regular hours frequently stayed up until midnight making the designs for his assistants, of whom he had secured several possessed of considerable skill, his fortune grew visibly, as did also his standing in his guild. With all this he had no spare time to keep in touch with the friend of his youth, who in the mean time had not been idle either, and who after a few years won the doctor's degree and returned to his native city. Nino's parents had also died meanwhile, and it was generally believed that, as soon as the young doctor had completed his year of mourning, he would take a wife from one of the first families of the town and present himself as a candidate for one of the high public offices in the community. For the old excessive love and intimacy with the neighbor's son was regarded as extinct, or at least considerably cooled, since the bosom friends had managed to live for such a long time without each other's companionship.

Instead of that, it soon became known that young del Garbo had made application to be received into the guild of lawyers, and that on the same day he had become engaged to the sister of his friend. For some time this caused much jeering comment, since the foolish tongues in Siena, like those in Florence, cannot at once cease wagging if a good subject is offered them. In time, however, this news, like any other, grew old and stale, since the closely united friends, now three in number — or four, if we include Aunt Brigida — were seldom seen, and, at most, Maso's lute was again heard in the quiet garden on moonlight or

starlight nights, accompanying the soft voice of the young
fiancèe. And as Nino also went about his business as reticent as ever, there even were many who asserted they had
always claimed that thus and not otherwise would matters
come to pass, and thus and not otherwise matters ought
to be, too.

The wedding had been deferred for half a year, as Liza-
betta had to make her trousseau herself and was very busy
with Brigida day after day. Now, for a lover to whom it
would have seemed that a thousand years must pass before
he could lead his loved one home to his richly appointed
house, this indeed would not have been sufficient reason
for such a long delay. Nino, however, although he made it
clear that he regarded the charming maiden as a jewel of
her sex, did not manifest the least impatience, so that it
even attracted the attention of the simple child, who at last,
with tears in her eyes, complained to her old foster-mother
about the coldness of her lover. It seemed to her he would
never have chosen her had she not been the sister of Maso,
who really was his only love. Thereupon the old nurse,
although she also regarded the affair with some suspicion,
tried to console her pet as well as she could; at the same
time she made a secret resolution to call the cold lover to
account and ask him whether he were a fish or a salamander
that could not warm up even in the fire of such tender
young eyes. But when he came in the evening with his
quiet, dreamy cheerfulness, and chatted as kindly, but also
as coolly, with little Lisabetta as though she had been his
own sister, she nevertheless had not the courage to show
her secret resentment, but thought that some day things
would surely change, when the flame of his own hearth
began to melt the ice.

Now it happened at carnival-time that Maso was called
to Venice by a very distinguished and wealthy nobleman to
give him advice regarding the bridal jewelry of the daughter of the house, who had been betrothed to a French duke.
The jewels, which in the family of the mother had for cen-

turies been bequeathed from mother to daughter, were to have a new setting and were to be completed by the most beautiful stones that could be procured from the Orient. Maso had expected to discharge this honorable commission within three weeks; but since his personality found great favor, just as his art justified its good reputation, he was detained from week to week, and always had his hands full making new designs and directing less skilled masters who were working under his instructions. More than a hundred times he cursed himself for having anything to do with the whole business.

When at last the month of March drew to a close and still the end was not in sight, he wrote to his people at home to prepare the wedding without waiting for him, have the banns published, and let him know the day fixed for the celebration, adding that he would come then even if they tried to bind him with golden chains to the Campanile of San Marco.

For something like two weeks no answer came to this letter, so that Maso, tortured by anxiety and impatience, could think of nothing better than to send a trusted servant as courier to Siena, with instructions to return to Venice without delay as soon as he had received an answer. This servant, however, could not have got further than Florence, when the so eagerly expected letter, which he had passed on his way, was delivered into the hands of the young master. Now this letter was neither in Nino's handwriting, who during the last months had been able to find no leisure at all for writing because of excessive pressure of business, as he had pretended, nor did the missive exhibit the daintily scrawled characters of the bride-to-be, either; but old Brigida herself, with halting pen and with evidently uncontrollable emotion, had written the following lines:

"Dearest nephew! Dearly beloved Maso! In the weeks that you have had to go without news from home things have been in a rather sad state here, and unless the good Lord and the blessed Virgin Mary should yet cause everything to turn out for the best, mirth and laughter will be silenced forever and the last days of your old Brigida will pass in sheer grief and distress. But because I know that the author of all this wretchedness and sadness is dearer to you than the light of your eyes, I have hesitated until now to tell you a single word about it, being well aware, dear Maso, that for your work away from home you need to be of good courage and to have a spirit free from care, so as to do yourself credit and put your detractors to shame. Now, however, I owe it to another person whom, next to that friend, you love most dearly, to break my silence, in order that when you learn in what danger and distress she is living you may yet find means of warding off the worst and of once more securing peace and happiness for us all.

" For I must make known to you, my dearest son, that your friend's heart has turned away from his affianced bride, your innocent sister, so that for three weeks now he has avoided her presence, nor has he sent her any message to explain his absence. A short time after you had left us there came to our city — rumor says from Empoli — a strange lady, a very youthful widow, Madonna Violante, the sister-in-law of our *podestà*, Messer Vitelli, whose brother had made her acquaintance some years ago on one of his business trips and subsequently married. He died soon after, and, not having anticipated such an early death, had not drawn up his last will in proper legal form. The widow did not enjoy the best reputation, and her husband's relatives here tried to put her off with a small sum. In order to protest against such action and at the same time to take possession of her late husband's country home — situated near the city — as her widow's dower, Madonna Violante came to Siena. As the relatives of the *podestà* to a man closed their doors against her, she applied to the court, and requested the services of the most learned and distinguished lawyer in the city. Public opinion designated your Nino as that man. In the beginning he devoted

himself with all conscientiousness to the case, and when he
still came daily to our garden for an hour's talk with little
Lisabetta he used to tell about the whole affair and the
beautiful plaintiff with as little embarrassment as if he
were reading it all from a printed book. After some weeks,
though, it was evident that he avoided this subject, and
whenever Lisabetta playfully alluded to it he became confused, and blushed. Finally the girl's jealousy was aroused,
and when one day with tears in her eyes she fell upon his
neck, begging him, for love of her, to intrust this ugly lawsuit to one of his friends and colleagues, since it threatened to rob him of his cheerfulness and her of his love, he
pressed her violently to his heart and in great agitation
stammered a few distracted words. Then he freed himself from her dear arms, and left her like a man pursued
by evil spirits.

" Since that day, dear Maso, he has not again appeared
under our roof, in spite of the proximity of our houses and
in spite of the approaching wedding, although I sent him
message after message. And when at last I entered his
house myself to tell him to his face that by this estrange-
ment he would break the young heart that was so devoted
to him and would burden his conscience with a mortal sin,
one of his clerks gave me to understand that his master was
unwell and could not receive anybody.

" You may be sure, my dear son, that I did not take this
subterfuge at its face value. On the contrary, with anxiety
and indignation in my old heart, which has only you two
beloved children left on this earth, I set myself to watch.
And that very same night, as soon as all good Christians
had retired to rest, I saw your fine friend, muffled up in his
cloak, steal out of his house—a fact that did not very
well agree with the report of his indisposition, which probably was nothing else than a violent love-fever, absolutely
proof against any winter night. Although my teeth were
chattering with anger and the cold, I nevertheless bravely
kept my place at the upper window, because I believed that

it was my duty to witness with my own eyes how this per-
fidious traitor was menacing the life of my dear child.
When finally, in the fourth hour after midnight, I saw
him slinking back along the street and into his house, I
could scarcely restrain myself from screaming in his face
what I thought of him, and that I hoped God's justice would
succeed in finding him.

"However, I bit my lips to prevent myself from pro-
claiming to the neighborhood the shame he had brought
upon us — especially as it came to my mind that it was your
duty, and nobody's else, to defend the happiness and honor
of your sister. I concealed from the girl what I had seen in
the night, although the proceeding was continued during the
following nights too, and although her poor heart, if it should
once realize that it had thrown itself away on an unworthy object, might perhaps find in this bitter knowledge a
means of recovery from its error. In this matter, as I am
old and no longer know what young people need and are
capable of, my judgment may perhaps lead me astray; and
for this reason I have finally decided, my dearest son, to
tell you everything faithfully and to leave to your judgment
what you deem it necessary to do. But now, before I commend you to the protection of the Holy Trinity and of all
the saints, I must implore you not to delay reaching a
decision. You will be alarmed to see how this sorrow has
gnawed at our darling's heart and destroyed the bloom of
her youthful beauty, so that she is walking about as if in
the shadow of death; and even entire strangers are touched
with pity at beholding this young affianced bride, once so
joyous, with head bowed to earth like a withered lily."

This letter, which was later found preserved among
Maso's papers, with plain traces of a hand that had violently crumpled it up during the reading, reached the young
master in the Piazza di San Marco as he was just on the
point of carrying to the nobleman who had ordered it a
magnificent silver vase richly ornamented with precious

stones and figures in relief. No sooner had he cast his eye over the letter than he directed his servant to go alone on the errand and to present his master's excuses, saying that a very urgent matter had necessitated his immediate departure for home. Within the same hour, without stopping to arrange his other affairs, he had himself rowed in a little skiff to the mainland, hired a horse, and galloped toward home by the shortest road. During the journey he allowed himself no more rest than he absolutely needed in order to arrive at home in the full possession of his faculties, as behooved a judge and an avenger.

In the last night, however, before reaching his destination, he could find no sleep on his couch; and, as he feared an illness might overtake him and detain him in that solitary inn, he rose without disturbing the host, saddled his horse, which was only half rested, without calling the hostler, and through the gray, frosty, February night rode along the road to Siena. When he beheld the beautiful city on the heights the early rays of the morning sun were just gilding the towers and battlements of the palaces — but in his soul it remained dark night. He left his horse at a small inn close to the city gate, then crept on foot to his house, choosing the most deserted alleys; for he had a feeling that he could look no one straight in the face, because the shameful conduct of his only friend weighed upon him as if it were his own guilt and dishonor, of which he ought to be ashamed in the eyes of God and the world.

Old Brigida herself was just opening the door of the little goldsmith-shop when she found herself face to face with Maso. She was about to rush into his arms with a loud cry, but he put his hand over her mouth commanding silence. Trembling in every limb, she obeyed when she saw his sunken cheeks and the haunted look in his eyes, dull from lack of sleep. Then he drew her into the kitchen, which was on the ground floor looking out upon the garden, and after he had tossed off a goblet of wine and repeatedly applied to his forehead a sponge with ice-cold water he listened to her account of the events of the last few days.

The situation had not changed, except that people in the city were already beginning to whisper about the affair, and some inquisitive gossips had visited the faithful old lady to find out whether there were any truth in the rumor. The good soul assured him that she had boldly denied everything, and had even invented an illness of her dear Lisabetta as a pretext, which, as a matter of fact, was not so very far from the truth; for many a person whose last hour had come felt less anguish than this poor creature.

Would he like to see her? She was upstairs in her room, and it was to be hoped that she had fallen into a light morning slumber after a restless night of sighing and weeping. Maso energetically shook his head. He had not the courage to look again into his sister's eyes until he could tell her that he had done a brother's duty by her. To this he now intended to proceed without delay.

"Oh, Maso," cried the old lady, wringing her hands, "think of the salvation of your soul and do not commit a deed of violence! Perhaps he is less guilty than we think, and has been compelled to yield to some hellish delusion. For several persons, whom I asked about this strange lady, have assured me that she is by no means a marvel of beauty and grace; and who knows whether Nino, when you remind him of everything as it used to be formerly between you—"

"Enough," he cried with a dark look, gnashing his teeth. "Look! Here I lay aside my sword and my dagger. I shall go to him unarmed. If the words from my lips cannot find a way to his heart then we will see what steps are to be taken later. But I must protect myself from my own fury, so that I may do nothing that I shall rue. Is he not Nino? Even after all the sorrow he has caused me, can I have the heart to go to him in arms as to an enemy?"

Then his eyes beheld upon the table a little box of ebony inlaid with mother-of-pearl, that Nino had presented to him years ago, and all at once his self-command, which he had maintained only with great effort, broke down, and the tears rushed to his eyes. But he immediately regained control over himself, rose, and shook hands with Brigida. "It has relieved me," he said, "and washed the mist from my eyes. You will see it was nothing; we have all misjudged him; everything will yet turn out well. Prepare my breakfast, for I hope to be back soon, bringing good news, and perhaps Nino himself."

Thereupon he went out of the door with a firm step, up to the gate of the *Casa del Gargo*. But when he heard the sound of the knocker his heart trembled. He mounted the well-known stairs, and, since no one dared to stop the friend of the master of the house, although it was not yet the hour for visitors, he quickly found the way to Nino's room, knocked in the manner arranged between them, and, without waiting for any "Come in," entered the chamber.

Nino started from his bed, in which he had been resting only a few hours. It seemed as if he did not immediately recognize his visitor. The latter, however, when he saw the pale face that he had loved so much staring at him from the dimly lighted corner, was not able to utter a single one of all the bitter words which he had resolved to speak. He advanced slowly to the middle of the room, his hat still on his head; and stopping by an arm-chair at the side of the bed and beginning slowly to take off his gloves, he nodded absent-mindedly to his friend as though bidding him not to disturb himself.

"Good morning, Nino," he said at length with an unsteady voice. "I come early. But I do not intend to stay long."

"Is that really you, Maso!" Nino exclaimed, only now rousing himself completely. "Oh, Maso, why did you not come sooner? Why did not some good spirit whisper to you what alone might perhaps have saved us? And yet — at last you are here — once more I see your face. It is strange, Maso, but I have long feared that you would enter here in this manner; and now, although it is not possible

that you can come with kind thoughts, I nevertheless feel
as though there were removed from my breast an anvil upon
which malicious demons have been hammering day and
night. I thank you for coming.''

He held out both hands toward him. But Maso, although
he felt an almost irresistible desire to rush into Nino's
arms, looked away from him, dropped into the arm-chair,
and riveted his eyes upon the carpet that covered the
floor; he dared not speak a word for fear of losing his
determination.

''You are right,'' said Nino, whose head sank back upon
his pillow. ''You cannot again clasp my hand in yours
before you know how wretched is the man whom you cannot but regard as the heedless destroyer of your happiness
and honor. Oh, believe me, Maso, every day I have said
to myself a hundred times that I am a scoundrel, more
guilty than a murderer or sacrilegist, that I need go but
twenty steps to confess my great crime and to atone for
it at the feet of the angel who has given me her heart. But
there are demons, Maso, that cling to the heels of a penitent sinner and hold him back, so that he can never walk
in the way of grace; and therefore it is well that you have
come. There upon the table lies the dagger which you
yourself forged for me and brought to Bologna; take it and
end my torments, and avenge your sister. With my last
breath I will proclaim that you have dealt rightly and
justly by me, and with your name upon my lips I will go
down to hell.''

After these words there ensued a long silence, interrupted only by the stifled moans of the wretched man who
had pressed his lips against the bolster of his bed. Then
he suddenly felt his friend's hand laid gently and tremb-
lingly on his own.

''Nino,'' whispered the latter, terribly shaken, in a voice
almost stifled with emotion, ''tell me everything. I ought
to have known indeed that you never could grieve me of
your own free will.''

Nino did not move, but lay for quite a while as if his spirit were far away. His breathing, however, became more regular, and his soul's agony seemed to find relief through the touch of Maso's hand. Then, suddenly supporting himself on his pillows, he said: "In the cathedral I have had masses said for the delivery of a poor soul from the snare of the devil, on my knees I have prayed to my patron saint, who knows far more than others what it means to be tempted — all in vain! She is a devil, but I have fallen into her power, soul and body. Three years ago, when I first entered the university, a fortune-teller warned me to beware of women marked with a birth-mark. At that time I laughed, as, until then, I had never been tempted by a woman. Now I have lived to learn that the sorceress prophesied the truth. You see, Maso, in the beginning, when I went to see her in the matter of the lawsuit — if any one had told me then that for the sake of this woman I should forfeit my eternal salvation, do such irreparable injury to my dearest friend, and betray the most innocent heart on earth, I should have treated his prattle as that of a madman, and should have considered myself invulnerable in the armor of my good conscience. And yet now it has gone so far that I have fallen under a spell that enslaves my free will, disarms my pride, and makes me appear to myself a wretch and scoundrel unworthy of mercy and pity, because I am too cowardly to flee what I despise and to grasp the hand that is desirous of saving me from damnation."

He covered his face with his hands, and again no word was spoken for a considerable time. Maso had risen and was pacing the room with long strides. Finally he stopped close by the bed.

"Do you intend to make her your wife?" he cried from the depths of his oppressed heart.

"The Madonna and all the saints defend me from such madness!" exclaimed the wretched man. "I tell you, Maso, this woman has no soul, and whoever gives himself up to her is surely damned, in this world and the next. Moreover, she does not love me, although now and then she makes me believe that she does. She loves nothing under the sun but her power over poor fools; and I know that I might writhe at her feet in the agony of death, and not a fibre of her heart would feel pity. All this I say to myself, and when I am away from her I call her by the wildest, the most wicked, the most shameful names. And then when the day draws to a close and all grows still about me, there rings distinctly in my ear her enticing voice, soft as the caresses of a little child; and all at once my defiance, my manliness, my anger are dissipated; I must go to her and drink life and death from her glances."

Maso made no reply. For a long time his eyes were riveted upon his friend's high, white forehead, over which the black locks hung disheveled. Then suddenly he stooped down, imprinted a hasty kiss upon Nino's head, and with averted face rushed from the room.

Not until he reached the hall downstairs did he remember that he had forgotten to ask something. But one of the clerks, who was just entering the house to begin his day's work, was able to reply to his question concerning the residence of Madonna Violante; however, he impressed upon the young man that he must not inform his master of his inquiry.

He took the nearest way to the house indicated, which was situated in one of the poorer quarters of the town; nevertheless it was an imposing building, formerly inhabited by one of the wealthier families that had subsequently died out, and the heirs, who did not care to live there, rented it as opportunity offered. When Maso caught sight of it he came to a sudden stop. He did not himself know whether some presentiment of evil rose within him, or whether he wished first to collect his thoughts for the meeting which was to decide the fate of them all. Thus he stood for a while in the middle of the street, attracting the astonished glances

of the passers-by, most of whom recognized him; but his look was so strange, his expression, at other times bright and open, so changed, that nobody ventured to address him. At length he seemed to have come to a decision, and walked resolutely up to the fatal house.

In answer to his knocking a servant pulled the cord, and met him half way up the steps with the question what his business was there at such an early hour. She informed him that her mistress had risen only that moment, and anyway was not in the habit of receiving strangers. The cunning, searching eyes of the girl, who was still young and not ugly, made a decidedly unfavorable impression upon him. But he put a sequin in her hand, and told her briefly that he had a message for Madonna Violante about a matter that would admit of no delay. After she had left him alone for a short time the maid returned and asked for his name. When he had mentioned it she seemed to hesitate a moment; but then she made him a sign with her eyes to follow her, and led him into a large, bare room, where she left him alone with his brooding thoughts.

In a spacious fireplace some logs of olive-wood were burning; on a few of the branches the leaves and withered fruits were still hanging. But the fire gave so little light that the figures of the tapestries with which the walls were covered were distinctly visible only when an occasional gust of wind, coming down the chimney, fanned the flames. Two arm-chairs stood facing each other before the fire; into one of them Maso dropped wearily and waited. As he thought how many nights Nino had probably sat in this place, listening to the words that had beguiled his soul, his heart became suddenly convulsed.

At the other end of the long room a door opened, and the dark figure of a lady entered. With measured steps she advanced toward the fireplace, where Maso had risen, but only after she had come quite near could he distinguish her features. At the first glance he too was surprised that the woman for whose sake his young sister had been sacri-

ficed was not more beautiful. The lady was of medium
height; her figure was rather concealed than displayed to
advantage by a black velvet dress trimmed with a fine gray
fur, especially as she had enveloped her neck and shoulders
in a long, closely woven, light veil of the color of a spider's
web, with slender gold threads running through it. This
veil she had drawn closely about her, as if she felt chilly,
so that her arms and hands were also hidden under it.
Above the folds of this fine-meshed wrap she held her head
erect and immovable; only her eyes, which were of a bluish
hue, moved restlessly under her heavy eyebrows. Her luxuriant hair, of a beautiful chestnut color, hung low on her
neck, arranged in a careless knot. Her face was pale, and
only when she drew back her lip slightly, which she did as
she welcomed her visitor with a scarcely perceptible inclination of the head, did Maso see her small white teeth
glisten; but this strange smile did not render her face any
more attractive in his eyes.

"Assuredly," he said to himself, " I begin to believe that
Nino is right when he says that a spell has been cast over
him. How could this very commonplace being have won
such power over him unless there had been some sorcery
about it? "

Without speaking a word the lady had seated herself in
the vacant chair opposite Maso and made a gesture to him
to resume his seat. She took an iron poker that was standing in a corner of the fireplace, began to stir up the flame,
and threw a fresh log on the fire. As she did this he noticed
her hand, which was not small, but very white and exquis-
itely slender. Upon her middle finger she was wearing a
ring with a blood-red stone.

" Signora Violante," he said at last, suppressing a deep
sigh, " I do not know whether you have ever heard my name
before, or whether you know that it is the name of the
brother of that young girl who in a few weeks, if it is God's
will, is to become the wife of my friend Nino del Garbo.
It would be useless to waste time with deceitful words

and subterfuges; after I have told you this much you probably know what has brought me here to you. You have
alienated the heart of the betrothed lover from his affianced
bride, and have drawn bitter tears from young eyes. It
is not my intention to reproach you for this, however much
or little you may have known of the state of affairs, for
what is done cannot be altered. But what is to happen
in the future, human wisdom, determination, and good will
may still direct into other channels; and for this reason I
have called upon you to ask you whether, and under what
conditions, you will consent to release Nino.''

For some time he waited for her reply. She, however,
as though all these words did not concern her in the least,
sat facing him with her head bent forward, constantly playing with the glowing logs, which she would now pull apart
with the poker, and then again pile one on another.

''I know,'' Maso continued after a silence of some
moments, '' that I am making an unpleasant demand upon
you. You have come to our city on account of your lawsuit, and you would regard it as a piece of great folly to
give up together with the lover who adores you the lawyer
who is to help you to secure your right. And yet I see
no other way out of this sad entanglement than for you to
leave the city as quickly as possible and renounce all intention of ever seeing your lawyer again.''

From the downcast eyes of the lady a quick glance flashed
at the speaker, and once more her lip curled contemptuously. At the same time there had appeared on her cheeks
a slight flush, which suddenly made her look more youthful.
It seemed as if she were on the point of saying something
in reply, but she only shrugged her shoulders, drew the gray
veil closer about her, and continued to poke the fire.

'' I thank you for listening to me quietly,'' Maso continued. '' The sacrifice that I expect of you seems exorbi-
tant, and I could not blame you if you had dismissed me
as a madman. But hear now, what compensation I have
to offer you. If you consent to leave the city I will induce

Nino to transfer your suit to two of the most skilled and influential among his colleagues, who in the future shall transact their business with you in writing. At the same time I will have a deed made out to you stipulating that, in case you should nevertheless lose the suit, I will be responsible with my whole fortune for any loss you may sustain; and if this fortune should not prove sufficient I will pursue my calling as a sort of personal bondman, solely for your benefit, until you have obtained to the last farthing everything that you now claim. In this way you run no risk of suffering any loss of your fortune through your departure. If you regard it as a loss to give up a lover — well, you are sufficiently young and beautiful to win in place of this one as many others as you like, without taking away from some one else what was her property, confirmed by holy vows.''

After that there was silence between them, while Maso with anxious heart tried to read in her impassive face what impression his earnest words had made. Beads of perspiration stood upon his forehead, and he was obliged to press his hand to his heart in order to subdue its tumultuous beating. For the longer he remained in her presence, the more uneasy he became; indeed, the lady's rather snub nose, the nostrils of which were twitching slightly, her small ears, and her soft dimpled chin were already beginning to appear to him more charming than at first, so that Nino's sin and folly no longer seemed to him sheer madness. Then she opened her lips for the first time, and he now heard that caressing child's voice which every day, when twilight came, Nino imagined he heard from a distance.

'' You speak like a sensible man and warm friend of your friend, Signor Buonfigli,'' she said calmly, without looking at him as she spoke. '' But what am I to do? If I leave the city and your friend is really as violently in love with me as you say, will he then be able all at once to adore his intended again as before? Suppose he would without hesitation transfer my lawsuit to others, will he also patiently consent to have my person pass over to some other lover,

as you so kindly take for granted? Come now, you are too
sensible a man to believe that! If you know of no better
means of keeping your sister's lover for her, matters are
in a sad state for the good child, whom I pity heartily,
although I do not know her and have received from you the
first intimation of her relation to Doctor Del Garbo.''

Maso had risen. The tone of her voice and the truth
of what she was saying did not allow him to keep his seat
opposite her. He was pacing the long dark room and letting his eyes wander along the walls, as though the figures
of the tapestries were to counsel him as to what he ought
to say and do. Suddenly he stopped again by his chair,
and said in a hollow voice, '' You will understand, Madonna,
that I cannot go away before I have brought this matter to
a successful issue and have wrested from your hands the
honor of my friend and the happiness of my sister. God
Almighty is my witness that, if I believed that Nino would
be happier with you than with my sister, I should try to
live down this sorrow and not stand between him and his
happiness. But neither do I believe this—nor does he
himself.''

A flaming glance from her eyes penetrated his very heart.
However, he summoned all his courage and continued, '' No,
Madonna, he does not believe it. He has himself assured
me by everything that is most sacred that he neither
believes in your love for him, nor regards his love for you
as something that will bring happiness and endure for a
lifetime. On the contrary he is firmly convinced that you
have fascinated him with magic arts, that you have cast
over him a spell which is not from heaven but—from hell.''

He stopped short after this word had escaped him, which
to his own dismay now reëchoed weirdly in the spacious
room. But the lady before the fire seemed to be entirely
unmoved. She only bent down a little lower, so as to push
back again a log that had rolled out of the fire. At this
moment, however, something dangerous happened. One
end of her gray veil, which was hanging down over her

knees, came too near the flickering flame. Instantly it blazed up, and as the weft was of extreme thinness the whole long veil was suddenly flaming like a fiery serpent around the dark figure, which for a few seconds stood in a red circle of fire and seemed lost beyond all hope of rescue. With a sudden cry Maso rushed toward her. As though she were proof against fire, however, and her hands of asbestos, she tore from her throat and shoulders with lightning rapidity the burning tatters that played about her, before the flames could ignite her dress. And while the glowing folds fell in red flakes at her feet, she suddenly stood with bare shoulders before the dumbfounded Maso; not a muscle of her face moved, nor did the slightest gesture characteristic of a weak woman betray that the danger had alarmed her.

Maso, however, whose heart was beating so loudly that he could not utter a sound, was unable to take his eyes off her. The sight of the most beautiful neck and perfectly formed shoulders seemed to have turned him to stone, but there was also something else that almost deprived him of his senses. Upon her left breast, the whiteness of which seemed even more resplendent by contrast with the black velvet, and was irradiated by the warm glow of the fire, he saw a strange, dark blue mark, similar to the trace which the claw of a small bird leaves in hard-frozen snow. This delicate impression upon the soft skin seemed to be alive, as it rose and fell with every breath; and it was impossible to avert one's glance, if one had once allowed it to stray thither. But all this lasted only a few moments, for suddenly she enveloped her shoulders in her hair, which from her rapid motions had fallen down, and the birth-mark too was hidden from view. Then with a cold triumphant smile which completely crushed Maso, and without addressing another word to him, with head erect and arms crossed over her breast she walked slowly from the room, just as she had come.

When, some time later, the young servant entered again, she found the strange visitor still standing immovable upon the same spot, his eyes directed toward the door through which her mistress had disappeared. Only the sound of her steps roused him from his revery. Hastily he gathered up his hat and cloak from the floor where they had fallen, and, paying no attention to the malicious tittering of the girl, he rushed out of the house.

Where he spent the next few hours he himself was afterward unable to remember. It seems that he must have roamed about senselessly in the neighborhood of the city, his eyes fixed on the ground before him and his soul filled only with inward fancies and visions. Some peasants who were on their way to the city claimed to have seen a man resembling Maso in stature and dress in the open fields about an hour's walk from town. They reported that this man had been beating the air with his arms in a strange manner, as if to ward off the attack of an evil spirit; then again he had thrown himself on the ground and pressed his forehead against the hard earth, like some unfortunate wretch imploring mother Earth to open her bosom to receive her despairing son.

About dusk, however, Maso entered the inn where he had left his horse in the morning, called for something to eat, and drank greedily of the wine which the host placed before him. Subsequently the man said that his guest had looked quite pale and ashen gray, and had occasionally talked to himself in an undertone; that during his soliloquy he had once burst into a laugh, but not a merry laugh such as people were accustomed to hear from Master Maso — for the host had easily recognized him; it had sounded rather like the laugh of an alien spirit from within an unfortunate person possessed. Then the guest had demanded to be shown to a room, where he had immediately thrown himself on the bed without taking off his clothes and fallen into a sound sleep.

As he had not closed his eyes during the preceding night, he lay in the quiet house for several hours in a profound deathlike sleep, which no dreams disturbed. But when a belated carter drove his team with jingling bells into the courtyard of the inn and awakened the host together with all his servants from their first sleep, Maso also was roused from his stupor. The first thing that presented itself to his returning consciousness was the spectre with the white shoulders that had pursued him during the day and drained his blood. He stumbled down the stairs, and for a moment the thought flashed through his brain that he should saddle his horse and ride to the end of the world. Then he heaved a deep sigh and turned in the direction of the city.

The gatekeeper admitted him, since he recognized Maso as a resident citizen. He walked slowly along through the deserted streets, ever as if reluctantly obeying a superior force. What he wished to do there, whither he felt himself drawn, he did not acknowledge to himself. Involuntarily he several times made the sign of the cross in the air with his right hand, and murmured short prayers; but his head was confused and dull, as if he had taken too much wine.

Then at last he saw the house of Madonna Violante, and twinkling from one of the upper windows a narrow streak of light, which showed that she had not yet retired. Only now did he begin to speculate whether he would be admitted, and whom he should find there. He felt a sudden pain in his heart, so that he was obliged to stand still to collect his spirits; but as he was considering further what he should do, he heard from the other side of the narrow street a hurried, soft footstep likewise approaching the house. He knew who it was that was coming, but was not glad, as formerly, to meet this wanderer unexpectedly. As one goes to meet a mortal enemy with whom one has an affair of life and death to settle, he went forward hurriedly, in order that the other person should not reach the fatal house before him. Directly in front of the steps that led up to the little gate they met.

"It is you, Maso!"

"I, and none other, Nino!"

"I have been waiting for you in vain all day, Maso. This is not the time when we can talk. Come tomorrow to my house. Now — I am expected here."

Saying this he started to pass Maso, and was already reaching with his hand for the knocker when he felt his arm pulled back with great violence, and heard these words uttered in a hoarse voice, "They will expect you here in vain today and all future days. Never shall you cross this threshold again, as surely as I pray Christ and his most holy Mother to have mercy on me."

When Nino found himself so forcibly restrained from entering he was silent for a moment; then he said with a sad but calm voice: "Oh, Maso, why did you not kill me this morning in your first anger, as it was your good right and my wish? Then we should not be obliged to face each other here in this manner! But now I cannot yield to you. Even if I wished it otherwise the spell has regained its power, and that is stronger than your arm which desires to hold me back, stronger than our old friendship, which impedes my footsteps like a leaden weight. Were there a bottomless abyss before my feet and this woman were standing on the other side and beckoning to me, I should rush on to meet her, and no one should be permitted to make bold to try to save me. If this seems madness to you, let it be so. Farewell, and leave the madman to his fate!"

"Stop," Maso cried, controlling his voice with difficulty. "One more word first, before matters come to the worst. Let me tell you that I have seen her and am a victim of the same madness. This whole long day I have tried in vain to escape from the net which this devil has thrown about my head. Now I am here to contest the right of every mother's son to her person, even though it were he whom I have loved above all other human beings. Who dares come between me and this woman is my mortal enemy, whom I hate, for whose blood I am thirsting, whom I with these hands of mine — "

He suddenly seized Nino by both shoulders and thrust
him away from the steps with such force that he was pushed
back tottering against the wall. In the next moment Nino,
merely uttering a suppressed groan of rage and resentment, had grappled with his opponent; and now there
began upon the steps a blind, furious wrestling, like that
of two shipwrecked persons, each of whom tries to push
the other into the deep when they find themselves drifting
upon a board too weak for both. Only a muffled, doleful
sigh, as if from a wounded heart, was heard now and then.
But suddenly in their pitiful embrace, which neither seemed
willing to relinquish until he had throttled his opponent,
they had clasped each other so tighly that their heated
cheeks touched. In that moment the dagger which Nino
wore in his belt, loosened through the violent movement,
fell clattering to the ground. Then it seemed as though
through the body and soul of both there passed an electric
shock, which suddenly roused from its torpor their old
love and fidelity which had been so unhappily stifled.
"Nino!" moaned the one; "Maso!" stammered the
other—and before they knew how it had all come about,
the hostile grip had changed to a stormy embrace of four
tenderly entwined arms, and while tears gushed from their
eyes their lips were pressed so close together that all
words of accusation and excuse were smothered.

In this embrace they held each other for possibly some
three minutes, during which time neither was able to say
anything else than: "O Nino, was it really possible?"—
"O Maso, can it have come to this?" But when their first
terrible bewilderment had somewhat subsided, when their
eyes no longer met through tears, and they had come to
realize their situation, Maso grasped the hand of his
friend, and said: "With this handclasp I here vow never
to allow any other love to have power over me than the
love for my Nino!" and Nino cried, "To my Maso I make
a similar vow, so help me God!" "Amen," Maso added.
Then he dried his forehead and eyes with his hand, cast a

look upward toward the light in the window, and said, " If
we really mean what we have just sworn there is only one
hope of safety — the sorceress who tried to come between
us must not live ! "

" You speak the truth," answered Nino. " If one could
kill with thoughts she were dead now."

" Behind the thought there must rise an arm, and a
weapon must be at its service," Maso said. " Which of
us is to put the sentence into execution ? "

Thereupon both were silent, but Nino collected himself
first. " I am the more guilty," he said, " and the more
tormented. God will pardon me sooner, if I revolt against
damnation and wipe this devil from the face of the earth."
With that he bent down to lift the dagger from the stones.

But Maso held him back. " We will draw lots," he said
hastily. " Upon whom it then falls, he shall nevertheless
be answerable for only one half of the bloody deed before
the Eternal Judge as well as before earthly justice. We
will both simultaneously reach for the weapon, which lies
so much in the dark that we cannot distinguish it clearly.
He who grasps the sheath shall not be destined to do the
deed. He who chances upon the hilt, let him be the one;
let him go up to her room and avenge us both upon this
accursed soul before she makes us enemies once more ! "

It was never known who grasped the sheath, and who
the hilt; who, after the door had been opened in answer
to the prearranged signal, then remained alone upon the
threshold with beating heart, straining his ears for something to announce that the ghastly deed had been done.
But everything remained as quiet as if the meeting upstairs
were only the meeting of two tender lovers, anxious to
keep their words and their caresses secret. It was not
very long, however, before stealthy steps came down the
stairs once more. He upon whom the bloody lot had fallen
appeared upon the threshold with face pale as death, and
for a moment fell upon his knees. " It is done," he gasped.
" God forgive us and her ! One second more and I should

no longer have had the strength. Even in death the spell was potent. I was weak enough to kiss away the blood from her bosom!''

Early the next morning the report spread through the city that Madonna Violante had been found murdered in her house; thereupon the prefect of police took eight or ten of his men with him and set out in great haste for the scene of the crime. Not without difficulty and the use of force was he able to press through the dense crowd that shoulder to shoulder filled the narrow street and the dark stairway of the house itself. Upstairs the murdered woman was found before the fireplace, in which the fire had gone out; she had fallen among the ashes trampled upon the floor. The upper part of her body was leaning back against one of the arm-chairs, upon which her rigid head was resting with hair much disheveled. The shoulders were bare; above the left breast, thrust down vertically so that it had reached the heart, was the dagger with the skilfully ornamented hilt; it had been driven into the tender flesh with such force that it could be withdrawn from the wound only with difficulty. But the birth-mark had disappeared; the three-edged steel had fitted exactly into the outline of that fatal bird's claw.

As everybody knew who had made the weapon and who had carried it, and, moreover, as the young servant, throwing herself with a scream upon the body of her dead mistress, loudly accused of the murder the only intimate friend of the house, the prefect with his men went without delay to the *Casa del Garbo*. A dense crowd surged after them. Still it seemed utterly incomprehensible to him and to everybody else that a man like Nino, of spotless reputation and himself a servant of justice, should have committed the nocturnal crime, especially as there was no reason to believe that rejected love could have driven him to such extremity. When they entered Nino's house they found him and his friend calmly sitting together before a table with a pitcher of wine and a single glass, from which both seemed to have been drinking. They had also a copy of the *Purgatory* of the great Dante Alighieri, out of which Nino was reading aloud to his friend in a sonorous voice, while the latter from time to time struck a few soft chords upon a lute which lay upon his knees. When asked whether this dagger belonged to him and whether he knew in what manner the widow, Madonna Violante, who was a stranger in Siena, had come to her death by means of this instrument, the lawyer replied without hesitation that the weapon belonged to him and that he and his friend had together decreed the death of this woman and executed the sentence, inasmuch as she was a sorceress and there had been no possibility of escape from her as long as she lived.

In this declaration they could not be shaken, even when they were brought before the judge and urgently adjured to confess the truth, since it seemed impossible that this one deadly thrust had been delivered by two allied murderers. For the senators were saddened at the thought that the expiation of this dreadful deed — an offense that, of course, could not be condoned — should at one stroke deprive the city of two such excellent and hitherto irreproachable citizens. However, the two friends refused to give any further information, and, too, when requested to make a more definite statement regarding the magic arts practised by the murdered woman, they simply preserved an obstinate silence. To Brigida alone, when she visited her unfortunate nephew and darling in prison, the latter opened his heart and disclosed to her how everything had happened; but even to her he refused to tell who had dealt the deadly thrust. He asked her to give his love to his poor young sister, who lay at home in a high fever and had been unconscious ever since the first news of the dreadful event had reached her, and sent word to her to seek refuge in some convent for a while, until time should have softened the effects of this blow. But Nino knelt down before the old woman without speaking a word, yet in such a humble attitude that, in spite of her anger and grief, she could not refrain from laying her hands upon the head of the author of such deep sorrow and commending him, amid falling tears, to the mercy of heaven.

On the eighth day after the deed the two condemned friends were led to the spot where they were to suffer punishment for their crime. Dressed in penitents' garb they went their bitter way hand in hand, without defiance, yet also without any dejection, and saluted gravely with a slight nod this friend or that among the crowd, who waved a last farewell to them. After they had mounted the scaffold draped in black, they once more rushed into each other's arms in such a fervent embrace that no eye among the spectators remained dry. Then, as a favor that Maso had asked of him, Nino knelt down first; and after he had prayed in a loud voice for his own and his friend's soul he received the fatal stroke without the least flinching. Then Maso tore open the garment at his throat and offering his neck to the sword cried, " I follow thee, most faithful and beloved soul, be it to salvation or to damnation; for without thee even Paradise would be a hell to me!" A few moments later his head also rolled down upon the bloody scaffold; and the story goes that, even in death, the two heads had sought and greeted each other with their eyes.

Lisabetta never left the cloister in which her faithful foster-mother took refuge with her. The writer of this story still remembers very well that, as a boy of twelve years, he saw at the feast of the patron saint a delicate slender figure who was pointed out to him as the abbess, and he was then told the strange story of the events that had driven her from the world into holy seclusion. Even at that time, although she was an old lady with features pale as wax, she seemed possessed of such noble, almost supernatural charm, that the boy could not believe that in her youth any one would have preferred to her another woman, who was not even regarded as beautiful. Through personal experience he later became sufficiently acquainted with the magic arts which women know, not to doubt any longer the literal truth of what has here been recorded.

THE SPELL OF ROTHENBURG * (1881)

By Paul Heyse

TRANSLATED BY C. L. TOWNSEND
Assistant Professor of German, Trinity College

IT was the Tuesday after Easter. The people who had celebrated the feast of the Resurrection by an excursion out into the open country and the balmy spring air were thronging back to their homes and to the daily round of toil which would begin again on the morrow. All the highways were alive with vehicles and pedestrians. The railroads were crowded in spite of the extra trains that had been put on, for no one could recall any such lovely settled Easter weather for many years. The evening express, too, which was standing in the station in Ansbach, ready to leave for Würzburg, had twice as many cars as usual, yet it seemed to be filled to the last seat, when a tardy traveler with a second-class ticket, who tried to find a place at the last minute, knocked in vain at all doors, peered into all the compartments, and everywhere met only with a shrug expressive of more or less annoyance or malicious amusement. At last the guard who was walking at his side came to a hurried decision, opened a first-class carriage, and shoved the late-comer into the dimly lighted compartment, slamming the door violently just as the train began to move.

A lady traveling alone, who had been dozing in the opposite corner, curled up like a black lizard, straightened up suddenly and cast a glance of rebuke at the unwelcome disturber of her solitude. But she seemed to find nothing worthy of notice in the blond young man clad in quiet Sunday garments, who had a portfolio under his arm and was

---

* By permission of the author, and J. G. Cotta, publisher, Stuttgart.

[105]

holding in his hand a well-worn carpet-bag with an old-fashioned design embroidered on it. At least, her only answer to his polite salutation and the words of apology which he stammered out was a proud, scarcely perceptible inclination of her head; she once more drew the black silk hood of her cape down over her forehead, and made ready to continue her interrupted nap with as little concern as if, instead of her new traveling companion, there had been shoved into the carriage only another piece of baggage. The young man, feeling like an intruder who was there only on sufferance, was careful not to remind her of his presence by unnecessary noise. Although he had been running hard, he held his breath as much as possible for the first five minutes and resolutely maintained the uncomfortable attitude which he had assumed on first taking possession of his corner seat. He did, however, take off his hat quietly and with a handkerchief wipe the sweat from his brow, glancing discreetly out of his window as though it was only by the most self-effacing behavior that he could obtain pardon for his emergence into a higher sphere. But the sleeper did not stir, and as the scenery gliding by outside had little attraction for him he finally ventured to turn his eyes toward the interior of the compartment. After admiring sufficiently the broad red-plush cushions and the mirror over the seats, he made bold to look more closely at the form of the stranger, even letting his glance steal cautiously and slowly from the point of the little shoe which peeped forth under the edge of her dress, up to her shoulder, and at last to what little of her face was turned toward him.

She must be a lady of rank — so much seemed at once beyond all doubt; and from a far country — a Russian, a Pole, or a Spaniard. Everything she wore and all her belongings bore the stamp of an aristocratic origin,— her garments, the dainty red traveling bag against which she braced her slender foot so carelessly, and the trim light-brown glove into which she had cuddled her cheek. Fur-

CITY HALL, ROTHENBURG-ON-THE-TAUBER

thermore, she was enveloped in a peculiar fragrance, not as of some aromatic essence, but as of Russian leather and cigarettes; indeed, there were lying about on the carpet of the compartment some half-smoked little white stubs which had scattered their ashes, and some Russian tobacco. A book had likewise slipped to the floor. He could not prevail upon himself to leave it lying there, and as he lifted it carefully and laid it on the seat he saw that it was a French novel. All this filled him with that mysterious yet agreeable tremor that is wont to steal over a young man who, having grown up in middle-class circles, one day unexpectedly comes into contact with a lady from the world of fashion. In that event there is added to the natural superiority of the woman over the man the romantic charm which the novel and more unconstrained manners of the higher class and the vague consciousness of its passionate joys and sorrows exercise upon a youth of the lower class. The very gulf which lies between the two serves but to increase this charm, as there is likely to be then kindled in the man a dreamy, audacious impulse to presume upon the privilege of his sex and leap for once across this apparently unbridgeable chasm.

The young traveler, to be sure, did not rise to such venturesome heights of audacity; but when he felt sufficiently assured that the sleep of his unknown neighbor was not feigned he drew softly from his breast pocket a little booklet bound in gray linen and made furtive preparations to sketch on a blank leaf with rapid strokes the pale, delicate, somewhat arrogant profile of the sleeper. It was not altogether an easy undertaking, although the roaring speed of the express train helped him over many a difficulty. He had to hold himself half poised over his seat, and make every stroke with decisive firmness. But the head paid him well for his trouble, and as the cheek, pressed against her hand and lightly framed by the folds of the hood, revealed itself to him in the dim evening glow, he thought that he had never seen more classic lines in any living being.

She seemed to have passed her first youth; her delicate lips quivered at times with a strange expression of bitterness or ennui, even now as she was dreaming. Marvelously beautiful, however, were her forehead and the curve of her brow, and the soft, abundant, wavy hair.

He had been drawing very industriously for perhaps ten minutes, and had almost finished his little sketch when the sleeper suddenly straightened up quietly, and in the best German addressed him with — '' Do you not know, sir, that it is forbidden to rob travelers in their sleep? ''

Caught in the act, the poor fellow let the sketch-book fall to his lap in great consternation, and flushing deeply, said, '' I beg your pardon, madam! I did not think — I supposed — it is only a very hasty sketch — only for a remembrance — ''

'' Who gives you any right to remember me and to help out your memory so offensively in the effort? '' replied the lady, looking him up and down somewhat coldly and scornfully with her sharp blue eyes. In the meantime she had sat bolt upright and her hood had fallen back upon her shoulders; he saw how delicate was the contour of her head, and in spite of his embarrassment he continued to study her with the eye of a painter.

'' I must indeed admit that I have behaved like a regular highwayman,'' he rejoined, trying to turn the matter into a joke. '' But perhaps you will let mercy take the place of justice if I restore my plunder, not for you to preserve, but merely that you may see how very little it is that I have appropriated.''

He handed her the open sketch-book, and she cast a quick glance at her likeness, then nodded approvingly, but with a quick gesture that refused the proffered book. '' It is a good likeness,'' she said, '' but idealized. You are a portrait painter, sir? ''

'' No, madam. Otherwise I should probably have made the sketch a better likeness. I paint architectural pictures for the most part. But just because I have a keen eye for the beauties of proportion and for pure lines — and these are not offered one every day by a human face — '' He was too confused to finish his sentence, stared at the toes of his boots, tried to smile again, and got redder than ever.

Without heeding this the lady remarked: '' In your portfolio there you doubtless have some of your drawings and paintings. May I look at them? ''

'' I should be pleased to have you.'' He handed her the portfolio, and spread its contents out before her, sheet after sheet. They were all water-color sketches, representing medieval buildings, Gothic turrets, and rows of high-gabled houses, executed with a skill and grace that showed a thoroughly artistic conception. The lady allowed them to pass in review before her, one after another, without addressing a single question to the young painter. Several of the sheets, however, she studied for some little time, and handed them back with an air of reluctance.

'' These things are not quite finished,'' was the excuse he made for a more hastily executed sketch here and there, '' but they all belong to the same series. I took advantage of the Easter holidays to discuss them with a print-seller in Nuremberg. I should like to issue all these sketches in a chromo-lithographic work. To be sure, I have many predecessors already, but even yet Rothenburg is not as well known as it deserves to be.''

'' Rothenburg? ''

'' That is the name. These are all Rothenburg views you see. I thought you knew it, madam, as you asked no questions.''

'' Rothenburg? Where is it situated? ''

'' Why, on the Tauber, not so very many hours' journey from here. But do you really not know the place? Haven't you even so much as heard its name? ''

'' You must excuse my ignorance in matters of geography, as I am not a German,'' she replied with a gentle smile. '' But though I have associated a great deal with Germans, I admit that I have never before heard the name of Rothenburg on the — what is it now? — on the Taube? ''

He laughed and had suddenly lost all embarrassment, as
if he had now realized that in one important respect he was
after all far superior to this great lady.

"Excuse me," said he, "I treat you as every Rothenburger does a stranger, though my own cradle did not
stand on the banks of the little river Tauber. We are all
so madly in love with our city that it is hard for us to
imagine what can occupy the mind of a person who knows
nothing at all about Rothenburg. When I first went there,
nine years ago, I did not myself know much more about the
ancient free city of the Empire than that it was situated,
like Jerusalem, upon a plateau rising to a considerable
height above the river valley, that it was still surrounded
by walls and towers just as it had been five centuries before,
and that it had had the honor of counting among its citizens
the remote ancestors of my family. For I shall make bold
to introduce myself to you — my name is Hans Doppler."
He smiled and bowed, with a questioning look at her, as if
he expected this name to rouse her to pleased interest, much
as though he had told her that his name was Hans Columbus
or Hans Guttenberg; but she betrayed not the least emotion.

"For Doppler," he continued with somewhat less assurance, "is the more modern spelling of the name ' Toppler '
which was adopted in the last century by the branch to
which I belong. It is proved by documents, however, that
the founder of our family was no less a personage than
Heinrich Toppler, the great burgomaster of Rothenburg,
of whom you have no doubt heard."

She shook her head, visibly amused by his naïve assurance.

"I regret that my knowledge of history is as fragmentary
as my knowledge of geography. But what did your ancestor
do that it is a disgrace not to know him?"

"Goodness!" said he, now laughing at his own presumption, "do not be afraid, madam, that from mere family
pride I might bore you with an extract from the annals
of Rothenburg. My family pride really has good cause for
feeling humbled, for I myself, as you see me here, have no

longer any authority in the ancestral seat of my family, but on the other hand I hope not to fare like my ancestor, who, after increasing the military prestige of the good city, was imprisoned by his fellow citizens and given over to death by poison or starvation. A dreadful end, was it not, madam, and a handsome reward for so many glorious deeds? — and all that because of a mere calumny. He is said to have lost the city to a prince in a game of dice, but there is not a word of truth in the story. It is true that in the old days ' dopple ' meant to cast the dice, and in our family coat of arms — "

He stopped abruptly, for it seemed to him that the lady's delicate nostrils were quivering as if she wished to hide a slight yawn. Rather offended, he turned to his water-color sketches and put them back again in the right order into the portfolio, which he was still holding in his hand.

"And how did you happen," she now asked, " to enter at last upon the inheritance of this unjustly murdered man? Did they wish to make reparation to you for the sins committed against your ancestor? "

" You mistake, madam," said he, " if you suppose the citizens of Rothenburg considered it an honor to have a Doppler among them once more, and paid out anything for this honor. When nine years ago, as I just told you, I strolled through the Röder Gate out of mere curiosity to make the acquaintance of the old fortress, not a soul there knew me, and even on the occasions when I told my name not much notice was excited. It was even very much doubted whether I belonged to the family at all, as I was born in Nuremberg and no longer spell my name with the hard T. But the world's history, as the poet says, is its own Judgment Day. The failure of the city fathers of Rothenburg to have me brought in in triumph, to restore to my possession the houses once owned by the great burgo-master, and to provide for me for the rest of my life as a living patron saint of the city, was rectified in a different way by Fate, or by the goodness of God, whichever you pre-

fer. I came to Rothenburg simply to make a few sketches
and to view an old nest which had remained behind the
times, and I found there my life's happiness and a new,
warm nest of my own, to which I am flying back again at
the present moment.''

" May I ask how that came to pass? ''

" Most certainly, if it interests you at all?   My parents
had sent me to the Academy at Munich. They were not
rich, but they nevertheless had the means to support me
respectably and to enable me to take the entire course.   I
intended to be a landscape painter and to enjoy a few years
of study in Italy after finishing my training at the Academy.
Absorbed in these plans, I had passed my twenty-first birthday, and I felt a longing to visit my good old mother in
Nuremberg before setting out on my great journey to
Italy (my father had died some time before). 'Hans,' she
said, 'before you make your pilgrimage to Rome, you
ought to make another pilgrimage — to the place where our
family-tree stood rooted before it was torn up and transplanted hither from East Franconia!' (you see, my good
mother was a genuine old patrician dame, and attached
much importance to grandiloquent genealogical terms).
Well I had no reason to delay; I took my pilgrim's staff
in hand and made my way slowly westward, sketching industriously on the road, too, as after all I felt for the time
being more affection for this German landscape of ours
than for the as yet unknown scenery to the south.   Now
that you have looked over the portfolio you will perhaps
understand why the German Jerusalem made an over-
whelming impression upon me, and why my eye and hand
were unable to sketch all even of what was most worthy
of notice.   But there was something in Rothenburg that
charmed me far more than even its precious antiquity.   In
brief — for I will not regale you with any long love-story —
at one of the weekly balls given by the so-called ' Harmony
Society ' I made the acquaintance of the young daughter
of a respected burgher and former member of the city coun-

cil. She was three whole years younger than I, and, I think I may venture to affirm, the prettiest girl in all the city. After the second waltz I knew how I stood — that is, with regard to my own feelings; but not yet, unfortunately, with regard to hers, or, what is of more importance, to the wishes of her respected papa. And so it might have turned out a very sad affair, and the descendant of the great Toppler might, like his ancestor, have had to pine away in his chains in the old Imperial free city, had not Fate, as I said before, intervened and caused me to cast a lucky throw with my family dice. At the end of three days I was certain that the girl loved me, and at the end of three weeks I was assured that her father too would overlook my raw youth and my immaturity in other respects, since he had, as the saying is, gone daft over me — for what reason, heaven only knows. The fact that I was a Doppler and that I could paint such delicately colored sketches of the prettiest nooks in the dilapidated old fortifications as well as of the quaint turrets and curious wells, contributed more than anything else to win me his heart, which was so loyal to Rothenburg. After a brief probationary period of a year, then, he gave me the hand of his only child, with the one stipulation, to be sure, that while he lived I should not take her away from his home and that I should apply my talent as an artist chiefly to the glorification of his beloved city. You will readily understand, madam, that I made no prolonged resistance. Not only was my father-in-law the prosperous owner of a house and garden, of vineyards and some cultivated fields; he was also the best-hearted man in the world, and was never put out save when some one happened to praise other old towns above their merits, or rank Nuremberg or Augsburg above the 'pearl of the Tauber valley.' He lived with us more than four years after our marriage, and each time that I sold a sketch of some Rothenburg building at an exhibition away from home he would bring up from the cellar a special bottle of Tauber wine and drink to my health. When he died, I was myself already much too comfortably settled in our old, many-cornered house to think of removing elsewhere. Besides, I had made a beginning on several pictures, and there was no lack of orders. But if the old gentleman had lived long enough to see the appearance of my series of water-color sketches, I believe he would have gone out of his mind for sheer joy."

After this lengthy account of his brief career he was silent for a time, and, filled with quiet emotion, gazed out of the window at the landscape which was constantly growing dimmer. But at length he was struck by the fact that the lady did not answer by so much as a syllable, which was the more remarkable as he felt that her eyes, from the dimly lighted corner, were fixed upon his face.

" I am afraid that I have bored you with this tale of life in a country town," said he; "but it was you who coaxed it out of me, and if you knew — "

" You are very much mistaken," she interrupted. " If I said nothing it was only because I was pondering a riddle."

"A riddle? One that I had given you to solve?"

" Yes, you, Mr. Hans Doppler. I have been asking myself how I am to reconcile the artist with whom I have become acquainted through this portfolio, with the domesticated young paterfamilias — you have children too, I suppose?"

" Four of them, madam — two boys and two little girls."

" Well, then, how am I to reconcile the artist with the young husband and father who has settled down to a life of happy monotony in Rothenburg, as in a snail-shell, and whose farthest excursion is to Nuremberg? For, you may believe me, your work shows quite unusual talent. I have seen the work of Hildebrandt, of Werner, and of the whole Roman school of Aquarellists, and I assure you that yours would attract attention if placed among theirs — it shows such freedom, such inspired lightness of touch, and such grace in the depiction of both landscape and figures. And then to think that such unusual talent is, during thirty or forty years, to have no other task to perform than to reproduce, with infinite variations, turrets, oriels, arched gateways and slanting roofs of a little medieval town, which gazes upon the world of our day just like a Pompeii excavated on German soil—but pardon my taking the liberty of criticizing your whole plan of life. However, as you wished to know what I was thinking about—it was the following problem: Can a genuine, free artistic soul really have its cravings completely satisfied by the prosaic happiness of domestic ties? I suppose it must indeed be possible, yet to me, accustomed as I am to a life of unlimited liberty, to unrestrained freedom of movement, it seems incomprehensible that you, scarcely thirty years old—"

"You are right!" he interrupted her, while his frank rosy face became suddenly overcast. "You have given expression to a thought which at first occurred to me often enough, but which I always forced back into a secret corner of my heart. Does it really seem to you that my sketches give promise of a capacity for something greater and higher? Heaven knows, I fear I lack the most essential qualification of a truly great artist. However—you know Schiller's poem, 'Pegasus in Harness?' An ordinary horse, though it be of good stock, shows that it has no wings by the very fact of allowing itself to be harnessed to the plough and remaining there. Still, perhaps it was good for something better than ploughing. But if you knew—if, for instance, you knew my Christel and the youngsters—"

"I do not doubt for a moment, Mr. Doppler, that you have a dear, good wife and the sweetest of children. Nothing is more remote from my thought than any intention to belittle your domestic happiness in your eyes. But that while you are still so young you should regard it as final—as something never to be interrupted, never to be subordinated for a time to a higher purpose, you who were already on your way to the Promised Land of art, and had surely heard and seen enough of it at the Academy to have some inkling of what joys await you there—and yet—"

"Oh, madam!" he cried, and started up as if he had

all at once felt the narrow compartment to be a sultry prison cell. "You are merely putting my own thoughts into words. How often when I wake up in the night — especially on a clear spring night — and hear the quiet breathing of my dear wife at my side — and the children are asleep in the next room, and the moonbeams glide so softly and eerily along the low walls, and the clock, which the old gentleman used to wind up so regularly and which harks back to the Thirty Years' War, ticks on so sleepily — I feel too restless then to stay in bed, and I have to jump up and gaze down into the valley through the little window with its round panes. And when the Tauber flows by so swiftly in its winding channel as if it could not escape soon enough from its narrow course and plunge into the Main, and with the Main into the Rhine, and finally into the sea — what a strange feeling then comes over me, how I clench my teeth, and at last steal back to bed, weary and sad at heart! I have never told any one of it. It seemed to me the blackest ingratitude toward kind Fate, which has made so soft a bed for me. But, as a rule, I cannot bear to touch a brush the day after, and when I read the word Rome or Naples in a newspaper the blood rushes to my head as if I were a deserter, who, caught on his flight, is being dragged back to barracks with handcuffs on his wrists."

He ran his fingers through his curly hair and dropped again upon his seat. During his melancholy oration she had watched him closely without taking her eyes from his face; now for the first time his countenance seemed interesting to her. The guilelessly youthful look had vanished, the clear, beautifully shaped eyes were flashing, and in spite of his very ordinary black jacket his slender form assumed an air of energy, almost of heroism, such as was meet for a descendant of the "great burgomaster."

"I understand your feelings," said the lady, as she took a cigarette from a silver case and composedly lit it at a wax candle, "but all the less do I understand your way of acting. Since childhood I have, of course, been accustomed to do only what is in harmony with my nature, with my spiritual needs. I submit to no bonds. Either they are weak, and then I break them, or they are too strong, and then they strangle me. But to be held fast in them and continue to live—that is for me an impossible idea. Do you smoke? Don't stand on ceremony. You see I am setting you the example.''

He declined with a shake of the head, and was all eyes and ears.

"As I said," continued the lady, slowly blowing the smoke into the air with her witty, beautiful lips, "I have no right to find fault with your plan of life. But you must permit me to be astonished that a man should prefer to complain rather than to extricate himself from an uncomfortable position, especially when it would be so easy to do so. Are you afraid, by any chance, that if you made a pilgrimage to the shrine of art, your wife might prove false to you in the meantime?"

"Christel? False to me?" In spite of his melancholy he could not help bursting into a ringing laugh.

"I beg your pardon," she said quietly, "I forgot that she is a German, and more than that, a daughter of Rothenburg. But all the less do I understand why you will yourself insist on condemning yourself to paint for the rest of your life only St. James' Church and the Klimper Gate or whatever its name is."

"Klingen Gate, madam."

"Well then, to reproduce all these stupid walls and this commonplace Gothic rubbish, as if there were no Coliseum, no Baths of Caracalla, no theatre at Taormina! What luxuriant vegetation, what splendid weeds there are among the holy ruins of the old temples! What pines, what cypresses, what clear outlines of seas and mountains on the horizon! I assure you that I myself as you see me here, though I am by no means an old woman, should have been dead and buried long ago if I had not one day taken flight from narrow, revoltingly dull surroundings, and taken refuge in the land of beauty and freedom.''

"You are not married, madam?"

She threw the glowing stub out of the window, clenched her little teeth, which were very white and even, for a moment, and then said in a tone of indescribable indifference: "My husband, the general, is the governor of a fair-sized fortress in the interior of Russia, and of course could not accompany me; besides, at his age, he would have missed his home comforts very much. So we have arranged that every other year we appoint a place of meeting somewhere on the frontier, and since then each of us has led a much more contented life.

"I know very well," she went on, as he looked at her in some surprise, "that this conception of marital happiness is diametrically opposed to sentimental German prejudices, but you may take my word for it that we barbarians are in many respects in advance of your own so progressive civilization, and for the political freedom that we lack we make up fully by our social freedom. If you were a Russian you would have emancipated yourself long ago and have followed the example of your river, only in the opposite direction. And besides, what would you lose by it? When, after a year or so, you came back with your artistic ability fully developed would you perchance not find your home still in the old spot, your wife still as domestic and virtuous as before? Your children, I admit, would have grown half a head taller, but would you not find them as well behaved and well cared for as when you left home?"

"It's true, only too true," he faltered, tugging constantly at his hair. "Oh, if I had only thought it over so clearly before!"

"Before! A young man like you, who is not yet past thirty! But I can see indeed that you are too well used to your fleshpots at Rothenburg. You are right! Stay at home and earn your daily bread honestly. The proposal I had on the tip of my tongue to make would seem to you just about as sensible as though I called upon you to journey to the wilderness and hunt tigers and crocodiles, instead of motifs for landscape paintings."

She discharged this sharp-pointed arrow at him with such quiet grace that he felt himself hurt and attracted at the same moment.

"No, madam," he exclaimed, "you must tell me what kind of proposal you had in mind. Though I have enjoyed the good fortune of knowing you for only a short time, I can nevertheless assure you that your personality — that every word you have spoken — has made a deep — yes, an indelible impression upon me. It is just as though a complete transformation were taking place within me, and this hour with you — "

He paused again and blushed. Though apparently looking beyond him, she noticed it and came to his aid in his embarrassment.

"My proposal," she said, "was by no means intended to make an entirely different man of you, but only to help the real man in you from the confinement of the shell. I am now on the way to Würzburg to visit a sick friend. After bearing her company for a couple of days, I shall return by the same route and make no stop before reaching Genoa, where I embark on a steamer to journey direct to Palermo — for I have not seen Sicily yet. Now in Goethe's *Italian Journey* I have always read with a feeling of envy what he has to say about his traveling-companion, the artist Kniep, whom he had engaged to reproduce for him at once, with a few magic strokes on a blank sheet, every spot along the route that appealed to him. I am neither a great poet nor a wealthy princess; but I do not have to limit my expenditures to such an extent that I could not also afford the luxury of such a traveling-companion. To be sure we have photography now, but to you least of all do I need to explain how much better it is to have the hand of an artist at one's disposal than any photographic apparatus. Now I thought it could do you no harm, either, to be introduced into this paradise by some one who can speak the language and is no longer a novice in the art of traveling. You would be fully entitled to remain with me just as long or as short a time as you pleased. The first article of our agreement would read: ' Freedom extending even to lack of consideration for the other party.' And if on the return journey you happened to wish to spend some little time in Rome and Florence, the means to do so—"

" Oh, madam! " he quickly interrupted, " under no circumstances would I think of abusing your kind generosity. I can afford to live in Italy for a year entirely at my own expense. And if I see the finger of Providence in your proposal it is only because the inspiration I have received from you, the prospect of seeing all these world-renowned wonders in your company, makes the decision so much the easier for me. I shall always be grateful to you for that. It is really just as you say—my wife and my dear children will in reality miss me less than I now imagine. Christel is so sensible, so self-reliant! She herself, if I put the whole case before her—or, better still, if you could say to her what you have said to me!— But of course you have to go to Würzburg; I cannot expect you to visit Rothenburg on the way. To one who has seen the Coliseum and the Baths of Caracalla, our modest little medieval town would surely—"

A whistle from the engine interrupted him. The train was slowing down, lanterns were appearing beside the track.

" Steinach! " said the painter, rising and taking up his traveling bag and portfolio. " Here is the parting of our ways. You go on toward the north, I change to a little local train which will bring me home in half an hour. O madam, if you would only tell me the day and hour, when, on your return journey—"

" I'll tell you! " she suddenly exclaimed, looking at her watch, " I have concluded that it would be more sensible to spend the night at Rothenburg and not continue my journey till tomorrow. I should arrive at Würzburg much too late to be allowed to see my friend today. Instead, as I happen to be so near, I will fill up the gaps in my his-

STREET IN ROTHENBURG

torical and geographical lore and take a look at your Jerusalem on the Tauber. You will be so kind as to play the cicerone a little for me tomorrow, if Madame Christel has no objection."

"Oh, my dear madam," he cried in joyous excitement, "I should never have dared to beg for such a favor. How happy you make me, and how shall I ever—"

The train stopped, and the door of the compartment was opened. The young painter respectfully helped out the patroness he had so quickly gained and accompanied her to a second-class carriage, into which she called a few words in Russian. An uncanny little creature, wearing a small hat with a plume on it, and laden with a multitude of boxes, bags and little baskets, worked her way out of the over-crowded compartment into the open air and inspected her mistress' fair-haired companion with a not over-favorable look in her little Kalmuck eyes. The lady seemed to be explaining the changed situation to her maid, without even a syllable in reply from that heavily-burdened creature. Then she took the arm of her young traveling-companion and strolled up and down the dark platform with him in lively conversation, telling of Italy, of Russia, of the German cities she had seen, with so much ease and cleverness, and with such a spice of graceful malice, that it seemed to her companion as though he had never in all his life been better entertained and could never grow weary of listening to this irresistible Sheherezade.

Did it not seem like a fairy-tale, that he should now be walking arm in arm with this beautiful lady whom he had never seen till an hour before, that she should have made up her mind to follow him to his little sleepy city which lay off of her direct road, and that all these seductive prospects were beckoning to him in the distance? Of course they knew him at the little station, but never had they lifted their caps so respectfully as today, when he appeared in this aristocratic company. In the flickering lamplight her pale face bore a still closer resemblance to that of some fairy princess. She had donned a strangely-shaped cap of black velvet edged with a reddish fur, and her short cape and hood were trimmed with the same material. Moreover she had removed her gloves, and on her little finger there gleamed a large sapphire, at which, as she had laid her hand on his arm, her young companion stole a glance from time to time out of the corner of his eye. It was long since he had looked upon so delicate a hand. It was white as a lily, and every finger seemed endowed with a soul and language of its own.

But when they had entered the little local train, which consisted merely of two light coaches besides the diminutive two-and-a-half horsepower engine, he could not help feeling somewhat ill at ease. As there was no first-class carriage the three sat together alone in the only one of the second-class, and glided slowly on in the soft, cloud-veiled moonlight. The maid had settled herself in the darkest corner and crouched there as if buried under the mountain of her hand-baggage. The light of the lamp on the ceiling fell full upon her mistress' face, and the young painter sitting opposite became more and more devoutly absorbed in contemplating those beautifully shaped features which corresponded almost perfectly to the ideal of beauty that had hovered before his mind's eye in the plaster-model drawing-class at the Academy. But the nearer the train drew to its destination, the more he was oppressed by anxiety and dread at the thought of how those wonderful eyes which had already seen half the world would regard the angularity of a country town like his old Rothenburg.

All at once everything there that he had known and been charmed by for years appeared to him wretched and petty in the extreme, and he thought with terror of the way her slender nose would turn up scornfully in the light of the next morning, when all the long-famous marvels of which he had been so proud passed in review before it. His alarmed imagination flew also to his own house, and unfortunately did not fare much better there either. What sort of impression would his little wife, who had never been away from the town, produce on this cosmopolitan — and his lads, who usually ran about with tousled curly heads, his little girls, who had still so elementary an idea of deportment!

He keenly regretted having made this venture into aristocratic society, and the fairy atmosphere had suddenly departed. Fortunately he did not need to impose any restraint upon himself; the lady had closed her eyes and seemed to be asleep in real earnest. From her hiding place, to be sure, the slit-eyed Kalmuck watched him continually, but did not say one word.

Then the train stopped; the sleeping lady started up, seeming to find it hard to recollect where she was, and then asked if there were a passable hotel in Rothenburg. All the patrician pride of her companion was roused by the contemptuous tone of her words. With dignified reserve he praised the Golden Stag, the omnibus of which, he said, was waiting at the station. She inquired whether his wife would not be there to meet him. He answered that he had told her not to, as it was so late — ten o'clock — and she did not like to leave the children with the maid alone. He hoped on the morrow to have the pleasure of presenting his family to her. The Russian lady made no reply to this; she was by no means in her previous good humor, and seemed, like him, to be repenting in silence of this over hasty side-trip.

Without another word being spoken all three drove in the narrow hotel carriage through the dark gate, swaying dangerously over the rough paving-stones into the sleeping city. Not until they reached the market-place did the lady glance out through the carriage window. Just then the moon emerged from the clouds. She expressed her satisfaction at the stately architecture of the town hall, which showed to the best advantage in the silvery moonlight. Thereby she roused her companion from his depression. He began to tell her something of this building, the pride of Rothenburg, and its erection after a great fire. It was, he said, an edifice in the best style of the Renaissance, and, particularly in summer, when the wide, projecting balcony which runs along the whole front was decorated with fresh flowers, nothing more stately and at the same time more delightfully cheerful could well be imagined.

He was still speaking when they stopped before the open door of the Golden Stag. Hans Doppler jumped out, and then helped out the lady, bidding the host good evening, and whispering to him to prepare his best room. "Numbers fifteen and sixteen are unoccupied," replied the landlord with a bow of polite familiarity.

"You will have a fine view of the river valley from there, madam," said the artist. "When the moon is higher, you will enjoy the view of the double bridge down in the valley and of the little Gothic church. I shall take the liberty of waiting upon you tomorrow morning to inquire how you have slept, and when you desire to set out on a tour of the city."

She noticed that he was a little cool and out of humor. At once she held out her hand to him, pressed his, while he respectfully carried her slender fingers to his lips, and she said, "Good by, then, till tomorrow, dear friend. But do not come too early. I am a night bird, and your Rothenburg moonlight along with the nixie of the Tauber will not suffer me to sleep yet awhile."

Thereupon she followed the landlord into the hotel. The maid, relieved by the porter of a part of her burden, slipped in behind her.

Not walking as briskly as was his wont on returning from one of his short trips, but with the air of a very weary, thoughtful man uncertain of the nature of his reception, Hans Doppler turned his steps toward his little home. This was a house near the Castle Gate, and was built into the city wall. It faced northwest, whereas the windows of the hotel he had just left, looked southwest. As he walked he racked his brains to determine which course would be

wiser—to make a full confession that very night, or to
put it off till the morrow. The moment he was free from
the spell of the dangerous stranger, the whole affair seemed
extremely awkward and almost wrong and criminal; but
he had already gone too far to be able to withdraw without deep disgrace. The morrow would have to be faced,
of course. But after that he would plead some urgent
obligation that detained him; in no event would he accompany her at once.

Having thus quieted his scruples in regard to his unsus-
pecting young wife, he felt somewhat more at ease. He
walked up the steep lane and through the market-place, and
then turned to the left, still with faltering steps, till he
reached the Castle Gate tower. But then, when he turned
into the narrow lane on the right which led to his home, he
saw, at a distance, a dark form standing beneath the round
arch of the gateway in the high garden wall, and had scarcely time to recognize that it was his little wife before
a pair of soft yet strong arms were clasped around his neck
and in the darkness warm lips sought his.

As he was carrying his portfolio and traveling-bag, he
could neither return her embrace nor ward it off as he felt
inclined to do, since he noticed some of the neighbors' windows standing open and feared that this tender reunion
might be observed. She perceived his embarrassment and
reassured him by saying that it was only such and such old
people, who had long known that they still loved each other
even after seven years of married life. Then, chattering
softly and delightedly of a hundred little happenings, she
drew him into the house where every one was already asleep.
It was a very ancient, dilapidated structure, the walls of
which had survived many an assault of the elements and of
turbulent warfare. Inside, its age was still more evident.
All the woodwork was cracked and black, the stairs were
warped and worn, and the walls, in spite of various props,
were rather out of joint; the whole venerable building
would have had to be razed to the ground and built anew

to repair all the defects, and the loyal Rothenburger who had previously possessed it could no more prevail upon himself to do this than could later his daughter and her young husband, in whose veins, after all, there flowed the blood of the " great burgomaster."

Furthermore it happened that night for the first time that Hans Doppler, climbing the narrow crooked staircase, found something to find fault with in this historic little house, which circumstance, it is true, he wisely kept to himself. The little sitting-room which he had entered, with its low-beamed ceiling, its very old-fashioned furniture, and the family pictures on the walls, seemed to him for the first time stuffy and shabby, pretty as the little brass lamp with the green shade looked as it stood on the table which was set for him, lighting up the neat plates and dishes that contained his frugal supper. At such a home-coming he was usually wont to bubble over with sprightly talk; this time he had nothing to say, though he smiled continually, if somewhat forcedly, and patted his pretty wife's cheek in a rather fatherly way, so that though she said nothing she was astonished at her husband's behavior. But in the room where the children slept his heart and lips seemed to be freed from the spell, especially as the younger boy, his favorite because he was the very image of his mother, woke up and, jumping out in his nightgown, threw his arms about his father's neck with a joyful shout. He gave him at once a toy he had bought for him in Nuremberg, and a large cake of gingerbread, though the child was only allowed a hasty glimpse of both, since the lamp was at once carried out again. Then he sat down opposite Christel, on the old sofa, the haircloth covering of which had never seemed to him so hard and cold. He ate a little, drank some of the red wine from his own vineyard, and during the meal related to his young wife, who sat opposite him resting her elbows on the table and eating nothing, the happy outcome of his business trip.

And then, he said he had chanced to travel from Ansbach with the wife of an old Russian general, the governor of some fortress. The lady had wished to see Rothenburg and had put up at the Stag. Unfortunately he should have to show her around the next day; he was even considering whether it wouldn't be necessary to invite her to dinner.

" You know, Hans," said the young woman, " that our Marie doesn't know much about cooking, and I myself, unless I have notice a little further ahead, cannot perform miracles. But why do you wish to issue a formal invitation at once to an old lady who is a perfect stranger? She has not even paid us a call yet, you know. Or have you some reason for showing her particular attention? Is it some old acquaintance whom you knew when you lived in Munich? In that case, of course, I should have to bestir myself."

" No," he answered, bowing his head rather low over his plate, " she is neither an old acquaintance, nor is she so very old. You are right, little one, we must wait for her to visit us. She will certainly do so, for I have told her so much about you and the children! You will find her an interesting woman who is quite a connoisseur in art — her recommendation may well be of use to me some day, for she knows half the world."

" Well, I am eager to meet her," replied the young woman. " Besides, the fact that now even Russians are beginning to notice Rothenburg — "

He blushed, knowing best how this suddenly awakened interest had been inspired. " Now just go to bed, dear," said he. " You should have been there long ago. I am still somewhat excited after my journey, but shall follow presently."

" You are right," she said with a hearty yawn that showed a mouth which, though not especially small, was fresh, rosy and full of white teeth. " I noticed right away that there was something the matter with you; your eyes

are darting rather restlessly this way and that. Open the
window, too, and sit in the cool air for a little while. Good
night!''

She kissed him quickly and went into the adjoining bedroom, leaving the door open. Then he arose, pushed back
the shutter, and opened the window with the little round
panes. The night breeze had quite frightened away all the
fog from the face of the moon, the winding valley with its
delicate trees and freshly ploughed fields lay at his feet in
the dim silvery light, and in the deep silence he could hear
the whispering of the swift waves of the Tauber as they
hurried past the little white water tower built by his ancestor. He began to feel very peaceful and contented. This
time his thoughts did not follow the course of the little
stream until it reached the boundless sea, although everything was again as it had so often been before; to the right
he heard the breathing of his rosy children, to the left the
soft footsteps of his little wife who had various tasks still
to perform before going to bed. But he felt as though the
Russian fairy-tale had been but a dream; for tonight, at
any rate, it should not spoil his rest.

When Hans Doppler awoke bright and early and missed
from beside him his little wife, who had been busy in the
nursery for some time, his first thought was of all that
awaited him that day in the company of his aristocratic
patroness.

Viewed in the sober light of day, his house, his historic
furniture, even his own dear wife, and his rosy-cheeked
children were far from affording him the delight which he
had felt in them on his return the night before. He found
his Christel's neat morning gown altogether too provincial
in cut, and noticed for the first time that the little trousers
of his son Heinz were mended with a patch that did not
quite match the rest of the goods in pattern and color.
With his own suit which he had worn the day before he was
also extremely dissatisfied. Its decorous blackness vied
with a clergyman's robe, for it had seemed advisable to the

young painter to conduct his business with the gentleman in Nuremberg in a garb that amply guaranteed his being a citizen of good standing. Even when going about the town he dressed like everybody else; for, being the only one of his species, he would have attracted attention everywhere by wearing the distinctive dress of an artist. But he did not wish to appear again in the sight of this woman of the world, dressed like a young Philistine; accordingly he brought up from the remotest depths of his wardrobe a velvet jacket, the very one he had worn when first he strolled into Rothenburg, and along with it a broad brimmed, black felt hat and a pair of very light-colored trousers. Christel opened her eyes in amazement when he appeared before her thus transformed and explained to her that it was really a pity that this good coat should be hanging up in the clothes press for the moths alone. He said, besides, that now, when his fellow citizens should learn at last that they were to be made famous far and wide by his art, he no longer wished to seem ashamed of his profession. The wise young wife made no reply to this, though she observed him constantly with a calm scrutiny.

On leaving her he casually suggested that she herself might likewise dress up a bit today, for there was no telling when the general's wife would pay her a call. The lady would be welcome at any time, answered Christel; besides, she herself was always presentable, and so were the children; any one who did not find them pretty enough in their little every-day suits had poor taste. In Russia, she had read, they ran about all ragged and unwashed besides, helter skelter with the precious cattle. As she said this she took little Lena in her arms, stroked back her fair, curly hair, and kissed her with proud confidence on the bright blue eyes which she had inherited from her father; Christel's eyes were brown. Hans Doppler suppressed a gentle sigh, endeavored to smile at his little brood, and then strode off briskly toward the Golden Stag.

VOL. XIII — 9

He thought he would be much too early even now, but he could not endure the confinement of the house and the secret consciousness of having done wrong. He wanted to stroll about a little while longer, before calling on the lady. But when he reached the market-place and glanced down the street toward the hotel, he saw the lady standing in the middle of the street opposite St. John's Chapel, attentively studying through her lorgnette its Gothic windows and old statues, among which a black St. Christopher was especially conspicuous.

He was startled at finding himself so late. But she, on seeing him hurrying toward her, nodded a cheery greeting from some distance away, and called out, " You see, dear friend, that the Rothenburg spirit is already haunting my brain. I am already deep in admiration of the brave days of old. For sheer impatience I could sleep only till seven, to the horror of Sascha, who is a regular dormouse. I jumped out of bed in my bare feet to admire in the glow of the morning the Cadolzeller—no, the Cobolzeller Chapel down in the valley and the Double Bridge, which had already enchanted me when seen by moonlight. Your Tauber nixie is a young lady of excellent taste. And then I at once received my first lesson in Rothenburg history and legend. When I praised the bread at breakfast, the head waiter quoted the old saying—

> At Rothenburg on the river
> The bread is good for the liver.

And when I stepped out of doors to see the lay of the land a bit by myself, the host at once informed me that this was the famous Schmiedegasse and that in the Peasants' War, when sixty of the rebel leaders were beheaded by some Margrave or other on the square before the town hall, the blood had flowed like a brook down the steep street here. If only I were to remain here three days I believe I should become a full fledged Rothenburger, for, really and truly, everything I see pleases me; you, too, please me much better

A GABLE AT ROTHENBURG

today than you did yesterday.   Do you know that your
artist's costume is very becoming?   But come, we must
not stay so long in one place.   You are not to show me
especially the so-called sights but the nooks which no
Bædeker has noted and marked with an asterisk.   And, as
my husband is governor of a fortress, I want to see the
towers and walls first of all, in case Russia should some
day lay siege to Rothenburg in revenge for its conquest of
me today.''

He had not taken his eyes from her while all this light
banter was falling from her nimble tongue.   She still wore
the traveling-costume of the previous day, but everything
was a little more coquettishly arranged, and the little fur
cap was cocked more saucily over one ear.   He now offered
her his arm and led her along little side lanes to the defen-
sive wall, which is still in a very fair state of preservation
and encompasses the whole area of the city.   He told her,
too, that the city had had as many towers as the year has
weeks.   Most of these were still standing, and for many
centuries, he said, they had been, in war times, the first
thought both of the citizens and their enemies, either as a
place of refuge for themselves and their belongings or as
a stone wall against which to break their heads.   She listened rather unresponsively to his lecture, but let her sharp
eyes rove about incessantly, merely interrupting him from
time to time by a joyful exclamation when they came upon
some quaint bit of masonry, a picturesque little cottage
hidden among the flying buttresses, or the end of a lane
through which one could look back at the hilly old town.
Then she mounted one of the little gray stairways that lead
to the top of the wall, and continued her walk under the low
projecting roof beneath which the sturdy citizens had so
often stood and answered the fire of the enemy's artillery.
Now and again she would stop at a loophole, peep out, ask
what point of the compass she was looking toward, and
what sort of roads ran into the country in that direction.
So they walked from the Faul Tower through the Röder

Gate to the White Tower, where she at last declared that she had now pursued her course in fortification long enough for the present, and wished to return to town. Only St. Wolfgang, who stands in a niche in the chapel named for him, so meek and so long-suffering, holding up his broken crozier and resting the other hand upon a model of his little church, detained her outside the walls for a little longer. "If I remained in Rothenburg," said she, "this holy man would be dangerous for me. Just see what a sweet innocent face he has, and yet so wise a one. I have always desired to meet a live saint some day, and then to play the temptress a little. Do you think this one could withstand me if I had designs upon his soul?"

He faltered some awkward word of jest. In sober earnest he felt as though neither saints nor children of the world could escape from this charming woman if she chose to cast her net for them. As he watched her slender form gliding through the shady walks along the wall and up and down the steps, while a sunbeam now and again flittered over her face, his heart beat with a strange commotion which he took for an ebullition of his artistic blood — only it surprised and almost offended him that she did not allude by so much as a word to her plan of yesterday for the journey to Sicily. For, in spite of all his resolutions of the night before, he could not help imagining himself already climbing the steps of the Taormina amphitheatre in spirit at her side, listening to exclamations of joy very different from those she uttered over an old watch-tower or sally-port here.

Now she was leaning on his arm again as they returned to the town, and he led her straight to the old church of St. James, the real cathedral of the town. However, she inspected the beautiful Gothic edifice with much slighter interest than he had expected, and even the three famous altars with their excellent carvings left her cold; only at the glass vessel on one of them, in which the holy blood is preserved, did she gaze for a long time, while she crossed herself. He thought he would impress her by telling her that the high altar, together with the paintings by Michael Wohlgemuth, had been given by Heinrich Toppler, and by showing her the great burgomaster's coat of arms with the two dice; but she yawned softly through her nose, and asked to be led outside.   Then her interest was roused again by the black spot on the arched roof of the passage beneath which the street runs right through the centre of the church. A peasant, he told her, who had cursed while driving his team through here, had been seized by the devil and hurled aloft against the vaulted roof; his body had fallen back, but his poor soul had stuck fast above.

Then she laughed, showing her gleaming teeth. "You men of Rothenburg have gone mad peddling old legends," she exclaimed. "And now, just show me your town hall, and that will be enough for today."

"Do you know," said she, as they were walking the short distance back to the market-place, "it seems to me as if this German Pompeii were inhabited only by good people, whose loyalty and honesty has been covered up for a few centuries, just like the old stones, and has now come to light again. I have not seen a single evil face here. They all speak to each other in passing; it is like a large, well-brought-up family, every member of which behaves becomingly because he is kept under the eye of all the others. You, too, probably once looked out more jauntily and boldly into the world; now you have the same sanctimonious expression. But you must not take it ill if I sometimes look a bit critical."

He eagerly assured her that, quite to the contrary, he was very much attracted by her brilliantly unconventional way of judging everything. He was at once put to a severe test on this point in the great hall of the town house. When the keeper's wife told the story of the Master-Drink, that oft-sung heroic rescue by old Burgomaster Nusch, who from the evil Tilly, the iron-hearted conqueror of the city, obtained the forfeited lives of the entire council and mercy for the inhabitants by accomplishing what had been deemed impossible — draining at one draught a bumper that held thirteen quarts, Bavarian measure — the lady could not repress her mirth, and burst into a ringing laugh. The excuse she afterward offered was that it was not so much the pleasing story that had appeared laughable to her, as the solemn, emotional delivery which had magnified this exploit into a deed of the most exalted heroism. It had struck her, too, that this legend was a counterpart of that of the Roman knight Curtius, only that the latter, to save his city, had been swallowed up by the gulf, whereas the Rothenburg Curtius had himself swallowed the gulf — and more such disrespectful quips. Regretfully Hans was forced to admit to himself that this lady, whom he regarded in other respects as a being of rare perfection, was almost entirely lacking in the ability to appreciate history.

" Should you like to climb the tower? " he asked. It is a bit hard on the nerves, though quite safe, for from the foundation to the very top the masonry is held by iron clamps, so that the square hollow pillar is bound firmly together; but often when there is a storm, the tall slender tower sways like a tree which is shaken back and forth by the winds."

" It's a pity that the air is so calm today," she replied. " Of course we will go up."

He now led the way, and they climbed the steep little wooden stairways until they had reached the very top, where, at their knock, a trap-door opened, and a little gray-haired man, who performed the duties of tower-watchman, greeted them in friendly fashion.

She looked about inquisitively in the airy room, into which the bright midday sunlight was streaming through four tiny windows, sat down on the stool from which the little man had risen, and engaged in a conversation which was sustained with great zeal by this lonely weathercock. Needle and thimble lay upon the little table, and a half finished waistcoat, for the watchman was a tailor by trade,

and was not only invested with a civic function but also
made the vestments of his fellow-citizens. She clapped on
the steel thimble in which her delicate finger-tip was fairly
lost, took a few stitches, and asked whether he would yield
his office and trade to her, for, so she said, he was the only
man in the world whom she envied, as, in spite of his lofty
position, he was not bothered by people, and, if he should
ever be struck by lightning during a storm, he had so much
shorter a distance to travel to Heaven. The little fellow
told her in return that he had a wife and children, and a
salary of but sixty pfennigs a day, so that his life was by
no means free from cares. And now he showed her the
fire-alarm signals, and complained of the fear he often
endured when the tower swayed so violently that the water
in his dish would splash over the edge. She then asked if
it were not possible to get out into the open air, out on the
gallery that runs around the spire. At once the watchman
took down a little ladder which was attached to the ceiling,
climbed up ahead of them, and opened a metal trap-door
which closed a rather small triangular hole. Would the
lady take the risk of worming through it? Of course she
would, said she, she was still just slender enough; only the
gentlemen were to go first.

Hans Doppler, who had never persuaded his little wife
to squeeze through the narrow opening, showed his admiration of her courage only by an ardent glance, and clambered
up hastily after the watchman. The next moment he saw
the fair lady pop up through the trap-door and held out his
hand to her to help her out. There they stood, drawing
deep breaths of satisfaction, shoulder to shoulder on the
narrow platform about the belfry, separated from the dizzy
depths merely by a slender railing. The city lay at their
feet as neatly arranged as if taken out of a Nuremberg
playbox. The towers of St. James' Church, round which the
swallows were flying, were far below them. They saw the
silvery Tauber wandering off into the countryside, and the
thin spirals of smoke from a hundred chimneys whirling

straight upward. It was noon, and the streets were almost deserted.

Suddenly she turned to her companion. "If two people exchange a kiss up here can it be seen from below?" she asked.

He flushed fiery red. "It depends on how good one's eyes are," he answered. "But so far as I know, nothing of the sort has been noticed hitherto."

"Hasn't it really?" she said, laughing softly. "Do not sweethearts come up here on the tower, or other people who are misled by their lofty stand-point into committing a trifling piece of folly? Just imagine how scandalized the good Philistines below would be if they squinted up here in the semi-twilight of the afternoon, and suddenly witnessed such a merry piece of impropriety. Perhaps the authorities would then have a notice posted up here, that kissing was forbidden under a penalty of three marks."

He laughed in an embarrassed fashion.

"Once," she continued, "I climbed to the top of the dome of St. Peter's. A young Frenchman who was my escort asserted that he absolutely must embrace me as we sat in the great copper dome — that this was a venerable old custom. But I would not allow it, just because up there one is quite safe from indiscreet observers; I could have been attracted only by the danger. We must have the courage of our follies, otherwise they are foolish and nothing more. Do you not think so too?"

He nodded an eager assent. He felt more uncomfortable and ill at ease every moment. At the same time, moreover, he felt more and more clearly the power this woman was acquiring over him.

"You were born for the heights of life," he faltered. "In your presence such a feeling of freedom and lightheartedness comes over me that I could imagine that, were I to stand here beside you for long, I should grow wings which would carry me far out beyond the humdrum."

She gave him a keen, penetrating, sidelong glance. " Well, then, why do you refuse to let yourself be carried? "

Confused, he contemplated the depths below. At this moment there were twelve booms from St. James' Church, and at once the little watchman also struck twelve blows on the great dark bell behind them. The lady shrugged her shoulders and turned away. " Come," she said coolly, " it is late, and your wife will be keeping the soup waiting for you." Then she smoothed down her dress at the hips, so that it clung close about her knees and ankles, and popped down again into the narrow opening, cautiously feeling with her little feet for the rungs of the ladder. His proffered assistance came too late. By the time he had himself regained the tower-room below she was already standing before the tailor's little mirror, which was not wider than a hand's breadth, putting her hair in order.

She seemed to have lost some of her good humor, and he secretly acknowledged to himself that he was to blame. He felt very much vexed at having behaved like a boor and not having seized his good luck quickly by the forelock — not that he could have brought himself to do anything very wrong or be guilty of real disloyalty to his good wife. But really only some frolicsome game had been meant, as in redeeming forfeits, and he had played the spoil-sport. What must she think of his Rothenburg lack of breeding? And would she care to trouble further about such a blockhead?

She had taken abrupt leave of the watchman, who had been almost petrified by the thaler she slipped into his hand. While descending the stairs they did not exchange a word, and even in the broad quiet Herrengasse where ordinarily he would surely have explained to her the tablets on the houses which indicated where and how long this or that lofty monarch had lodged in the old imperial fortress, he walked silently at her side. She perceived that vexation and remorse sealed his lips, and as, after all, she liked him very well in his embarrassment she began once more to chat in her confidential manner. Then, when they passed through the Castle Gate out to the narrow hill planted with trees and graceful shrubs, which leads to the plateau that centuries before had been the site of the real Rothenburg (Red Castle), she expressed an eager delight in the still leafless branches, the old Pharamund Tower, and the view to right and left. Then he too became more cheerful again, and pointed out to her now the small water tower down in the valley which had been built by Heinrich Toppler and within the modest compass of which he had offered hospitality to King Wenceslaus. "And up yonder," said he, "where you see the four small windows — the wall of the house forms part of the city wall — that is where I live, and if you will do me the honor — "

"Not just now," she quickly interrupted. "I have been dragging you about too long already. I shall now go back to the hotel by myself, for even now I could find my way about the town on a foggy night, and if I were to get lost, so much the better. Nothing is more tiresome than to be always treading familiar paths. *La recherche de l'inconnu* — that has always been my life-work. So go home now; I shall invite myself to drink a cup of coffee with you and your wife this afternoon. But you are not to call for me, do you hear? Farewell!" She held out her hand to him, but he could not bring himself to kiss merely her glove now, after trifling away so short a time before the chance to kiss her lips. So he left her with a strange feeling of agitation.

When Hans Doppler got home, he found that Christel had not kept dinner waiting for him, though she had put aside his share in case he should care for it. She had supposed, she explained, that he would dine with his old general's wife at the hotel, and the children had felt hungry. Now she set the plain repast before him after the rest had finished, but for the first time it failed to tempt his appetite. As he ate, she again sat opposite him and chatted in her quiet, cheery way about things, which that day, after he had been standing upon the "heights of human experience," seemed to him thoroughly insipid and unprofitable. The children, except the eldest, who was already going to school, were playing in the garden and were not dressed up at all.

"Listen, dear," he said, "you might, perhaps, put another ribbon in your hair, and dress Lena in her blue dress. The general's wife intends to come and have a cup of coffee with us."

"Don't you think my bow good enough any more?" she asked in reply, looking at herself in the mirror. "I made it only a week ago. Why are we to make such ceremonial preparations when an old Russian lady wishes to make our acquaintance?"

"H'm," he remarked, "I have told you already that she is not so very old, between thirty and forty, and extremely elegant. And when we really have the means, why should we choose to affect an air of greater poverty than necessary? We cannot, to be sure, exchange our old furniture for new, but at least you should remove these little spoons that are worn so very thin and brittle and take the newer ones instead; and even if you don't wish to put on one of your best dresses — "

He grew confused, although she had not interrupted by so much as a word; but her glance, seeking to read his inmost thoughts, troubled him.

"Why, Hans, you seem to be in a queer state," she said. "Has not everything here seemed to you attractive and appropriate until now, and haven't you said yourself that you would never part with this old sofa on which we sat when our betrothal was celebrated? And was not the little coffee-spoon good enough for you when I put the first preserved cherry into your mouth with it? The new ones, as you well know, belong to Heinz. His godfather is going to give him one every year till the dozen is completed. Am I to borrow something from our laddie, to make a display of it before a stranger? My coffee is renowned throughout the town. Marie shall run to the pastry-shop and fetch fresh cake. Then, if your Russian is not satisfied with what we have, I am sorry for her. Besides, you seem not to have examined her birth certificate very closely until today; so much the better if she's not an old hag. Tell me, has she any children?"

"I believe not. She did not mention it."

"No matter. Her silver spoons may be finer than mine. As far as our children are concerned — they, I think, will bear comparison with the children of any Russian general. I will just clean their hands a bit — they are digging up their little garden. Besides, earth is not dirt."

At this she went down into the garden, while he, glad to be alone, inspected the room to see where something ought to be removed or arranged a little more in accordance with his sense of the picturesque. From the attic which he had transformed into a studio by means of a half-masked window looking toward the north, he brought down a few water-color paintings and hung them on one of the walls in place of the pastel picture of a scarcely remembered great-aunt. He carried an easel to the corner by the little window and placed an oil sketch upon it. He would have liked to banish entirely the glass case with its miscellaneous glasses, cups, nosegays of artificial flowers, and little alabaster figures, even if he had had to fling it out of the window and down on the rampart. But he knew that this treasure-house, full of tasteless souvenirs, was so precious to his wife that she would never forgive him such an outrage. At last he surveyed the fruits of his work and sighed; the little room looked much as it had before. He had to admit that the stamp of self-satisfied provincialism had been too deeply impressed upon his life to be eradicated in a twinkling. But then, of course, this cage was too confined to permit an ambitious artist to soar. He must escape, if the veil which had hitherto concealed all this wretched tastelessness from his eyes were not to be bound over them forever.

OUTSIDE THE ROTHENBURG WALLS

Then Christel came in again, cast a glance of surprise at the easel and the new pictures on the wall and smiled a little, but said nothing. She spread a dainty cloth over the table and took her best cups out of the glass case. These, too, it must be confessed, were already somewhat advanced in years and ornamented with the decorations of an earlier period. The chief treasure of her modest array of silverware, a little sugar bowl, on the lid of which a swan was spreading its wings, was placed between the two plates which the maid was now filling with fresh cakes. The little woman did not seem much surprised that her Hans was sitting in silence by her sewing-table at the window, pretending to read a book which he was holding in his hand. She soon left him alone again, with the same quiet smile, which greatly enhanced the beauty of her round pretty mouth. But he had no eyes for such things now.

The better part of an hour slipped thus away. He heard her bustling about in the kitchen and talking to the maid, but her quiet gentle voice which he had hitherto loved so dearly, tortured him now, he did not himself know why. Suddenly the front door opened downstairs. He started up and rushed out into the hall. There Christel met him.

"Must you really meet her at the foot of the stairs, as if she were a princess?" she remarked with perfect composure. "Surely we are not such insignificant people as that."

"You are right," he replied, somewhat taken aback. "All I wanted was to be sure that you were here."

She preceded him back to the sitting-room, and the caller entered immediately after. Christel received her with unembarrassed friendliness, while the young husband bowed silently. The lady seemed almost to ignore him, too, devoting herself exclusively to the young wife, who invited her to sit down beside her on the little hard sofa, and thanked her for having taken the time and trouble during so brief a stay to call upon her. "Our little old house," she went on, " is not one of the wonders of Rothenburg. Our paneling is not so beautiful as that in the drawing-room of the Weisz-bäcker house, and although everything we have is old, that does not make it pretty. Of course it pleases me because I have seen it ever since my childhood, and have seen people I loved sitting on every one of these plain chairs. But my husband "— and she threw him a roguish glance — "would not be sorry to see all our furniture depart for the second-hand dealer's, or put into the fire. The best things we own are common property, and are outside in front of the window. You must look at our view. Then you will understand how even an artist found it possible to be satisfied with this old nest — though, to be sure, who knows how long he will continue so?"

Once more she shot a mischievous glance at her husband, who was now pushing aside the little sewing-table to show their visitor the view. But the lady kept her seat, saying she had already observed the Tauber valley carefully from the Castle and had come solely on Christel's account. Evidently she intended to be very gracious and affable and to give the shy young wife every encouragement; but when she perceived that the latter stood in no need of encouragement, she became somewhat diffident herself. Contrary to her usual procedure she remained silent for some time, listening to the simple-hearted talk of her hostess, in which the husband joined only by an occasional remark. The maid brought in the coffee and Christel served her guest without any unusual ceremony. Meanwhile she sharply scrutinized the stranger's countenance, and the result of this inspection seemed to make her every moment more cheerful and more self-possessed. Then she asked the lady about her travels, about her husband the general, and whether she had any children; but at a quick shake of the head from her caller she dropped this subject. Just after this, however, the three older children rushed up the stairs and into the room, the eldest boy carrying his baby sister, who had just turned two. All four looked pretty and rosy and were only a little shy when their mother called them to her to shake hands with the lady. The latter inspected them with apparent kindliness through her lorgnette, but evidently did not feel quite at ease with them. Then, with a glance at a small faded piano which stood against the rear wall, she abruptly inquired whether Christel were also a musician.

The latter answered that she had played in her girlhood, but at present was too busy with the housekeeping, and opened the piano only once in a while to accompany her children when they sang. Of course the caller begged to be favored with such a family concert, and although the father remarked that the pleasure was but a moderate one, the young wife nevertheless did not wait very long to be urged. She gently put down the baby, who had climbed on her lap, and placed her in the corner of the sofa. Then she went to the piano, struck a few chords with an unpractised, yet musical hand, and played the air of the song: "Afar in a shady valley." The two boys and little Lena had quietly taken their places behind her, and began to sing, rather timidly at first. But on the second stanza the young voices rang out fresh and clear, and now the mother sang, too, with a beautiful deep alto voice which permeated the tender melody with a strange and powerful fervor.

Hans was sitting by the window, casting an occasional furtive glance at the visitor, whose face, as she listened, grew sterner and more unhappy every moment. When the song was at an end she still remained silent. Christel rose and whispered something to the children, whereupon they bowed politely and stole out of the room. Then she took up the baby, who had fallen asleep, and carried her out to the maid. When she returned the other two were still sitting, wrapped in silent meditation.

"Aren't you going to show the lady your studio too?" she asked cheerily. "There really is more to see there than down here." He rose at once, and the visitor did likewise. "You have no idea how well you sing," she said, holding out her hand to Christel. "Only music always

makes me melancholy — not the great, tumultuous operas
and concerts, but a pure, warm, human voice. And now
let us enter art's workshop.''

Hans led her up a small, dark, breakneck flight of steps, and
opened the door of the so-called studio. The whitewashed
walls of the roomy garret were covered with sketches and
studies dating from his days at the Academy. A sketching
table stood close by the window where he did his work in
water-colors. On a couple of easels stood oil paintings —
one finished, the other with only the first coat laid on —
views of Rothenburg, of course. But today her interest in
such things seemed to have cooled a good deal, for she
honored but few of the sketches with a remark. Presently
she turned to the window through which they could look
across the gentle green slopes of the plateau down the
Tauber to the little village, where the old church-steeple
towered among tall, still leafless trees into the faint haze
of the spring air.

'' There is no special beauty in these colors and lines,''
he remarked, '' only they do fairly well as a setting for the
panorama of the city. How different it must be to stand
on the Capitol and look out over the imperial palaces and
the Forum at the beautiful, classic outlines of the Alban
Mountains. Of course I only know it from pictures,'' he
concluded with a sigh.

'' Well, you will some day see it, too, as it really is —
that, and other beautiful things besides. In the meantime,
this is not to be despised, either. Each is good in its own
way.''

Then she changed the subject. It was enough for him,
however, that she had at last again mentioned his journey
to Italy, for the first time in all that day. He was just
considering how to enlarge upon the topic she had broached,
when she broke off the conversation and requested him to
take her downstairs again. She explained that she still
had some letters to write before her departure, as she would

be better able to write in peace here than in Würzburg. She asked when the evening train left.

"At eight," he replied.

"Very well. I suppose I shall see you again at the station? I am going back to my room now."

When they descended to the sitting-room Christel was not there. The maid, who blushed and could not possibly be induced to accept what the caller tried to put into her hand, said that her mistress was in the garden. There Christel came to meet them, carrying in her hand hyacinths and other spring flowers which she had just cut off and twined in a simple little nosegay.

"You must be content with these just now," said she; "I cannot yet offer you any of my roses, of which I am very proud. But this yellow hyacinth, you know, with the greenish bells, I raised myself. I have good luck in raising children and flowers — that is my sole accomplishment."

The caller accepted the bouquet and embraced the giver, kissing her on the cheek. She allowed herself to be shown about the little garden, which was surrounded by high walls and was not at this season receiving the full benefit of the sun's light. But a thick ivy-vine had taken pity on the black walls and clothed them in a mass of dark green against which the young shoots of the fruit trees and the flower beds with their primroses, crocuses, and hyacinths stood out in cheerful contrast. The children were playing in one corner, where they kept at work on a topsy-turvy little garden of their own, without letting themselves be disturbed by the caller.

"Now I must take leave of you," said the stranger. "Unfortunately, I cannot invite you to pay me a return visit at my so-called home. Our fortress does not wear a fresh and smiling aspect like this place, and I have never tried to see whether I have good luck in raising children and flowers. But I thank you for these pleasant hours. I shall never forget them; they have afforded me more joy and more pain than anything has done for a long time. Good-by!''

She embraced Christel once more, this time kissing her upon the mouth. Then she nodded to the young husband with an almost inaudible *"Au revoir!"* and hastily left the garden by way of the gray arched gate.

It was only half-past seven, and the sun had hardly set, when the 'bus of the Golden Stag rolled through the east gate of the town and shortly afterward drew up in the square behind the little station. But even before the porter could open the door the young man in the black artist's hat, who had been waiting there, sprang forward to help out first the lady, and then the Kalmuck maid with her load of bandboxes and satchels.

He himself had a light overcoat flung over his shoulders, a thick package was peeping from the pocket, and he was carrying a large sketch-book under his arm. His face was somewhat flushed, his glance shifting and excited. He asked whether the tickets had been secured already, and then hurried to the ticket office, from which he quickly returned again. Two tickets he handed to his patroness, a third he put in his own pocket.

"You are going along?" asked the lady, coming suddenly to a halt, while Sascha lugged her traps toward the waiting room.

He merely nodded, looking at her in astonishment and some excitment.

"Where are you going, pray, seeing that you got back only yesterday?"

"Where? I hope to learn that from you, madam."

She looked at him for a moment, as if some madman had spoken to her.

"Did you not convincingly demonstrate to me," he continued, his heart throbbing violently, "that I owe it to myself to see a little of the world first, before settling down for good in this little out-of-the-way place? And were you not kind enough to desire to have me for your traveling-companion, that I might everywhere sketch for you the landscapes which especially took your fancy? After mature consideration I have come to the conclusion that you are right — that I have no time to lose if I wish to take up again the plans I let slip; and so I am here and at your service."

Still she said nothing, but now turned her eyes from him to the evening sky, where Venus was just rising in mild radiance.

"Does your wife know of your decision, and approve it?"

"My wife — I simply told her that I wished to bid you good-by at the station. I intend to telegraph her from Steinach not to expect me today, as I am going on a short journey for purposes of study before returning; from Würzburg I shall write her in detail, explaining the reasons why I stole away from her in this fashion. It would have meant needless heartache for both of us, and in a year or so, God willing, we shall meet again well and happy. She is a very sensible woman, quicker and surer by far than I in making a decision, and loves me too well not to desire what is best for me. In the last twenty-four hours I have arranged it all in my mind. Have you changed your views in the meantime? — I have brought with me only what was absolutely necessary," he continued hesitatingly; "I did not wish to attract attention. I have a sufficient supply of money, I shall buy a trunk during the journey — but why do you look at me so strangely, madam?"

"Dear friend," she quietly said, "do you know that unless I show more sense than you, you are about to commit an act of positive madness — yes, a crime against yourself and your life's happiness?"

"For heaven's sake, madam — "

"Silence! Don't say a word, but listen to me. First, however, answer me a simple question, but honestly and truthfully — haven't you fallen a little bit in love with me?"

"Why, madam," he faltered in the utmost embarrassment. He dropped his sketch-book, stooped for it, and took a long time to pick it up again and brush off the dust.

"You are right," she said without smiling. "It is an awkward question, and I am the more ready to spare you the answer as I know it already. Of course I am not angry with you for that, and you are not the first one, either. Yes, it has happened to me often, when I had less reason to be vain over it. But what in the world have you thought would be the outcome?"

He made no reply and, giving him a sidelong glance, she enjoyed for a little while his helplessness and dismay.

"I'll tell you the answer," she went on. "It seemed to you quite romantic to suffer yourself, as it were, to be abducted, to act out a little story of travel in rambling chapters, and to illustrate it with pretty Italian landscapes. I admit, too, that I liked you just well enough to find your society very desirable, since I am a lonely, dissatisfied, and, as yet, not entirely resigned creature. Yes, just to tell you the truth — for I will not give myself credit for virtue that I do not possess — I took a little trouble — though, to be sure, not much was needed — to turn your head a bit. You seemed to me really too good for a philistine provincial life in dressing-gown and slippers at the side of a demure little goose such as I imagined your wife to be. I even fondly fancied that I had something like a mission to fulfil in saving an artist's life from the curse of becoming commonplace and countrified, or whatever one wants to call it. But I have been frightfully put to shame."

"My wife — " he said.

"Don't speak of her," she interrupted hastily. "Do you know that you are not at all worthy of such a woman? To think, that after the way you spoke of her I expected to meet a good, honest, insignificant creature, and instead — why, the whole of your famous Rothenburg can show nothing more worthy of note than this little woman. And you were willing to leave a woman like her in the lurch in order to run after a perfect stranger? Don't be angry with me, but you were on the right road to become an utter fool, and I am not vain enough to see any special extenuating circumstance in the fact that it is I with whom you happen to have become madly infatuated.''

Her voice rang stern and harsh; by its sound he knew that it expressed the feelings of a sorely wounded heart. Then he tried to compose himself and said, as he grasped her hand and pressed it softly in his, '' I thank you for all the kind things you have just said to me, and for those that hurt.   I will be no less frank than were you; yes, you have bewitched me, yet really not in the most ordinary sense of the term, but by revealing to me the heights of life and art, the attaining of which I had renounced so soon to seek my happiness modestly half way up the slope.   I have indeed found it, and am truly not so blind and ungrateful as to esteem it lightly.   But shall one not strive to mount higher? Shall one be content with what you yourself called ' a life of happy monotony in Rothenburg,' especially when one has dedicated his life to art, rather than seek ' the unknown? ' ''

'' Strive to mount higher? '' she interrupted. '' ' The unknown? ' Bless your fate that you have not hitherto taken these fine phrases seriously.   They are will-o'-the-wisps that lure us into swamps and over precipices.   Shall I tell you a tale?   Once upon a time there was a beautiful young girl, the daughter of a petty serf, who was loved by a good young man, the tutor in the house of the lord of the estate.   He resembled you a little, only his hair and beard were not arranged with such an eye to the pictur-esque.   He wished to marry the girl, and as he had a small competency, it would have been a very nice match.   But the proud creature wished to ' mount higher,' and even then, though as yet ignorant of French, cherished an inclina-tion in her heart for *la recherche de l'inconnu*.   Then a general came on a visit to the estate.   He likewise thought the young girl strikingly pretty, paid court to her, and finally offered to marry her.   Well, that was the mounting higher of which she had dreamt, and the unknown as well;

for the fashionable world of St. Petersburg was to open its doors to her. So she forsook her faithful suitor and became a general's wife, and when she viewed the height by daylight it was low and vulgar, and when she came to know the unknown it was insipid triviality. To be sure, the cravings of her heart would probably not have been satisfied by the happiness of life with a simple schoolmaster, yet she would not have felt quite so utterly miserable nor have made others so unhappy. Of course others were willing to help rectify her error, and there was one among them who might very likely have succeeded. Unhappily, though, the general had a sure hand with the pistol, and did not consider it beneath him to give one of his young officers with his own hand a lesson which struck the poor fellow's name from the rank-list of the living. But the wife, fool that she is, has known no peace since that, and hunts the world over for the 'unknown,' or, when she feels really inclined to self-deception, strives to 'mount higher.' Do you know that up to the present she has found nothing higher than the calm, kindly face of your clever little wife, the peace of your old-fashioned sitting-room, and that good luck in raising children and flowers, the witchery of which has invested both with such bright colors?

"There! Now, I have nothing more to say to you. If you still believe your happiness depends on sketching the old stones of the Castle of Sant Angelo instead of the old stones of the White Tower, or on trying your hand at the great and the sublime, though you are scarcely cut out for a Raphael, then board the train with me. The road is open and long enough, perhaps, to cure me of my very unselfish whim. But if you are wise you will postpone your journey for the study of art until the children are so far grown that you can some day leave them under the care of others for a few months. Then take your Christel under your arm and cross the Alps in her company, and I assure you that, even though she is only a child of Rothenburg, you will not disgrace yourself by exhibiting her on the Monte

Pincio. I am assuming that you yourself will not under-estimate her, but will make her a partner in your life and aspirations, for when we women are good we are what you make of us. Otherwise we are, of course, what we make of ourselves — but neither good nor happy. And with that we'll stop. Good-by, and my compliments to Madam Christel. When your book on Rothenburg comes out, send it to me at Rome, in care of the Russian Embassy. I will subscribe for three copies. I will spread the fame of the German Pompeii.''

She held out her hand to him, and he pressed it to his lips with irresistible emotion. She then drew down her veil and hurried to the train, which was about to start, and when she had taken her place in the compartment she waved her hand once more. The little engine whistled, and the black snake glided slowly off along the gleaming track. The lady retreated to the dark corner of the compartment and for a long time sat staring into vacancy like a statue. Suddenly she opened one of her Russian leather bags, groped about in it, and at last drew out a case. '' There, take it,'' she said in Russian to the sullen maid. '' You have always admired this bracelet so much, Sascha; I'll make you a present of it — for once I am in the mood to be generous! I only wish generosity never cost me more than a bright toy like that.''

Sascha fell on her knees before her and kissed her hand. Then, playing with the gift, she again withdrew into her corner. She fancied she heard her mistress weeping softly under cover of her veil, but did not venture to ask the reason.

About the same time Hans Doppler returned to his little wife. The children were already asleep. He was strangely gentle, moved, and tender. Again and again he stroked the curly brown locks that fell so prettily over the delicate ears. Without going into a full account of what had occurred at the parting, he had given her their visitor's parting message. But several times, as they sat together at supper, he started to make a full confession. At last he merely remarked, "Do you know, sweetheart, the general's wife had quite seriously formed the purpose of carrying me off for a journey in her company to study art all through Italy and Sicily? What would you have said to that?"

"Well, Hans," she replied, "I should not have kept you from going if it had really been your wish. To be sure, I do not know how I could have borne it; I can hardly imagine living without you now. But if your happiness had depended upon it—"

"My happiness? That depends on you alone!" the dissembler affirmed, trying to conceal a blush. "But you should just have heard her making clear to me my good luck and your qualities. But you—wouldn't you really have grown a little jealous?"

"Of whom? Of that old Russian?"

"Old? With that hair and that complexion?"

"Oh, Hans, how blind you are!" she cried with a hearty laugh, pulling his hair. "Is it possible that you didn't see that this dangerous Muscovite was powdered ever so heavily, and had a thick switch? But even if everything about her had been genuine, do you suppose I should not have trusted myself to cope with her? And besides—the Tiber may be a very beautiful river but, after all, it certainly cannot compare with our Tauber!"

RÖDER GATE TOWER, ROTHENBURG

THE LIFE OF JOSEPH VICTOR VON SCHEFFEL

By MAX WINKLER, PH.D.

Professor of German Literature, University of Michigan

 OSEPH VICTOR SCHEFFEL was born in Karlsruhe, the capital of the Grand Duchy of Baden, February 16, 1826. He was descended of pure Alemannic stock, and various members of his family had for generations occupied honorable positions in Suabian lands. His immediate family belonged to the cultivated well-to-do middle class, was conservative in its political and social life, and was loyally attached to the reigning house. His father had entered the military service of his country, attained in course of time the rank of major in the engineering corps of the army of Baden, and won the confidence and esteem of the government by the high efficiency of his service and the integrity of his character. By training and temperament he was an old-fashioned bureaucrat, and as such regarded a fixed position in one of the higher branches of governmental service as the natural career for his son to follow. The poet's mother, Josephine, was a much more gifted nature. She was a woman of broad sympathies, was thoroughly sound and practical in the manifold duties of her family and social life, was endowed with a keen sense of humor and had a strong bent toward poetry, to which she gave occasional expression in verse and tale and dramatic composition. Thus she was by nature well able to appreciate the poetic aspirations and achievements of her son and help him by counsel and deed in the many problems and inner conflicts of his whimsical career. She had the deepest insight into his nature, and hence her judgments upon him are among the most suggestive and helpful for our interpretation of his life and art. Both parents were

liberal Catholics and were in close touch with the best thought of the time. In the gymnasium of Karlsruhe Scheffel received an excellent education, developed a decided aptitude for linguistic study and became very well acquainted with the best productions of the literature of his country. Even in his boyhood he became very fond of the history, legends and Volkslieder of Suabia, and read with much interest the lyrics and novels of the romantic movement, especially the poems of Uhland and Heine and the works of Hauff and Walter Scott. Upon finishing the gymnasium at the age of seventeen, he would by preference have devoted himself to painting, but he yielded, for a time at least, to the wishes of his father, who insisted upon his study of law. Speaking many years later of this enforced choice of vocation the poet said: "By endowment and preference I should have become a painter. Training and circumstance turned me to the service of justice. The unfulfilled longing for the painter's art in its contrast to the barrenness of a mechanical calling awakened the poetical sentiment."

He spent four years (1843–47) in the universities of Munich, Berlin, and Heidelberg, devoting himself partly to his professional studies, which he pursued with vigor and success, and partly to the more congenial labors in literature, history, and art. He also entered with hearty enthusiasm into the social life of the students, made frequent pleasure tours to the Black Forest with merry companions, became a prominent member of several student organizations and formed many friendships by his jovial humor and genuine convivial spirit. It was during this joyous period of his life that he began to publish student songs, the excellence of which was soon recognized throughout Germany.

He passed his State examination and took his doctor's degree with high credit in the stormy years of 1848 and 1849. Although a liberal and nationalist in politics, his temperament and family traditions made it impossible for him to join his countrymen in their efforts to obtain by revolutionary means the much needed reforms. Moreover, the revolutionists of Baden, though animated by high motives, seemed to him too vague and visionary in their aims and too weak in their organization to win his real sympathy and respect. To be sure, he was for a time secretary of K. J. Welcker, one of the intellectual leaders of the movement, but as the revolution progressed his attitude became distinctly critical and conservative.

In 1850 he accepted a government appointment as "Amtsrevisor" in Säkkingen, an ancient and beautiful town on the Rhine in the southern part of the Black Forest. The two years he spent there were among the happiest in his life. His official duties were not too burdensome, so that he had ample time and opportunity to make excursions to the various neighboring towns and villages and become thoroughly acquainted with that charming region. With warm sympathy he observed the manners and customs of the people, mingled with them in their social affairs, and felt that the whole life of that country was intimately bound up with the traditions of his family and with his own deepest being. The quiet life in Säkkingen proved indeed most fruitful for his poetical career; the impressions which land and people made upon him stirred his imagination, quickened his historical consciousness and awakened his latent artistic powers. Some of his impressions of land and people in and about Säkkingen he published in a series of articles entitled: *From the Jauenstein Black Forest,* which show close observation and keen historical sense.

Upon leaving Säkkingen (1851) he spent several months in governmental service in Bruchsal, and then, notwithstanding his long and excellent legal preparation and his good prospects for a distinguished career in the government of Baden, his artistic longings had become so strong that a further continuation of legal work seemed unbearable to him. He, accordingly, decided to give up for a time, at least, his professional work, and devote himself to landscape painting. The father, though seriously disappointed by this sudden and radical change of his son's vocation, was finally prevailed upon to give his consent, and so in the spring of 1852 Scheffel set out for Italy, firmly believing that in spite of his meager preparation he would soon justify his strange conduct by producing landscape paintings of acknowledged artistic value. In June he arrived in Rome, and began at once to sketch from nature under the direction of Willers, a highly talented German painter. In the midst of a circle of congenial friends he worked at his art with much diligence and enthusiasm, convinced for a time that he had finally found his true vocation. But his friends soon realized that with his inadequate training he could, at best, attain but moderate results as a painter, even after years of serious effort. On the other hand, they discovered in him a remarkable natural talent for telling stories, and so they candidly advised him to devote his productive energy to poetry. At first he was much irritated and dejected by their judgment, but gradually felt obliged to acknowledge his limitations, and decided, before returning to his home, to achieve something worthy in the field of poetry. With this end in view he directed his imagination to his delightful experiences in Säkkingen and to the life and traditions of that region. Thus, stimulated by the artistic environment of Italy and encouraged by his friends he sketched in the fall of 1852 with much ease the *Trumpeter of Säkkingen,* and in February of 1853 withdrew to Capri and Sorrento to complete that work. Here his good fortune brought him in contact with the youthful Paul Heyse who was then working upon his *L'Arrabbiata.* A sincere friendship soon sprang up between the two poets, which reacted most favorably upon their poetic labors. The several weeks which Scheffel spent with Heyse were perhaps the happiest in his life. The long suppressed poetic powers of Scheffel, deflected for a time in Rome into false channels, now found their full and free expression. With sure instinct Scheffel developed in his first larger work his characteristic poetic style and manner, and produced an epic which several years after its appearance became one of the most popular works in modern German literature.

As Scheffel's fame rests, in part, upon the *Trumpeter of Säkkingen,* a short analysis and characterization of this poem will here be in place. The ease with which he conceived and completed this work was doubtless due to the fact that the theme was so familiar and congenial to him that he could readily identify himself with it and animate it with his own poetic spirit. In the churchyard of Säkkingen there was a moss-covered gravestone with a Latin inscription which had aroused Scheffel's curiosity and about which a local legend had developed. It was the story of the love of the young and handsome Werner Kirchhof, a son of a citizen of Säkkingen and a skilled musician, for the only daughter of the Baron of Schönau who lived in the castle near the town. Upon discovering this attachment the baron forbade Werner to enter the castle, and determined to take his daughter to Vienna to become a maid of honor at the court of that city. Before her departure Werner managed to see her again and find out the plans of the baron. The lovers agreed to meet in Vienna, and the girl promised to inform Werner of her presence in the great city by writing her initials on the door of the church she happened to attend. Werner then joined a band of roving musicians, went with them through the various lands of the Holy Roman Empire and finally reached Vienna, where his musical talents attracted attention and won for him the position of musical director at the imperial cathedral. There he one day discovered the initials of his beloved one. At the close of the service he stationed himself at the entrance of the cathedral, and as the royal party was coming out, he noticed among the maids of honor the daughter of the Baron of Schönau. The girl fainted at the unexpected joy of seeing her lover, her swoon attracted the attention of the court, and the emperor himself inquired with much concern about the occurrence. Then the maiden told the romantic story of her love, and the emperor, roused to sympathy, conferred the patent of nobility upon Werner and brought about the union of the lovers.

Into this simple love story Scheffel has introduced typical romantic motives as we find them in Hauff's *Lichtenstein,* which doubtless influenced the spirit of the work. The hero is filled with a genuine devotion to Nature and finds in her various manifestations living symbols of the moods and feelings of his heart. In his wanderings Nature is his constant friend, ever revealing to him the deeper meanings of life, ever ready to give him solace, encouragement, and inspiration. In true romantic fashion the glory of art and the free life of the artist are here exalted and contrasted with the philistinism of the work-a-day world. A fresh patriotic spirit and especially a deep love for the beauty of the Rhenish country permeates the poem. Reflections upon the sad aspects of life with deep suggestions of its seriousness and mystery are finely interwoven with the joyous experiences of the hero, thus giving to the poem a greater wealth and dignity of content. All these romantic features of the story are individualized, heightened and transfigured by the poet's delightful humor which always enables him to rise superior to moods of melancholy and pessimism and to strengthen his faith in the essential beauty and goodness of life.

The background of the story is the baroque period after the Thirty Years' War, and Scheffel with his unusually fine historical insight and vivid imagination sketches with the sure hand of an artist the characteristic features of that period, picturesque even in its decadence. Unlike so many historical novelists and dramatists who but too often make their works a means for displaying their historical erudition, Scheffel in this and his other productions rarely yields to this temptation, but in a masterly way makes his descriptions an organic part of the central theme. The form of the poem shows unmistakable traces of the influence of Heine's *Atta Troll.* The imperfections of the style and meter of the

Trumpeter have been noticed and even satirized, but the poem has such vitality that all adverse criticisms have been unable to injure it in the estimation of the public.   The work is written with such lightness and grace, the trochaic tetrameter is handled with so much skill and is so melodious, the freshness of tone is so well sustained that the occasional carelessness of expression and verse, far from disturbing the reader, contributes to that spirit of freedom and naturalness which is one of the chief charms of the poem.   Scheffel himself did not take this first production of his too seriously.   Only youthful and extravagant admiration would accord to it a place beside the great classics of German literature.   It does, however, express one of the soundest phases of later German romanticism, and appearing several years after the revolutionary outbreaks of 1848–49, it gave to the German youth of that time just what they needed, a work, which through its genuine German sentiment and sound humor reawakened that spirit of optimism which was then so necessary for the further spiritual and political development of Germany.

In May, 1853, Scheffel returned to Karlsruhe, determined not to resume the practice of law, but still uncertain as to the choice of some other occupation that would appeal to his real tastes and talents.   In the fall of that year he decided to prepare himself for an academic career, and with that end in view went to Heidelberg to devote himself there to the study of the Middle Ages and produce in time a monograph on some subject in historical jurisprudence by which he might habilitate himself as *docent* in that university.   Under the influence of Adolf Holtzmann, who was then professor of German literature in the University of Heidelberg, Scheffel soon became interested in old German history and literature, and in the midst of his studies became deeply impressed by the chronicle of the monastery of St. Gallen of the tenth century — the *Casus Sancti Galli*. This naïve account of the various aspects of monastic life of the tenth century stimulated his imagination and doubt-

less gave the first impulse to the production of his masterpiece — *Ekkehard*. At the suggestion of Holtzmann he
undertook in the winter of 1853-54 to translate the most
famous Latin epic of the Middle Ages — *Waltharius manu
fortis*, written by Ekkehard I. of St. Gallen, and later revised by Ekkehard IV. While working upon this trans-
lation he developed the action of his novel with astonishing
rapidity. His creative impulse reached its highest strength
during this period and found the Ekkehard theme especially
well adapted to his literary talents. For several decades
scholars of early German history and literature had worked
assiduously to increase our knowledge of the beginnings of
German culture, and yet, notwithstanding their vast and
minute investigations, none of them had succeeded in
organizing that learned material and in presenting a vivid
and accurate picture of any phase of early German culture.
Scheffel was preëminently fitted for a work of this kind in
that he was not only excellently versed in early German
history, literature, and law, but also possessed a strong and
remarkably true historical imagination and powers of expression which could forcibly depict or suggest the local
color and the sentiment of a vital period of the civilization
of his country. It was a favorite thought of his that the
novel should, on the basis of careful historical study, represent that which was typically great and beautiful in certain
important epochs of the national life and thus, to some
extent, serve the same function that the great national
epochs had had in the life of early peoples. The possibility
of deliberately creating historical novels to serve the function of national epics has been justly questioned, especially
in view of our present knowledge of the origin and development of national epic poetry, and not even the most ardent
admirer of Scheffel would claim today that *Ekkehard* has
the characteristics we usually associate with a great
national epic. On the other hand, it may be safely asserted
that among the great mass of historical novelists that Germany and other European countries have produced, there

are few, if any, that have grasped so deeply and represented so artistically the spirit of the periods they have treated as Scheffel has done in his novel of the tenth century. This novel is, therefore, not to be interpreted in the light of a national epic, but rather from the point of view of the training, the ideals, the personal experiences, the methods of work, and the peculiar poetic endowments of Scheffel. His original purpose in taking up the study of early German history and institutions was to produce some treatise on historical jurisprudence that might serve his professional ends, and, indeed, the various excellent descriptions of old Germanic law and custom in which the novel abounds show unmistakably the poet's legal training and interests. However, as the poet became absorbed in the study of the chronicle of the monastery of St. Gallen, he found in that work many passages that suggested to him his own experiences, struggles and aspirations, so that his imagination unconsciously constructed out of these crude records of a distant past a story permeated with his own spirit. Thus the scholar's interests were transformed and merged into the larger interests of a struggling soul longing to liberate itself from the bondage of passion by a life of free and wholesome activity.

The theme in the chronicle which seems to have stirred the poet's imagination was the story of how Hadwig, the widowed duchess of Suabia, in her castle Hohentwiel tried to acquire a knowledge of Latin through the study of Virgil, under the direction of the handsome young monk and scholar, Ekkehard of St. Gallen. According to the poet's fancy this relation between the young teacher and the beautiful duchess develops into an ardent passion and causes the intensest soul conflicts. Insuperable and unnatural barriers of rank and station on the part of the duchess, and of stern ascetic vows on the part of the monk of St. Gallen, separate the lovers. Each in his own way struggles mightily against the snares and the temptations that beset the course of duty and honor as demanded by social and his-

torical conventions or by religious ordinances. The action
in the novel often calls forth passions so intense and elemental that the hero and heroine must strain to the utmost
their moral energy to retain their self-mastery. Finally
by a mighty act of will the monk severs a relation which
has so often bewildered his soul, regains his calmness
of spirit through the contemplation of the sublimity of
nature about him, and feels inspired to give expression
to his purified being by writing a poem glorifying the
simple natural heroism of old Germanic legend. And
after the conquest of his passion his religious life becomes also freed of all ecclesiastical ambition and dog-
matic narrowness. He casts off the scholastic subtle-
ties in which he has hitherto been involved, and finds the
simple faith of the Gospel fully adequate to his moral and
religious needs. His experiences and inner struggles have
aroused in him a contempt for the mere conventions of
life, he can no longer submit to the constraints of the Benedictine rules, and resolves henceforth to lead a free natural
life devoted to high practical ends. How symbolic is all
this of Scheffel's own experiences and aspirations! His
novel does not end, therefore, in melancholy resignation,
as some have asserted, but in a spiritual clarification re-
sulting in wholesome practical activity. The necessity of a
natural life is the ideal that the poet would impress upon
us in this his greatest novel. To accentuate this ideal he
presents to us in contrast to the passions of the monk and
the duchess the charming idyllic relation between Audifax
and Hadumoth. These children of nature live for and
enjoy their innocent love as long as fortune smiles upon
them, but when adversity comes and separates them, it is
this simple natural love that comforts and animates their
whole being, triumphantly overcomes all obstacles and leads
to their happy reunion. In the character of Hadumoth,
Scheffel has beautifully delineated his ideal of genuine love,
free of all romantic ornamentation or fantastic sentimentality. Simple and pure, implicitly trusting her unerring

instincts, she stands before us as one of the most clearly conceived and charming creations of Scheffel's imagination.

Much has been written about the style and local color of this famous novel. The poet studied with the greatest care the history and inner life of the tenth century and by dint of his true imagination constructed for himself a faithful picture of the leading events of that period. He appended a number of notes to his work which show that he had gained full mastery of the material he was to use in his novel. However, he never allows his learning to interfere with his artistic ends, but freely introduces such deviations from history as the spirit of the work requires. The many archaic High German and Alemannic expressions of the novel are used with great skill and discrimination to suggest the atmosphere of the time. In short, the poet has so thoroughly identified himself with the life and manners of the tenth century, the characters and their environment stand out so clearly before him, and his powers of expression are so strong and accurate that his *Ekkehard* must be regarded in form and thought as a masterpiece of objective art. The manner in which he translates the *Waltharius manu fortis* is quite in keeping with the spirit of the novel. He rejects the style of Virgil, which the medieval monkish scholar tried so anxiously to follow, and gives us a free and much condensed rendition of the poem, not in hexameters, but, as far as possible, in the language and manner of the old Germanic folk-epic.

Ekkehard appeared in 1857 and marks the zenith of Scheffel's creative powers. The great and concentrated labors he had expended upon this novel had so exhausted his strength that never again could he produce a work of equal artistic value. He now definitely abandoned all thought of continuing his legal career, and went with his friend, the painter Anselm Feuerbach, to Venice in the hope of regaining his strength and of obtaining inspiration for a new historical novel the theme of which was suggested to him by Feuerbach's painting " The Death of Arretino."

The principal characters of this novel were to be Titian and
his brilliant pupil, Irene von Spielberg, whose personality, the poet believed, resembled in some respects that of
his beloved sister Marie. Undaunted by the intense heat,
and the cholera which was then raging in Venice, he remained there for some time planning his novel, but finally
felt obliged to leave, and withdrew to a small place near
Meran, where he fell into a serious illness. After he had
partially recovered, he moved in the summer of 1856 to
Avignon, and, feeling still too weak to resume his work upon
his proposed novel, he wrote in the latter part of that year
a series of delightful letters describing his impressions of
Southern France. Shortly afterward he went to Munich in
the hope of finding there the stimulus he needed for his ambitious poetical labors. The distinguished artists and poets,
whom King Maximilian of Bavaria had called to his capital, received him so heartily and the city proved so attractive that he decided to establish himself there, and prevailed
upon his parents to allow his sister Marie to join him. She
was a charming, talented woman and soon won the admiration of his friends, so that Scheffel had every reason to
hope that with her help his home would soon become one
of the social centres of the artistic life of Munich and that
he would realize there his much cherished poetic ambitions.
However, his happiness was of short duration. Several
weeks after her arrival in Munich Marie was stricken with
typhoid fever and died. It took many years for the poet
to recover from this cruel blow of fortune. He brooded
greatly over it, and for a long time could not get rid of the
thought that indirectly he had been responsible for this
great calamity which had befallen him and his family.

Immediately after the death of his sister he left Munich,
went to Karlsruhe and then settled for a time in his beloved Heidelberg where he was always sure to find a hearty
welcome from the members of his club, which called itself
Der Engere. It was a small informal club of men of ability,
wit and learning who in their meetings cast aside all con-
straint and freely surrendered themselves to mirth and

good humor. Scheffel's life in Heidelberg was most closely associated with this club. Conventional society was obnoxious to him and he avoided it as much as possible, but in the inner circle of his Heidelberg friends he gave free vent to his wit and sentiment and fancy. This convivial circle of friends inspired some of his finest drinking songs, the remembrance of the many hours he had spent in their midst cheered him in his lonely wanderings, and to them he addressed numerous letters in which he disclosed his innermost being.

Scheffel's works were steadily growing in popularity and attracted the attention of the Grand Duke Karl Alexander of Saxe-Weimar, who, inspired by the example of his grandfather, wished to attach to his court poets and artists of promise and distinction. He was especially impressed with the superior worth of *Ekkehard* and showed his appreciation by inviting Scheffel, in August, 1857, to come to Weimar to attend the unveiling of the Goethe-Schiller monument. Shortly afterward he invited the poet to come as his guest to the Wartburg, which was then being redecorated and restored. This invitation to the Wartburg strongly appealed to the poet, but about the same time, through the influence of his mother, he was tendered the position of court-librarian at Donaueschingen, and felt it his duty to accept it. The library of Donaueschingen, which belonged to the Prince of Fürstenberg, had been recently enriched by the collection of rare books and manuscripts of Baron von Lassberg, and Scheffel was commissioned to examine and catalogue this very valuable literary material. He held the position from the end of 1857 till the spring of 1859. Although at times he found his work monotonous, he performed his duties with the utmost care, and published the results of his investigations in a monograph which bears testimony to the thoroughness of his scholarship.

In the meantime his cordial relations to the Grand Duke of Weimar continued. He made several visits to the Wartburg and conceived the plan of writing a comprehensive historical novel which was to represent the noblest phases

of medieval German culture, and the action of which was
to centre in the glorious poetic legends of the Wartburg.
In full confidence in his poetic strength he practically promised the Grand Duke of Weimar to write this Wartburg
novel, which, he believed, would far excel *Ekkehard* in the
greatness of its thought and in its national significance.
He made most comprehensive studies of the life and culture
of the period to be covered by his novel, undertook journeys to various places in Upper Austria and Thuringia,
to Passau and especially to the Wartburg in order to get
into close touch with his theme, and endeavored in every
way to stimulate his imagination so as to be able to construct a well defined action and clearly conceived characters
and situations.   After a time he began to feel that his
creative powers were unequal to the task he had undertaken.
His scholarly labors in medieval German history and literature presented so many difficult and perplexing problems
that he could not solve them.   The vast material which he
had so conscientiously accumulated, overburdened and im-
paired his imagination, and impeded the creative work upon
his novel.   Under these circumstances he gradually lost
confidence in himself, brooded much over the decline of
his genius and became possessed with the idea that he had
lost the favor of the Grand Duke of Weimar because of
the slow progress of the novel.   At last, utterly exhausted
by his strenuous but futile labors, he became so seriously
ill that for a time his mind was despaired of.   When the
well disposed Grand Duke heard of his sufferings, he released him of his promise to write the Wartburg novel and
thus partly contributed to his recovery.

It would lead us too far to analyze here the manifold
reasons which made it so difficult for him to complete his
ambitious work.   Chief among these was his desire to
adjust the demands of severe scholarship to his high artistic
ideals.   He saw in the German life of the twelfth and
thirteenth centuries a typical conflict between the native
vigor and grandeur of old German art as embodied in the

Nibelungenlied and the superficial imitation of French culture as represented in the German court epics and lyrics. The novel was to develop the essential features of this conflict and glorify the truth and simplicity of the Germanic epic. As in his *Ekkehard,* naturalness was to triumph over artificiality. But the theme here was a vastly more complex one and, according to the conception of the poet, involved the very perplexing question of the character and personality of the poet of the *Nibelungenlied.* Scheffel followed most closely the scholarly investigations on that subject, attaching himself to no school but trying to arrive at independent conclusions which he wished to embody in his novel. But the farther he proceeded, the more difficult he found it to make his learning subserve his poetical ends. In short, in his work upon the Wartburg novel he was unable to attain that fine balance between scholarship and art which so distinguishes the *Ekkehard* from other historical novels.

During the years 1861 and 1862 after a series of solitary wanderings he partially recovered his health. In 1863 he decided to publish a collection of poems entitled: *Frau Aventiure aus Heinrich von Ofterdingens Zeit,* which are the chief results left to us from his Wartburg novel, and which he probably intended to incorporate in that work. Some of these poems have been much admired, and certainly reveal to us in their thought and sentiment the inner conflicts and the deep personality of the poet. Most of them, however, are rather successful imitations of a scholar who has finely observed the manner and style of medieval poetry than independent creations of a true artist.

After the publication of these poems Scheffel withdrew from his retirement and solitary broodings and regained something of his former freshness of spirit. From his correspondence it appears that in previous years he had had several love experiences, but we know very little about them except that they had given him much disappointment and sorrow. In December, 1863, he became engaged to

Karoline von Malzen, a young friend of his mother and the daughter of the Bavarian ambassador at the court of Baden. In her he thought that he had found a woman of deep sympathy whom he could really love. She certainly had a fine appreciation of art, was a genuine admirer of Scheffel's poetry and seemed to understand and appreciate his character and aspirations. They married in the summer of 1864. A few months after the marriage the poet's excellent mother died, and Scheffel returned with his wife to Karlsruhe to take charge of his sickly and crippled brother and give what comfort he could to his aged father. The happiness that he had expected of his marriage was of brief duration. Several months after he and Karoline had settled in Karlsruhe they discovered that they were essentially incompatible natures. Both were persons of mature years, fixed in their social habits and views of life and unable in character and temperament to adjust themselves to the new relations. Karoline, thoroughly aristocratic by birth and training, could not renounce the social life and conventional forms to which she had been accustomed. The great inner conflicts of the poet, often verging on the tragic, had, on the other hand, developed in him an aversion to all conventional society. Half-broken in spirit, he was often moody and melancholy and inclined to isolation and brooding, and whenever his social instincts reasserted themselves, he preferred his former boon companions and the free convivial life of his earlier years. It is not surprising, then, that two years after the birth of their son Victor, they decided upon a voluntary separation. Karoline moved to Munich, and the poet remained with his son and father in Karlsruhe until the death of the latter in 1869.

In 1867 Ludwig Häusser, the historian, who for many years had been Scheffel's most faithful friend and who, perhaps, better than any one else, appreciated the temper and genius of the poet, died. With his death the jovial Heidelberg club, *Der Engere,* which had so often stimulated the brilliant wit and light song of Scheffel, was prac-

Permission Berlin Photo Co., New York

ANTON VON WERNER

JOSEPH VICTOR VON SCHEFFEL

tically dissolved. It seems that the poet felt that this period of his life had closed when in that same year he collected and published the many student songs of his youth under the significant title of *Gaudeamus* and fittingly dedicated them to his departed friend. Besides the works already mentioned, he published in 1866 *Juniperus,* a crusader's tale, which, like *Frau Aventiure,* had been originally intended as a part of the Wartburg romance, in 1870 the *Bergpsalmen,* and in 1883 *Hugideo,* a most touching memorial to his sister Marie.

After the death of his father he bought a small estate at Radolfszell on Lake Constance, built a picturesque villa there, and lived partly in his new home and partly in Karlsruhe and Heidelberg. Gradually the former restlessness, which had so often impelled him to roam to all sorts of places in pursuit of health or in the hope of gaining poetic inspiration, subsided, leaving, however, a certain acerbity of manner which often surprised those who expected to find in him something of that hearty, jovial, care-free spirit which he had celebrated in his song. The fact was that the poet who had once aspired to the highest artistic ideals and had hoped to produce works of serious national import and enduring value had with much effort resigned himself to the limitations which his nature and talents had imposed upon him. He devoted himself with love and care to the education of his son, found some comfort in the admiration and gratitude which students expressed for his poetry and in the honors which universities conferred upon him, and was especially touched by the continued friendship of the Grand Duke Karl Alexander toward him. He never again undertook a larger poetical task, but limited himself henceforth to occasional poems treating of events of more or less vital importance.

Naturally he followed the historical development of his country with keen interest, but for many years he was unable or unwilling to adjust himself to the course which Prussia had assumed in the affairs of the nation. When, however, after

the **Franco-Prussian War** Germany attained her political
unity, he became a devoted adherent of the great chancellor
and expressed his admiration for him in unequivocal terms.
The popularity of his works continued to grow amazingly,
and his fiftieth birthday was celebrated by his countrymen
with an enthusiasm which but few German poets have ever
called forth. It was on that occasion that the patent of
hereditary nobility was conferred upon him by the Grand
Duke of Baden. He accepted the honor, not in a feeling
of vanity, as his detractors have represented it, but chiefly
for the sake of his son who had chosen to prepare himself
for the career of an officer in the German army. In the last
decade of his life the circle of his friends naturally became
more restricted. Among those who stood closest to him
was the painter Anton von Werner, who had most successfully illustrated his works and who had a very sympathetic
appreciation of his character and temperament. Werner's
correspondence with Scheffel is, therefore, a very valuable
source of information for our knowledge of the poet.

Scheffel's health, seriously undermined by his former
inner struggles, declined rapidly during the last years of
his life. He sought alleviation for his malady in various
places, but all in vain. In the fall of 1885 he settled again
in Heidelberg, where he composed his famous song in honor
of the five-hundredth anniversary of his beloved university,
which was to take place in the following year. It was
destined to be his swan-song; he died April 9, 1886, a few
months before the celebration at which he was to be one
of the noted figures. It was a great comfort to him that
shortly before his death his long estranged wife hastened
to his bedside and became reconciled to him. His last composition, nobly set to music, was sung at the Heidelberg
celebration and was one of the deeply impressive episodes
of the festival. It was a peculiarly fitting and touching
tribute to the poet who had succeeded better than any one
else in glorifying the joys and beauties of that ancient and
famous seat of learning. The grateful German people

erected monuments to his memory in Heidelberg, Säkkingen, and near the castle Hohentwiel.

I have tried to some extent to analyze in this brief sketch Scheffel's two longer finished works: the *Trumpeter* and the *Ekkehard,* and to explain the causes of their great popularity and success. I wish now to characterize in a few words his student songs, which, although written with least effort, and in the lightest mood, are regarded by many as his finest contributions to German lyrical poetry. It has been justly observed that the typical German student songs, like many Volkslieder, are permeated with a light tone of parody or irony. In convivial moments, when the student feels free from the severe tasks of learning, he playfully and frivolously turns against the rigid bonds of academic lore that have held in check his buoyant spirits, and in contrast glorifies the cheer and abandon and freedom of youth. Now, Scheffel, himself an excellent boon companion, takes up in his drinking songs this mood, and through his intimate knowledge of academic life, gives it a richness and variety of content and treats it with a freshness and spontaneity of spirit rarely found in lyrics of this class. Moreover, his metrical skill and great natural powers of poetic expression enable him to find for each of his songs just the form best suited to the mood. He rarely falls into the vapid conventional manner of his predecessors. His irony gains in point and significance because of the weightiness of the subjects he attacks. The most serious branches of the learning of his day he introduces into his lyrics, and with a brilliant flash of wit reveals to us the weakness, futility, or emptiness of the erudition of contemporary scholarship. Indeed, there is something of the spirit of Aristophanes in these songs of Scheffel. We find in them, as in the Greek comic poet, that fine blending of the rollicking mood and the serious thought of a man whose candid sceptical spirit will tolerate no shams or half-truths, even when paraded under the guise of ponderous academic learning. It is not surprising, then, that the

academic youth of Germany soon discovered that these
songs were unique of their kind, and have ever since
regarded them as among the most brilliant student songs
in German literature.

Scheffel's literary activity represents the soundest
aspects of later German romanticism. His profound and
sympathetic knowledge of the Middle Ages, his genuine
devotion to Nature and his fine appreciation of the influence
she exerts upon the spiritual life of man, his love of art
and his exalted conception of the mission of the true artist,
the naturalness and freedom of his poetical expression, his
impatience with all that is conventional and commonplace
in life — all these elements which we find in his life and
writings are characteristic of German romanticism. On
the other hand, his humor and sound realistic sense
enabled him to avoid the morbid phases of the movement,
its excessive sentimentality, its overwrought religious
broodings, its reactionary political tendencies, its fantastic
extravagance, and its poetic formlessness. Gifted as he
was, we naturally deplore the meagreness of his poetic
productions. Some of the causes of it I have indicated in
this sketch, but the chief cause of his failure to become a
more productive poet no one saw so well as his mother.
It lay in his "Tasso nature." Indeed, Scheffel's innermost personality could not be more truly characterized. In spirit and temperament he is most closely
akin to Goethe's Tasso, an artist impelled by his very
nature to strive after an ideal far surpassing his creative genius, and hence doomed to disappointments and
the deepest spiritual sufferings. It is possible that if he
had not been born to wealth and had been unable to indulge
his moods, that if he had been compelled to struggle with
poverty and practice self-control, he might have come out
victorious from his inner conflicts and have produced more
works of enduring value. But all this is idle speculation.
Such as he was, Scheffel will never fail to win our deepest
sympathy and respect because of the high seriousness and
nobility of his artistic endeavor.

JOSEPH VICTOR VON SCHEFFEL

EKKEHARD* (1857)

TRANSLATED BY SOFIE DELFFS

REVISED AND ABRIDGED BY RUDOLF TOMBO, JR., PH.D.
Professor of German Literature, Columbia University

CHAPTER I

HADWIG, THE DUCHESS OF SUABIA

T the time when our story begins, almost a thousand years ago, the Hohentwiel was already crested by stately towers and walls. This fortress had been held during his lifetime by Sir Burkhard, Duke of Suabia. He had been a valiant knight, and performed many a good day's fighting in his time. In Suabia it was said that he reigned like a true despot; and in far off Saxony the monks wrote down in their chronicles that he had been an almost "invincible warrior."

Before Sir Burkhard was gathered to his forefathers, he had chosen a spouse for himself in the person of the young Princess Hadwig, daughter of the Duke of Bavaria. But the evening-glow of a declining life is but ill matched with the light of the morning-star. Such a union is against nature's laws, and Dame Hadwig had accepted the old Duke of Suabia merely to please her father. It is true that she had nursed and tended him well and held his gray hairs in honor; but when the old man laid himself down to die grief did not break her heart.

Dame Hadwig now lived all alone in the castle of Hohentwiel. She remained in possession of the entire landed property of her husband, with the full right to do with it

* Permission of Bernhard Tauchnitz, Leipzig.

what she pleased. Besides this she was lady patroness of the bishopric of Constance and all the cloisters near the lake, and the emperor had given her a bill of feoffment signed and sealed by his own hand, by which the regency of Suabia remained her own as long as she kept true to her widowhood. The young widow possessed a very aristocratic mind and no ordinary amount of beauty. Her nose, however, was a trifle short, the lovely lips had a strong tendency to pout, and in her boldly projecting chin the graceful dimple so becoming to women was not to be found. All those whose features are thus formed unite to a clear intellect a not over tender heart, and their disposition is more severe than charitable. For this reason the Duchess, in spite of her soft beautiful complexion, inspired many of her subjects with a sort of trembling awe.

On that misty day mentioned before, the Duchess was standing at one of her chamber windows, looking out into the distance. There are days when one is dissatisfied with everything and everybody, and if one were suddenly transported into paradise itself even paradise would not give contentment. It is a belief in those parts that the universal contrariety of such days arises from people having stepped out of bed with their left foot foremost, which is held to be in direct opposition to nature. Under the spell of such a day the Duchess was laboring just now. She wanted to look out of the window, and a subtle wind blew the mist right into her face, which annoyed her.

Spazzo the chamberlain had come in meanwhile and stood respectfully waiting near the entrance. The wolf-dog of the knight of Friedingen had killed two lambs of the ducal herd upon which Master Spazzo intended to make his dutiful report; but before he had reached the end of his speech he saw the Duchess make a sign, the meaning of which could not remain unintelligible to a sensible man. She put her forefinger first up to her forehead, and then pointed with it to the door, and the chamberlain perceived that it was left to his own wits, not only to find the best expedient

with regard to the lambs, but also to take himself off as
quickly as possible; so with a profound bow he accordingly
withdrew.

In clear tones Dame Hadwig called out, " Praxedis! "—
and when the person thus named did not instantly make
her appearance she repeated in sharper accents, " Praxedis! "

It was not long before Praxedis with light graceful steps
entered the closet. Praxedis was waiting-maid to the
Duchess of Suabia. She was a Greek, and a living proof that
the son of the Byzantine Emperor Basilius had once asked
the fair Hadwig's hand in marriage. He had made a present of the clever child, well instructed in music and the art
of the needle, together with many jewels and precious
stones, to the German duke's daughter, and in return had
received a refusal. Praxedis had a small head with pale
delicate features, out of which a pair of large dark eyes
looked into the world, unspeakably sad one moment and
in the next sparkling with merriment. Her hair was arranged over her forehead in heavy braids, like a coronet.
She was very beautiful.

" Praxedis," said the Duchess, " go and bring me my
trinkets. I wish to put on a bracelet." When the Duchess
opened the casket, the rich jewels sparkled and glittered
beautifully on their red velvet lining. She put on the bracelet, which represented two serpents twisted together and
kissing each other. On the head of each rested a tiny crown.

" Canst thou tell me why I have donned these glittering
ornaments today? " inquired Dame Hadwig.

" God is all-knowing," replied the Greek maid; " I cannot tell."

After this she was silent. So was Dame Hadwig, and
there ensued one of those long, significant pauses generally
preceding self-knowledge. At last the Duchess said, " Well
to tell the truth I don't know myself! "— and looking dis-
mally at the floor, added, " I believe I did it from ennui.
But then the top of the Hohentwiel is but a dreary nest —

especially for a widow. Praxedis, dost thou know a remedy against dullness? "

" I once heard from a very wise preacher," said Praxedis, " that there are several remedies, sleeping, drinking, and traveling — but that the best is fasting and praying."

Then Dame Hadwig rested her head on her lily-white hand, and, looking sharply at the quick-witted Greek, said, " Tomorrow we will go on a journey."

CHAPTER II

THE DISCIPLES OF ST. GALLUS

THE next day the Duchess crossed the Bodensee in the early glow of the morning sun, accompanied by Praxedis and a numerous train. Nobody knew where the end of the journey was to be, but they were accustomed to obey without questioning.

When they approached the bay at Rorschach, the Duchess commanded them to land; so the prow was turned to the shore, and soon after she crossed lightly over the rocking plank and stepped on land. The horses, which had been secretly sent ahead, in the night, stood waiting, and when all were in the saddle Dame Hadwig gave the word of command, " To the holy Gallus." Then her servants looked at each other with wondering eyes, as if asking, " What business can we have there? " But there was not even time for an answer, as the cavalcade was already cantering over the hilly ground toward the monastery itself.

When Romeias, the guard on the watch-tower, heard the tramp of horses' feet in the neighboring firwood, he quickly dropped down the portcullis from the gate, drew up the little bridge leading over the moat, and then seized his horn and with all his might blew three times into it.

The Abbot Cralo jumped up from his chair and limped to the open bow-window, but when he beheld who it was that had occasioned all this disturbance he was as unpleasantly surprised as if a walnut had dropt on his head, and exclaimed, "St. Benedict save us! My cousin the Duchess!" He then quickly adjusted his habit and descended into the courtyard.

A bugle now sounded and the chamberlain Spazzo, in the capacity of herald, rode up close to the gate, and called out loudly: "The Duchess and reigning sovereign of Suabia sends her greeting to St. Gallus. Let the gates be opened to receive her."

The Abbot heaved a deep sigh, then climbed up to Romeias' watch-tower and, leaning on his staff, gave his blessing to those standing outside, speaking thus: "In the name of St. Gallus, the most unworthy of his followers returns his thanks for the gracious greeting. But his monastery is no Noah's ark into which every species of living thing, pure and impure, male and female, may enter. The presence of a woman, although the noblest in the land, and the frivolous speech of the children of this world would be too great a temptation for those who are bound to strive first after the kingdom of Heaven and its righteousness."

But Dame Hadwig called out laughingly: "Spare yourself all your fine words, Cousin Cralo, for I will see the cloister."

[Sir Cralo insisted upon putting the case before the assembled brotherhood, and after much discussion one of the brothers rose and asked to be heard.]

"Speak, Brother Ekkehard!" called out the Abbot; and the noisy tumult was hushed, for all liked to hear Ekkehard speak. He was still young in years, of a very handsome figure, and he captivated everybody who looked at him by his graceful mien and pleasing expression. Besides this he was both wise and eloquent, an excellent counselor and a most learned scholar. At the cloister-school he taught Virgil, and had been intrusted with the office of custodian.

A scarcely perceptible smile had played around his lips while the others were disputing. He now raised his voice and spoke thus: "The Duchess of Suabia is the monas-

tery's patron, and in such capacity is equal to a man; and
as our monastic rules strictly forbid that a woman's foot
shall touch the cloister-threshold she may easily be carried
over.''

Upon this the faces of the old men brightened up, as if
a great load had been taken off their minds. A murmur
of approbation ran through the assembly, and the Abbot
likewise was not insensible to the wise counsel.

''Verily, the Lord often reveals himself, even unto a
younger brother! Brother Ekkehard, you are guileless
like the dove, and prudent like the serpent; so you shall
carry out your own advice. I give you herewith the necessary dispensation.'' A deep blush overspread Ekkehard's
features, but he quietly bowed his head in sign of obedience.

''And what about the female attendants of the Duchess?''
asked the Abbot. But here the assembly unanimously
decided that even the most liberal interpretation of the
monastic laws could not grant them admittance. The evil
Sindolt proposed that they should meanwhile pay a visit to
the recluses on Erin-hill, because when the monastery of
St. Gallus was afflicted by a visitation it was but fair that
the pious Wiborad should bear her share of it. After
having held a whispering consultation with Gerold the
steward about the supper, the abbot descended from his
high chair, and, accompanied by the brotherhood, went out
to meet his guests, and forthwith communicated the condition on which she was to enter.

Then Dame Hadwig replied smilingly, '' During all the
time that I have wielded the sceptre in Suabia such a
proposition has never been made to me. But the laws of
your order shall be respected. Which of the brothers have
you chosen to carry the Sovereign over the threshold?''

Ekkehard had been trying meanwhile to compose an
address, which in faultless Latin was intended to justify
the strange liberty he was about to take; but when she
stood before him, proud and commanding, his voice failed
him, and the speech remained where it had been con-

THE ARRIVAL OF THE MONKS OF ST. GALL

ceived — in his thoughts. Otherwise, however, he had not lost his courage, and so he lifted up his fair burden with his strong arms, who, putting her right arm around his shoulder, seemed not displeased with her novel position.

Cheerfully he thus stepped over the threshold which no woman's foot was allowed to touch, the Abbot walking by his side and the chamberlain and vassals following. The serving ministrants swung their censors gaily into the air, and the monks, marching behind in a double file as before, sung the last verses of the unfinished hymn. It was a wonderful spectacle, such as had never occurred, either before or after, in the monastery's history.

"I suppose that you found me very heavy?" said the Duchess.

" My liege lady, you may boldly say of yourself as it has been written, ' My yoke is easy and my burden is light,' " was the reply.

" I should not have thought that you would turn the words of Scripture into a flattering speech. What is your name?"

" They call me Ekkehard."

" Ekkehard, I thank you," said the Duchess with a graceful wave of her hand.

Meanwhile two of the brothers had carried down a box, which now stood open in the passage. Out of this the Abbot drew a monk's habit, quite new, and said, " Thus I ordain our monastery's mighty patron a member of our brotherhood, and adorn him with the holy garb of our order."

Dame Hadwig complied, lightly bending her knee on receiving the cowl from his hands, and then she put on the garment, which became her well. The beautiful rosy countenance looked lovely in the brown hood.

[Thereupon the Abbot led his guests into the church, while Romeias accompanied the Duchess' waiting women, led by Praxedis, to the cell of the pious Sister Wiborad.]

CHAPTER III

IN THE MONASTERY

AFTER Dame Hadwig had performed her devotions at the grave of the holy Gallus, she asked the Abbot to show her the treasures of the church, so they went to the sacristy, whence they directed their steps by and by toward the garden, which occupied a considerable space and produced much vegetable and fruit for the kitchen as well as useful herbs for medicines. In the orchard a large portion was divided off and reserved for wild animals and numerous birds, such as were to be found in the neighboring Alps; and rarer ones which had been sent as presents by stranger guests from foreign countries.

Dame Hadwig took great pleasure in looking at the rough, uncouth bears, which were funny enough when climbing about on the tree in their prison. "That is our Tutilo," said the evil Sindolt, pointing to a bear, which had just thrown down one of its companions; "that, the blind Thieto," he continued, pointing to a wild goat nearby; and he was just about to honor the Abbot with some flattering comparison when the Duchess interrupted him by saying, "As you are so clever in finding similes, will you find one for me also?"

Sindolt became embarrassed. Luckily his eye now fell on a beautiful silver-pheasant, which was in the midst of a troop of cranes, basking in the sunshine that lighted up its pearly gray feathers.

"There," cried Sindolt.

But the Duchess turned round to Ekkehard, who gazed dreamily at the bustle and life before him.

"What do you think of it?" asked she.

He started up. "Oh, mistress!" said he in soft tones, "who is so audacious as to compare you to anything that flies or crawls?"

"But if we desire it?"

"Then I know of only one bird," said Ekkehard. "We

do not have it, nor has any one; in starlit midnights it flies high over our heads, brushing the sky with its wings. The bird's name is Caradrion, and when its wings touch the earth a sick man is healed. Then the bird, inclining toward the man, opens its beak over his mouth, and taking the man's sickness unto itself rises up to the sun, and purifies itself in the eternal light; and the man is saved.''

Then the singing of sweet boyish voices was heard. The voices were those of the younger cloister-pupils who came to do homage to the Duchess. Children as they were, the little fellows wore already the monk's habit, and several even the tonsure on their eleven-year-old heads. When the procession of the little rosy-cheeked future abbots came in sight, with their eyes cast down and singing their sequences so seriously, a slight mocking smile played round Dame Hadwig's lips, and with her strong foot she upset the nearest of the baskets, causing the apples to roll about enticingly on the ground in the midst of the boys. But unabashed they continued their walk; only one of the youngest wanted to bend down and take up the tempting fruit, which his companion forcibly prevented by taking a good hold of his girdle.

Much pleased, the Abbot witnessed the young folks' excellent behavior, and said, ''Discipline distinguishes human beings from animals, and if you were to throw the apples of Hesperides among them they would remain steadfast.''

Dame Hadwig was touched. ''Are all your pupils so well trained?'' asked she.

'' If you would like to convince yourself with your own eyes,'' said the Abbot, '' you will see that the elder ones know quite as well the meaning of obedience and submission.''

The Duchess, nodding an assent, was then led into the the outer cloister-school, in which the sons of noblemen and those who intended to join the secular clergy were educated.

After a visit to one of the school-rooms the Abbot offered to show the Duchess the library of the monastery, but she was tired by this time and declined, so Sir Cralo conducted his guest to his apartments. On going along the cross-passage they passed a small room, the door of which was open. Close to the bare wall stood a pillar, from the middle of which hung a chain. Over the portal, in faded colors, was painted a figure holding a rod in its lean hand. "Him whom the Lord loveth, he chastiseth," was written under it in capital letters.

Dame Hadwig cast an inquiring look at the Abbot.

"The scourging room!" replied he.

"Is none of the brothers just now liable to punishment?" asked she. "It might be a warning example."

Then the evil Sindolt's feet twitched as if he had trodden on a thorn. He turned round as if he had been attracted by a voice calling to him, and exclaiming, "I am coming," quickly vanished into the darker parts of the passage. He well knew why he did so.

Notker, the stutterer, after the labor of years, had at last completed a psalm-book, adorned with dainty drawings. This book the envious Sindolt had destroyed at night, cutting it to pieces and upsetting a jug of wine over it. On account of this he had been sentenced to be flogged three times, and the last instalment was still due. He knew the room and the instruments of penance hanging on the walls well enough, from the nine-tailed "scorpion" down to the simple "wasp."

The Abbot hurried on. His state-rooms were richly decorated with flowers. Dame Hadwig threw herself into the primitive arm-chair, to rest from the fatigue of all the sight-seeing. She had received many new impressions within the space of a few hours. There was still half an hour left before supper.

And now resounded the tinkling of that bell, the sounds of which were not heard without a pleasurable sensation, even by the most pious of the brethren, as it was the signal for the evening meal.

The duty of reader for that week, before the meals, had to be performed by Ekkehard, the custodian. In honor of the Duchess he had chosen the forty-fifth psalm. He arose and said, " O Lord, open thou my lips, that my mouth may speak forth thy praise," and all repeated these words in a low murmur, as a sort of blessing on his reading.

After that he lifted his voice and began reciting the psalm, which Scripture itself calls a beautiful one.

" My heart is inditing a good matter; I speak of the things which I have made, touching the king; my tongue is the pen of a ready writer.

" Thou art fairer than the children of men; grace is poured into thy lips; therefore God hath blessed thee forever.

" Gird thy sword upon thy thigh, O most mighty, with thy glory and thy majesty.

"And in thy majesty ride prosperously because of truth and meekness and righteousness. * * *

" Thou lovest righteousness and hatest wickedness; therefore God, thy God, hath anointed thee with the oil of gladness above thy fellows.

"All thy garments smell of myrrh, and aloes and cassia."

The Duchess seemed to understand the latent homage, and, as if she herself were being addressed in the words of the psalm, she fastened her eyes intently on Ekkehard. But the Abbot likewise had noticed this, and made a sign to interrupt the reading; and thus the psalm remained unfinished, and every one sat down to supper.

Sir Cralo could not, however, prevent Dame Hadwig's ordering the zealous reader to sit down by her side. Next to Ekkehard came Spazzo the chamberlain, and after him the monk Sindolt.

The meal began. The Abbot did his best to entertain his princely cousin. He first began to sing the praises of her late husband Sir Burkhard, but Dame Hadwig's responses were but scanty and cold, so that the Abbot found out that everything has its time — especially the love of a widow for her late spouse; so he changed the conversation, and praised the art of logic as a weapon to protect God's church. "With such arts heretics were wont to attack believers," he continued, "but now we fight them with their own arms; and, believe me, good Greek or Latin is a much finer instrument than our native language, which even in the hands of the ablest is but an unwieldy bludgeon."

"Indeed," said the Duchess, "must we still learn from you what is to be admired? I have existed until now without speaking the Latin tongue, Sir Cousin."

"It would not harm you if you were still to learn it," said the Abbot, "and when the first euphonious sounds of the Latin tongue shall have gladdened your ear you will admit that, compared to it, our mother-tongue is but a young bear, which can neither stand nor walk well before it has been licked by a classical tongue. Besides, much wisdom flows from the mouths of the old Romans. Ask your neighbor to the left."

"Is it so?" asked Dame Hadwig, turning toward Ekkehard, who had silently listened to the foregoing conversation.

"It would be true, liege lady," said he enthusiastically, "if you still needed to learn wisdom."

Dame Hadwig archly held up her forefinger. "Have you yourself derived pleasure from those old parchments?"

"Both pleasure and happiness," exclaimed Ekkehard with beaming eyes. "Believe me, mistress, you do well in all positions of life, to come to the classics for advice. The Gospel is the guiding-star of our faith; the old classics, however, have left a light behind them which, like the glow of the evening-sun, sends refreshment and joy into the hearts of men."

Ekkehard spoke with emotion. Since the day on which the old Duke Burkhard had asked her hand in marriage, the Duchess had not seen any one who showed enthusiasm

for anything. She was endowed with a high intellect, quick
and imaginative. She had learned the Greek language very
rapidly, in the days of her youth, on account of the Byzantine proposal. The name of Virgil, besides, had a certain
magic about it.

In that hour the resolution was formed in Hadwig's
heart to learn Latin. She had plenty of time for this, and
after having cast another look on her neighbor to the left
she knew who was to be her teacher.

After the meal, in accordance with the rules of the order
a chapter out of the lives of the holy fathers had to be read
for the general edification.

The day before Ekkehard had begun a description of
the life of St. Benedict, which had been written by Pope
Gregory. The brothers drew the tables closer together,
the wine-jug came to a dead stop, and all conversation was
hushed. Ekkehard continued with the second chapter:
" One day when he was alone, the Tempter approached him;
for a small black bird, commonly called a crow, came and
continually flew around his head, finally approaching so
near that the holy man might have captured it with his
hand. He, however, made the sign of the cross, and the
bird flew away. No sooner, however, had the bird flown,
when a fiercer temptation than the holy man had ever yet
experienced assailed him. Some time previous he had
beheld a certain woman. This woman the Evil One caused
to appear before his mental eyes and to influence the heart
of God's servant to such a degree that a devouring love
gnawed at his heart, and he almost resolved to leave his
hermit-life, so strong was the longing and desire within
him. But at that moment a light from heaven shone on
him, compelling him to return to his better self. He then
beheld on one side a hedge of brambles and nettles; so he
undressed and threw himself into the thorns and stinging
nettles, until his whole body was lacerated, and thus the
wounds of the skin had healed the wound of the spirit, and,
having conquered sin, he was saved.''

Dame Hadwig was not greatly edified by this lecture.

She let her eyes wander about in the hall, and then inclined her head toward Ekkehard, asking in a half whisper, "Would you be willing to teach me Latin, young admirer of the classics, if I felt inclined to learn it?"

Then Ekkehard heard an inner voice, whispering like an echo of what he had read — "Throw thyself into the thorns and nettles, and say no!" But, heedless of the warning voice, he replied, "Command and I obey."

The Duchess gazed once more on the young monk with a furtive searching look, then turned to the Abbot and talked of indifferent things.

The cloister inmates did not seem inclined as yet to let this day's unusual liberty end here. In the Abbot's eyes there was a peculiarly soft and lenient expression, and the cellarer also never said "nay" when the brothers descended with their empty wine-jugs into the vaults below.

Presently Master Spazzo slunk away to the building in which Praxedis and her companions were installed, and said, "You are to come to the Duchess, and that at once."

The maidens followed him into the refectory, as there was no one to hinder their entrance; and as soon as they became visible at the open door a buzzing and murmuring began, as if a dancing and jumping were now to commence such as these walls had never before known.

Sir Cralo the Abbot, however, looked at the Duchess and exclaimed, "My Lady Cousin!" uttering the exclamation with such a touching, woe-begone expression that she started up from her reverie. And suddenly she looked with different eyes than before on the chamberlain and herself, in their monks' habits, as well as on the rows of carousing men. The faces of the more distant ones were hidden by their projecting hoods, and it seemed as if the wine was being poured down into empty cowls; in short, the entire scene and the boisterous music appeared to her like a mad masquerade that had lasted too long already — so she said, "It is time to go to bed," and went with her suite over to the schoolhouse where she was to rest that night.

Chapter IV

EKKEHARD'S DEPARTURE

EARLY the next morning the Duchess and her attendants mounted their steeds to ride homeward; and when she declined all parting ceremonies the Abbot did not press her to remain, but came over himself, knowing well what good manners demanded. Two of the brothers accompanied him. One of them carried a handsome crystal cup, the other a small jug of old wine. The Abbot pouring out some into the cup, then wished good speed to his cousin, begging her to drink the parting-draught with him and to keep the cup as a small remembrance.

Dame Hadwig took the proffered cup, feigned to drink a little, and then, handing it back, said, " Pardon me, dear cousin, what shall a woman do with that drinking-vessel? I claim another parting gift. Did you not speak of the wells of wisdom yesterday? Give me a Virgil out of your library! "

"Always jesting," said Sir Cralo, who had expected a more costly demand. " What good can Virgil do you, as you do not know the language? "

"As a matter of course, you must give me the teacher with it," seriously replied Dame Hadwig.

But the Abbot shook his head in sign of displeasure. " Since what time are the disciples of St. Gallus given away as parting-gifts? "

Upon this the Duchess resumed, " I suppose you understand me. The fair-haired custodian shall be my teacher; and three days hence, at the latest, he and the volume of Virgil shall make their appearance at my castle! Remember that the settlement of the disputed land in the Rhine valley, as well as the confirmation of the monastery's rights, are in my hands, and that I am not disinclined to erect on the rocks of the Hohentwiel a small cloister to the disciples of St. Gallus! And so farewell, Sir Cousin! "

Dame Hadwig gracefully extended her right hand to him,

the mares pawed the ground, Master Spazzo took off his hat with a flourish, and the little cavalcade turned their backs on the monastery, setting out on their way homeward.

Slowly the Abbot went back to the monastery, and as soon as he got there he sent for Ekkehard the custodian.

"A dispensation has come for you. You are to take a volume of Virgil to the Duchess Hadwig, and become her teacher. Tomorrow, you will set out on your journey. 'Tis with regret that I lose you, for you were one of the best and most dutiful here. The holy Gallus will not forget the service which you are rendering him."

" The vow of obedience," said Ekkehard, " obliges me to do the will of my Superior, without fear or delay, without regret or murmur."

He bent his knee before the Abbot and then went to his cell, walking as if in a dream, for since yesterday almost too much had occurred. He bent his steps to the library, thence to fetch the Virgil, and when he stood all alone in the high-arched hall, among the silent parchments, a feeling of melancholy came over him. The books were his best friends. He knew them all, and knew who had written them. Some of the handwriting reminded him of companions whom death had already gathered.

" What will the new life, which begins tomorrow, bring to me? " he thought, while a solitary tear started into his eye. He took the Virgil from the book-shelf, and then started to his cell to prepare himself for the journey.

In the night he prayed at the grave of St. Gallus, and early in the morning he bid good-by to all. The volume of Virgil was packed up in his knapsack, which also held the few things besides that he possessed. In a ship, laden with corn, he crossed the lake; a favorable wind filling the sail, and courage and the love of travel swelling his bosom.

At dinner-time the castle of Constance, as well as the cathedral with its towers, became more and more distinct.

With a joyous bound, Ekkehard sprang on shore, and his heart beat with pleasure, as he briskly walked along.

His path took him through meadows and past high reeds. A long and narrow island, called Reichenau, extended itself in the lake. The towers and cloister-walls were mirrored in the placid waters, and vineyards, meadows, and orchards testified to the industry of the inhabitants. Ekkehard resolved to pay a visit to this rival of his monastery. On the white sandy shore of Ermatingen a fisherman was standing in his boat, baling out water, to whom Ekkehard, pointing with his staff toward the island, said, " Ferry me over there, my good friend."

[After Ekkehard had been ferried over he directed his steps toward the monastery, which he reached unobserved.]

In the court all was hushed and silent. A large dog wagged its tail at the stranger, without giving a single growl, for it knew better than to bark at a monk's habit. All the brotherhood seemed to have been enticed by the beautiful weather into the open air.

Ekkehard entered the vaulted room for visitors, near the entrance. Even the door-keeper's chamber next to it was empty. Open tuns were standing about, some filled already with the newly pressed wine. Behind these, near the wall, was a stone bench, and Ekkehard, feeling tired from his long walk, the fresh breeze having blown about his head and made him sleepy, he put his staff against the wall, lay down on the bench, and soon fell asleep.

As he lay thus a slow step approached the cool recess. This was the worthy brother Rudimann, the cellarer. He carried a small stone jug in his right hand, and had come to fulfil his duty by tasting the new wine. The smile of a man, contented with himself and with the world, was on his lips, and his stomach had thriven well, like the household of an industrious man. Over this he wore a white apron, and at his side dangled a ponderous bunch of keys. Meanwhile Kerhildis, the upper maid-servant, passed the door, carrying a tubful of grapes to the press.

" Kerhildis," whispered the cellarer, " take my jug and fill it with wine from the Wartberg, which you will find over there, that I may compare it with this."

Kerhildis put down her load, went away, and speedily returning stood before Rudimann with the jug in her hand. Archly looking up at him she said — "To your health!" Rudimann took a long pious draught.

"It will all be sweet and good," said he, lifting his eyes with emotion; and that they then fell on the maid-servant's beaming countenance was scarcely the cellarer's fault, as she had had plenty of time in which to retire. So he continued with unction, "But when I look at thee, Kerhildis, my heart becomes doubly glad, for you also thrive as the cloister-wine does this autumn, and your cheeks are like the pomegranates, waiting to be plucked. Rejoice with me over the goodness of this wine, best of all maids." So saying, the cellarer put his arm round the waist of the dark-eyed maid, who did not resist very long; for what is a kiss at vintage-time?

The sleeper started up from his slumbers on the stone bench. A peculiar noise, which could be caused by nothing else than a well-meant and well-applied kiss, struck his ear, and looking through the opening between the vats he saw the cellarer's garments covered with flowing tresses which could not well belong to that habit. Snatching up his strong hazel wand he quickly advanced, and with it struck a powerful blow at the cellarer; and before the astonished Rudimann had recovered from the first shock there followed a second and third blow of the same description. The cellarer dropped his pitcher, which was shattered to pieces on the stone floor, while Kerhildis fled.

"In the name of the pitcher at the marriage at Cana!" cried Rudimann, "what is the meaning of this!" and, turning round on his assailant, the two looked into each other's faces for the first time.

"'Tis a present which the holy Gallus sends to St. Pirmin,"* replied Ekkehard fiercely, again rising his stick.

---

* Patron saint of the monastery at Reichenau.

"Well, I might have guessed as much," roared the cellarer—"St. Gallish crabapples! You may be recognized by your fruits. Rough ground, rough faith, and rougher people! Just wait for the present I shall make thee in return!" Looking about for some weapon and perceiving a good-sized broom, he took it up and was just about to attack the disturber of his peace when a commanding voice called out from the gate: "Stop! Peace be with you!" It was the Abbot Wazmann who had commanded peace, and he desired to hear the case before him, that he might settle it.

After the Abbot had heard both sides, he said, "You, brother cellarer, may look on the received blows as the just retribution for your forgetfulness; and you, stranger, I might well bid to continue your journey, for the laws say, 'Whenever a stranger monk enters a monastery he shall be satisfied with everything he meets there, allowing himself only to reprove mildly, and not making himself officious in any way.' In consideration of your youth, however, as well as the blameless motive of your action, you shall be allowed to pass an hour's devotion at the chief-altar of our church, in expiation of your rashness, and after that you will be welcome as the guest of the monastery."

The Abbot and his sentence fared as many an impartial judge has fared before. Neither of the two was satisfied. They obeyed, but were not reconciled.

What Kerhildis, the upper-maid, related that evening to her companions, by the flickering light of the pine-wood, in the sewing-room at Oberzell where they had to make a dozen new monks' habits, was couched in such very insulting terms regarding the disciples of the holy Gallus that it had better not be repeated here!

Early the next morning Ekkehard stood at the threshold of the cloister, ready to continue his journey. The Abbot was also up betimes and was taking a walk in the garden. The serious look of the judge was no longer visible on his face. Ekkehard said good-by to him. Then the Abbot, with a meaning smile, whispered in his ear, "Happy man, to teach grammar to such a fair pupil." These words stabbed Ekkehard to the heart and an old story rose in his memory; for even within cloister-walls there are evil gossiping tongues, and traditional stories which go round from mouth to mouth.

"You are probably thinking of the time," replied he tauntingly, "when you were instructing the nun Clotildis in the act of dialectics, Sir Abbot."

After this he went down to the boat. The Abbot would much rather have taken a quantity of pepper for his breakfast than have had that fact called up to his mind. "A happy journey!" he called out after his departing guest. From that time Ekkehard knew that he had incurred the enmity of the monks at Reichenau, but this he little heeded.

As he was being rowed down the lake by the boatman of Ermatingen a large stone-built castle could be seen through the willow-bushes, but Ekkehard's eyes were riveted on a more distant point. Proud and grand, in steep bold outlines a rocky mountain-peak, the Hohentwiel, rose above the hills on the shore like a mighty spirit, which, ponderous and pregnant with action, towers over the insignificant objects around. The morning sun was casting faint gleams of light on the rocky edges and steep walls. A little to the right several lower hills of the same shape stood modestly, like sentinels of the mighty one.

[The shores of Radolfszell were soon reached. Here Ekkehard was the guest of the old Irish priest Moengal, who, after a hearty repast, offered to accompany his confrere to the borders of his district.]

It was a long distance through the pine-wood, and no sound was stirring. Where the trees were less crowded together, they could see the dark mass of the Hohentwiel, throwing its shadow over them. Moengal's sharp eyes now looked searchingly along the path, and shaking his head, he muttered: "There's something coming." They had proceeded but a short way when Moengal seized his companion's arm, and pointing forward said: "These are neither wild ducks nor animals of the forest!"

At the same moment was heard a sound like the neighing of a horse in the distance. Moengal sprang aside, glided through the trees, and, lying down on the ground, listened intently. "Strange!" cried the old man. "Three armed men are coming toward us."

"Most likely they are messengers sent by the Duchess to receive me," said Ekkehard with a proud smile.

"Oho!" muttered Moengal, "you've not hit the mark there; that is not the livery of the Duchess' vassals. The helmet has no distinguishing mark, and no one on the Hohentwiel wears a gray mantle!" He stood still.

"Forward," said Ekkehard. "He whose conscience is clear is protected by the angels of the Lord."

"Not always, at least in the Hegau," replied the old man. There was no more time for continuing the dialogue, for the tramp of horses' feet and the clattering of arms was heard, and the next moment three men on horseback, with closed visors and drawn swords, became visible.

"Follow me!" cried the priest, "*maturate fugam?*" An attack was made and Moengal escaped, but Ekkenhard was seized, his hands tied behind his back and a handkerchief bound over his eyes. He was carried to the opening of the wood, where four men were waiting with a sedan-chair. Into this they threw their victim and then the band sped onward, Ekkehard noticing by the tramp of the horses' feet that his captors remained at his side. Ekkehard thought of dying. With his conscience he was at peace, and death itself had no terror for him, but yet in his heart there arose the faint murmur, "Why not a year later, after my foot has trod the Hohentwiel?"

At last his bearers moved more slowly, as they were walking uphill. Into which of their robbers' nests were they carrying him? They had ascended for about half an hour, when the tramp of the horses' feet made a hollow sound as if they were going over a wooden bridge. Still everything was quiet; there was no call even of the watchman on the tower. The decisive moment was close at hand, and Ekkehard felt new courage and confidence rising within his heart, as he remembered the words of the psalmist:

"He that dwelleth in the secret place of the most High shall abide under the shadow of the Almighty.

"I will say of the Lord, He is my refuge and my fortress: my God; in Him will I trust."

Another bridge was crossed, then a gate opened and the sedan-chair was put down, after which they took out their prisoner. His foot touched the ground; he felt grass, and heard a faint whispering, as if there were many people around him. At the same time the cords were loosened.

"Take away the bandage from your eyes," said one of his companions. He obeyed, and — O heart, do not break with too much happiness! — he stood in the courtyard on the Hohentwiel.

The wind was rustling in the boughs of the old linden-tree to which a tent-like linen cloth was fastened and from which garlands of ivy and vine-leaves were hanging. All the inhabitants of the fortress were assembled, and on a stone bench in the midst sat the Duchess; from her shoulders the princely mantle of dark purple descended in heavy folds, and a sweet smile softened her haughty features. The stately woman rose and advanced toward Ekkehard. "Welcome to Hadwig's domains!" she said.

Ekkehard had as yet scarcely realized his position. He was about to kneel before her, but she prevented him by graciously extending her hand to him. Throwing aside his gray mantle, the chamberlain Spazzo also came forward and embraced Ekkehard like an old friend. "In the name of our gracious mistress, please to receive the kiss of peace," he cried.

A faint suspicion that he was being played with crossed Ekkehard's mind; but the Duchess now called out laughingly, "You have been paid in your own coin. As you did not allow the Duchess of Suabia to cross the threshold of

St. Gallus otherwise, it was but fair that she also should
have the man of St. Gall carried through the gateway into
her castle.''

Dame Hadwig now took her guest by the hand and showed
him her airy castle with its beautiful view of the Bodensee
and the distant mountain peaks. Then all the people belonging to the castle came and asked for his blessing, among
them also the lancers; and he blessed them all.

The Duchess accompanied him to the entrance of his
chamber, where new clothes and other comforts awaited
him, and told him to rest himself from the fatigues of the
journey; and Ekkehard felt happy and light-hearted after
his strange adventure.

CHAPTER V

VIRGILIUS ON THE HOHENTWIEL

EKKEHARD's room was a spacious chamber, with arched
windows supported on pillars, and was entered by the same
passage as the one which led to the Duchess' hall and chambers. Now the impressions which a man takes with him
from his lonely cloister-cell are not to be shaken off in a
single night, and Ekkehard reflected how often he might be
disturbed in his meditations if the tread of armor-clad men,
or the softer footsteps of serving maids, were to pass his
door; he might even hear the mistress of the castle passing
up and down in her chambers. So he addressed himself to
the Duchess saying simply, '' I have a favor to ask of you,
my liege lady.''

'' Speak,'' said she mildly.

'' Could you not give me, besides this grand room, a more
distant and solitary little chamber, no matter whether it be
high up under the roof or in one of the watch-towers? One
great requirement for the study of science, as well as the
exercise of prayer, is perfect quiet, according to the rules
of the cloister! ''

On hearing this a slight frown overshadowed Dame Hadwig's fair brow. '' If you wish often to be quite alone,''

said she with a satirical smile, "why did you not stay at St. Gall?"

Ekkehard bowed his head and remained silent.

"Stay," cried Dame Hadwig, "Your wish shall be granted. You can look at the room in which Vincentius, our chaplain, lived till his blessed end. He also had the taste of a bird of prey, and preferred being the highest on the Hohentwiel to being the most comfortable. Praxedis, get the large bunch of keys and accompany our guest."

Praxedis obeyed. Slowly she ascended the winding staircase, followed by Ekkehard. The chamber of the late chaplain was high in the square tower of the castle. The key grated in the long unused lock, and, creaking on its hinges, the heavy door swung back. They entered—but what a sight was before them! A storm had broken the little window, and Vincentius' room, after his death, had been open to sunshine and rain, to insects and birds. A flock of pigeons, taking undisputed possession, had snugly settled down among all the wisdom-imparting books.

Ekkehard examined the books on the shelves. "I am sorry for the pigeons, but they will have to go."

"Why?"

"They have spoilt the whole of the first book of the Gallic Wars; and the Epistle to the Corinthians is hopelessly and irreparably damaged."

"Is that a great loss?" asked Praxedis.

"A very great loss!"

"Oh, you naughty doves," said Praxedis jestingly. "Come to me, before yonder pious man drives you out among the hawks and falcons," and she called the birds which had quietly remained in their niche. Then she began to sing softly a Greek melody.

Ekkehard started up with surprise from the codex he was reading. "What are you singing," he asked, "it sounds like a foreign language."

"Why should it not be foreign?"

"Greek?"—

"And why should I not sing Greek," pertly rejoined Praxedis.

"By the lyre of Homer," exclaimed Ekkehard, full of surprise, "where in the name of wonder did you learn that, the highest aim of our scholars?"

"At home," quietly replied Praxedis.

Ekkehard cast upon her another look, full of shy respect and admiration. While reading Aristotle and Plato he had hardly remembered that any living persons still spoke the Greek tongue. "I thought I had come as a teacher to the Hohentwiel," said he almost humbly, "and I find my master here. Would you not now and then deign to bestow a grain of your mother-tongue on me?"

"On condition that you will not drive away the doves," replied Praxedis. "You can easily have a grating put up before the niche, so that they do not fly about your head."

"For the sake of pure Greek—" Ekkehard was beginning to say, when the door opened and the sharp voice of Dame Hadwig was heard.

"What are you talking here about doves and pure Greek? Does it take so much time to look at four walls?—Well, Master Ekkehard, does the den suit your taste?"

He bowed in the affirmative.

"Then it shall be cleaned and put in order," continued Dame Hadwig. "Be quick, Praxedis, and see about it— and, to begin with, let us drive away these doves!"

Ekkehard ventured to put in a word on their behalf.

"Indeed!" said the Duchess, "you desire to be alone, and yet wish to keep doves! Shall we perhaps hang a lute on the wall and strew rose-leaves into your wine? Well, they shall not be driven out; but they shall appear roasted on our supper-table this evening."

"And what was that about the pure Greek?" inquired the Duchess. So Ekkehard simply told her the favor he had asked of Praxedis, upon which the frown returned to Dame Hadwig's forehead. "If you are so very anxious to learn," said she, "you can ask me; for I also speak that language.'' Ekkehard made no objection, for in her speech there was a certain sharpness which cut off all replies.

The Duchess was strict and punctual in everything. A day or two after Ekkehard's arrival she worked out a plan for learning the Latin language, and so it was settled that they should devote one hour each day to the grammar, and another to the reading of Virgil. To mitigate the bitterness of the grammar, Ekkehard could find no means. Every day he wrote a task for the Duchess on parchment, and she proved a very eager and industrious pupil; for each morning when the sun rose over the Bodensee and cast its early rays on the Hohentwiel she stood already at her window, learning her task — silently or aloud as might be. Once her monotonous reciting of *amo, amas, amat, amamus,* etc., reached even Ekkehard's ear in his chamber.

In the evening the Duchess came over to Ekkehard's room, where everything had to be ready for the reading of Virgil.

The first evening the door of Ekkehard's room, leading into the passage, was left wide open by Praxedis. He rose and was about to shut it when the Duchess prevented him by inquiring, '' Do you not yet know the world?'' But Ekkehard could not understand the meaning of this.

He now began to read and translate the first book of Virgil's great epic poem. Æneas the Trojan rose before their eyes; they heard how he had wandered about for seven years on the Tyrian sea, and what unspeakable pains it had cost him to become the founder of the Roman people. Then came the recital of Juno's anger, when she went to intreat Æolus to do her bidding, promising the fairest of her nymphs to the God of the winds if he would destroy the Trojan ships. Thunder-storms, tempests, and dire shipwrecks — the turbulent waves scattering weapons and armor, beams and rafters, of what had once been the stately fleet of the Trojans, while the roar of the excited waves reached the ears of Neptune himself, who, rising from his watery depths, beheld the dire confusion! The winds of

THE HOHENTWEIL

Æolus are ignominiously sent home, the rebellious waves settle down, and the remaining ships anchor on the Lybian shores!

So far Ekkehard had read and translated. His voice was full and sonorous, and vibrating with emotion; for he perfectly understood what he had read. It was getting late; the lamp was flickering in its socket, and Dame Hadwig rose from her seat to go.

"How does my gracious mistress like the tale of the heathen poet?" asked Ekkehard.

"I will tell you tomorrow," was the reply.

To be sure she might have said it there and then, for the impression of what she had heard was already fixed in her mind; but she refrained from doing so, not liking to hurt his feelings.

"May you have pleasant dreams," she called out as he was departing.

Ekkehard went up to Vincentius' room in the tower, which had been restored to perfect order; all traces of the doves had been removed. He wanted to pray and meditate, as he was wont to do in the monastery; but his head began to burn, and before his soul stood the lofty figure of the Duchess. What was to come of all this? He went to the window, where the fresh autumn air cooled his forehead, and looked out at the dark vast sky stretching out over the silent earth. For a long time he stood thus, until he began to shiver; but he felt as if the stars were attracting him upwards, and that he must rise toward them as on wings.

The next day Dame Hadwig came with Praxedis to take her grammar lesson. She had learned many words and declensions, and knew her task well; but nevertheless was absent-minded.

"You still owe me your opinion of Virgil," said Ekkehard.

"Well," returned Dame Hadwig, "if I had been a queen in Roman lands I do not know whether I should not have burnt the poem and imposed eternal silence on the man—"

Ekkehard stared at her, full of amazement.

" I am perfectly serious about it," continued she, " and do you wish to know why?—because he reviles the gods of his country. I paid great attention when you recited the speeches of Juno yesterday. That she, the wife of the chief of all the gods, feels a rankling in her mind because a Trojan shepherd boy does not declare her to be the most beautiful,—and, being powerless to call up a tempest at her will to destroy a few miserable ships, must first bribe Æolus by the offer of a nymph! And then Neptune, who calls himself the king of the seas, allows strange winds to cause a tempest in his realms, and only notices this transgression when it is well-nigh over—what is the upshot of all that? I can tell you that in a country whose gods are thus abased and defamed I should not like to wield the sceptre!"

Ekkehard could not very readily find an answer. All the manuscripts of the ancients were for him stable and immovable as the mountains, and he was content to read and admire what lay before him—and now such doubts!

" Pardon me, gracious lady," he said, " we have not read very far as yet, and it is to be hoped that the human beings of the Æneid will find greater favor in your eyes."

Ekkehard was only provoked into greater zeal, by the Duchess' opposition. With enthusiasm he read, on the following evening, how the pious Æneas goes out to seek the Lybian land; how he meets his mother Venus, dressed in the habit and armor of a Spartan maid, the light bow hanging over her shoulder and her fair heaving bosom scarcely hidden by the looped-up garment; and how she directs her son's steps toward the Lybian princess. Further he read how Æneas recognized his divine mother, but too late— calling after her in vain; how she wrapped him up in a mist so that he could reach unseen the new town, where the Tyrian queen was building a splendid temple in honor of Juno. There he stands transfixed with admiration, gazing at the representation of the battles before Troy, painted by the hand of the artist; and his soul is refreshed by the recollections of past battles.

And now Dido, the mistress of the land, herself approaches, urging on the workmen and performing her sovereign's duties.

"And at the gate of the temple, in Juno's honor erected,
There on her throne sat the queen, surrounded by arms-bearing warriors,
Dealing out justice to all, and dividing the labors among them,
With an impartial hand, allotting his share to each one."

" Read that again," commanded the Duchess. Ekkehard complied with her wish.

" Is it written thus in the book? " asked she. " I should not have objected if you had put in these lines yourself; for I almost fancied I heard a description of my own government. Yes, with the human beings of your poet I am well satisfied."

" It was no doubt easier to describe them than the gods," said Ekkehard. " There are so many men in this world! "

She made him a sign to continue. So he read on, how the companions of Æneas came to implore her protection, and how they sang the praises of their leader, who, hidden by a cloud, stood close by. And Dido opens her town to the helpless ones; and the wish arises in her that Æneas their king might also be thrown by the raging waves on her shores — whereupon the hero feels a great longing to break through the cloud that is veiling him.

But when Ekkehard began with —

" Scarce had she uttered this wish, when the veiling cloud floated backwards."—

a heavy tread was heard, and the next moment Master Spazzo the chamberlain came in. Most likely he had been sitting with the wine-jug before him, for his eyes were staring vacantly, and the salutation-speech died on his lips.

" Stop there," cried the Duchess, " and you Ekkehard continue! "

He read on with his clear expressive voice —

" Showing Æneas himself, in all the bloom of his beauty,
High and lofty withal; godlike, for the heavenly mother
Having with soft flowing locks and glorious features endowed him,

Breathing into his eyes sereneness and radiance forever,
Like as the ivory may, by dextrous hands, be embellished,
Or as the Parian stone, encircled by red, golden fillets.
Then he, addressing the queen, to the wonder of all the surrounders,
Suddenly turned, and said: Behold then, him you were seeking—
Me, the Trojan Æneas, escaped from the Lybian breakers."

Master Spazzo stood there, in utter confusion, while an arch smile played around the lips of Praxedis.

"When you honor us next with your presence," called out the Duchess, "please choose a more suitable moment for your entrance, so that we be not tempted to imagine you to be 'Æneas the Trojan escaped from the Lybian breakers!'"

Master Spazzo quickly withdrew, muttering, "Æneas the Trojan! Has another Rhinelandish adventurer forged some mythical pedigree for himself? Troy!—and clouds floating backward!—Wait, Æneas the Trojan; when we two meet we shall break a lance together! Death and damnation!"

CHAPTER VI

THE WOMEN OF THE WOOD

IN those times there also lived on the Hohentwiel a boy whose name was Audifax. He was the child of a bondsman, and had lost both his parents early in life. As he grew older he was intrusted with the care of the goats; and this office he fulfilled faithfully enough, driving them out and home again every day. He was a shy and silent boy, with a pale face and short-cut fair hair, for only the freeborn were allowed to wear long, waving locks.

It was now late in the autumn, but the sun was still shining brightly, and Audifax was driving his goats as usual down the rocky mountain slope. Through the dark fir-trees he could see the glittering surface of the Bodensee. All around, the trees were already wearing their autumnal colors, and the winds were playing merrily with the rustling red and yellow leaves on the ground. Heaving a deep sigh, Audifax after a while began to cry bitterly.

At that time a little girl, whose name was Hadumoth, was minding the geese and ducks belonging to the castle poultry-yard. She was the daughter of an old maid-servant, and had never seen her father. This Hadumoth was a very good little girl, with bright red cheeks and blue eyes; and she wore her hair in two tresses falling down on her shoulders. The geese were kept in excellent order and training, and though they would stick out their long necks sometime and cackle like foolish women, not one of them dared disobey its mistress. Often they picked their herbs in company with the goats of Audifax; for Hadumoth rather liked the short-haired goatherd, and often sat beside him. At the moment when Audifax sat weeping Hadumoth was coming down the hill with her geese, and on hearing the tinkling of the goat-bells looked about for the driver. Then she beheld him in his distress, sitting on a rock, and, going up to him, sat down by his side and asked, "Audifax, what makes thee cry?"

" There is something within me that makes me cry," said Audifax. Then he took one of the stones, such as were lying about plentifully, and threw it on the other stones. The stone was thin and produced a ringing sound.

" Didst thou hear it?"

" Yes," replied Hadumoth, " it sounded just as usual."

" Hast thou also understood the sound?"

" No."

"Ah, but I understood it, and therefore I must cry," said Audifax. " It is now many weeks ago that I sat in yonder valley on a rock. There the meaning first came to me. I cannot tell thee how, but it must have come from the depths below; and since then I feel as if my eyes and ears were quite changed, and in my hands I sometimes see glittering sparks. Whenever I walk over the fields I hear it murmuring under my feet, as if there were some hidden spring; and when I stand by the rocks I see the veins running through them; and down below I hear a hammering and digging, and that must come from the dwarfs, of whom my grandfather has told me many a time.   And sometimes I even see a red glowing light shining through the earth.— Hadumoth, I must find some great treasure, and because I cannot find it, therefore I cry.''

Hadumoth made the sign of the cross, and then said: '' Thou must have been bewitched somehow, Audifax.''

He hung down his head again, and began to cry afresh. '' What must I do to find the treasure? '' sobbed he.

'' Be sensible,'' said Hadumoth; '' what wouldst thou do with the treasure if thou couldst find it? ''

'' I should buy my liberty, and thine also; and all the land from the Duchess, mountain and all; and I should have made for thee a golden crown, and for every goat a golden bell, and for myself a flute of ebony and pure gold.''

'' Of pure gold,'' laughed Hadumoth.   '' Dost thou know what gold looks like? ''

Audifax pointed with his fingers to his lips.   '' Canst thou keep a secret? ''   She nodded in the affirmative. '' Then promise me with your hand.''   She gave him her hand.

'' Now I will show you how pure gold looks,'' said the boy, diving into his breast-pocket and pulling out a piece like a good-sized coin, but shaped like a cup.   On it were engraven mystic half-effaced characters.   It glistened and shone brightly in the sun, and was really gold.   Hadumoth balanced it on her forefinger.

'' That I found in yonder field, far over there, beyond the thunder-storm,'' said Audifax.   '' Whenever the many-colored rainbow descends to us there come two angels who hold out a golden cup so that its ends should not touch the rough and rain-drenched ground; and when it vanishes again they leave their cups on the fields, as they cannot use them twice for fear of offending the rainbow.''

Hadumoth began to believe that her companion was really destined to obtain some great treasure.   ''Audifax,'' said she, giving him back his rainbow cup, '' this will not help thee.   He who wants to find a treasure must know the spell.''

" Oh, yes, the spell! " said Audifax with tearful eyes.
" If I only knew that! "

" Hast thou yet seen the holy man? " asked Hadumoth.
" No."

" For some days a holy man, who is sure to know all
spells, has been in the castle.   He has brought a great book
with him out of which he reads to the Duchess; in it is
written everything — how one conquers all the spirits in
air, earth, water, and fire. The tall Friderun told the men-
servants about it, and related how the Duchess had made
him come to strengthen her power and to make her remain
forever young and beautiful, and live to eternity."

" I will go to the holy man, then," said Audifax.

The following day Ekkehard was going over the courtyard when Audifax came to him and asked to know the
spell.   An inclination to allow himself an innocent joke came
into Ekkehard's serious mind, and he laughingly quoted to
the goatherd the following words from Virgil —

> "Auri sacra fames, quid non mortalia cogis
>   Pectora? "

With stubborn patience Audifax repeated the foreign words
over and over again, until he had fixed them in his memory.

" Please to write it down, that I may wear it on me," he
now intreated.

Ekkehard, wishing to complete the joke, wrote the words
on a thin strip of parchment and gave it to the boy, who,
gleefully hiding it in his breast-pocket, again kissed the
monk's garment, and then darted off, with innumerable mad
gambols outrivaling the merriest of his goats.

In the night Audifax and Hadumoth set out to seek the
treasure, but were greatly disappointed, for the spell did
not prove efficacious.   They concluded that Ekkehard did
not pray to the right god and decided to look up some one
else, who knew all about spells and charms and prayed to
the old god — the woman of the wood.   When they reached
the top of the Hohenkrähen they found the woman's stone

hut empty, but near by they came upon a party of men engaged in heathen rites, an old haggard woman presiding over the ceremony. After the sun had risen and the men had gone, the children stepped out of their hiding-place and confronted the old woman. Audifax had taken out the slip of parchment — but the hag, snatching up a brand, approached them with so threatening a look that the children hastily turned round and fled down the hill as fast as their feet could carry them. Nobody at the castle had noticed their absence.

After a time they made up their minds to go to Ekkehard and complain of the woman of the wood. So they went to him and told him all that they had beheld that night on the Hohenkrähen. He listened kindly to their tale, which he repeated to the Duchess in the evening. Dame Hadwig smiled.

"They have a peculiar taste — my faithful subjects," said she. "Everywhere handsome churches have been erected in which the Gospel is preached to them. Fine church music, great festivals and processions through the waving corn-fields, with cross and flag at their head — all this does not content them. So they must needs sit on their mountain-tops in cold chilly nights, not understanding what they're about except that they drink beer. 'Tis really wonderful! What do you think of the matter, pious Master Ekkehard?"

"Annihilate them," said Ekkehard. "He who forsakes his christian faith and breaks the vows of his baptism shall be eternally damned."

"Not so fast, my young zealot!" continued Dame Hadwig. "My good Hegau people are not to lose their heads because they prefer sitting on the cold top of the Hohenkrähen, on the first night of November, to lying on their straw-mattresses."

"With the devil there can be no peace," cried Ekkehard hotly. "Are you going to be lukewarn in your faith, noble Mistress?"

" In reigning over a country," returned she with a slight sarcasm in her voice—" one learns a good deal that is not in books. To be sensible is not to be lukewarm. Why should we wage war so fiercely against the miserable stragglers of the olden times? "

" Then you had better reward them," said Ekkehard bitterly.

" Reward them? " quoth the Duchess. " Between the one and the other there is still many an expedient left. Perhaps it were better if we put a stop to these nightly trespasses. No realm can be powerful in which two different creeds exist, for that leads to internal warfare, which is rather dangerous as long as there are plenty of outward enemies. Besides, the laws of the land have forbidden them these follies, and they must find out that our ordinances and prohibitions are not to be tampered with in that way. To-morrow you shall ride over to the Hohenkrähen and try to discover whether the woman of the wood is a Circe. We give you full authority to act in our name, and are truly curious to ascertain what your wisdom will decree."

" It is not for me to reign over a people and to settle the affairs of this world," replied he evasively.

" That will be seen," said Duchess Hadwig. " I do not think that the power of commanding has ever embarrassed any one, least of all a son of the Church."

So Ekkehard submitted—the more readily as the commission was a proof of confidence on her part. Early the next morning he rode over to the Hohenkrähen on horseback, taking Audifax with him to show him the way.

"A happy journey, Sir Chancellor! " called out a laughing voice behind him. It was the voice of Praxedis.

They soon reached the old hag's dwelling, which was a stone hut, built on a projecting part of the high rock, about half way up. Mighty oaks and beech-trees spread their boughs over it, hiding the summit of the Hohenkrähen. Three high stone steps led into the inside, which was a dark but airy chamber. On the floor there lay heaps of dried herbs, giving out a strong fragrance.   Three bleached horse skulls grinned down fantastically from the walls, and beneath them hung the huge antlers of a stag; in the doorpost was cut a double, intricate triangle, and on the floor a tame woodpecker, and a raven with cropped wings were hopping about.

The inhabitant of this abode was seated beside the flickering fire on the hearth, sewing some garment.   By her side stood a high, roughly hewn, weather-beaten stone.   From time to time she bent down to the hearth and held out her meagre hand over the coals; for the cold of November was beginning to be felt, especially on the mountains.

Ekkehard had left the saddle and had tied his horse to a neighboring fir-tree.   He then stepped over the threshold, shyly followed by Audifax.

The woman of the wood threw the garment she had been working upon over the stone, folded her hands on her lap, and looked fixedly at the intruder in his monk's habit, but did not get up.

"Praised be Jesus Christ!" said Ekkehard, by way of greeting, and also to avert any possible spell.   Instinctively he drew in the thumb of his right hand, doubling his fingers over it, being afraid of the evil eye and its powers.   Audifax had told him how people said that with one look she could wither up a whole meadow.   She did not return his greeting.

"What are you doing there?" began Ekkehard.

"I am mending an old garment that is getting worn," was the answer.

"Have you been baptized?" continued Ekkehard.

"Aye, they will have baptized me, likely enough."

"And if you have been baptized," he said raising his voice, "and have renounced the devil with all his works and allurements, what is the meaning of all this?"   He pointed with his stick toward the horses' skulls on the wall. "Woman!" cried Ekkehard, approaching her closer, "thou exercisest witchcraft and sorcery!"

Then she arose and exclaimed with a frowning brow and

strangely glittering eyes —" You wear a priest's garment, so you may say this to me; for an old woman has no protection against such as you!   Otherwise it were a grave insult you have cast on me, and the laws of the land punish those that use such words."

At that moment Ekkehard's eye fell on the stone by the hearth.   It was a Roman altar, on which some strange figures were carved.   A youth in a flowing mantle and with Phrygian cap was kneeling on a prostrate bull—he was the Persian god of light, Mithras.

" You worship that man on the bull? " cried the monk vehemently.   " How does the stone come to be here? "

" Because we took pity on it," replied she.   " You who wear the tonsure and monk's habit probably will not understand that.   The stone stood outside, on yonder projecting rock, which must have been a consecrated spot on which many have probably knelt in the olden times.   ' The sight of the stone grieves me,' said my mother one day.   ' The man in the flowing mantle looks as if he were freezing with the cold.'   So we took it up and placed it beside the hearth, and it has never harmed us as yet.   We know how the old gods felt when their altars were shattered; for ours also have been dethroned.   You need not begrudge its rest to the old stone."

" Your gods! " echoed Ekkehard.   " Who are your gods? "

" That you ought to know best, for you have banished them into the depths of the lake.   We can see them no more, and know but the places where our fathers have worshipped them before the Franks and the cowl-bearing men had come. But when the winds are shaking the tops of yonder oak-tree you may hear their wailing voices in the air; and on consecrated nights there is a moaning and roaring in the forest and a shining of lights, while serpents are winding themselves round the stems of the trees; and over the mountains you hear a rustling of wings of despairing spirits that have come to look at their ancient home."

Ekkehard crossed himself.

" I tell it thus as I know it," continued the old woman. " I do not wish to offend the Savior, but he has come as a stranger into the land. You serve him in a foreign tongue which we cannot understand. If he had sprung from our own ground, then we might talk to him and be his most faithful worshippers; and maybe things would then fare better in Allemannia."

" Woman!" cried Ekkehard wrathfully, " we will have thee burned!"

" If it be written in your books that trees grow up to burn old women with, very well! I have lived long enough. The lightning has lately paid a visit to the woman of the wood "—pointing to a dark stripe on the wall—" but the lightning has spared the old woman."

After this she cowered down before the hearth and remained there motionless, like a statue. The flickering coals threw a fitful varying light on her wrinkled face.

" 'Tis well!" murmured Ekkehard, as he left the chamber. Audifax was very glad when he could again see the blue sky over his head. " There they sat together," said he pointing upward.

" I will go and look at it, while you return to the Hohentwiel and send over two men with hatchets. Tell Otfried, the deacon of Singen, to come, and direct him to bring his stole and mass-book with him."

Audifax bounded away, while Ekkehard went up to the top of the Hohenkrähen, where he inspected the scene of the nightly revel, of which but few traces remained. The earth around the oak-tree was still wet and reddish looking, and a few coals and ashes indicated where the fire had been.

Two men with hatchets soon came up. " We have been ordered to come here," they said.

" Good," said Ekkehard. " You are to cut down this oak for me. Begin at once and make haste, for before nightfall the tree must be felled to the ground."

The deacon of Singen had also arrived with stole and

mass-book. Ekkehard beckoned to him to go with him into the hut of the woman of the wood. She was still sitting motionless as before, beside her hearth. "Woman of the wood," called out Ekkehard imperiously, "put your house in order and pack up your things, for you must go!"

"Who is it that is insulting me," growled she; "and who wishes to cast me out of my mother's house, like a stray dog?"

"In the name of the Duchess of Suabia," continued Ekkehard solemnly, "and on account of your practising heathenish superstitions and nightly idolatries, I banish you herewith from house and home, and bid you leave the land. Your chair shall be placed before the door of your hut, and you shall wander restlessly about as far as the sky is blue and Christians visit the church, as far as the falcon flies on a day of Spring when the wind is carrying him along. No hospitable door shall be opened to you; no fire be lighted to give you warmth; and may the wells deny you water until you have renounced the powers of darkness and made your peace with the almighty God."

The woman of the wood had listened to him without showing great emotion. She scraped her scanty belongings together, making a bundle of them, and, taking her staff, prepared to go. The heart of the deacon of Singen was touched. "Pray God through his servants to have mercy on you, and perform some christian penance," he said, "so that you may find forgiveness."

"For that, the woman of the wood is too old," she replied. "Be cursed, ye dogs!" continued she. Then, followed by her birds, she took the path leading into the woods, and disappeared.

Just as all was over, the tramping of horses' feet was heard. It was the Duchess, accompanied by a single servant. Ekkehard went out to meet her, and the deacon directed his steps homeward.

"You were so long away that I had to come hither myself, to see how you had settled everything," graciously called out the Duchess.

Ekkehard then told her about the life and doings of the woman of the wood, and how he had driven her away.

" You are very severe," said Dame Hadwig.

" I thought I was very mild," replied Ekkehard.

" Well, we approve of what you have done. What do you intend to do with the deserted hut," casting a hasty look at the stone walls.

" I mean to consecrate it as a chapel to St. Hadwig."

The Duchess looked at him with a well pleased expression. " How did you hit upon that idea? "

" The thought struck me just now.— The oak I have had cut down."

" We will examine that spot, and I think that we shall approve also of the felling of the oak."

She climbed the steep path leading up to the top of the Hohenkrähen, accompanied by Ekkehard. There lay the oak on the ground, its mighty branches almost preventing their further ascent. A flat stone, but a few paces in circumference, crowned the top of the strangely shaped hill. They stood silently on the rocks, looking at the splendid view before them. Dame Hadwig was touched, for her noble heart could feel and appreciate nature's beauty and grandeur, and at that moment a certain tenderness pervaded her whole being. Her looks from the snowy Alpine peaks fell on Ekkehard. " He is going to consecrate a chapel to St. Hadwig," something whispered within her, over and over again. She advanced a step, as if she were afraid of becoming giddy, and putting her right arm on Ekkehard's shoulder, leaned heavily on him; her sparkling eyes looking intently into his. " What is my friend thinking about? " cooed she in soft accents.

Ekkehard, who had been lost in thought, started. " I have never before stood on such a height," said he, " and I was reminded of the passage in Scripture — 'Afterwards the devil, taking him up into a high mountain, shewed unto him all the kingdoms of the world in a moment of time. And the devil said unto him: All this will I give Thee, and the glory of them, if thou wilt worship me. But Jesus answered and said unto him: Get thee behind me Satan, for it is written, thou shalt worship the Lord thy God, and Him only shalt thou serve.'"

With a strange look the Duchess stepped backward, the light in her eyes changing as if she would have liked to push the monk down into the abyss.

"Ekkehard!" cried she, "you are either a child—or a fool!"

Then she turned round, and hastily and disgruntedly descended the path. Mounting her horse, she rode back to the Hohentwiel at a gallop so furious that her servant could scarcely follow her. Ekkehard, full of consternation, remained where he was. He passed his hand over his eyes as if to remove a mist from before them.

When, late at night, he sat in his tower on the Hohentwiel, thinking of all that had happened that day, he beheld a distant gleam of fire. He looked out and saw that the fiery blaze arose from the fir-trees on the Hohenkrähen. The woman of the wood had been paying her last visit to the future chapel of St. Hadwig.

Chapter VII

CHRISTMAS

The evening on the Hohenkrähen cast a gloom over the following days. Misunderstandings are not easily forgiven—least of all by him who has caused them. For this reason Dame Hadwig spent some days in a very bad humor, in her own private apartments. Grammar and Virgil both had a holiday. Ekkehard came to ask whether he were to continue his lessons. "I have a toothache," said the Duchess. Expressing his regret, he attributed it to the rough autumnal weather. Every day he asked several times how she was, which somewhat conciliated the Duchess.

Ekkehard all this time felt quite at his ease; for the

idea that he had given an unsuitable answer to the Duchess never entered his head. He had really been thinking of that parable in Scripture, and failed to see that in reply to the timid expression of a friendly liking it might not always be quite the right thing to quote Scripture. He reverenced the Duchess, but far more as the embodied idea of sublimity than as a woman. That sublime beings demand adoration had never struck him; and still less did it occur to him that even the sublimest personage is often perfectly satisfied with simple affection.

"It was really a grand sight we had, that evening, from the Hohenkrähen," said she one day to Ekkehard. "But do you know our weather-signs on the Hohentwiel? Whenever the Alps appear very distinct and near, the weather is sure to change; so we have had some bad weather since. And now we will resume our reading of Virgil." Upon this, Ekkehard, highly pleased, went to bring his heavy metal-bound book, and their studies were resumed, not to be interrupted again until the early winter.

[As Christmas came on, every one became busily engaged in the preparation of presents. Even Dame Hadwig, putting aside the grammar, took to sewing and embroidery. Balls of gold thread and black silk lay about in the woman's apartments; and when Ekkehard once came in unawares Praxedis rushed up and pushed him out of the door while Dame Hadwig hid some needlework in a basket. This aroused Ekkehard's curiosity, and he arrived at the not unreasonable conclusion that some present was being made for him, and, casting about for the best way of making an adequate return, sent word to his friend and teacher, Folkard, at St. Gall, to send him parchment, colors, and brushes, as well as some precious ink. As soon as these materials arrived he sat up many an hour at night in his tower, pondering over a Latin composition which he wanted to dedicate to the Duchess, and which was to contain some delicate homage. He finally wrote a poem, as if Virgil had appeared to him in his solitude, expressing delight that his poetry was living again in German lands and thanking the high-born lady for thus befriending him. This poem he wrote down on parchment and adorned it with a picture whose central figure is the Duchess, with crown and sceptre, sitting on her throne. She is accosted by Virgil in white garments, who inclining his bay-crowned head, advances toward her, leading Ekkehard. The latter represents himself as modestly walking by Virgil's side, as the pupil with the master, and both are humbly bowing before the Duchess.]

In the kitchen on the Hohentwiel there was great bustle and activity, such as there is in the tent of a commander-in-chief on the eve of a battle. Dame Hadwig herself stood among the serving maidens. She did not wear her ducal mantle, but a white apron, and stood distributing flour and honey for the gingerbread. Praxedis was mixing ginger, pepper, and cinnamon to flavor the paste with.

"What cutting-mold shall we take?" asked she. "The square with the serpents?"

"No, the big heart is prettier," said Dame Hadwig. So the gingerbread was made in the shape of hearts, and the finest was stuck with almonds and cardamom by the Duchess' own hand.

Christmas Eve had arrived. All the occupants of the castle were assembled, dressed in their best; for on that day there was to be no distinction between masters and servants. Ekkehard read to them the story of Christ's nativity, and then they all went, two and two, into the great hall, where the Christmas-tree, with its many candles, lighted the room brilliantly. On large tables the presents for the serving people were laid out — a piece of linen, or cloth, and some cakes. They rejoiced at the generosity of their mistress, which was not always so exercised. Men and maid-servants then offered their thanks to the Duchess, and went down again to the servants' hall.

Dame Hadwig, taking Ekkehard by the hand, led him to a little table apart. "This is meant for you," said she.

Between the almond-covered, gingerbread heart and the basket, there lay a priest's cap of handsome velvet, and a magnificent stole. Fringe and ground-work were of gold thread, and embroideries of black silk, interwoven with pearls, ran through the latter; the whole would have been worthy of a bishop.

"Let me see how it becomes you," said Praxedis, and in spite of their ecclesiastical character, she put the cap on his head and threw the stole over his shoulders. Ekkehard cast down his eyes. "Splendid!" exclaimed she; "you may offer your thanks!"

Shyly Ekkehard put down the consecrated gifts, and then drawing the parchment roll from beneath his ample garment timidly presented it to the Duchess. The painting at the beginning told its story fairly well, for any doubt of its meaning was dispelled by the superscription of the names: Hadwigis, Virgilius and Ekkehard. A bold initial, with intricate golden arabesques, headed the poem.

[Ekkehard then read and explained the poem and received the thanks of the Duchess, who was highly pleased by the monk's gift.]

After Ekkehard had gone up to his little chamber, the Duchess and Praxedis still sat up together, and the Greek maid fetched a basin filled with water, some pieces of lead, and a metal spoon. "The lead-melting of last year portended well," said she. "We could not at that time quite understand what the strange shape was which the lead assumed in the water; but now I am almost sure that it resembled a monk's cowl—and that, our castle can now boast of."

The Duchess had become thoughtful. She listened to hear whether Ekkehard was returning. "It is nothing but an idle amusement," said she.

"If it does not please my mistress," said the Greek, "then she might order our teacher to entertain us with something better. His Virgil is no doubt a far better oracle than our lead, when opened on a consecrated night with prayers and a blessing. I wonder now what part of his epic would foretell to us the events of the coming year."

"Be silent!" commanded the Duchess. "He spoke but lately so severely on witchcraft; he would laugh at us."

"Then we shall have to content ourselves with the old way," returned Praxedis, holding the spoon with the lead in it over the flame of the lamp. The lead melted and trembled; and, muttering a few unintelligible words, she poured it into the water, the liquid metal making a hissing sound.

Dame Hadwig with seeming indifference cast a look at it when Praxedis held the basin up to the light. Instead of dividing into fantastic shapes, the lead had formed a long pointed drop. It glimmered faintly in Dame Hadwig's hand.

"That is another riddle for time to solve," laughed Praxedis. "The future this time closely resembles a pine-cone."

"Or a tear," mused the Duchess seriously, leaning her head on her right hand.

The remainder of the winter passed by monotonously, and in consequence swiftly enough. They prayed and worked, read Virgil and studied the grammar, every day. March had come, and heavy gales blew over the land. On the first starlight night a comet was seen in the sky; and the stork which had lived comfortably on the castle-gable flew away. A strange, uncomfortable feeling took possession of all minds.

A man of Augsburg, coming to the Reichenau, also brought evil tidings. Bishop Ulrich had promised a precious relic to the monastery — the right arm of the holy Theopontus, richly set in silver and precious stones. He now sent word that as the country was unsafe at present he could not risk sending it. The Abbot ordered the man to go to the Hohentwiel, there to inform the Duchess of the state of things.

"What is the good news?" asked she, on his presenting himself.

"There's not much that is good. They are again on the road, between the Danube and the Rhine."

"Who?"

"The old enemies from other parts—the small fellows with the deep-set eyes and blunt noses. A good deal of our meat will again be ridden tender under the saddle this year."

"The Huns?" exclaimed the Duchess, in startled tones.

"They have already swum over the Danube," said the messenger, "and will be falling like locusts into the German lands, and as swift as winged devils. May the plague take their horses!"

She dismissed the man from Augsburg with a present. Then she sent for Ekkehard.

"Virgil will have to rest a while," said she, telling him of the danger that was threatening from the Huns. "What is to be done? To meet them in open battle? Even bravery is folly, when the enemy is too numerous. To obtain peace by paying tribute and ransom, thus driving them over to our neighbors' territory? Others have done that before, but we have other ideas of honor and dishonor. Are we to barricade ourselves on the Hohentwiel, and leave the land at their mercy, when we have promised our protection to our subjects?—Never! What do you advise?"

"My knowledge does not extend to such matters," sorrowfully replied Ekkehard.

The Duchess was excited. "Oh, schoolmaster," cried she reproachfully, "why has Heaven not made you a warrior? Many things would be better then!"

Ekkehard, deeply hurt, turned to go. The words had entered his heart like an arrow, and remained there. The reproach had some truth in it, so it hurt him all the more.

"Ekkehard," called out Dame Hadwig, "you must not go. You are to serve the country with your knowledge, and what you do not know as yet you may learn. When the enemy threatens, we'll prepare, and when he attacks us, beat him."

Chapter VIII

THE APPROACH OF THE HUNS

THE exciting and dangerous prospect put the Duchess in high spirits. They were all busy making preparations for the reception of the enemy. The Hohentwiel was to be headquarters, nature herself having made it a fortress. Swift messengers were riding on horseback through the Hegau, and people began stirring everywhere in the land.

Ekkehard went to the peaceful little island of Reichenau, as the Duchess desired it; he was to carry an invitation to the brotherhood to come to the Hohentwiel in case of danger. When he arrived there he found everybody in a state of excitement.

"I should have asked for this invitation myself," said the Abbot, "if you had not come." He had seized a long sword, and made such a cut in the air with it that Ekkehard started back a pace or two. "Yes, 'tis getting serious," continued he. "Down in Altdorf the Huns have already effected an entrance, and we shall soon see the flames of Lindau reflected in the water."

With his back leaning against an apple-tree, stood Rudimann the cellarer, an ominous frown on his forehead. Ekkehard went up to him, wishing to embrace him as a sign that a general calamity was wiping out the old quarrel; but Rudimann, waving him off, said: "I know what you mean." Then drawing a coarse thread out of the seam of his garment, he threw it to the ground and placed his foot on it. "As long as a Hunnic horse is treading German ground all enmity shall be torn out of my heart, as this thread is out of my garment; but if we both outlive the coming battles we will take it up again, as it is meet we should."

On a clear moonlight night the monks of the Reichenau ascended the Hohentwiel, where they found everything prepared for their reception.

The courtyard, the next morning, was transformed into a bustling bivouac. Some hundred armed vassals were already assembled, and from the Reichenau ninety more combatants were added to their number. They were all eagerly preparing for the coming contest.

Ekkehard came up to the hall. He had exercised with the others, and his face was glowing with the unwonted exertion, while a red stripe on his forehead showed where his helmet had heavily pressed. In the excitement of the moment he had forgotten to leave his lance outside the door.

With evident pleasure Dame Hadwig stood looking at him. He was no longer the timid teacher of Latin. Bowing his head before the Duchess he said, " Our brothers in the Lord, from the Reichenau, bid me tell you that a great thirst is besetting their ranks."

Dame Hadwig laughed merrily. " Let them put a tun of cool beer in the courtyard. Until the Huns are all driven out of the country, our cellarer is not to complain about the emptying of his tuns."

[After a few days Simon Bardo's men were so well drilled that he could let them pass muster before the Duchess — and it was time, for ominous portents had disturbed their recent slumbers. A bright red light was illuminating the sky far over the lake. Like a fiery cloud the dread sign hung there for several hours, the conflagration being probably far off in Helvetia.

While the muster was in progress Master Spazzo observed a dark line approaching in the valley. The strangers proved to be the monks of St. Gall, headed by their Abbot, Cralo, and they made their way directly to the castle where they were welcomed by the Duchess.]

" May God bless you, most noble cousin," said the Abbot, bowing his head before the Duchess. " Who would have thought half a year ago that we should return your call with the whole of the brotherhood? "

Dame Hadwig held out her hand to him with visible emotion. " Yes, these are times of trial," said she. " Be welcome! "

As soon as an opportunity offered, Abbot Cralo told them what had happened at his monastery.

"This time," he began, "the danger came upon us almost unawares. Scarcely had one spoken of the Huns when the ground was already resounding with the tramp of their horses' hoofs. We had made ourselves a sort of stronghold as a refuge. In a narrow fir-grown valley we found an excellent hiding-place, which we thought no heathenish bloodhound would ever sniff out. There we built ourselves a strong house, with towers and walls, but we had scarcely finished it when the messengers from the lake came crying, 'Fly, the Huns are coming!' Then there came others from the Rhine valley, and 'Fly!' was again the word. The sky was already red from conflagrations and camp-fires, the air was filled with the shrieks of people fleeing and the creaking of retreating cart-wheels, and there was nothing for us to do but to repair in great haste to our retreat in the wood. On the road the brothers discovered that we had left the blind Thieto behind in his cell; but nobody ventured to return for him, as the ground was almost literally burning under our feet, and we remained for several days quietly hidden in our fir-wood. One evening a clear voice demanded admittance, and in came Burkhard, the cloister-pupil, haggard and tired to death. Out of friendship for Romeias, the cloister-watchman, he had remained behind without our noticing it. He was the bearer of evil tidings.

"Romeias, the best of all watchmen, had not left the monastery with us. 'I will keep my post to the last,' said he. He then barred and locked all the gates, hid all that was valuable, and went his round on the walls, accompanied by Burkhard the cloister-pupil; the rest of the time he kept watch on the tower, his arms by his side. Soon after we had left, a large body of Huns on horseback, carefully prying about, approached the walls. Romeias gave the ordinary bugle sounds, and then quickly running to the other end of the courtyard, blew the horn again there, as if the monastery were still occupied and well prepared. ' Now the time has come for us to depart also,' said he to the pupil. The two went over to the blind Thieto, who, being loth to leave his accustomed corner, was placed on two spears and thus carried away. Letting themselves out by a secret little gate they fled up the Schwarzathal.

" But soon the Huns were on their track. Wild cries came up the valley and soon afterward the first arrows whizzed through the air. They reached the rock of the recluses indeed; but here even Romeias was surprised, for, as if nothing uncommon had happened, Wiborad's hollow psalm-singing was heard as usual. ' My cell is the battle-field on which I have fought against the old enemy of man-kind, and like a true champion of the Lord I will defend it to the last breath,' said she; and so she remained quite alone in that desolate spot, though all others left it. As the cloister's refuge in the fir-wood was too far to be reached, Romeias picked out a remote little hut and in it carefully deposited the blind Thieto, letting him in by the roof. Before leaving him he kissed the old man, and then told the cloister-pupil to save himself.

" ' You see something may happen to me,' he said, ' and so you must tell those in the refuge to look after the blind one.' Burkhard in vain besought him to flee likewise. ' I should have to run too fast,' replied Romeias, ' and that would make me too warm, and give me pains in the chest. Besides, I should like to speak a word or two with the chil-dren of the devil.'

" He then went up to Wiborad's cell, and knocking at the shutter, called out, ' Give me thy hand old dragon, we will make peace now,' upon which Wiborad stretched out her withered right hand. Finally Romeias blocked up the nar-row passage of the Schwarzathal with some huge stones, and then, taking his shield from his back and holding his spears ready, he seized his big bugle-horn to blow once more upon it. With flying hair he thus stood behind his wall, expecting the enemy. At first the sounds were fierce

and warlike, but by degrees they became softer and sweeter,
until an arrow, flying right into the opening, produced a
sharp dissonance. The next moment a whole shower of
arrows covered him and stuck fast in his shield, but he
shook them off like rain-drops. Here and there one of the
Huns climbed up the rocks to get at him, but Romeias'
spears brought them quickly down. The attack became
fiercer and louder, but, undaunted, Wiborad was still chant-
ing her psalm:

"'Destroy them in Thy anger, O Lord. Destroy them
that they do no more exist, so that the world knows that
God is reigning in Israel, and over the whole earth, Selah!'

"So far Burkhard had witnessed the fighting; then he
had turned and fled. On hearing his account in the refuge
we were all very much grieved, and sent out a troop that
very night to look after the blind Thieto. Perfect quiet
reigned on the hill of the recluses when they reached it.
The moon was shining on the bodies of the slain Huns,
and, among them, the brothers found also the dismem-
bered body of Romeias. His head had been hewn off and
carried away by the enemy. May God reward him; for he
whose life was lost in doing his duty is surely worthy to
enter heaven! Wiborad's shutter was knocked at in vain,
and the tiles of her roof were mostly broken. So one of
the brothers climbed up, and, looking down, beheld the
recluse lying in her blood before the little altar of her cell.
Three wounds were visible on her head, which proved that
the Lord had deemed her worthy to die a martyr's death
by the hands of the heathen."

Every one was too much moved to speak. Dame Hadwig
also was deeply touched.

"Only Thieto, the blind one," continued Sir Cralo, "had
remained unharmed. Undiscovered by the enemy, he was
found soundly sleeping in the little hut by the rock. 'I
have been dreaming that an eternal peace had come over
the world,' said he to the brothers when they awoke him.
But even in our remote little valley we were not to have

peace much longer, as the Huns found their way to us also. Our walls were strong and our courage likewise, but hungry people soon get tired of being besieged. The day before yesterday our provisions were gone, and when the evening came we saw a pillar of smoke rise from our monastery; so in the middle of the night we broke through the enemy, the Lord being with us and our swords helping likewise. And so we have come to you,''— with a bow toward the Duchess —'' homeless and orphaned, like birds whose nest has been struck by lightning, and bringing nothing with us but the tidings that the Huns, whom may the Lord destroy, are following on our heels.''

'' The sooner they come the better,'' defiantly cried the Abbot of the Reichenau, raising his goblet.

'' Here's to the arms of God's own champions,'' added the Duchess, ringing her glass against his.

The opportunity for valiant deeds was no longer very far off.

Chapter IX

THE BATTLE WITH THE HUNS

Good Friday had come; but the anniversary of our Savior's death was not kept on the Hohentwiel this time in the silent way which the ordinances of the church require. Late in the night a war-council was held, at which it was determined that they should go out to meet the Huns in open battle.

In his closet up in the watch-tower Ekkehard was silently pacing up and down, his hands folded in prayer. A highly honorable commission had devolved on him. He was to preach a sermon to the united forces before they went out to battle, and so he was now praying for strength and inspiration, that his words might be like sparks, kindling the warlike flame in each breast. Suddenly the door opened and the Duchess entered, unaccompanied by Praxedis. Over her morning-dress she had thrown an ample cloak to protect herself against the cool air, perhaps also that she might not be recognized by the stranger guests while going over to the watch-tower. A faint blush mantled on her cheeks when she thus stood alone, opposite her youthful teacher.

"You are also going out to battle today?" asked she.

"Yes, I go with the others," replied Ekkehard.

"I should despise you if you had given me any other reply," said she, "and you have justly presumed that for such an expedition it would not be necessary to ask my leave. But have you not thought of saying good-by?" added she in low reproachful accents.

Ekkehard was embarrassed. "There are many nobler and better men leaving your castle today. The abbots and knights will surround you; how then could I think of taking special leave of you, even if —" His voice broke off. The Duchess looked into his eyes. Neither uttered a word.

"I have brought you something which is to serve you in battle," said she after a while, drawing from under her mantle a precious sword with a rich shoulder-belt; a white agate adorned the hilt. "It is the sword of Sir Burkhard, my late husband. Of all the arms he possessed he valued this the most. You will wear it today with honor."

She held out the sword to him; Ekkehard received it in silence. His coat-of-mail he had already put on under his habit. Now he buckled on the shoulder-belt, and then seized the hilt with his right hand as if the enemy were already facing him.

"I have something else for you," continued Dame Hadwig. On a silk ribbon she wore a golden locket round her neck, and this she now drew forth. It was a crystal, covering an insignificant looking splinter of wood.

"If my prayers should not suffice, this relic will protect you. It is a splinter of the holy cross, which the Empress Helena discovered. May it bring a blessing to you in the coming battle."

She leaned toward him to hang the jewel round his neck. Quickly he bent his knees to receive it; but after it had long been hanging round his neck he still knelt before her. She passed her hand lightly over his curly hair, and there was a peculiarly soft and half sad expression on the usually haughty countenance.

Ekkehard had bent his knee before, at the name of the holy cross, but now he felt as if he must kneel down a second time before her who was thus graciously thinking of him. A budding affection requires some time to understand itself clearly, and in matters of love he had not learned to reckon and count, as in the verses of Virgil, or he might have guessed that she who had taken him away from his quiet cloister-cell—that she who on that evening on the Hohenkrähen, had looked on him so tenderly, and now again on the morning of battle was standing before him, as Dame Hadwig was at that moment, might well have expected some words out of the depth of his heart—perhaps even more than words only.

His thoughts quickly followed one another, and all his pulses were throbbing. When on former occasions anything like love had stirred his heart the reverence for his mistress had driven it back, nipping it in the bud, as the cold winds of March wither and blight the early spring flowers. At this moment, however, he was not thinking of that reverence, but rather how he had once carried the Duchess boldly over the cloister-yard. Neither did he think of his monastic vow, but he felt as if he must rush into her arms and press her to his heart with a cry of delight. Sir Burkhard's sword seemed to burn at his side. "Throw aside all reserve, for only the bold will conquer the world." Were not these words to be read in Dame Hadwig's eyes?

He stood up—strong, great and free; she had never seen him look so before. But it lasted only a second. As yet not one sound betraying his inward struggle had escaped his lips, when his eye fell on the dark, ebony cross which Vincentius had once hung up on the wall. "It is the day of the Lord, and thou shalt open thy lips today before his people." Then the remembrance of his duty drove away all other thoughts, like a frost on a clear morning, under whose withering blight grass and leaves and blossoms became black and seared. Yet shyly, as in former times, he took Dame Hadwig's hand. "How shall I thank my mistress?" murmured he in broken accents.

She cast a searching look at him. The soft expression had vanished, and the old sternness had returned to her brow, as if she meant to say: "If you don't know how, I am not going to tell you." But she said nothing, and Ekkehard lingeringly held her hand in his. Finally she drew it back.

"Be pious and brave," said she, turning to leave the chamber. It sounded like mockery.

Scarcely longer than a person needs to say the Lord's prayer had the Duchess been with him, but far more had happened in that time than he realized.

[Ekkehard preached the sermon at the divine service that was held the next morning, and the assembly listened to his inspiring words with breathless attention.]

At the conclusion of the sermon every one who had not yet taken the holy sacrament went up to the altar to receive it. But now from the watch-tower was suddenly heard the cry, "To arms! to arms! the enemy is coming! A dark mass of riders and horses are moving toward us from the lake!" And now there was no longer any possibility of keeping back the eager men who were all pressing toward the gate, Abbot Wazmann having scarcely time to pronounce a blessing over them.

Thirsting for the coming battle the troops left the court-yard, each heart swelling with the soul-stirring conviction that a great and important moment was at hand. The monks of St. Gall mustered sixty-four, those of the Reichenau ninety, and of the arrier-ban men there were more than five hundred. Close by the standard of the cross of the brotherhood of St. Gall walked Ekkehard, bearing a crucifix veiled in black crape and long black streamers, as the monastery's banner had been left behind.

On the balcony stood the Duchess, waving her white handkerchief. Ekkehard, turning round, looked up at her, but her eyes evaded his, and the parting salutation was not meant for him.

The Huns had left the monastery of Reichenau at early dawn. The provisions were all consumed, the wine drunk, and the cloister pillaged; so their day's work was done. And now they were riding through the dark fir-wood toward the Hohentwiel. But as they were thus cantering along, heedless of all danger, here and there a horse began to stagger, and arrows and other sharp missiles flew into their ranks, sent by invisible hands. The vanguard began to slacken rein and to halt; but Ellak, the Hunnish leader, giving the spurs to his horse, cried out, " Why do you care for the stinging of gnats? Forward! The plain is a better field of battle! "

Far ahead rode Ellak, accompanied by the Hunnic standard-bearer, who was waving the green and red flag over his head. Uttering a piercing cry, the chieftain lifted himself high in the saddle and dispatched the first arrow, thus opening the battle according to old custom; and then the bloody fight began in good earnest. Little availed it to the Suabian warriors that they stood firm and immovable like a wall of lances, for although the horses recoiled before it, showers of arrows were sent at them from the distance. Half rising in the stirrups, with the reins hanging over their horses' necks, the Huns took aim, and generally their arrows hit the mark.

Then came the moment for the light troops to come out of the fir-wood and attack the Huns from behind. The sound of the bugle again assembled them, and they advanced — but quick as thought their enemies' horses were turned around, and a shower of arrows greeted them. They staggered, only a few advancing, but these were also soon thrown back; and finally Audifax was left alone, bravely marching along. Many an arrow whizzed round his head, but without minding them, or once looking back, he blew

his bag-pipe, as was his duty; thus he came right into the
midst of the Hunnic riders. But his piping stopped suddenly, for, in passing, one of the Huns had thrown a noose
over his head. Trying hard to resist Audifax looked
around, but not a single man of his troop was to be seen.
"Oh, Hadumoth!" cried he mournfully. The rider took
pity on the brave fair-haired boy; so, instead of splitting
his head, he lifted him into the saddle, and galloped away
to the place where the Hunnic train had stopped, under the
shelter of a hill. With erect figure the woman of the wood
stood on her cart, intently gazing at the raging battle.
She had dressed the wounds of the first Huns who fell,
pronouncing some powerful charms over them to stop the
bleeding.

"Here I bring you some one to clean the camp-kettles!"
cried the Hunnic rider, throwing the boy over into the cart
and at the feet of the old woman.

"Welcome, thou venomous little toad!" cried she
fiercely; "thou shalt get thy reward, sure enough, for
having shown that cowl-wearer the way to my house!"
She had recognized him at once, and, dragging him toward
her, tied him fast to the cart.

Audifax remained silent, but scalding tears fell from his
eyes. He did not cry on account of being taken prisoner,
but from another heavy disappointment. "Oh, Hadumoth!" sighed he again. Yesterday at midnight he had
sat together with the young goose-driver, hidden in a
corner of the fireplace. "Thou shalt become invulnerable,"
Hadumoth had said, "for I will give thee a charm against
all weapons!" She had boiled a brown snake, and
anointed his forehead, shoulders, and breast with its fat.
"Tomorrow evening I shall wait for thee in this same
corner, for thou wilt surely come back to me safe and sound.
No metal can do anything against the fat of a snake."
Audifax had squeezed her hands, and had gone out so joyously into battle — and now!

The fighting was still going on in the plain, and the

Suabian combatants, not being used to battle, began to tire. With an anxious expression Simon Bardo was watching the state of affairs; and with an angry shake of the head, he grumbled to himself, " The best strategy is lost on these Centaurs, who come and go and shoot at a distance, as if my threefold flanks stood there only to amuse them. It would really be well if one were to add a chapter to Emperor Leo's book on tactics, treating of the attacks of the Huns."

He approached the monks, and, dividing them again into two bodies, ordered the men of St. Gall to advance on the right, and those of Reichenau on the left, then to wheel about, so that the enemy, having the wood at his back, was shut in by a semicircle. "If we do not surround them they will not let us get at them," cried he, flourishing his broad sword in the air. "And now to the attack!"

In the middle of the arrier-ban fought Master Spazzo, the chamberlain, heading a troop. The slow advance had rather pleased him, but when the fight seemed to come to no conclusion, and men were clinging to each other like the hounds to the deer in a chase, it became rather too much for him. A dreamy pensive mood came over him in the midst of the raging battle, and only when a passing rider pulled off his helmet as an acceptable booty was he roused from his meditations; but when another, renewing the experiment, tried to drag off his mantle, he cried out angrily, " Is it not yet enough, thou marksman of the devil?" dealing him at the same time a thrust with his long sword, which pinned the Hun's thigh to his own horse. Master Spazzo then thought of giving him the death-blow, but on looking into his face, he found it so very ugly that he resolved to bring him home to his mistress as a living memento of the battle; so he made the wounded man his prisoner. His name was Cappan; and putting his head under Master Spazzo's arm in sign of submission, he grinned with delight, showing two rows of shining white teeth, when he perceived that his life had been spared.

HEIDELBERG CASTLE

Round the standard of St. Gall a select body of men had rallied. The black streamers still floated in the air from the image on the cross, but the contest was doubtful. By word and action Ekkehard encouraged his companions not to give way, but it was Ellak himself who fought against them. The bodies of slain men and horses cumbered the ground in wild disorder. Sir Burkhard's sword had received a new baptism of blood in Ekkehard's hands; but in vain had he fiercely attacked Ellak the chieftain; for after having exchanged a few blows and thrusts they were separated again by other combatants.

The Hunnish leader was presently slain, however, and his death caused a panic among the Huns, who fled in wild disorder in the direction of the Rhine. The conquerors returned to the Hohentwiel, their helmets adorned with green fir-twigs, and leaving twelve of the brothers behind to watch the dead on the battlefield. Of the Huns, one hundred and eighty had fallen in battle, whilst the Suabian arrier-ban had lost ninety-six; those of the Reichenau eighteen, and those of St. Gall twenty.

Chapter X

HADUMOTH

MASTER SPAZZO, whose tongue had not been lazy in recounting his warlike deeds — and the number of the Huns he had slain increased with every recital, like a falling avalanche — now said with emphasis, "I have still a wartrophy to present, which I have destined for my gracious mistress herself."

He then went down to the under apartments, in one of which Cappan his prisoner lay on a bundle of straw. His wound had been dressed, and had proved not to be dangerous. "Get up, thou son of the Devil!" cried Master Spazzo, adding a rude kick to this invitation. The Hun rose, his face wearing a somewhat dubious expression. "Forward!" said Master Spazzo, indicating the direction in which he was to go. So they went upstairs and entered the hall. Here an imperious "Stop!" from Master Spazzo made the unfortunate wretch stand still, casting his eyes around with evident surprise.

With kindly interest Dame Hadwig looked at the strange specimen of humanity before her. Praxedis also had come near, and, turning to Master Spazzo, said, "One cannot say much for the beauty of your war-trophy, but it is curious enough."

The Duchess folded her hands. "And this is the nation before which the German empire has trembled!" exclaimed she. "You have queer fancies," she added, turning to Spazzo; "however, it was gallant of you to think of me, even in battle."

Meanwhile Ekkehard had been silently sitting at the window, looking out over the country. "In order to humiliate us," thought he, "the Lord has sent over the children of the desert, to be a warning to us and to teach us, even on the ruins of that which is perishable, to think of that which is eternal; the earth which covers the bodies of the slain is still fresh, and those left behind are already jesting, as if all had been but an empty dream."

Praxedis had approached him, and now playfully said, "Why did you not likewise bring home some keepsake from the battle, Professor? A wonderful Hunnic Amazon is said to have skirmished about there, and if you had caught her we should now have a nice pair of them."

"Ekkehard had to think of higher things than Hunnic women," said the Duchess bitterly, "and he knows how to be silent, as one who has taken a vow for that purpose. Why should we need to know how *he* fared in battle!"

This cutting speech deeply wounded the serious-minded man. Silently he walked out to fetch Sir Burkhard's sword, and, drawing it out of the scabbard, he laid it on the table before the Duchess. Fresh red spots were still glistening on the noble blade, and the edge showed many a new notch here and there. "Whether the schoolmaster was idle all the time, this sword may bear witness! I have not made my tongue the herald of my deeds!"

The Duchess was startled. She still bore him a grudge in her heart, and was sorely tempted to give it vent in an angry outburst; but the sword of Sir Burkhard called up manifold thoughts. So, restraining her passion, she held out her hand to Ekkehard. " I did not wish to offend you," said she.

The mildness of her voice was like a reproach to him, and he hesitated to take the proffered hand. He almost wanted to ask her pardon for his roughness, but the words clove to his tongue — and at that moment the door opened and he was spared the rest.

Hadumoth the little geese-driver came in. Shyly she stopped at the door, not venturing to speak. Her face, which was pale from want of sleep, bore the traces of recent tears.

" What is the matter with thee, my poor child?" called out Dame Hadwig. " Come hither!"

Then the little maiden came forward and kissed the Duchess' hand. She tried to speak, but violent sobs prevented her.

" Don't be afraid," said the Duchess, soothingly. Then she found words, and said, " I cannot take care of the geese any more; I must go away, and thou must give me a gold-piece, as big as thou hast. I cannot help it, but I must go!"

"And why must thou go, my child?" asked the Duchess. " Has any one wronged thee?"

" He has not come home again!"

" There are many who have not come home again; but thou must not go away on that account. Those who have fallen are now with our dear Lord in heaven. They are in a large beautiful garden, and are much happier than we are."

But Hadumoth, shaking her young little head, said, "Audifax is not with God; he is with the Huns. I have searched for him down in the valley, and he was not among

the dead men.   Besides, the charcoal-burners' boy from
Hohenstoffeln, who also went out with the archers, saw him-
self how he was taken prisoner.   I must go to fetch him.
I can find no peace if I don't!"

"But how wilt thou find him?"

"That I don't know.   I shall go where the others went.
They say that the world is very wide, but in the end I shall
find him; I feel sure of it.   The gold piece which thou art
to give me I will give to the Huns, and will say —'Let me
have Audifax for this,' and when I have him we shall both
come home again."

Dame Hadwig delighted in all that was extraordinary.
"From that child we might all learn something," she said,
lifting up the shy little Hadumoth to imprint a kiss on her
forehead.   "God is with thee, without thy knowing it.
Therefore, thy thoughts are great and bold."   The Duchess
then gave a large golden thaler to the child.   "Go out then,
with the Lord; it is a decree of providence."

All were deeply touched, and Ekkehard put his hands on
the little maiden's head as if to bless her.   "I thank you!"
said she, turning to go; then, once more looking round, she
added, "But if they will not let me have Audifax for one
gold piece only — ?"

"Then I will give thee another," said the Duchess.

Upon this, the child confidently walked away.

And Hadumoth really went out into the unknown world.
The gold piece, sewn up in her bodice, her pocket filled with
bread, and in her hand the staff which Audifax had once cut
for her from the dark green holly-bush.   That she did not
know the way and that her finding food and a shelter for
the night were doubtful things, she had not time to trouble
herself about.   The Huns have gone away toward the setting sun and have taken him with them, was her sole
thought.   The flowing Rhine and the setting sun were her
only waymarks, and Audifax her goal.

By and by the scenery became strange to her; the Bodensee looking smaller and narrower in the distance, and for-

eign hills rising before her, to hide the proud and familiar shape of the hill which was her home; but, nodding a last good-by to her Hegau mountains, Hadumoth walked on undauntedly.

Hadumoth spent the night in the cottage of an old deaf woman, but before the day had well dawned, she had already set out again on her journey. She noticed from a height, that the Rhine was flowing onward in large circuits; so she cut across the mountains, thus to get the start on the Huns. Two days she thus wandered on, sleeping one night in the open air on the mossy ground, and scarcely meeting a human being all the time, but in spite of all terrors and difficulties, she never once lost her courage.

[After much arduous wandering she finally met a fisherman, who led her within sight of the Hunnic camp at the entrance of a valley near the Rhine. It consisted of some tents and a few larger huts made of branches and straw, the horses being lodged in blockhouses of pine logs.]

In his tent lay Hornebog, who was now sole leader since Ellak's death; but in spite of all the cushions and carpets heaped around, he could find no rest. Erica, the flower-of-the-heath, was sitting by his side, playing with a golden bauble, which she wore round her neck on a silk ribbon.

Then there entered one of the Hunnic sentinels, accompanied by Hadumoth and Snewelin of Ellwangen as interpreter. The child had entered the camp, bravely passing the posts and not heeding their calls until they stopped her. Snewelin then explained Hadumoth's wish with regard to the prisoner boy.

"Tell them also that I can pay them a ransom," said Hadumoth, undoing the seam of her bodice to get at the gold piece. She handed it to the chieftain, who laughed immoderately, joined by Erica.

"What a crazy land!" exclaimed Hornebog, when his laughter had subsided. "The men cut off their hair, and the children do what would honor a warrior. If, instead of this little maiden, the armed men from the lake had followed us, it would have put us into an awkward position."

A sudden suspicion now crossing his mind, he cast a searching look at the child. "If she were a spy—!" exclaimed he. But Erica now rose and patted Hadumoth's head. "Thou shalt stay with me," said she, "for I want something to play with since my black horse is dead and my Ellak is dead—"

"Take the brat away!" Hornebog now called out angrily. "Have we come here to play with children?" Then Erica saw that a storm was brewing in the chieftain's bosom, and, taking the little maiden by the hand, led her out.

Where the camp receded toward the mountain, between some sheltering pieces of rock, a temporary cooking-place had been erected, which was the undisputed realm of the woman of the wood. Audifax was kneeling before the biggest of the kettles, blowing into the fire; but now he jumped up and gave a loud shriek, for he had beheld his little friend. He had become pale and haggard, and his eyes were dimmed by tears, which had touched nobody. "Mind that thou dost not hurt the children, old baboon!" cried Erica.

Then Hadumoth went over to where the boy was, who silently held out his hand to her; but out of his dark blue eyes there came a look which told its own story of woe and suffering and the longing wish to regain his liberty. Hadumoth, likewise, stood quietly before him. She had often imagined a joyous and touching meeting, but all these pictures had faded away now. The greatest joy sends its gratitude up to heaven in a voiceless prayer.

When it became dark and his tyrant went away, Audifax's tongue loosened. "Oh, I have so much to tell thee, Hadumoth!" whispered he. "I know where the treasure of the Huns is! The woman of the wood has it in her keeping. Two big boxes stand under her couch in yonder hut; I have looked into them myself, and they were quite full of jewels and diadems and golden trinkets. I have paid dearly for seeing them, though!"

He lifted up his leathern hat. One half of his right ear had been cut off.

"The woman of the wood came home before I could close the lid again. It has hurt me a good deal, Hadumoth, but I shall pay her back some day!"

"I will help thee," said his companion.

For a long time the two whispered on together, for no sleep came to the eyes of the happy ones. The noise in the camp was hushed now, and the shadows of night brooded over the valley. They sat quietly together for a while; then Audifax gave a violent start, and Hadumoth could feel the trembling of his hand. On the other side of the Rhine, on the summit of the black looking mountains, a sudden light shone out. It was like a torch swung around, and then thrown away.

From the height of the Bötzberg another flame darted up, likewise describing a fiery circuit in the air. It was the same signal. And yonder, over in the Black Forest, on the same place where the burning torch had first been visible, there now arose a mighty flame, lighting up the dark starless night. The guard in the valley uttered a piercing whistle, and the inhabitants of the camp began to stir everywhere. The woman of the wood came back also, and threateningly called out, "What art thou dreaming about, boy? Quick, put the nags to the cart and saddle my sumpter-horse!"

Audifax silently obeyed her orders.

The cart stood ready, and the sumpter-horse was tied to a stake. Carefully the old woman approached it with two panniers, which she hung over its back, and then, bringing out the two boxes from her hut, put one in each, covering them up afterward with some hay. When she had done this she peered out anxiously into the darkness. Everything was quiet again. The wine had insured a sound sleep to the Hunnic warriors.

" 'Tis nothing," muttered the woman of the wood, "we can take the horses back again;" but the next moment she started up, almost blinded. The mountains rising behind the camp had suddenly become alive with hundreds of

torches and fire-brands; and from all sides there resounded
the loud and terrific cry of battle. From the Rhine dark
masses of armed men were swiftly approaching; on all the
mountain summits tremendous bonfires were burning. Up
now, ye sleepers!—It was too late, for already the fire-
brands came flying into the Hunnic camp. Pitifully sounded
the frightened neighing of the horses, whose large shed
was already burning. Dark figures stormed the camp on
all sides. This time King Death was coming with blazing
torch-light, and he who brought him was the old Knight
Irminger, the owner of the Frickgau.

"Lost, everything lost!" muttered the woman of the
wood, lifting her hand up to her forehead. Then she untied
the sumpter-horse, to harness it likewise before her cart.
Meanwhile Audifax was standing in the dark, biting his
lips that he might not scream out with delight at this
unexpected turn of affairs. A trembling reflection of the
flames played on his excited countenance; everything was
boiling within him. For some time he stood there, gazing
fixedly at the tumult and the fighting of the dark figures
before him. "Now I know what I must do," whispered he
into Hadumoth's ear. He had taken up a big stone, and,
springing up at the woman of the wood with the agility of
a wild cat, he struck her down. After this he quickly
pulled away the sumpter-horse, upon the saddle of which
he placed the trembling Hadumoth with the sudden strength
of a man. "Take hold of the pommel!" cried he. Then,
jumping up himself, he seized the reins, and the horse no
sooner felt the unwonted burden than it galloped off into the
night, frightened by the glare and noise around. Audifax
never staggered, though his heart was beating wildly. The
blinding smoke made him shut his eyes, and thus they sped
onward—over the corpses of the dead and through the
crowds of fighting men. After a while the noise became
fainter in the distance, and the horse began to slacken its
pace. It was taking the children toward the Rhine—they
were saved!

Thus they rode on through the long dark night, scarcely once daring to look about them. At dawn the two children stood before the falls of the Rhine. Then Audifax jumped to the ground, and, taking down the tired little Hadumoth, as well as the two baskets, allowed the brave animal to graze.

Presently the sun cast his first rays on the dashing waters, which caught them and built them up into a glittering, many-colored rainbow. Then Audifax went up to the baskets, to take out one of the boxes; this, on being opened, disclosed its glistening contents of pure gold and silver. The long-coveted treasure was found at last, had become his own—not by spells and nightly conjurations, but by the use of his hands and by seizing the favorable opportunity.

Of every kind of article it contained he picked out four —a casket, a ring, a coin, and a bracelet, and with them approached the brink of the waters.

"Hadumoth," said he, "here I think that God must be; for His rainbow is hovering over the waters. I will make Him a thank-offering."

Stepping on a projecting rock, he flung in with a strong hand first the casket, then the ring, coin, and bracelet; and then kneeling down, Hadumoth kneeling by his side, they prayed for a long time, and thanked God.

Chapter XI

THE RETURN OF THE CHILDREN

There was a great deal to arrange and put in order, after the driving away of the Huns. The widows and orphans of the slain arrier-banmen, as well as all those whose houses had been burnt and whose harvests had been destroyed, came to sue for assistance. Help was given to every one, as far as this was possible. With Reichenau and St. Gall there was also much business to transact, for ecclesiastics seldom forget to present their bills for any services that they have rendered. Far away in the Rhine valley, where the Breisach mountain with its dark, scorched rocks narrows the bed of the river, the Duchess owned some property, called Saspach, and this would have suited the pious brothers of the Reichenau admirably.

One day, when Dame Hadwig had not appeared quite disinclined to make the donation, was followed by the arrival of the Subprior in the early morning, bringing a parchment with him on which the whole formula of the donation was written down.

"The Lord Abbot wanted to save our gracious sovereign the trouble of writing the donation herself," said the Subprior, "and it would be a very desirable thing for the Abbot if I could bring him back the deed, signed and sealed by Your Highness, today. It is only on account of the order and precision in the monastery's archives, the Abbot said."

Dame Hadwig, casting a haughty look at the man, then said, "Tell your Abbot that I am just now summing up the account of how much the quartering of the brothers on the Hohentwiel has cost me in kitchen and cellar. Tell him likewise that we have our own scriveners, if we should feel so inclined, to give away landed property on the Rhine, and that"—she wanted to add a few more bitter words, but the Subprior here fell in coaxingly, telling her a number of cases where Christian kings and princes had done the same. But the Duchess, turning her back on him, left him standing in the hall. Having reached the entrance she turned round once more, and, with an indescribable movement of the hand, said, "If you wish to go, you had better go at once!" So he made his retreat.

[Cappan, the captured Hun, has won the affections of Friderun, a maiden who worked in house and garden. In due time the Hun is baptized and the marriage ceremony is performed the same day. In connection with the wedding a rustic festival is arranged, which is attended also by Dame Hadwig and Ekkehard.]

It was one of those soft, balmy evenings, such as Sir Burkhart of Hohenvels enjoyed in later times from his huge tower on the lake "when the air is tempered and mingled with sun-fire;" the distance was shrouded in a soft glowing haze. He who has ever looked down from those quiet mountain-tops, when, on a bright radiant day, the sun is slowly sinking down, arrayed in all the splendor of his royal robes, when heaven and earth are palpitating with warmth and light, while dark purple shadows fill up the valleys, and a margin-glory, like liquid gold, illumines the snowy alpine peaks, he will not easily forget that aspect; and perchance when sitting later within his dusky walls, the memory of it will rise in his heart, as soft and bewitchingly sweet as a song uttered in the melting tones of the South.

Ekkehard was sitting there with a serious expression on his countenance, his head supported by his right hand.

"He is no longer as he used to be," said Dame Hadwig to the Greek maid; whereupon she approached Ekkehard. He started up from his mossy seat, as if he saw a ghost.

"All alone, and away from the merry-makers?" asked she. "What are you doing here?"

"I am wondering where real happiness may be found," replied Ekkehard.

"Happiness?" repeated the Duchess. "'Fortune is a fickle dame, who seldom stays long anywhere,' says the proverb. Has she never paid you a visit?"

"Probably not," said the monk, riveting his eyes on the ground. With renewed vigor the music and noise of the dancers struck the ear.

"Those who lightly tread the green meadow-lands, and know how to express with their feet what oppresses their hearts, are happy," continued he. "Perhaps one requires very little to be happy; but, above all"—pointing over to the distant glittering Alpine peaks—"there must be no distant heights which our feet may never hope to reach."

"I do not understand you," coldly said the Duchess; but her heart thought otherwise than her tongue. "And how fares your Virgil?" asked she, changing the conversation. "During those days of anxiety and warfare I am afraid that dust and cobwebs may have settled on it."

"He will always find a refuge in my heart, even if the parchment should decay," replied he. "Only a few moments ago his verses in praise of agriculture passed through my mind. With a feeling almost of envy Virgil's picture rose before me —

'Simple and artless, his life is with many a blessing surrounded,
  Rich with many a joy and peaceful rest after labor —
  Grottoes and shady retreats, affording a shelter for slumber.'"

"You well know how to adapt his verses to life," said Dame Hadwig. "And then the joys of winter, when the snow rises like a wall up to the straw-thatched roof, so that daylight is sorely perplexed through what chink or crevice it may creep into the house." * * *

"Even such a dilemma I could bear with composure, and Virgil too knows how this may be done."—

"Many a one, in the winter, will sit by the glare of the fire,
  Late in the evening then; the light-giving torches preparing —
  During the time that his wife his favorite ditties is singing,
  Throwing the shuttle along, with a dextrous hand, through the texture."

"His wife?" maliciously asked the Duchess. "But if he has no wife!"—

"And *may* not have a wife?" said Ekkehard absently. His forehead was burning; he covered it with his right hand. Wherever he looked, the sight pained him. Yonder, the loud joy of the wedding-guests; here, the Duchess; and, in the distance, the glittering mountains. An inexpressible pain was gnawing at his heart, but his lips remained closed. "Be strong and silent," he said to himself.

He was in reality no longer as he used to be. The undisturbed peace of his lonely cell had forsaken him. The late

battle, as well as all the excitement brought on by the
Hunnic invasion, had widened his thoughts; and the signs
of favor which the Duchess had shown him had called up
a fierce conflict in his heart. Day and night he was haunted
by the recollection — how she had stood before him, hanging
the relic round his neck and giving him the sword that had
been her husband's; and in evil moments, self-reproaches
— misty and unexpressed as yet — that he had received
these gifts so silently, passed through his troubled soul.
Dame Hadwig had no idea of all that was stirring in his
heart. She had accustomed herself to think more indifferently of him since she had been humiliated by his apparent
misunderstanding of her; but as often as she saw him
again, with his noble forehead clouded by grief and with
that mute appealing look in his eyes, then the old game
began afresh.

"If you take such delight in agricultural pursuits," said
she lightly, "I can easily help you to that. The Abbot of
Reichenau has provoked me. To think of asking for the
pearl of my estates, as if it were a mere crumb of bread
which one shakes down from the tablecloth without so much
as looking at it!"

Here something rustled in the bushes behind them, but
they did not notice it. A dark brown color might have
been seen between the foliage. Was it a fox or a monk's
garment?

"I will appoint you steward of it," continued Dame Hadwig. "Then you will have all that, the lack of which has
made you melancholy today; and far more still."

Ekkehard's eyes were still resting on the ground.

"I can also give you a description of your life there,
though I have not Virgil's talent for painting. Fancy that
autumn has come. You have led a healthy life, getting
up with the sun and going to bed with the chickens — and
so vintage-time has arrived. From all sides men and maids
are descending, with baskets full of ripe luscious grapes.
You stand at the door looking on —"

Again the rustling was heard.

"—And wondering how the wine will be, and whose health you are going to drink in it. Then you see a cloud of dust rising on the highroad from Breisach. Soon after, horses and carriages become visible, and — well, Master Ekkehard, who is coming?"

Ekkehard, who had scarcely followed her recital, shyly echoed, "Who?"

"Who else but your mistress, who will not give up her sovereign right of examining her subjects' doings!"

"And then?"

"Then? Then I shall gather information about how Master Ekkehard has been fulfilling his duties; and they will all say: 'He is good and earnest, and if he would not think and brood quite so much, and not read so often in his parchments, we should like him still better.'"

"And then?" asked he once more. His voice sounded strange.

"Then I shall say in the words of Scripture: 'Well done, thou good and faithful servant; thou hast been faithful over a few things, I will make thee ruler over many things.'"

Ekkehard stood there like one but half conscious. He lifted one arm and let it fall again; a tear trembled in his eye; he was very unhappy.

* * * At the same time a man softly crept out from the bushes. As soon as he felt the grass again under his feet he let his habit, which had been gathered up, drop down. Looking stealthily back once more at the two standing there, he shook his head like one who has made a discovery. He had certainly not gone into the bushes to gather violets!

The wedding-feast had by slow stages reached that point where a general chaos threatens. The mead was having its effect on the different minds. Suddenly the tall Friderun gave a loud shriek, upon which all heads were turned round to see what might have caused it.

Audifax and Hadumoth were there, on their way back from the Huns, and had been discovered first by the tall bride. Audifax led the horse that carried the treasure-boxes, by the reins, and with beaming faces the two children walked side by side. They now caught sight of the Duchess, standing with Ekkehard under the pine-tree. The wild burst of joy had interrupted their agricultural conversation. Praxedis came bounding along to impart the wondrous news, and, following on her heels, the two youthful runaways walked hand in hand. They both knelt down before Dame Hadwig, Hadumoth holding up her thaler and Audifax two big gold coins. He tried to speak, but his voice failed him. Then Dame Hadwig, with lofty grace, addressed the surrounding group.

" The silliness of my two young subjects affords me an opportunity to give them a proof of my favor. Be witnesses thereof.''

Breaking off a hazel-wand from a neighboring bush, she approached the children; and after first shaking the golden coins out of their hands, so that they flew into the grass, she touched their heads with the branch, saying, ''Arise, and scissors shall never cut off your hair again. As vassals belonging to the castle of Hohentwiel, ye have knelt down; as freedmen, stand up again; and may ye be as fond of each other in your free state as you were before!''

The two children arose. They had well understood what had happened. A strange dizzy feeling had seized the little goatherd's brain. The dream of his youth — liberty, golden treasure — had become true; a lasting reality, for all days to come!

When the mist before his eyes had cleared away again, he beheld Ekkehard's serious countenance, and throwing himself at his feet with Hadumoth, he cried, '' Father Ekkehard, we thank you also for having been good to us! ''

Ekkehard let his blue eyes rest for a while on the two children. Laying his hands on their heads and making the sign of the cross over them, he softly said to himself, '' Where is happiness? ''

Late at night Rudimann the cellarer rode back to his monastery. The ford being dry he could cross it on horseback. From the Abbot's cell a gleam of light still fell on the lake. So Rudimann knocked at his door, and, but half opening it, said, "My ears have taken in more today than they liked to hear. 'Tis all over with the Saspach estate on the Rhine. She is going to make that milksop of St. Gall steward of it." * * *

"*Varium et mutabile semper femina!* Woman is ever fickle and changeable!" murmured the Abbot, without looking round. "Good night!"

CHAPTER XI

GUNZO VERSUS EKKEHARD

DURING the time in which all that has been so far related was happening on the shores of the Bodensee, far away in the Belgian lands, in the monastery of the holy Amandus *sur l'Elnon*, a monk, Gunzo by name, had been sitting in his cell. Day after day, whenever the convent rules permitted it, he sat there transfixed as by a spell. In his cell every article of furniture, nay, even the floor, was covered with parchments, for almost all the monastery's books had emigrated to his chamber. There he sat reading, and thinking, and reading again, as if he wanted to find out the first cause of all being. On his right lay the psalms and holy Scriptures; on his left the remains of heathenish wisdom. Everything he peered over assiduously, now and then a malicious smile interrupting the seriousness of his studies, upon which he would hastily scribble some lines on a narrow strip of parchment.

On a soft, balmy, summer evening, when his pen had again flitted over the patient parchment, like a will-o'-the-wisp, emitting a soft creaking sound, it suddenly began to slacken its pace — then made a pause; a few strokes more, and he executed a tremendous flourish on the remaining space below, so that the ink made an involuntary shower of spots,

like black constellations. He had written the word *finis,*
and with a deep sigh of relief he rose from his chair, like a
man from whose mind some great weight has been taken.
Casting a long look on what lay before him, black on white,
he solemnly exclaimed, "Praised be the holy Amandus!
We are avenged!"

At this great and elevating moment he had finished a libel,
dedicated to the venerable brotherhood on the Reichenau,
and aimed at—Ekkehard the custodian at St. Gall. When
the fair-haired interpreter of Virgil took leave of his monastery and went to the Hohentwiel, he would never, though
he had searched the remotest corners of his memory, have
had an inkling of the fact that there was a man living whose
greatest wish and desire was to take vengeance on him; for
he was inoffensive and kindhearted. And yet so it was.
The work of Brother Gunzo, which never benefited any of
the few who read it, has come down to posterity. Let the
monstrous deed, which so excited the Gallic scholar's ire,
therefore be told in his own words.

"For a long space of time"—thus he wrote to his friends
on the Reichenau—"The revered and beloved King Otto
had carried on negotiations with the different Italian
princes with the view of letting me come over to his lands.
But as I was neither of such low birth nor so dependent
upon any that I could have been forced to this step, he himself sent a petition to me, of which the consequence was that
I pledged myself to obey his call. Thus it happened that,
when he left Italy, I soon followed him, and when I did so I
did it with the hope that my coming, whilst harming no one,
might benefit many; for what sacrifices does the love of
one's fellow-creatures, and the desire to please, not entice
us into? Thus I traveled onward, not like a Briton, armed
with the sharp weapons of censure, but in the service of
love and science.

"Over high mountain-passes and steep ravines and valleys I arrived at last at the monastery of St. Gall, hoping
to find a peaceful resting-place within the monastic walls

—a hope which was strengthened on beholding the frequent bending of heads, the sober-colored garments, soft-treading steps, and sparing use of speech prevalent there.

"Among their numbers there was also a young convent-pupil and his uncle, who—well, who was no better than he should be! They called him a worthy teacher of the school; although to me he appeared rather to look at the world with the eyes of a turtle-dove. Of this languid-looking wiseacre I shall presently have to say more. Listen, and judge of his deed!

" Walking up and down, he instigated the convent-pupil to become a partaker of his base design.

'Night had come, and with it the time for grief-stilling slumber:
  After the sumptuous meal Bacchus exacted his rights'—

when an evil star prompted my making a mistake in the use of a *casus,* in the Latin table-speeches we held together—using an *accusativus,* where I ought to have put an *ablativus.*

" Now it became evident in what kind of arts that far-famed teacher had instructed his pupil, all day long. ' Such an offense against the laws of grammar deserved the rod,' mockingly said that little imp to *me,* the well-tried scholar; and he further produced a rhymed libel, which his fine teacher must have prompted him to, and which caused a rough cisalpine burst of laughter in the refectory at the expense of the stranger guest.

" Judge now, ye venerable brothers, what insults have been heaped on me, and what must be the character of the man who can upbraid his fellow-creature for mistaking an *ablativus!* "

The man who, intending only a harmless jest, had committed this fearful crime, was Ekkehard. Only a few weeks before the sudden turn in his fate brought him to the Hohentwiel the terrible deed had been done! With the coming morn on the next day he had forgotten the conversation that had taken place at supper with the overbearing Italian, but in the bosom of him who had been

convicted of the wrong *ablativus* was matured a rancor
as fierce and gnawing as that which, caused by the war-
deeds of Achilles, drove the Telamonian Aïas to destroy
himself, and which followed him even into Hades.

Therefore Gunzo was bent on taking his revenge on
Ekkehard, and he had an able and sharp pen, and had spent
many a month over his work, so that it became a masterpiece of its kind. It was a black soup made up of hundreds
of learned quotations, richly seasoned with pepper and
wormwood and all those spicy, bitter things which, before
all others, give such a delicious flavor to the controversies
of ecclesiastical men.

The treatise was divided into two parts, the first serving
to prove that only an ignorant and uncultivated mind could
be shocked by so slight an error as the mistaking of a
casus; while the second was written in order to convince
the world that the author himself was the wisest, most
learned, and at the same time most pious, of all his contemporaries. For this end he had read the classics and
the holy Scriptures in the sweat of his brow, so that he could
make a list of all the places in which the caprice or negli-
gence of the author had also misplaced an *ablativus*.

"Praised be the holy Amandus!" exclaimed Gunzo once
more, when the last word of his work* had been written
down. Then he walked up to his metal looking-glass, and,
gazing for a long time at his own reflection, as if it were
of the greatest importance for him to study the countenance of the man who had annihilated the Ekkehard of
St. Gall, he finally made a deep bow to himself.

When the meal was over, he invited some of his friends
to come up to his cell in as mysterious a way as if they
were about to dig for some hidden treasure, and when they
were all assembled he read his work over to them. The
monastery of St. Gallus, with its libraries, schools, and
learned teachers, was far too famous throughout all Chris-

---

* The major portion of which is here omitted.

tendom for the disciples of St. Amandus not to listen to the whizzing of Gunzo's arrows with a secret joy. Cleverness and a blameless life are often far more offensive to the world than sin and wickedness. Therefore they nodded their hoary heads approvingly, as Gunzo read out the choice bits.

The next day Gunzo packed up his epistle in a tin box, and this again in a linen bag. The way of a bondsman of the monastery led up the Rhine. So Gunzo put the tin case round his neck, and a few weeks later it was delivered safe and sound into the hands of the gate-keeper at Reichenau. As Gunzo well knew his friends there he had dedicated the libel to them.

When he had come to the description of Ekkehard's curly hair and fine shoes, the Abbot was nearly convulsed with laughter. "Rudimann!" he called out through the passage. Rudimann instantly made his appearance.

"I suppose you remember the last vintage-time," began the Abbot, "as well as a blow given to you by a certain milk-sop to whom a fanciful Duchess is now about to give certain lands?"

"I remember the blow," replied Rudimann with a bashful smile, like a maiden who is questioned about her lover.

"That blow has been returned by some one, with a strong and unrelenting hand. You may be satisfied. Read this," handing Gunzo's parchment to him.

"By your leave," said Rudimann, stepping up to the window.

"What a precious gift from above is extensive knowledge and a fine style," exclaimed he. "The brother Ekkehard is done for. He cannot dare show his face again."

"'Tis not quite so far yet," said the Abbot. "But then, that which now is not may yet be in the future. The learned brother Gunzo is helping us. His epistle must not be allowed to rot unread: so you can have some copies taken—better six than three. That fine young gentleman must be driven away from the Hohentwiel. I am not over fond of yellow-beaked birds, who pretend to sing better than their elders. Some cold water poured on his tonsure will benefit him. We will send a note to our brother in St. Gall, urging him to command his return. How is it with the list of his sins?"

"The custodian of St. Gallus has become subject to haughtiness and insolence, since the day on which he left his monastery. Without moving his lips to frame a greeting, he passes by brothers whose age and intellect ought to claim his reverence. Moreover, he presumed to preach the sermon on the holy day when we beat the Huns, although such an important and solemn office ought to have been performed by one of the abbots. Further, he presumed to baptize a heathenish prisoner, albeit such a baptism should have been superintended by the regular priest of the parish and not by one who ought to attend at the gate of the monastery of St. Gallus.

"What may still arise out of the constant intercourse of the forward youth with his noble mistress, He who searcheth all hearts alone can tell! Already, at the wedding-feast of that baptized heathen, it was observed that he did not shun meetings in solitary places with that beauteous dame, and that he heaved frequent sighs, like a shot buck. Likewise it has been remarked with heartfelt sorrow that a Greek maiden, as fickle and unstable as a will-o'-the-wisp, is flickering about him; so that, what is left undone by the mistress may be finished by her hand-maiden, of whose orthodoxy even one is not fully assured. Now a frivolous woman is bitterer than death, according to Scripture; she is a bait of the evil one, and her heart is a net, and only he who pleases God can escape her wiles."

It was a most becoming and just thing for Rudimann, the protector of the uppermaid Kerhildis, to be so well versed in the words of the Preacher.

"Enough," said the Abbot. "Chapter Twenty-nine, treating of the calling back of absent brothers! It will do, and I have a sort of presentiment that the fickle lady will

soon flutter about on her rock, like an old swallow whose
nestling has been taken away. Good-by, sweetheart. And
Saspach will yet become ours!''

"Amen!'' murmured Rudimann.

Chapter XIII

THE MISSION OF MASTER SPAZZO, THE CHAMBERLAIN.

EARLY on a cool pleasant summer day, Ekkehard walked
out of the castle-gate into the breezy morning air. He had
passed a sleepless night, during which he had paced up
and down in his chamber. The Duchess had called up a
host of wild thoughts in his heart, and in his head there
was a buzzing and humming as if a covey of wild ducks
were flying about there. He shunned Dame Hadwig's
presence, and yet longed every moment that he was away
to be near her. The old happy ingenuousness had taken
wing. His ways had become absent-minded and variable;
in short, the time which has never been spared yet to mortal
man, and which Godfrey of Strassburg describes '' as an
everpresent pain in a continual state of bliss '' had come
for him.

At the foot of the hill there lay a piece of weather-
beaten rock, over which an elder-tree spread its boughs,
richly laden with luxuriant white blossoms. Ekkehard sat
down on the rock, and after dreamily gazing into the distance for some time drew out from under his habit a neatly
bound little book, and began to read. It was neither a
breviary nor the Psalter. It was called, '' The Song of
Solomon,'' and it was not good for him to read it. To be
sure, they had once taught him that the lily-scented song
expressed the longing for the church, the true bride of the
soul, and in his younger days he had studied it, undisturbed by the gazelle eyes and the dovelike cheeks and
waist, slender as the palm-tree, of the Sulamite woman —
but now — now he read it with other eyes. A soft dreami-
ness came over him.

" Who is it that looketh forth as the morning, fair as
the moon, clear as the sun, and terrible as an army with
banners? " He looked up to the towers of the Hohentwiel,
which were glittering in the first rays of the morning sun,
and there found the answer. And again he read: " I sleep,
but my heart waketh; it is the voice of my beloved, that
knocketh, saying: ' Open to me my sister, my love, my dove,
for my head is filled with dew, and my locks with the drops
of night.' " A stirring breeze shook down some of the
white blossoms on the little book. Ekkehard did not shake
them off. He had bent down his head, and was sitting
there immovable.

[Ekkehard is disturbed in his reveries by the loud shrieks
of Cappan, who has been accused by a convent-farmer of
having made the storm that has destroyed the farmer's
crops. The farmer and his servants are on the point of
stoning the converted Hun, when Ekkehard arrives in the
nick of time and shields Cappan with his own body.]

This had its effect.

The men looked at one another dumbfounded, until one
of them turned round to go away, and the others following
his example the convent-farmer was soon left standing
there all alone.

" You are taking the part of the land-destroyer! " he
cried angrily, but as Ekkehard gave no answer, he likewise
dropped the stone from his hand and went away grumbling.

Poor Cappan found himself in a most pitiable condition;
a stone had caused a wound on his head which was bleeding profusely. Ekkehard first washed his head with some
rain-water, made the sign of the cross over it to stop the
bleeding, and then dressed the wound as well as he could.
He thought of the parable of the Good Samaritan. The
wounded man looked up at him gratefully, and soon Ekkehard was able to lead him slowly to the castle. The foot
that had been wounded in the late battle also began hurt-
ing Cappan again, so that he limped on, with suppressed
groans.

On the Hohentwiel their arrival was the cause of great and general excitement, for everybody liked the Hun. The Duchess descended into the courtyard, bestowing a friendly nod on Ekkehard as recognition of his kindliness and compassion. The trespass of the monastery's vassal against her subject raised her just resentment.

"That shall not be forgotten," said she. "Be comforted, for they shall pay thee damages for thy wounded pate, that will equal a dowry. And for the broken peace of the realm we shall decree the higest possible fine. A few pounds of silver shall not be sufficient. These convent-people grow to be as insolent as their masters!"

But the most indignant of all was Master Spazzo, the chamberlain.

"What if he was our enemy before? Now he is baptized and I am his godfather, and bound to take care of the welfare of his soul as well as of his body. Be content, god-child!" cried he, rattling his sword on the stone flags, "for as soon as thy scratch has been mended I shall accompany thee on thy first walk, and then we will settle accounts with the convent-farmer. Hail and thunder, that we will, in a way to make the chips fly off his head!"

"Where was the trespass committed?" asked the Duchess.

"They dragged him from the boundary stone with the raised half-moon, to the Hunnic mound," said Ekkehard.

"Consequently the deed has been done, even on our own ground and territory," indignantly exclaimed the Duchess. "That is too much! Master Spazzo, you must to horse!"

"We must to horse!" echoed the chamberlain fiercely.

"And demand even today that the Abbot of Reichenau shall pay us both damages and fine for the peace which has been broken, and also give us all possible satisfaction. Our sovereign rights shall not be trampled upon by monastic insolence!"

"Shall not be trampled upon by monastic insolence!" repeated Master Spazzo, still fiercer than before.

His green velvet waistcoat and gold-bordered chamberlain's mantle he quietly left in his wardrobe, choosing, instead, an old and shabby gray suit. After having donned this he put on the large greaves he had worn on the day of the battle. Fastening on them the largest spurs he possessed, he tramped up and down a few times to try their effect. Finally he stuck three waving feathers in his steel cap, and hung his sword over his shoulders. Thus arrayed, he came down into the courtyard, and in less than an hour and a half he had reached the cloister-gate.

Master Spazzo strode over the cloister-yard to the gate, which, through the cross-passage, led into the interior. He had assumed his heaviest tread. The bell that announced dinner was just ringing. One of the brothers now came quickly across the yard, and Master Spazzo seized him by his garment.

"Call down the Abbot!" said he. The monk looked at him in mute astonishment, then, casting a side look at the chamberlain's worn hunting-suit, replied, "It is the hour for our midday meal. If you are invited, which however seems rather doubtful to me"—with another ironical look at Master Spazzo's outward man; but he was spared the end of his sentence, for the chamberlain dealt the hungry brother such a genuine cuff that he was sent reeling into the yard again, like a well-thrown shuttle-cock. The midday sun shone on the smooth tonsure of the prostrate man.

The Abbot had already been informed of the violent assault which the convent-farmer had made on one of the Duchess' subjects. He now heard the noise in the courtyard and, on stepping up to the window, was just in time to see the pious brother Ivo sent flying out into the yard. "Happy is he who knows the secret causes of things," says Virgil, and Abbot Wazmann was in that happy condition. He had seen Master Spazzo's feathers nodding over at him with a threatening aspect, from the sombre cross-passage.

"Call down the Abbot!" was again shouted up from the courtyard, in a tone that made the panes of the little cell-windows vibrate.

Abbot **Wazmann** had sent for Rudimann the cellarer. "All this annoyance we surely owe to that green-beak of St. Gall! Oh, Gunzo, Gunzo! No one ought to wish ill to his neighbor, but still I cannot help revolving in my mind whether our strong-handed yeomen had not done better to hurl their stones at that hypocrite Ekkehard, rather than at the Hunnic wizard!"

A monk now shyly entered the Abbot's room.

"You are desired to come down," said he in low accents. "There is somebody down stairs who shouts and commands, like a mighty man."

"There's no time to be lost," said the Abbot. "Set out as quickly as you can, Cellarer, and express our deep regret to the Duchess. Take some silver coins out of the convent-box as smart-money for the wounded man, and say that we will have prayers offered for his recovery. Get along! You are his godfather and a clever man."

"It will be a rather difficult task," said Rudimann. "She is sure to be downright exasperated."

"Take her some present," said the Abbot. "Children and women are easily bribed."

"What sort of a present?" Rudimann was about to ask, when the door was thrown open and Master Spazzo came in. His face wore the right expression.

"By the life of my Duchess!" exclaimed he. "Has the Abbot of this rats' nest poured lead into his ears, or has the gout got hold of his feet, that he does not come down to receive his visitors?"

"We are taken by surprise," said the Abbot. "Let me welcome you now!" He lifted his right forefinger to give him the blessing.

"I need no such welcome," returned Master Spazzo. "The Devil is the patron saint of this day. We have been insulted, grossly insulted! We exact a fine—two hundred pounds of silver at the least. Out with it! Murder and rebellion! The sovereign rights shall not be trampled upon by monastic insolence! We are an ambassador!"

He rattled his spurs on the floor. " Pay me at once, so that I can go on again. The air is bad here, very bad indeed."

"Allow me," said the Abbot, " but we never permit a guest to depart in anger from our island. You are sharp and urgent because you have not yet dined. Don't disdain a meal, such as the monastery can offer, and let us talk of business afterward."

That a fellow in return for his rudeness is kindly pressed to stay to dinner made some impression on the chamberlain's mind. " The sovereign rights shall not be trampled upon by monastic insolence," muttered he once more; but the Abbot pointed over to the open cloister-kitchen. The fair-haired kitchen boy was turning the spit before the fire and smacking his lips, for a delicious smell of the roast meat had just then entered his nostrils. Some covered dishes, calling up pleasant anticipations, were standing in the background, while a monk, bearing a huge wine-jug, was just coming up from the cellar. The aspect was too tempting to be resisted any longer; so Master Spazzo laid aside his frown and accepted the invitation.

When he had arrived at the third dish his insulting speeches became more rare, and when the red wine of Meersburg was sparkling in the beaker they ceased entirely. The red wine of Meersburg was good.

Meanwhile Rudimann rode out of the convent-gate. The fisherman of Ermatingen had caught a gigantic salmon, which lay, fresh and glittering, in the vaults below; this fish had been selected by Rudimann as a suitable present for appeasing the Duchess. Master Spazzo had ridden over in the haughtiest fashion, whereas Rudimann now assumed his most humble expression. He spoke shyly and in low accents, when he asked for the Duchess. " She is in the garden," was the reply. "And my pious confrere Ekkehard?" asked the cellarer.

" He has accompanied the wounded Cappan to his cottage on the Hohenstoffeln, where he is nursing him; he is not expected home before night.''

'' This I am truly sorry to hear,'' said Rudimann, with an evil expression of spite hovering about his lips. He then had the salmon unpacked and put on the granite table in the middle of the courtyard. '' He does not come home before nightfall,'' muttered Rudimann, breaking off a strong branch from the tree, a piece of which he put between the jaws of the fish, so that it remained with wide open mouth. With some of the leaves he carefully lined the inside, and then, diving down into his breast-pocket, drew out the parchment leaves of Gunzo's libel; rolling them up neatly, he then stuck them between the jaws of the salmon.

The Duchess was now seen approaching them. Humbly Rudimann walked forward to meet her, and, imploring her indulgence for the convent's bondsman, told her how sorry the Abbot was, and spoke with appreciation of the wounded man. '' And may an unworthy present show you at least the good will of your ever faithful Reichenau,'' concluded he, stepping aside, so that the salmon could shine out in full glory. The Duchess smiled, half reconciled already; and now her eye caught the parchment roll. ''And that?'' said she inquiringly.

'' The latest production of literature!'' said Rudimann. With a deep bow he then took leave, and, remounting his mule, hastily set out again on his way home.

The red wine of Meersburg was good, and Master Spazzo was not accustomed to treat drinking as a thing that could be done quickly. He persevered before the wine-jug like a general besieging a city, and, sitting immovably on his bench, drank like a man, silently, but much.

'' The red wine is the most sensible institution of the monastery. Have you more of it in the cellar?'' he inquired of the Abbot when the first jug was emptied. His desire to drink more was meant as a politeness, and a sign of reconciliation. So the second jug was brought up, and this was followed by others, until Master Spazzo's tongue was silent. A sweet placid smile now settled on the chamberlain's lips. He stepped up to the Abbot to embrace him.

" Friend and brother, much beloved old wine-jug! What if I were to dig out one of thine eyes?" he tried to say with stammering tongue, but he could only utter some unintelligible sounds. He pressed the Abbot vehemently to his bosom, treading on his feet at the same time with his heavy boots. Abbot Wazmann had already been deliberating within himself whether he should not offer a bed for the night to his exhausted guest, but the embrace and the pain in his toes changed his hospitable designs, and he took care that the chamberlain set out on his return.

Master Spazzo's horse stood ready saddled in the cloister-yard. He pressed the steel-cap down on his head, and tightly grasped the reins. Something was still weighing on his mind which made him struggle with his heavy tongue. At last he recovered some of his lost strength. He lifted himself in the stirrups, and his voice obeyed now.

"And the sovereign rights shall not be trampled upon by monastic insolence!" cried he, so that his voice rang loudly through the dark and silent cloister-yard.

At the same time Rudimann informed the Abbot of the success which his mission had had with the Duchess.

Master Spazzo rode away. The cool night air was fanning his heated face. He burst out laughing. The reins he still held tightly in his right hand. The moon was shining brightly, while dark clouds were gathering round the peaks of the Helvetian mountains. Presently it became intensely dark; the pine-trees had assumed a strange weird look, and everything was silent around. An unshapely cloud now stealthily approached the moon and soon covered her up entirely. Then Master Spazzo recollected that his nurse had told him in his earlier infancy how the bad wolf Hati and Monagarm the moon-dog persecuted the radiant astre. Looking up, he clearly recognized both wolf and moon-dog in the sky. With their teeth they had just taken hold of the gentle comforter of belated travelers. Master Spazzo was convulsed with pity; he drew his sword.

" *Vince, luna!* conquer, O moon!" cried he, at the top of his voice, and rattling his sword against his greaves. " *Vince, luna; vince, luna!* "

His cries were loud and his jingling metal sounded fierce enough, but the cloud-monsters did not loosen their hold on the moon; only the chamberlain's horse became frightened, and galloped at full speed through the dark wood with him.

When Master Spazzo awoke the next morning he found himself lying at the foot of the Hunnic mound. On the meadow he saw his mantle, while, at some distance, his black steed was indulging in a morning walk. The saddle was hanging down on one side, and the reins were torn, Falada, however, was eating the young grass and flowers with evident enjoyment. Slowly the exhausted man lifted his head and looked about, yawning. The convent-tower of Reichenau was mirrored in the distant lake as peacefully as if nothing whatever had happened. He tore up a bunch of grass and held the dewy blades to his forehead. " *Vince, luna!* " said he with a bitter-sweet smile. He had a racking headache.

Chapter XIV

BURKHARD THE CLOISTER-PUPIL

Rudimann the cellarer was no bad logician. A roll of parchment-leaves in the jaws of a salmon must beget curiosity. While Master Spazzo had been drinking the cloister-wine his mistress and Praxedis sat in their private room, spelling out Gunzo's libel. Ekkehard's pupils had learned enough Latin to understand the chief part, and what remained grammatically obscure they guessed at, and what they could not guess they interpreted as well as they could. Praxedis was indignant.

" Is the race of scholars then everywhere like that at

Byzantium?" exclaimed she. "First, a gnat is metamorphosed into an elephant, and then a great war is made against the self-created monster! The present from the Reichenau is as sour as vinegar."

Dame Hadwig was beset by strange feelings. A certain something told her that the spirit which pervaded Gunzo's libel was not a good one, and yet she felt some satisfaction at Ekkehard's humiliation.

"I think he has deserved this reprimand," said she.

Then Praxedis stood up: "Our good teacher needs many a reprimand, but that should be our business. If we manage to cure him of his shy awkwardness we shall have done him a good service; but if some one who carries a beam in his own eye reproaches his neighbor with the moat in his—that is too bad! The wicked monks have merely sent this to slander him. May I throw it out of the window, gracious mistress?"

"We have neither requested you to complete Ekkehard's education, nor to throw a present we have received out of the window," sharply said the Duchess. So Praxedis held her peace.

The Duchess could not so easily tear away her thoughts from the elegant libel. Her ideas with respect to the fair-haired monk had undergone a great change since the day on which he carried her over the cloister courtyard. Not to be understood in a moment of excited feeling is like being disdained; the sting remains forever in the heart. Whenever her eyes now chanced to light on him, it did not make her heart beat any quicker. Sometimes it was pity which made her gaze kindly on him again, but not that sweet pity out of which love springs, like the lily out of the cool soil; it contained a bitter grain of contempt.

Through Gunzo's libel even Ekkehard's learning, which the women until then had been wont to treat with great respect, was laid prostrate in the dust—so what was there now left to admire? The silent working and dreaming of his soul was not understood by the Duchess, and by others a

delicate timidity is but too often considered folly. His
going out into the fields in the fresh morning to read Solomon's song came too late. He should have done that last
autumn.

Evening had come.

" Has Ekkehard returned home yet? " asked the Duchess.

" No," said Praxedis. " Neither has Master Spazzo
returned."

" Then take yonder candlestick," said Dame Hadwig,
" and carry up the parchment-leaves to Ekkehard's tower.
He must not remain ignorant of the works of his fellow-
brothers."

The Greek maid obeyed, but unwillingly. In the closet
up in the tower the air was close and hot. In picturesque
disorder, books and other things were strewn about. On
the oak table the gospel of St. Matthew lay open at the
following verses:

" But when Herod's birthday was kept, the daughter of
Herodias danced before them and pleased Herod.

" Whereupon he promised with an oath to give her what-
soever she would ask.

"And she, being before instructed of her mother, said,
' Give me here John the Baptist's head on a charger.' "

The priestly stole, the Duchess' Christmas-gift to Ekkehard, lay beside it. Praxedis pushed back the other things,
placing Gunzo's libel on the table. When she had arranged
everything she felt sorry. Just as she was about to go she
turned back once more, opened the window, and, gathering
a branch of the luxuriant ivy which was winding its garlands round the tower, threw it over the parchment-leaves.

Ekkehard came home very late. He had been nursing
the wounded Cappan, but had found it far harder work to
comfort his tall spouse.

In the silence of night Ekkehard read the leaves which
the Greek maid had put on his table. His hand played with
a wild rose he had culled in the fir-wood when riding home,
while his eyes took in the spiteful attacks of the Italian
scholar.

"How is it," thought he, inhaling the soft fragrance of the flower, "that so much that is written with ink cannot deny its origin? All ink is made of the gall-nut, and all gall-nuts spring from the poisonous sting of the wasp."—

With a serene countenance he finally laid aside the yellow parchment-leaves. "A good work, an industriously good work!—Well, the peewit is also an important personage among the feathered tribe, but the nightingale does not heed its singing!"—He slept very well after he had read it.

On coming back from the castle-chapel the next morning he met Praxedis in the courtyard. "You ought to be thinking about the reply," said Praxedis. "Boil the crab till it gets dark red; then he will not bite you again."

"The answer to this," replied Ekkehard, "has been given already by another: 'Whosoever shall say to his brother, Raca, shall be in danger of the council: but whosoever shall say, thou fool, shall be in danger of hell fire.'"

"You are extremely mild and pious," said Praxedis, "but take care how you get on in the world with that. Whoever does not defend his skin will be flayed, and even a miserable enemy should not be considered quite harmless. Seven wasps together will kill a horse, you know."

The Greek maid was right. Silent contempt of an unworthy antagonist is easily interpreted as weakness. But Ekkehard acted according to his nature.

Praxedis, approaching him still closer, so that he started back, now added, "Shall I give you another piece of advice, most reverend Master?" He silently nodded in the affirmative.

"Then let me tell you that of late you have again become far too serious. To look at you one would think that you were going to play at nine-pins with the moon and stars. We are now in the middle of summer, and your habit must be exceedingly warm. Get yourself some linen garment, and perhaps it would not harm you either to cool your head a little in yonder spring. But above all be merry and cheerful; the Duchess might otherwise become indifferent toward you."

Ekkehard wanted to take her hand. Sometimes he felt as if Praxedis were his good angel; but at that moment Master Spazzo on horseback entered the courtyard at a slow and lingering pace. His head was bent toward the pommel, and a leaden smile rested on his tired features. He was half asleep.

"Your face has undergone a great change since yesterday," called out Praxedis to him. "Why do not the sparks fly out any more from under your steed's hoofs?"

With a vacant stare he looked down at her. Everything was dancing before his eyes.

"Have you brought home a fair amount of smart-money, Sir Chamberlain?" asked Praxedis.

"Smart-money? For whom?" stolidly muttered Master Spazzo.

"For poor Cappan! Why, I verily believe that you have eaten a handful of poppy-seed, not to know any better for what purpose you rode out."

"Poppy-seed?" repeated Master Spazzo in the same drowsy tone. "Poppy-seed? No. But wine of Meersburg, red wine of Meersburg, unmeasured quantities of red Meersburg, yes!"

Heavily he dismounted, and then retired into the privacy of his apartments. The report about the result of his mission was not given.

"Do look, you radiant star of science!" Praxedis now said to Ekkehard. "Who may that dainty ecclesiastical little man be, who is coming up here?"

Ekkehard bent over the wall and looked down the steep rocky hill-side. Between the hazel-bushes bordering the footpath that led up to the castle, walked a boy with wavy brown locks, wearing a monk's habit that came down to his ankles. It was Burkhard the cloister-pupil, the son of Ekkehard's sister, who had come over from Constance to pay a holiday visit to his youthful uncle.

After Praxedis had brought some refreshments to the weary traveler, she turned to Ekkehard. "The Duchess bids me tell you," she said with mock earnestness, "that she feels inclined to return to the study of Virgil, and we are to begin again this very evening. Remember that you are to wear a more cheerful expression than the present one," added she in a lower key, "as it is a delicate attention, extended in order to show you that in spite of a certain treatise her confidence in your learning has not been destroyed."

This was a fact; but Ekkehard received the news with a start of terror. To be again together with the two women as hé used to be — the mere thought was painful. He had not yet learned to forget a certain Good Friday morning.

He now slapped his nephew on the shoulder, so as to make him start, and said, "Thou hast not come here to spend thy holidays merely with fishing and bird-catching, Burkhard. This afternoon we will read Virgil with the gracious Duchess, and thou shalt be present also."

He thought to place the boy like a shield between the Duchess and his thoughts.

"Very well," replied Burkhard. "I much prefer Virgil to hunting and riding, and I shall request the Lady Duchess to teach me some Greek. After that visit when they took you away with them, the cloister-pupils often said that she knew more Greek than all the venerable fathers of the monastery put together. They say that she learned it by sorcery. And although I am the first in Greek—"

"Then you will certainly be Abbot in five years, and in twenty, holy father at Rome," said Praxedis mockingly.

At the fourth hour of the evening Ekkehard was waiting in the pillared hall below, ready to resume his reading of the Æneid. More than six months had gone by since Virgil had been laid aside. Ekkehard felt oppressed. He opened one of the windows through which the pleasant cool air of evening came streaming in.

The cloister-pupil was turning over the leaves of the Latin manuscript.

"When the Duchess speaks to thee, mind to be very polite," said Ekkehard. But he replied with a complacent air, "With such a grand lady I shall speak only in verse."

Hereupon the Duchess entered, followed by Praxedis. She greeted Ekkehard with a slight bend of the head. Without appearing to notice the boy she sat down in her richly carved arm-chair. Burkhard, from the lower end of the table, where he stood, had made her a graceful bow.

Ekkehard had opened the book, when the Duchess said indifferently, "Why is that boy here?"

"He is but a humble auditor," said Ekkehard, "who, inspired by the wish to learn the Greek language, ventures to approach such a noble teacher. He would be very happy, if from your lips he could learn—"

But before Ekkehard had ended his speech Burkhard had approached the Duchess. With eyes cast down, and a mixture of shyness and confidence, he said with a clear intonation of the rhythm:

"Esse velim Graecus, cum vix sim, dom'na *, Latinus."

It was a faultless hexametre.

Dame Hadwig listened with astonishment; for a curly-headed boy, who could make an hexametre was then an unheard-of thing in the Allemannic lands. And, moreover, he had improvised it in her honor. Therefore she was really pleased with the youthful verse-maker.

"Let me look at thee a little nearer," said she, drawing him toward her. She was charmed with him, for he had a lovely boyish face, with a red and white complexion, so soft and transparent that the blue veins could be seen through it. Then Dame Hadwig put her arms round the boy, and kissing him on both lips and cheeks, fondled him almost like a child, and finally pushing a cushioned footstool close to her side, bade him sit down on it.

"To begin with, thou shalt gather something else than Greek wisdom from my lips," said she jestingly, giving him

---

*Abbreviation of *domina*.

another kiss. "But now be a good boy, and quickly say some more well-set verses."

She pushed back his curls from his blushing face; but the cloister-pupil's metrical powers were not discomposed even by the kiss of a Duchess. Ekkehard had stepped up to the window, where he looked out toward the Alps, while Burkhard, without hesitation, recited the following lines:

> " Non possum prorsus dignos componere versus,
> Nam nimis expavi duce me libante suavi."

He had again produced two faultless hexametres.

The Duchess laughed out gaily. " Well, I verily believe that thou didst greet the light of this world with a Latin verse, at thy birth! That flows from thy lips as if Virgil had arisen from his grave. But why art thou frightened when I kiss thee?"

" Because you are so grand, and proud, and beautiful," said the boy.

" Never mind," replied the Duchess. " He who with the fresh kiss yet burning on his lips can improvise such perfect verses cannot be very much terrified."

Making him stand up before her, she asked him, "And why art thou so very eager to learn Greek?"

" Because they say that if a man knows Greek he can become so clever that he will hear the grass grow," was the ready answer. " Ever since my fellow-pupil Notker, with the large lip, has vaunted himself that he was going to learn all Aristotle by heart and then translate it into German, I have been uneasy in my mind."

Dame Hadwig again laughed merrily. " Let us begin then! Dost thou know the antiphon, ' Ye seas and rivers, praise the Lord?' "

" Yes," said Burkhard.

" Then repeat after me, 'θάλασσι καὶ πόταμι, εὐλογιτε τὸν κύζιον.'"

The boy repeated it.

" Now sing it!" He did so.

Ekkehard looked over reproachfully at them. The Duchess interpreted the look aright.

"So, now thou hast learnt six words already," she said
to Burkhard, "and as soon as thou wilt ask for it in hexametres, thou shalt be taught some more. For the present,
sit down there at my feet and listen attentively. We will
read Virgil now."

Then Ekkehard began the fourth canto of the Æneid,
and read of the sorrows of Dido, who is ever beset by
thoughts of the noble Trojan guest whose words and looks
are all deeply engraven on her inmost heart.

But Dame Hadwig had not much sympathy with the sorrows of the Carthaginian widowed queen. She leaned back
in her arm-chair and looked up at the ceiling. She no
longer found any similarity between herself and the desolate woman in the book.

"Stop a moment," cried she. "How very clear it is,
that this is written by a man. He wants to humiliate
women! It is all false! Who on earth would fall so madly
in love with an utter stranger?"

"You are right," said Ekkehard to Dame Hadwig, " 'tis
all wrong. Dido ought to laugh, and Æneas to go and kill
himself with his sword. That would be quite natural."

She gazed at him with an unsteady look. "What is the
matter with you?" asked she.

"I cannot read any more," replied he.

The Duchess had also risen.

"If you do not care to read any longer," she said with
an apparently indifferent expression, "there are still other
ways and means to pass one's time. What say you if I
were to ask you to tell us some graceful tale—you may
choose whatever you like. There are still many grand and
beautiful things besides your Virgil. Or, you might invent
something yourself. I see that you are oppressed by some
care. You neither like to read nor to go out into the
country. Everything hurts your eyes, you say. I think that
your mind lacks some great task which we will now give
you."

"What could I invent?" replied Ekkehard. "Is it not

enough happiness to be the echo of a master, like Virgil?''
He looked with a veiled eye at the Duchess. ''I should only
be able to chant elegies—very sad ones too.''

''Nothing else?'' mused Dame Hadwig reproachfully.
''Have our ancestors not gone out to war and let their
bugles sound the alarm through the world, and have they not
fought battles as grand as those of Æneas? Do you believe
that the great Emperor Charles would have had all the old
national songs collected and sung, if they had been nothing
but chaff? Must you, then, take everything out of your
Latin books?''

''I know nothing,'' repeated Ekkehard.

''But you *must* know something,'' persisted the Duchess.
''If we, who live here in this castle, were to sit together of
an evening and talk of old tales and legends, I shouldn't
wonder if we produced something more than the whole of
the Æneid contains? Do tell us such a story, Master Ekkehard, and we will gladly spare you your Virgil with his
love-sick queen.''

But Ekkehard's thoughts were quite differently occupied.
He shook his head like one who is dreaming.

''I see that you want some stimulant,'' said the Duchess.
''Above all, a good example will inspire you. Praxedis,
prepare thyself, and likewise tell our chamberlain that we
are going to entertain ourselves tomorrow with the telling
of old legends. Let everybody be well prepared.''

She took up Virgil and threw it under the table, as a sign
that a new era was to begin forthwith.

Ekkehard left the hall with hasty steps.

[In the cool hours of the evening the Duchess holds court
in a small garden within the castle-walls, having taken
much pleasure in her idea and adorned herself with particular care.]

Dame Hadwig was really a dazzling apparition, as she
proudly sailed along in her flowing robes. On her head she

wore a soft transparent tissue, a sort of veil, fastened to a
golden head-band. Pulling out a rose from Burkhard's
nosegay, she stuck it in between the head-band and the veil.

Praxedis and Master Spazzo entered after her. The
Duchess, casting her eyes hastily about, then asked, "Has
Master Ekkehard, for whose especial benefit we have ap-
pointed this evening, become invisible?"

"My uncle must be ill," said Burkhard. "He paced up
and down in his room with hasty steps yesterday evening,
and when I wanted to show him the different constellations,
such as the bear and Orion and the faintly glittering
Pleïads, he gave me no answer whatever. At last he threw
himself on his couch with all his clothes on, and talked a
good deal in his sleep.

"What did he say?" asked the Duchess.

"He said, 'Oh, my dove that art in the clefts of the
rock, and in the secret places of the stones; let me see thy
countenance, let me hear thy voice. For sweet is thy voice
and thy countenance is lovely.' And another time he said,
'Why do you kiss the boy before my eyes? What do I hope
still, and why do I tarry yet in the Lybian lands?'"

"That is a nice state of things, I declare," whispered
Master Spazzo into the Greek maid's ear. "Does that rest
on *your* conscience?"

The Duchess, however, said to Burkhard, "I suppose
that thou hast been dreaming thyself. Run up to thy uncle
and make him come down, as we are waiting for him."

She sat down gracefully on her throne-like seat. The
cloister-pupil soon came back with Ekkehard, who was looking very pale, while his eyes had something wild and sad
about them. He silently bowed his head, and then sat down
at the opposite end of the table. Burkhard wanted to place
his stool again at the Duchess' feet, as he had done the day
before, when they had read Virgil — but Ekkehard rose and
pulled him over by the hand. "Come hither!" said he.
The Duchess let him do as he wished.

[Master Spazzo draws the shortest straw and is called on
to relate the first tale, and he tells the story of Weland, the

smith. He is followed by Praxedis, who narrates the adventures of King Rother.]

Praxedis had spoken a long while.

"We are well satisfied," said the Duchess, "and whether smith Weland will carry off the prize, after King Rother's history has been told, seems to me rather doubtful."

Master Spazzo was not annoyed at this.

"The waiting-women at Constantinople seem to have eaten wisdom with spoons," said he. "But although *I* may be conquered, the last tale has not yet been told." He glanced over at Ekkehard who was sitting lost in thought; he had not heard much of King Rother. All the time that Praxedis had been speaking, his eyes had been fixed on the Duchess' head-band with the rose in it.

The evening had set in. The moon had risen, shedding her pale light over hills and plain. Strong fragrant perfumes filled the air, and the fireflies, in the bushes and crevices of the rocks round about, were getting ready for flight.

A servant came down with some lights, which, being surrounded by linen saturated with oil, burned brightly and steadily. The air was mild and pleasant.

Dame Hadwig was not yet inclined to go indoors. "Ekkehard!" she exclaimed sharply, "you are to relate something!"

"I am to relate something?" murmured he, passing his right hand over his forehead. It was burning, and underneath it was a storm.

"Ah yes — relate something. Who is going to play the lute for me?"

He stood up and gazed out into the moonlit night, while the others looked at him in mute wonder; and then he began in a strange, hollow voice:

"'Tis a short story. There once was a light, which shone brightly, and it shone down from a hill, and it was more radiant and glorious than the rainbow. And it wore a rose under the head band —"

"A rose under the head band?" muttered Master Spazzo, shaking his head.

"And there was once a dusky moth," continued Ekkehard, still in the same tone, "which flew up to the hill, and which knew that it must perish if it flew into the light. But it did fly in all the same, and the light burned the dark moth so that it became mere ashes — and never flew any more. Amen!"

Dame Hadwig sprang up, indignantly.

"Is that the whole of your story?" asked she.

"'Tis the whole of it," replied he with unchanged voice.

"It is time for us to go in," proudly said the Duchess. "The cool night-air produces fever."

She walked past Ekkehard with a disdainful look.

The chamberlain patted him on the shoulder. "The dark moth was a poor fool, Master Chaplain!" said he compassionately.

A sudden gust of wind here put out the lights. "It was a monk," said Ekkehard indifferently; "sleep well!"

CHAPTER XV

REJECTION AND FLIGHT

EKKEHARD had remained sitting in the bower for a long time after the others had gone away, and when at last he also rose he rushed out into the darkness. He did not know whither his feet were carrying him. In the morning he found himself on the top of the Hohenkrähen, which was silent and deserted since the woman of the wood had left it.

Ekkehard burst into a wild laugh. "The chapel of St. Hadwig!" he cried, striking his breast with his clenched hand. "This it must be!" He upset the old Roman stone, and then mounted the rock on the top of the hill. There he threw himself down, pressing his forehead against the cool ground which had once been touched by Dame Hadwig's foot. Thus he remained for a long time, and toward evening he came back to the Hohentwiel, looking hot

and excited and having an unsteady gait. Blades of grass
clung to the woolen texture of his habit.

The Duchess had noticed his absence without making any
inquiries about him. He went up to his tower and seized
a parchment as if he would read; it happened to be Gunzo's
libel. "Willingly would I ask you to try the effect of healing medicine, but I fear that his illness is too deeply
seated," was what he read. He laughed. The arched ceiling threw back an echo, which made him jump up as though
he wanted to find out who had laughed at him. Then he
stepped up to the window and looked down into the depth
below. It was deep, far deeper than he had imagined, and
overcome by a sudden giddiness he started back.

"I will pray to be delivered from temptation," said Ekkehard. He slowly descended the winding staircase to the
castle-chapel, and knelt before the altar-steps, his forehead
resting on the cold stone flags. Thus he remained, wrapt in
prayer. "Oh Thou, who hast taken the sins and sufferings
of the whole world on Thyself, send out one ray of Thy
grace on me, unworthy object." He looked up with a fixed
stare as if he expected the earnest figure to step down and
hold out his hand to him.

"I am here at thy feet, like Peter, surrounded by tempest, and the waves will not bear me up! Save me, oh Lord!
save me as Thou didst him, when Thou walkedst over the
raging billows, extending Thy hand to him and saying,
'O thou of little faith, wherefore dost thou doubt?'"

But no such sign was given him.

Ekkehard's brain was giving way.

A rustling like that of a woman's garments now became
audible, but Ekkehard did not hear it.

Dame Hadwig had come down, impelled by a strange
impulse. Since her feelings for the monk had undergone
a change, the image of her late husband recurred oftener
to her inward mind. This was but natural. As the one
receded into the background, the other must come forward
again. The latter reading of Virgil had also its share in

this, as so much had been said about the memory of Sichæus.

The following day was the anniversary of Sir Burkhard's death. The old Duke lay buried in the chapel below, and today the Duchess intended to pray on her husband's grave. The reigning twilight concealed Ekkehard's kneeling figure. She did not see him.

Suddenly she started up from her kneeling posture. A laugh, soft yet piercing, struck her ear. She knew the voice well. Ekkehard had risen and recited the following words of the Psalms:

"Hide me under the shadow of thy wings, from the wicked that oppress me, from my deadly enemies, who compass me about. Arise, O Lord, disappoint them, cast them down."—

He said it in an ominous tone: It was no more the voice of prayer.

Dame Hadwig bent down once more, beside the sarcophagus on which she would gladly have placed another, to hide her from Ekkehard's view. She no longer had any wish to be alone with him. Her heart beat calmly now.

He went to the door, about to go, when suddenly he looked back once more. The everlasting lamp was softly rocking to and fro, over Dame Hadwig's head. Ekkehard's eye pierced the twilight this time, and with one bound he stood before the Duchess. He cast a long and penetrating look at her. Rising from the ground and seizing the edge of the stone sarcophagus with her right hand, she confronted him, while the everlasting lamp over her head was still gently swinging to and fro on its silken cord.

"Thrice blessed are the dead, for one prays for them," said Ekkehard, interrupting the silence.

Dame Hadwig made no reply.

"Will you pray for me also, when I am dead?" continued he. "Oh, no, you must not pray for me — but you must let a goblet be made out of my skull, and, when you take another monk away from the monastery of St. Gallus, you must offer him the welcome draught in it — and give him my greeting! — You can also put your own lips to it; it will not crack. But you must then wear the head-band with the rose in it.'' * * *

'' Ekkehard!'' said the Duchess, '' you are trespassing!''

He put his right hand up to his forehead.

''Ah yes!'' said he in a soft, mournful voice, '' ah yes! — The Rhine is trespassing also. They have stopped its course with gigantic rocks, but it has gnawed them all through and is now rushing and roaring onward, carrying everything before it, in its glorious newly won liberty! — And God must be trespassing also, methinks, for He has allowed the Rhine to be, and the Hohentwiel, and the Duchess of Suabia, and the tonsure on my head.''

The Duchess began to shiver. Such an outbreak of long repressed feeling she had not expected. But it was too late — her heart remained untouched.

'' You are ill,'' she said.

He threw himself at Dame Hadwig's feet, clasping the hem of her garment. His whole frame was convulsed with trembling.

Dame Hadwig was touched against her will; as if from the hem of her garment, a feeling of unutterable woe thrilled her up to her very heart.

'' Get up,'' said she, '' and try to think of other things. You still owe us a story. You will soon have conquered this weakness.''

Then Ekkehard laughed through his tears.

''A story!'' cried he; '' yes, a story! But it must not be told. Come, let us act the story! From the height of yonder tower one can see so far into the distance, and so deep into the valley below — so sweet and deep and tempting. What right has the ducal castle to hold us back? Nobody who wishes to get down into the depth below need count more than three — and we should flutter and glide softly into the arms of Death, awaiting us down there. Then I should be no longer a monk, and I might wind my arms around you — and he who sleeps here in the ground below,'' striking Sir Burkhard's tombstone with his clenched hand, '' shall not prevent me! And we will float up to the tower again and sit where we sat before, and we will read the Æneid to the end, and you must wear the rose under your head-band as if nothing whatever had happened. The gate we will keep well locked against the Duke, and we will laugh at all evil backbiting tongues, and folks will say when sitting at their fireplaces of a winter's evening — ' That is a pretty tale of the faithful Ekkehard, who became a monk at St. Gall and is sitting now beside a proud, pale woman, reading Virgil to her.' And at midnight may be heard the words, ' If thou commandest, O Queen, to renew the unspeakable sorrow.' And then she must kiss him, whether she will or not, for death makes up for the pleasures denied us in life.''

He had uttered all this with a wild, wandering look in his face; and now his voice failed with low weeping. Dame Hadwig had stood immovably all this time. It was as if a gleam of pity were lighting up her cold eye, as she now bent down her head toward him.

'' Ekkehard,'' said she, '' you must not speak of death. This is madness. We both live, you and I!''

He did not stir. Then she lightly laid her hand on his burning forehead. This touch sent a wild thrill through his brain. He sprang up.

'' You are right!'' cried he. '' We both live, you and I!''

A dizzy darkness clouded his eyes as he stepped forward, and, winding his arms round her proud form, he fiercely pressed her to his bosom, his kiss burning on her lip. Her resisting words died away, unheard.

Raising her high up toward the altar, as if she were an offering he was about to make, he cried out to the dark and solemn looking picture, '' Why dost thou hold out thy gold glittering fingers so quietly, instead of blessing us?''

The Duchess had started like a wounded deer. One moment, and all the passion of her hurt pride lent her strength to push the frenzied man back and to free herself at least partly from his embrace. He still had one arm round her waist, when the church-door was suddenly opened and a flaring streak of daylight broke through the darkness — they were no longer alone. Rudimann, the cellarer from the Reichenau, stepped over the threshold, while other figures became visible in the background of the courtyard.

The Duchess had waxed pale with shame and anger. A tress of her long dark hair had become loosened and was streaming down her back.

" I beg your pardon! " said the man from the Reichenau, with grinning politeness. " My eyes have beheld nothing."

Then Dame Hadwig, ridding herself entirely from Ekkehard's hold, cried out, " Yes, I say! — yes, you *have* seen a madman, who has forgotten himself and God! — I should be sorry for your eyes if they had beheld nothing, for I would have had them torn out! " It was with an indescribably cold hauteur that she pronounced these words.

Then Rudimann began to understand the strange scene. " I had forgotten," said he in a cutting tone, " that the man who stands there is one of those to whom wise men have applied the words of St. Hieronymus, when he says that their manners were more befitting dandies and bridegrooms than the elect of the Lord."

Ekkehard stood there, leaning against a pillar, with arms stretched out in the air, like Odysseus when he wanted to embrace the shadow of his mother. Rudimann's words roused him from his dreams.

" Who dares come between her and me? " cried he, threateningly. But Rudimann, patting him on the shoulder with an insolent familiarity, said, " Calm yourself, my good friend; we have only come to deliver a note into your hands. St. Gallus can no longer allow the wisest of all his disciples to remain out in this shilly-shallying world. You are called home! — And don't forget the stick with which you are wont to ill-treat your confreres who like to snatch a kiss at vintage-time, you chaste censor," he added in a low whisper.

Ekkehard stepped back. Wild longings, the pain of separation, burning passionate love, and cutting taunting words — all these overwhelmed him at once. He made a few steps toward the Duchess, but the chapel was already filling. The Abbot of Reichenau had come himself to witness Ekkehard's departure.

"It will be a difficult task to get him away," he had said to the cellarer. It was easy enough now. Monks and lay brothers came in after him.

"Sacrilege," Rudimann called out to them. "He has laid his wanton hand on his mistress, even before the altar!"

Then Ekkehard could not restrain himself any longer. To have the most sacred secret of his heart profaned by insolent coarseness — a pearl thrown before swine! — He tore down the everlasting lamp, and swung the heavy vessel over his head. The light went out, and the moment after a hollow groan was heard, and the cellarer lay with bleeding head on the stone flags; the lamp lay beside him. Then there followed a fierce struggle, fighting, confusion — all was coming to an end with Ekkehard. They had the better of him, and, tearing off the cord which served him as a belt, they tied his hands together.

There he stood, the handsome youthful figure, now the very picture of woe, resembling the broken-winged eagle! His eyes sent one mournful, troubled, appealing look at the Duchess — who turned her head away.

"Do what you think right," said she to the Abbot, sweeping proudly through the ranks of those looking on.

It was a dreary, uncomfortable evening. The Duchess had locked herself up in her bedroom, refusing admittance to every one.

Ekkehard meanwhile, by the order of the Abbot, had been dragged into a dungeon. A bundle of straw had been thrown in for him, and a monk was sitting outside to guard the entrance.

At the well in the courtyard Rudimann the cellarer was standing, letting the clear water flow over his head. Ekkehard had given him a sharp cut, out of which the dark blood was slowly trickling down into the water. Praxedis was the only being who had sincere heartfelt pity for the prisoner. She went up to the Duchess, intending to implore her compassion for Ekkehard on her knees; but the door remained locked against her. Dame Hadwig was deeply hurt. If the monks of the Reichenau had not come in upon them she might have pardoned Ekkehard's frenzy — all the more as she herself had sowed the seeds of all this; but now it had become a public scandal which demanded punishment.

The Abbot had sent her the letter from St. Gall. " St. Benedict's rules," so the letter ran, " exacted not only the outward forms of a monastic life, but the self-denial of heart and soul, which forms the spirit of it! " Ekkehard was to return. From Gunzo's libel some parts were quoted against him.

It was all perfectly indifferent to the Duchess. What his fate would be if he were delivered into the hands of his antagonists she knew quite well; yet she was determined to do nothing for him. Praxedis knocked at her door a second time, but again it was not opened.

" Oh thou poor moth," said she sadly.

Ekkehard meanwhile lay in his dungeon like one who had dreamt some wild dream. Now and then he shivered as with cold. By degrees a melancholy smile of resignation settled on his lips, but this did not always remain there; bursts of anger, which made him clench his fists, interrupted it. But Ekkehard's heart was not yet broken; it was still too young for that. He began to reflect on his position. The view into the future was not very cheering. He well knew the rules of his order, and that the men from Reichenau were his enemies. With long strides he paced up and down the narrow space. " Great God, whom we may invoke in the hour of affliction, how will this all end? "

He shut his eyes and threw himself on the bundle of

straw. Confused visions passed before his soul. His thoughts were inclined to dark and despondent doubts. Yet hope does not entirely forsake even the most miserable.

He now heard a slight noise in the antechamber of his dungeon. A stone jug was put down. "You are to drink like a man," said a voice to the lay brother on guard, "for on St. John's night all sorts of unearthly visitors people the air and pass over our castle; so you must take care to strengthen your courage There's another jug set ready, when this is finished."

It was Praxedis who had brought the wine. Ekkehard did not understand what she wanted. "Then she also is false," thought he. "God protect me!"

He closed his eyes and soon fell asleep. Some hours later he awoke. The wine had evidently been to the lay-brother's taste, for he was lustily singing a song, beating time on the stone flags with his heavy sandal-clad foot. Ekkehard heard that another jug of wine was brought in. The singing became always louder and more uproarious. Then the lay brother held a soliloquy, until he suddenly ceased talking and his snoring could be heard very plainly through the stone walls.

Everything was silent around. It was about midnight. Ekkehard lay in a half-slumbering state until he heard the bolts of the door softly withdrawn. He remained lying where he was. A muffled figure came in, and a soft little hand was laid on the slumberer's forehead. He jumped up. "Hush!" whispered Praxedis; for it was she.

When everybody had gone to rest, Praxedis had kept awake. "The bad cellarer shall not have the satisfaction of punishing our poor melancholy teacher," she had said to herself; and woman's cunning always finds some way and means to accomplish its schemes. Wrapping herself up in a gray cloak she had stolen down on tip-toe; no special artifices were necessary, for the lay brother was sleeping the sleep of the just.

"You must fly!" said she to Ekkehard. "They mean to do their worst to you."

"I know it," replied he sadly.

"Come, then."

He shook his head. "I prefer to submit and to suffer," said he.

"Don't be a fool," whispered Praxedis. "First you built your castle on the glittering rainbow, and now that it has all tumbled down you will allow them to ill-treat you into the bargain? As if *they* had a right to drag you away and to flog you! And you will let them have the pleasure of witnessing your humiliation?—It would be a nice spectacle for them, to be sure!"

"Where should I go?" asked Ekkehard.

"Neither to the Reichenau nor to your monastery," said Praxedis. "There is still many a hiding-place left in this world." She was getting impatient, and, seizing Ekkehard by the hand, she dragged him on. "Forward!" whispered she. He allowed himself to be led.

They slunk past the sleeping watchman; and now they stood in the courtyard, where the fountain was splashing merrily. Ekkehard bent over the spout and took a long draught of the cool water.

"All is over now," said he. "And now away!"

It was a stormy night. "As the bridge is drawn up you cannot go out by the doorway," said Praxedis, "but you can get down between the rocks, on the eastern side. Our shepherd-boy has tried that path before."

They entered the little garden. A gust of wind was rocking the branches of the maple-tree to and fro. Ekkehard felt as if he were in a dream.

He mounted the battlement. Steep and rugged the gray rocks sloped into the valley, that now looked like a dark yawning abyss. Black clouds were chasing each other along the dusky sky—weird uncouth shapes, resembling two bears pursuing a winged dragon. After a while the fantastic forms united into one shapeless mass, which the wind drifted onward toward the Bodensee, that glittered faintly in the distance. The whole landscape could be seen only in indistinct outlines.

"Blessings on your way!" whispered Praxedis.

Ekkehard sat perfectly motionless on the battlement, still holding the Greek maiden's hand clasped in his. His lips could not express the feelings of gratitude which pervaded his whole being. Suddenly he felt her cheek pressed against his, and a trembling kiss imprinted on his forehead, followed by a pearly tear. Softly Praxedis then drew away her hand.

"Don't forget," said she, "that you still owe us a story. May God lead your steps back again to this place, some day, so that we may hear it from your own lips."

Ekkehard now let himself down. Waving one last farewell with his hand, he soon disappeared from her sight.

She crossed herself and went back, smiling through her tears. The lay brother was still fast asleep. While crossing the courtyard Praxedis spied a basket filled with ashes, which she seized, and, softly stealing back into Ekkehard's dungeon, she poured out its contents in the middle of the room, as if this were all that was left of the prisoner's earthly remains.

Chapter XVI

ON THE WILDKIRCHLEIN

From the lowlands of the Bodensee the Säntis stretches out grandly into the blue air, smilingly looking down into the depths below, where the towns of men shrivel up to the size of ant-hills. All around him there is a company of fine stalwart fellows, made of the same metal, and there they put their bold heads together, and jestingly blow misty veils into one another's faces. Over their glaciers and ravines a mighty roaring and rustling is heard at times; and what they whispered to one another respecting the ways and doings of mankind had already a somewhat contemptuous tinge, even a thousand years ago — and since then it has not become much better, I fear.

About ten days after the monks of the Reichenau had found nothing but a heap of ashes, instead of their prisoner,

in the castle-dungeon, and had debated a good deal whether
the Devil had burnt him up at midnight, or he had escaped,
a man was walking up the hills along the white foaming
Sitter.

He wore a mantle made of wolves' skins over his monkish
garb, a leathern pouch at his side, and he carried a spear in
his right hand. Often, he pushed the iron point into the
ground and leaned on the butt end, using the weapon thus
as a mountain-stick. The path which was followed by our
traveler became steeper and rougher.

Leaning with his left hand on the stone wall, the man
continued his way, which, however, became narrower with
every step he took. The dark precipice at his side approached nearer and nearer, a giddy depth yawning up at
him—and now all trace of a pathway ceased altogether.
Two mighty pine-trunks were laid over the abyss, serving
as a bridge.

"It must be done," said the man, boldly stepping over it.
Heaving a deep sigh of relief when his feet touched ground
again on the other side, he turned round to inspect the
dangerous passage somewhat more at his leisure.

"Ye mountains and vales, praise the Lord!" exclaimed
the wanderer, overwhelmed by the grandeur of the spectacle
before him. Many hundreds of mountain-swallows flut-
tered out of the crevices between the rocks; their appearance was like a good omen for the lonely traveler.

He advanced some steps forward. There the wall of
rocks had many a fissure, and he saw a twofold cavern. A
simple cross, made of rudely carved wood, stood beside it.
The stranger knelt down before the cross and prayed there
a long while.

It was Ekkehard—and the place where he knelt was the
"Wildkirchlein."

It was getting late. What now?—The cravings of hunger drew off his attention for the moment. Still having
provisions for three days, he sat down before a cavern and
took his evening meal, moistening his bread with the tears
he could not restrain.

"As long as the cross stands on yonder rock I shall not
be entirely forsaken," said he. He then collected some
grass that grew outside and prepared himself a couch.
Sleep is the best cure for the sufferings of youth, and in
spite of heartache and loneliness it soon closed Ekkehard's
eyelids.

The first dawn of morning rose over the head of the
Kamor, and only the morning star was still shining brightly
when Ekkehard started up from his slumbers. It was as
if he had heard the merry tones of a herdsman's shout, and
on looking up he saw a light shining out from the darkest
recess of the cavern. He believed himself to be under the
delusion of a dream — that he was still in his dungeon and
that Praxedis was coming to free him. But the light came
nearer and proved to be a torch of pine-wood. A young
girl, with high looped-up petticoats, was carrying this primitive candle. He jumped up. Without showing either fear
or surprise she stood before him, and cried, " God's welcome to you! "

It was a bold half wild looking maiden, with olive complexion and fiery sparkling eyes. Her dark abundant
tresses were fastened behind by a massive silver pin,
fashioned in the shape of a spoon. The braided basket on
her back, and the Alpine stick in her right hand, marked
her as being an inhabitant of the mountains.

" Holy Gallus, protect me from new temptation," thought
Ekkehard; but she called out cheerfully, "Again I say, be
welcome! My father will be very glad to hear that we
have a new mountain-brother."

It did not sound like the voice of a female demon.

Ekkehard was still sleepy and yawned.

" May God reward you! " ejaculated the maid.

" Why did you say, ' May God reward you? ' " asked he.

" Because you have not swallowed me up," laughed she;
and before he could put any more queries she ran away with
her torch-light and disappeared in the back of the cavern.

Presently she returned, however, followed by a gray-bearded herdsman, wrapped in a mantle made of lambs' skins.

"Father will not believe it!" cried she.

The herdsman now took a deliberate survey of Ekkehard. "So you are going to be our new mountain-brother?" said he, good-naturedly extending his hand. "Well, that's right! You shall get milk and cheese, and three goats which may graze wherever they like. In return you will preach us a sermon each Sunday, and pronounce a blessing over meadows and pasture-grounds so that storms and avalanches will cause no harm. Further, you have to ring the bell to announce the hours."

"I am a homeless wanderer, whom the Abbot has not sent out hither," said Ekkehard sadly.

"That's all the same to us," replied the other. "If but we and the old Säntis over there are satisfied, then nobody else need be asked. The Abbot's sovereignty does not extend here. Look there!" pointing out a gray mountain-peak, which in solitary grandeur rose from far-stretching ice-fields—"that is the high Säntis, who is the Lord and master of the mountains. We take off our hats to him, but to nobody else."

The herdsman inspired Ekkehard with confidence. Independent strength as well as a kindly heart could be perceived in his words. His daughter, meanwhile, had gathered a nosegay of Alpine roses, which she held out to Ekkehard.

"What is thy name?" asked he.

"Benedicta."

"That is a good name," said Ekkehard, fastening the Alpine roses to his girdle. "Yes, I will remain with you."

Upon this the old man shook his right hand until he winced, and then, seizing the Alpine horn which hung suspended on a strap at his side, he blew a peculiar signal.

From all sides answering notes were heard, and soon the neighboring herdsmen all came over—strong wild-looking men—and assembled around the old man, whom, on account of his good qualities, they had elected master of the Alps and inspector of the meadows on the Ebenalp.

"We have a new mountain-brother," said he. "I suppose that none of you will object?"

After this address they all lifted their hands in sign of approval, and then stepping up to Ekkehard bade him welcome — an action which touched his heart, and he made the sign of the cross over them.

Thus Ekkehard became hermit of the Wildkirchlein, scarcely knowing how it had all come about. And on the following Sunday he preached a sermon on the transfiguration, and told the herdsmen and their families how every one who ascended the mountain-heights with the right spirit became, in a certain sense of the word, transfigured also.

"And though Moses and Elijah may not come down to us," he cried, "have we not the Säntis and the Kamor standing beside us? — And they also are men of an old covenant, and it is good for us to be with them!"

His words were great and bold; and he himself wondered at them, for they were almost heretical, and he had never read such a simile in any of the church fathers before. But the herdsmen were satisfied, and the mountains also; and there was nobody to contradict him.

At noon Benedicta, the herdsman's daughter, came up. A silver chain adorned her Sunday bodice, which encircled her bosom like a coat of mail. She brought a neat milking-pail, made of ashwood, on which, in simple outlines, a cow was carved.

"My father sends you this," said she, "because you have preached so finely, and have spoken well of our mountains — and if anybody should try to harm you you are to remember that the Ebenalp is near."

She threw some handfuls of hazel-nuts into the pail. "These I have gathered for you," added she; "and if you like them I know where to find more."

Before Ekkehard could offer his thanks she had disappeared in the subterranean passage.

> " Dark-brown are the hazel-nuts,
> And brown, like them, am I;
> And he who would my lover be
> Must be the same as I! "

she sang archly, while going away.

A melancholy smile rose to Ekkehard's lips. The tempest in his heart had not yet been quite appeased. Faint murmurs were yet reverberating within — like the thunderclaps of an Alpine storm, which are repeated by innumerable echoes from the mountains.

A huge flat piece of rock had fallen down beside his cavern. Melting snow had undermined it in the spring. It resembled a grave-stone; and he christened it inwardly, the grave of his love. There he often sat. Sometimes he fancied the Duchess and himself lying under it, sleeping the calm sleep of the dead; and he sat down upon it, and looked over the pine-clad mountains far away toward the Bodensee — dreaming. Often his heart was brimful with bitter angry pain; often again in the evening hour he would strain his eyes in the direction of the Untersee, and whisper soft messages to the passing winds. For whom were they meant?

His dreams at night were generally wild and confused. He would find himself in the castle-chapel, and the everlasting lamp was rocking over the Duchess' head as it did then; but when he rushed toward her she had the face of the woman of the wood, and grinned at him scoffingly. When he awoke from his uneasy slumbers in the early morning, his heart would often beat wildly, and the words of Dame Hadwig, " Oh, schoolmaster, why didst thou not become a warrior? " persecuted him till the sun had risen high in the sky, or the appearance of Benedicta would banish them.

Ekkehard was as yet not ripe for the healing delights of solitude. The ever-present recollection of past suffering had a strange effect on him. Whenever he sat all alone in his silent cavern, he fancied he heard voices that mockingly talked to him of foolish hopes and the deceits of this world. The flight and calls of the birds in the air seemed to him the shrieks of demons, and all his praying would avail nothing against these fantastic delusions.

[Presently he falls seriously ill; the herdsmen nurse him and the Alpine air hastens his recovery. A great shock had been necessary to restore his bodily as well as mental equilibrium.] Now he was all right again, and neither heard voices, nor saw phantoms. A delicious feeling of repose and recovering health ran through his veins. It was that state of indolent pleasant weakness, so beneficial to persons recovering from melancholy. His thoughts were serious, but had no longer any bitterness about them.

"I have learnt something from the mountains," said he to himself. "Storming and raging will avail nothing, though the most enchanting of maidens were sitting before us; but we must become hard and stony outside, like the Säntis, and put a cooling armor of ice round the heart, and sable night herself must scarcely know how it burns and glows within."

By degrees, all the sufferings of the past months were shrouded and seen through a soft haze. He could think of the Duchess and all that had happened on the Hohentwiel, without giving himself a heartache.

Ekkehard had never before cast a retrospective glance on the days of his youth, but he now loved to fly there in his thoughts as if it had been a paradise out of which the storm of life had driven him. He had spent several years in the cloister-school at Lorsch on the Rhine. In those days he had no idea what heart-and-soul-consuming fire could be hidden in a woman's dark eyes; in that era of his life the old parchments were his world.

One figure out of that time had, however, been faithfully kept in his heart's memory, and that was Brother Conrad of Alzey. On him, who was his senior by but a few years, Ekkehard had lavished the affection of a first friendship. Their roads in life afterward became different; and the days of Lorsch had been forced into the background by later events. But now they rose warm and glowing in his thoughts, like some dark hill on a plain when the morning-sun has cast his first rays on it, and so Ekkehard's thoughts now recurred often to his faithful companion.

"Look over yonder!" Conrad had once said to his young friend, when they were looking down over the land from the parapet of the garden. "Here, on the shores of the Rhine, we stand on hallowed ground, and it is time that we set to collecting what has grown on it, before the tedious *trivium* and *quadrivium* has killed our appreciation of it."

In the merry holiday-time Conrad and he had wandered through the Odenwald, where, in a valley, hidden by green drooping birch-trees, they had come to a well. Out of this they drank, and Conrad had said, "Bow down thy head, for this is the grove of the dead, and Hagen's beech-tree, and Siegfried's well. Here the best of heroes received his death-wound from the spear of the grim Hagen, which entered his back, so that the flowers around were bedewed with the red blood." And he told him all about the princely castle at Worms, and the treasure of the Nibelungen, and the revenge of Chriemhildis, and Ekkehard listened with sparkling eager eyes.

"Give me thy hand!" he cried, when all was over, to his young friend. "When we have become men, well versed in poetry, then we will erect a monument to the legends of the Rhine. Nobody will dare chant another Iliad after Homer, but the song of the Nibelungen has not yet been sung, and my arm is young and my courage undaunted, and who knows what the course of time may bring. For thee I also know a song, which is simple and not too wild, so that it will suit thy disposition, which prefers the notes of a bugle to the roar of thunder. Look up! Just as today towers of Worms shone and glistened in the sun, when the hero Waltari of Aquitania, flying from the Hunnic bondage, came to Franconia. Here the ferry-man rowed him over, with his sweetheart and his golden treasure. Through

yonder dark, bluish-looking wood he then rode, and there
was a fighting and tilting, a rattling and clashing of swords
and spears, when the knights of Worms, who had gone
out in his pursuit, attacked him. But his love and a good
conscience made Waltari strong, so that he held out
against them all, even against King Gunther and the grim
Hagen.''

Conrad then told him the whole legend with its details.
'' Couldst thou not sing the Waltari? ''

But Ekkehard preferred at that time to throw pebbles,
making them skim the water, and he took in only half the
meaning of what his friend had said. But a good seed-
corn may for a long time lie hidden in a human heart, and
yet at last germinate and bud, like the wheat from Egypt's
mummy-graves.

That Ekkehard now delighted in dwelling on these recollections was a proof that he had undergone a considerable
change. And this was well. The caprices of the Duchess
and the unconscious grace of Praxedis had refined his shy
and awkward manners. The time of stirring excitement
he had gone through during the invasion of the Huns
had given a bolder flight to his aspirations and had taught
him to despise the paltry intrigues of petty ambition;
besides, his heart had received a mortal wound which had
to be treated and healed; and so the cloister-scholar, in
spite of cowl and tonsure, had arrived at a happy state of
transition, in which the monk was about to become a poet.

Summer came back once more to the mountains with
heart-stirring warmth, and a peaceful Sabbath quiet lay
over the highlands. The sun was standing over the Kron-
berg, inclining toward the west, and deluging the heavens
with a flood of golden light. He likewise sent his rays into
the mists over the Bodensee, so that the white veil slowly
dissolved, and in soft delicate blue tints the Untersee
became visible. Ekkehard strained his eyes and beheld
a filmy dark spot, which was the island of Reichenau, and
a mountain which scarcely rose above the horizon, but he
knew it well — it was the Hohentwiel.

Then Ekkehard's soul glowed and brightened. His thoughts flew away, over into the Hegau, and he fancied himself once more sitting with Dame Hadwig on the Hohenstoffeln when they celebrated Cappan's wedding, and saw Audifax and Hadumoth, who appeared to him the very embodiment of earthly happiness, coming home from the Huns. There arose also from the dust and rubbish of the past what the eloquent Conrad of Alzey had once told him of Waltari and Hiltgunde. The joyous spirit of poetry entered his soul. He rose and jumped up into the air in a way which must have pleased the Säntis. In the imagery of poetry the poor heart could rejoice over that which life could never give it—the glory of knighthood and the felicity of wedded love.

" I will sing the song of Waltari of Aquitania!" cried he to the setting sun, and it was as if he saw his friend Conrad of Alzey standing between the Sigelsalp and Maarwiese, in robes of light and nodding a smiling approval to this plan.

So Ekkehard cheerfully set to work, a goat-boy being dispatched on a secret mission to Burkhard, the cloister-pupil. Two days afterward he returned from his expedition, and unpacked the contents of his wicker-basket before Ekkehard's cavern. A small harp with ten strings, colors and writing material, and a quantity of clean soft parchment-leaves with ruled lines, all lay carefully hidden under a mass of green oak-leaves.

Ekkehard took up the harp, and sitting down at the foot of the crucifix before his cavern played a joyous air. It was a long time since he had last touched the chords, and it was an unspeakable delight for him, in that vast solitude, to give vent in low tuneful melodies to the thoughts and feelings that were oppressing his heart. And the fair lady *Musica* was *Poetry's* powerful ally; and the epic song of Waltari, which at first had limned itself only in misty outlines, condensed into clearly defined figures, which again grouped themselves into warm life-glowing pictures. Ekkehard closed his eyes to see them still better, and then he beheld the Huns approaching — a race of nimble merry horsemen, with less repulsive faces than those against whom he had himself fought but a few months ago; and they carried off the royal offspring from Franconia and Aquitania, as hostages — Waltari and the fair Hiltgunde, the joy of Burgundy. And as he struck the chords with greater force, he also beheld King Attila himself, who was of tolerable mien and well inclined to gaiety and the joys of the cup. And the royal children grew up at the Hunnic court, and when they were grown up a feeling of home-sickness came over them, and they remembered how they had been betrothed to each other from the days of their childhood.

Then there arose a sounding and tuning of instruments, for the Huns were holding a great banquet; King Attila quaffed the mighty drinking-cup, and the others followed his example until they all slept the heavy sleep of drunken-ness. Now he saw how the youthful hero of Aquitania saddled his war-horse in a moonlit night, and Hiltgunde came and brought the Hunnic treasure. Then he lifted her into the saddle, and away they rode out of Hunnic thraldom. In the background, in fainter outlines, there still floated pictures of danger, and flight, and dreadful battles with the grasping King Gunther. In large bold outlines the whole story which he intended to glorify in a simple heroic poem stood out before his inward eye.

That very same night Ekkehard remained sitting up with his chip-candle and began his work; and a sensation of intense pleasure came over him when the figures sprang into life under his hand. The next day found him eagerly busying himself with the first adventures. Some days were thus spent in industrious work. In the Latin verse of Virgil the figures of his legend were clothed, as the paths of the German mother-tongue struck him as being still too rough and uneven for the fair measured pace of his epic. Thus his solitude became daily more peopled, the song proceeding steadily.

One midday Ekkehard had just begun taking his usual walk on the narrow path before his cavern, when a strange visitor met his view. It was a bear, which sat down timidly before the cavern, steadfastly gazing in. The wish to recite the creation of his mind to some living being had for a long while been strong within him. Here, in the vast solitude of the mountains, he thought that the bear might take the place which under other circumstances would have required some learned scholar. So he stepped into his blockhouse, and, leaning on his spear, read out the beginning of his poem;* he read with a loud enthusiastic voice, and the bear listened with commendable perseverance.

Chapter XVII

THE LAST ECHO, AND END

Our tale is drawing to its close.

Perhaps some of our readers would be pleased to hear that Ekkehard, after having completed his song, died a peaceful death. It would verily have been a most touching conclusion—how he had reclined before his cavern, with eyes strained toward the Bodensee, his harp leaning against the rock, the parchment-roll in his hands—and how his heart had broken!—Further, one might have added some fine simile—how the poet was consumed by the burning flames of his genius, like the torch which is burnt to ashes while it gives its light; but this touching spectacle, I am sorry to say, Ekkehard did not afford to posterity.

Genuine poetry makes a man fresh and healthy. So Ekkehard's cheeks had assumed a brighter color during his work, and he often experienced a feeling of well-being which made him stretch out his arm as if he were about to strike down a wolf or bear with one blow of his fist.

But when his Waltari had bravely conquered all dangers

---

* "The Song of Waltari," translated by Scheffel from the Latin original, is omitted here for lack of space.

and deathly wounds he gave a shout of delight which made the stalactite walls of his cavern reëcho. That evening he sat on the Ebenalp in the cottage of the old herdsman, and they did not spare the jug; then Ekkehard seized the huge Alpine-horn, and, mounting a rock, blew a mighty strain in the direction of the hazy distant Hegau mountains; and the notes swelled out loud and triumphantly as if they wanted to reach the Duchess' ears, so as to make her step out on her balcony, followed by Praxedis, whom he then would have liked to greet with a laugh.

By and by autumn began. Fresh snow was glistening on all the peaks around, and was evidently not intending to melt again that year. Ekkehard had preached his last sermon to the herdsmen, and after it Benedicta sauntered past him. "Now 'tis all over with our merry-making up here," said she, "for tomorrow man and beast will betake themselves to their winter quarters."

The next morning they went down the valley in gay procession, and when herdsmen, cows, and goats had disappeared, Ekkehard entered his hermitage. During his solitary life in the mountains he had learned to understand that solitude is only a school for life, and not *life* itself; and that he who in this busy active world will only be a passive spectator, wrapped up in himself, must in the end become a useless being.

"There's no help for it," said he; "I too must return to the valley! The snow is too cold, and I am too young to remain a hermit."

He seized his knapsack, and in it put his scanty belongings. His most precious thing, the Waltari song, carefully wrapped up, was placed on the top. Firmly setting the point of his spear into the ground he walked down the well-accustomed giddy path.

At the Bodensee, people prepared for the coming vintage. One fine evening Dame Hadwig sat in her garden, with the faithful Praxedis by her side. The Greek had unpleasant times now. Her mistress was out of tune, discontented, and reserved. Today was another period when she could not entice her into a conversation. It was a day of evil remembrances.

"Today it is just a year," Praxedis began, with seeming indifference, "that we sailed over the Bodensee and paid a visit to St. Gallus."

The Duchess made no reply. "A great deal has happened since then," Praxedis was going to add; but the words died on her lips.

"And have you heard, gracious mistress, what people are saying of Ekkehard?" resumed she, after a considerable pause.

Dame Hadwig looked up. Her mouth was working.

"And what do people say?" she asked carelessly.

"Master Spazzo has lately encountered the Abbot from the Reichenau," said Praxedis, "who accosted him thus: 'The Alps have been highly favored, for the walls of the Säntis reverberate with the sound of the lyre and poetical twitterings; for a new Homer has built his nest up there.' And when Master Spazzo, shaking his head, replied, 'How does that concern me?' then the Abbot said, 'The poet's no other than your Ekkehard. This news has reached us from the cloister-school at St. Gall.' Master Spazzo then rejoined laughingly, 'How can a man sing who is not able to tell a story even?'"

The Duchess had risen. "Be silent," said she; "I won't hear anything more about it." Praxedis understood the wave of her hand, and sorrowfully went away.

Dame Hadwig's heart, however, had different feelings than the words her tongue uttered would lead one to expect. She stepped up to the garden-wall and looked over toward the Helvetian mountains. Dusk had set in, and long, heavy, steel-gray clouds stood immovably over the evening-red that glowed and trembled beneath them.

In looking at the beauty and softness of the waning day her heart was softened also. Her eyes were riveted on the Säntis, and it was as if she saw a vision in which the Heavens opened and sent down two angels, who, descending to those heights, lifted up a man in a well-known monk's habit — and the man was pale and dead, and an aureole of light, clear and beautiful, surrounded the airy procession.

But Ekkehard was not dead.

A low hissing sound made the Duchess start up from her reverie. Her eyes glided over the dark rocky wall down which the prisoner had once made his escape, and beheld a dark figure disappearing in the shade, the while an arrow sped toward her and dropped heavily at her feet.

She bent down to take up the curious missile. No hostile hand had sent it from the bow. Thin parchment-leaves were rolled round the shaft, and the point was covered with some wild flowers. She untied the leaves and did not fail to recognize the handwriting. It was *The Song of Waltari.* On the first page was written in pale red ink: "A parting salutation for the Duchess of Suabia!" and beside it the words of the apostle James: "Blessed is the man who has conquered temptation."

Then the proud woman inclined her head and wept bitterly.

Ekkehard went out into the wide world, and never set eyes again on the Hohentwiel, nor did he ever return to the monastery of St. Gall. It is true that when he descended from the Alps and approached the well-known walls he reflected whether he should not enter it again as a penitent; but at the right moment an adage of the old Master of the Alps occurred to him, "When a man has once been master, he does not like to become a servant again," and so he passed by.

Later, a good deal was bruited about concerning a certain Ekkehard at the court of the Saxon Emperor, who was said to be a proud, strong-willed, and reserved man; who to great piety united great contempt for the world — but was contented, active, and well-versed in all the arts. He became the Emperor's chancellor and tutor of his young son, and his counsel was of great influence in all the affairs of the realm. It has not been ascertained whether this was the same Ekkehard of our story.

The Duchess Hadwig never married again; and in her pious widowhood reached a considerable age. Later, she founded a humble little convent on the Hohentwiel, to which she bequeathed her territories in the Allemannian lands. Ekkehard's name was never permitted to be mentioned before her; but *The Song of Waltari* was read very often, and she evidently derived much pleasure and comfort from it. According to an assertion of the monks from the Reichenau — an assertion quite unwarranted, however — she is said to have known it almost by heart.

Praxedis faithfully served her mistress for some years more, but by degrees an irresistible longing for her bright sunny home took possession of her, and she declared that she could not bear the Suabian air any longer. Richly dowered, the Duchess let her go from her.

Audifax, the goatherd, learned the goldsmith's art, and settled down in the bishopric of Constance, where he produced much fine workmanship. The companion of his adventures there became his wedded spouse, and the Duchess was godmother to their first little son.

Burkhard, the cloister-pupil, became a celebrated Abbot of the monastery of St. Gallus, and on all great occasions he still manufactured many dozens of learned Latin verses, from which, however — thanks to the destroying powers of time — posterity has been spared.

And all have long since become dust and ashes. Centuries have passed in swift procession over the places where their fates were fulfilled; and new stories have taken the place of the old.

IN THE RHAETIAN ALPS*

By Joseph Victor von Scheffel

TRANSLATED BY A. I. DU P. COLEMAN, A.M.

Professor of English Literature, College of the City of New York

HE evening bells had fallen silent, and the faint glow which, like a last greeting, had been reflected from the distant, soaring summits, of the Rhaetian chain into the Tavetsch valley, was fading into the cloudy gray of the twilight as we came down from the heights of Chiamut and Rueras into the old town of Disentis. One who has clambered over the dangerous passes of the Oberalp into the Grisons valleys is apt to think at evening both of the rough beauty of the mountain paths he has left behind and of finding adequate shelter for his weary bones. This he will discover in satisfactory abundance at Disentis, at the foot of the lofty monastery walls.

Over the spicy Valtellina wine, to whose inevitable recurrence in this corner of the mountains the wanderer gladly resigns himself, and the tender roast chamois, the earliest spoils of the open season beginning the first of September, the memories of racked bones disappear; and in the warmth of the primitive stove, as if it were a winter evening at home, old stories come readily to the tongue. For these there is ample material in Disentis itself and the part of the Oberland just traversed — although unfortunately the turmoil of the French Revolution has destroyed the documentary sources of much of the old monastic history of this region. When in 1799 the " Landsturm " of the Confederation went out to meet the French and chased the unwelcome visitors from the whole valley of the Vorder Rhine down to the neighborhood of Chur, some

---

* From the *Reisebilder* (published, after Scheffel's death, in 1887).
Permission A. Bonz & Co., Stuttgart.

prisoners were shot down by the levies at Disentis, in a narrow street which is still pointed out. Lecourbe came up again to avenge this deed, and laid in ashes the village and the monastery; and all the treasures of ancient manuscripts which the library possessed perished in the flames. Much may still be deciphered, however, from the indestructible sources of history, the names of places and people.

That these remote parts of the valley of the Rhine remained, until within the first centuries of the Christian era, a desolate wilderness, into which the Celtic aborigines penetrated for hunting or grazing, is shown by the name of the monastery, " Desertina," the desert cloister. The same conclusion may be drawn from the names of the villages down the valley, Somvix and Surrhen (*summus vicus* and *summum Rheni*), whose few houses were once the last outposts of the dwellers in the valley, until the unequaled insight of the early servants of the Church chose this wilderness as the place from which to win for the Cross and Christian civilization the uppermost reaches of the Vorder Rhine and the wild lateral valleys at the foot of the Cornera and the Piz Medel.

Many a colony went out from the monks of Disentis, and the colonists were the devoted servants of the mother house. Thus to this day the chief official of these mountain villages bears the Romansch title of *mistral* (*ministerialis*). The original inhabitants, however, who gave names to the mountains and valleys before the Christian immigration, were certainly of Celtic stock. Some one who is working at the gradual building up of old Celtic history, whose stock has gone up notably of late through the labors of Mone, Keferstein, Brosi, and others, may subject these names to a closer investigation. The jagged crests of Sixmadun and Badüs, the peak on which the Medel glacier lies, the Bernatsch, the Tavetsch valley, named from its green, grassy bottom, and such places as Sedrun and Rueras, got their names from no Roman or Teutonic sponsors.

Even today the mountaineer of the Grisons for the most part bears a Celtic family name. The Celts named their tribes from the cluster of houses they inhabited — hence the frequency of names beginning with *Ca* (house). Thus those who belonged to the house of the chief were called Caflisch (Belgo-Celtic *flisch*, lord); those whose huts stood on marshy soil (*risch*) were called Carisch — and thus the zealous scholar, Professor Carisch of Chur, has a hereditary vocation to the philological studies in the speech of the Grisons whose results he has set forth in his Romansch dictionary and grammar. Similar formations account for the names of Cadusch, Camenisch, Carim; and in later days, when Latin Christian names came into the valley, those who abode in the house of Jacobus or of Albertus, for example, by the old Celtic analogy, were called Cajacob and Cadelbert.

To those who have become so enamored of Celtic studies that they put the rest of the ancient and modern world far behind the primitive Celts in wise organizing of the individual life and of social economy, we may leave the task of demonstrating that the simple village constitutions which developed, in the various federations of the Grisons, into a political whole of such distinct characteristics had their origin in the Celtic blood of the ancestors of the Cajacob and Caflisch of today; that indeed the striving after " legal freedom and popular sovereignty, ordered community life combined with the rights of property," as Brosi teaches at length in his *Celts and Old-Helvetii* (Solothurn, 1851), is nothing but the principle of Celtic Life.

Downstairs in the public room sat the young guide from Rueras, a trim black-haired fellow, who was perfectly willing to let the Celts and the old monastic history sleep the sleep of the dead, while he occupied himself with things of a different sort. At least he sang, with a comrade, a fine song in the Tavetsch dialect of a " tender, fair, and rosy maid " (*una zarta, bialla cotschna*), to whom a bold youth

sued for her favors, to be repulsed with the same contemptuous answer as the suitor in the German popular
song:

> " Oh, back you may go, by the road you came to me,
> And tie up your horse to an old dry tree!"

His song floated mockingly over, now and then, into the
midst of the learned discussions, as though he would command all philological and historical studies to beat a retreat.

After a sound sleep, the sort of sleep a man ought to have
who has come across the Oberalp, with no dreams either of
the beasts of the wilderness or of the ghosts of the Celtic
inhabitants of these valleys, I made an inspection of the
abbey and church.

In the abbey, where then only ten Benedictine fathers
were living, there were many traces of the fire which a few
years before had made another attempt at its destruction.
In the cells and the refectory carpenters were busily at
work; and experts were laboring to provide the cells with
the peculiar traditional stoves that can scarcely be found
anywhere except in the Grisons Oberland. On low stone
feet heavy squares of a stone resembling granite are built
up into a cube and covered with another huge stone, so that
the stove is not unlike an ancient sarcophagus. If its sides
were bedecked with reliefs of fabulous animal forms, in the
style of the grotesques found over the doors and windows
of the houses of the Engadine, the antiquary would be
tempted to freshen up his ancient Rhaetian or Etruscan
recollections and demonstrate the transition from the
coffin of the Lucumo to the Oberland stove of today. The
abbey church, not very old, though spared by the recent
fire, has nothing remarkable to offer in the way of architecture or monuments.

Veils of gray cloud trailed down into the valley from the
mountain-peaks when we took our way along the Vorder
Rhine, brawling in its youthful strength, toward Ilanz and
Reichenau. The good friends of the evening before, the

jagged Sixmadun and the soaring Crispalt, as well as the
distant Rhaetian chain, were pleased to be invisible.

The road to Truns is one of wild beauty in its details.
Fragments of rock chaotically heaped on every side remind us that even the peaks of the mountains grow old,
crumble, and fall into the valleys. Over picturesque piles
of such ruins, often extending down to the Rhine, grow
the fir and that finest of the conifers, the larch. Rude
bridges span the torrents which from every cleft and fold
in the hills bring new additions to the infant Rhine. Everywhere are studies for the landscape painter, such as he will
not find in like profusion in his usual haunts of the Tyrol
and the Bavarian Highlands. At the foot of the great
Medel mass, on the right bank of the Rhine, there bursts
forth from the Conflons gorge a dashing torrent which is
unfairly made equal to the other two confluents under the
name of Middle Rhine. Along the path which it cleaves the
Frankish hosts under Pepin marched long ago into the
Valle Leventina and down into Italy.

At many points along the road the vegetation is overwhelmed by tremendous landslides; against these and the
avalanches the dwellers in the valley contrive a frail de-
fense with bulwarks and walls, and often themselves fall
victims to the rush of the mighty mass. Passing Com-
padiels, where in the old Gothic church there are all sorts
of votive tablets in thanksgiving for deliverance from
avalanches and other perils, and Somvix, we reach the village of Truns. To the left of the road, just before you
reach the village, stands a chapel, and near it a venerable
witness of ancient days, a solitary maple-tree. The inner
parts of it are long since vanished; but far around the
outer bark of the hollow tree still rears the same giant
form above its deep roots. Gipsies used to find ample
room for their night encampment within its circumference;
now, modern piety has surrounded it with a protecting
fence. The top and the boughs have long since withered

away, but on one side a gnarled offshoot has grown up and
surrounds with fresh verdure the hoary trunk. That here
we are at the Grütli of the Grisons may be seen both in
word and picture at the neighboring Chapel of St. Anne.

From the Carolingian era the German feudal system took
root even in the wild valleys of the Rhaetian Oberland. As
counts of the Empire and vassals of the bishops of Chur,
beside the abbot of Disentis German lords held sway from
their castles over the Romanic territory. All the ruins of
the fallen castles bear German names — Saxenstein, Rin-
kenberg, Pultlingen, and the like. But in the valley of the
Vorder Rhine and on the heights, in tiny villages or distant herdsmen's cottages, still lived the Rhaetian-Romanic
peasantry, heavily oppressed, down to the least of them,
under the hand of the lords.

From Gothic or Frankish days there had been growing
up here a simple communal life, with some joint organization of the separate communes. Each village developed its
own law, which the " Dorfmeister " executed; single ham-
lets, united by ecclesiastical ties into a parish, set at their
head an "Ammann," who, with sworn assistants, regulated
their small affairs. For the adjustment of more serious
differences, for the judgment of crime and the promotion
of general peace, several communities would join to set up
a " high court " — a federation which was not the product
of any artificial abstract system, but grew directly out of
the nature and the needs of life among the mountains.

At the epoch when the bailiffs were exercising their cruel
sway on the other side of the mountains in Schwyz, Uri, and
Unterwalden, the Rhaetian lords also furnished notable
examples of oppression of their peasantry. Whether a
strain of German melancholy provoked them to abnormal
savagery in these wild defiles of the mountains, against a
population speaking another tongue and strengthened by a
strangely perfumed foreign wine, no romantic writer has
as yet arisen to decide for the clearing of their fame.

The lord of the Bärenburg near Andeer, who spat into

the broth cooking on the fire for the peasants' noonday meal; the bailiff of Guardavall in the Engadine, who attempted to seduce the daughter of Adam of Camogask; Donatus of Vatz, and other ruffians of the Rhaetian Alps, will, it is to be hoped, find their poets in time, who will discover the cause of their reprehensible conduct in some mighty soul-sorrow, and set it forth with as much tragic pathos as has been bestowed upon Count Golo by his apologist Hebbel in the account of his conduct toward Geneviève, the pious Duchess of Brabant.

But the Rhaetian peasant, who had learned to recognize his real master in the terror of the avalanche and the winter storm on the Alpine heights, who had evolved a rude and stubborn self-consciousness as with difficulty he wrested a scanty livelihood from the mountain wilderness, was neither resigned nor romantic enough to have a taste for the brutalities of his lords. Like Tell in the "Hohle Gasse" at Küssnacht, the peasants of the Engadine and the Schams valley also struck down their tyrants; Guardavall, Fardün, and Realt were laid in ruins, and the lord of the Bärenburg was forced to drink the soup which he had "seasoned" for John Caldar.

Here in the Oberland, however, the peasants adopted more civilized methods. When the strife between their rulers put them in peril, when the bishop of Chur called in Austrian aid against his city, the mountaineers of the Vorder Rhine came down to the wood of Truns, and under the old maple-tree founded a league for the maintenance of the common freedom. With order and moderation they sent to their lords delegates who should, in the words of the Chronicle, "remind them in friendly terms that injustice, violence, and shameful wantonness must be banished from their borders, letting them know that if they would not appoint upright judges for the administration and preservation of justice, the commons would no longer endure unrestrained wickedness — though otherwise they were ready to render obedience in all fit and proper things." Unfortunately there was no newspaper in the Grisons to urge the taking of energetic measures to suppress such presumption; the nobles gave their assent to the league — whether in a moment of Girondist inspiration, or with an eye to what lurked in the background of the petition, the chronicle does not tell us.

So in March, 1424, the abbot of Disentis, the counts of Werdenberg and Sax, and Baron Bruno of Rhäzüns rode up to the maple of Truns and swore to the heads of the village communities to grant shelter and sanction to the "Hochgerichte" or high courts which the peasants had established, to renounce private warfare, to abstain from violence and to be true confederates "as long as the hills and valleys endured." They took the oath before Peter of Pultlingen, abbot of Disentis; and they kept it like honest men.

This was the Upper or Gray League — *la lia grischa*. The confederation included the valley of the Rhine as far as Reichenau, the lateral valleys of Medel, Safien, and Lugnetz, down to where the Hinter Rhine flows out of the glaciers of the Rheinwald and the Val Mesocco stretches off in the direction of Italy. It endured in the strength of honorable manhood and had good repute in all the countryside — a model for the later League of God's House and the League of the Ten Jurisdictions in the Prättigau and Davos.

In memory of these events, the chapel near the maple has on either side of the door two frescoes, representing the foundation of the League and the last repetition of the oath in the year 1778. The modern representatives in their wigs and their smart rococo dress offer a lively commentary on the old rhyme which puts in a nutshell the story of the League's foundation and closes with

> This league of freedom still
> Endures to our own day —
> Whether for good or ill,
> Let each his own mind say.

It need not be said that the paintings, restored by a painter of the name of Kühlental, remind a connoisseur less of modern historical painting than of the style in which, according to the *Fliegende Blätter*, mural decoration is practiced in Breslau; for art also, several thousand feet above sea-level, suffers the fate which, according to Livy, befell the Italian immigrants in the Alpine regions — *quos loca ipsa efferarunt,* "they took on the savage nature of the place itself."

The league of Truns, like the other leagues, has come to an end since those days; but the old maple still stands "like the hills and valleys" of the Alps, held in superstitious veneration by the people about — and when the marksmen of the Oberland go down to Chur or to their camp at Thun, not one of them fails to stick in his cap a green twig from it.

If the ancient trunk has put forth its new shoots as a symbol of the modern confederate Swiss constitution, it must know why it has done so — since the days of the lords of Rhäzüns and Sax, it has had a chance to acquire much knowledge in silence — and no valid objection can be raised to the proceeding, although as a general rule it would not be fitting that even the trees should acquire the habit of making political demonstrations.

In the meantime the sky had opened its floodgates, and was pouring forth so much water that I decided at the inn, over a Homeric meal of goat's flesh, to make the rest of the journey on wheels, although a regular postroad does not begin until Ilanz is reached. That the manner of driving and the style of the charioteers had still preserved their primitive characteristics in these Celtic valleys was soon to be impressed on me.

An open vehicle which struck a happy mean between a carriage and a cart was soon provided — in shape and construction probably differing little from the *esseda* in which, at the battle of Sentinum long ago, according to Livy, the Celtic Gauls drove into the midst of the cavalry engage-

ment with " snorting of horses and din of wheels," to the
terror of the Romans.

A pony was hitched to a simple pair of shafts, the place
of reins being supplied by leather thongs cut out of raw
ox-hide. These were in the hands of the most dignified of
all coachmen — Joseph Antony was the worthy's name.

A warm woolen peaked cap covered his head, and on
top of this sat a peculiar sharply-pointed felt hat. Short
leather breeches reaching to his knees, rough blue stock-
ings, and shoes with wooden soles were other components
of his costume which pointed more or less to a Teutonic
origin. But his coat was of decidedly archaic form, sharply
cut away and furnished with long indented lapels, pointing
forward. It was quite clear to us that one more fragment
of ancient history was concealed in this coat; this was
assuredly the " peculiarly lengthened jacket of the Celtic
hand-barrow men," the *caricella*, from his preference for
which a Roman emperor got his nickname of Caracalla.

The institution of the whip had not yet penetrated these
regions; Joseph Antony was armed with an umbrella,
which, with equal skill, he used to belabor or to goad his
steed. Thus he was the venerable type of the Celtic house-
servant and coachman, as he sat with secure decision on
the front seat of the singular conveyance. "*Alto! alto!
hé bougre!*" he cried in affectionate objurgation to his
nag; and with the soothing conviction that King Rhaetus
at the head of his Etruscans entered the Engadine no more
proudly over the Maloja, we began our journey. No accident could upset the old man's equanimity; at most he
gave utterance to his feelings in the Romansch of the
Oberland, the " Schalauer Sprache " as the inhabitants of
other Romansch valleys call it in derision. " *Schliatt'
aura — schliatt' aura* " (bad weather), he muttered with a
shake of his head when torrents of rain poured from the
eaves of the houses. When the nag threatened to stand
still, he growled out something about a " liderlich cavaigl "
or " liderlich kerli," from which we deduced with satisfac-

tion that the abundance of Romansch terms of reproach owes notable enrichments to the German tongue.

Shall I describe at greater length the jolting drive over all manner of obstacles, and recall the peculiar mood which develops so harmoniously out of a thorough wetting and half-broken bones? *Infandum regina jubes renovare dolorem!* Past Tavanasa, past the German-speaking village of Waltensburg, perched on the mountain-top in the midst of a Romansch district, past the mouth of the grim Panixer Pass, where Suwarow taught his Russians the art of mountain-climbing, the track led us on to Ilanz, "the first town on the Rhine," where mine host of the "Cross" looked pityingly down upon our conveyance with the self-complacency of a postmaster.

Warm Valtellina wine and a huge salmon-trout at the inn compensated for the hardships of the journey, and we emptied a glass, with historical respect, to the health of our charioteer. When all the rest of the world has been completely covered with a network of railways, then perhaps the time may come for a postroad to be constructed from Ilanz to Truns and the Oberalp, and future travelers may gaze there upon the last postillion with the same feelings as ours for old Antony. And when even the railways elsewhere are reckoned among antiquities, and traveling by balloon is the fashion, it is possible that even the iron road may penetrate the last corner of the Rhine valley, and the descendants of Joseph Antony may shout "*Alto! hé bougre!*" to their locomotives as vigorously as their ancestor today to his nag. We attempted to open such a perspective into the changing course of the future for the excellent Antony's benefit; but he shook his gray head dreamily and went off to the stable.

We spent but a few minutes inspecting the time-stained walls and towers of Ilanz. But we had a glimpse of the simplicity of the forms with which democracy is administered today in the Grisons Oberland when we looked into the visitors' book. Among the sparsely-scattered names of travelers, we saw here and there an entry stating that the delegates of the "Hochgericht" of the Grisons had met here and held the election,—which according to the constitution takes place every two or three years,—for the functionaries of the district court, jurors, and the like. The result of the election is set down, with the names of the fortunate candidates and the number of votes given for each, and the record is closed. The visitors' book thus takes on the dignity of a public document and an election bulletin at once.

The road leads from the left bank of the Vorder Rhein at Ilanz to one side, climbing the mountain in great curves. By two bright little lakes lies the village of Laax, with some old houses of the better class. That the nobility of these parts was connected with the later period of Suabian knighthood is shown by an escutcheon on the house once belonging to John de Corays von und zum Seblen (1617), who describes himself as "Knight of the Holy Roman Empire and of the Knighthood of the Quarter on the Neckar, the Schwarzwald, and the Ortenaw."

Near Flims a streamlet coming down from the Tschingelshorn has chosen its way through a wild defile, and brawls along, far below the road, on its way to find the Vorder Rhine in its narrow valley.

Another turn, by the old mills of Trins, and above a steep precipice rise the ruins of the castle of Hohentrins, built by Pepin the Frank as a base and shelter for Lombard expeditions. The village nestles up to the mountain in terraces, and far below opens the valley through which the Hinter Rhine comes from the Splügen, to join the other branch at Reichenau. Nowhere in the Grisons is there a more splendid panorama.

Behind stretch the lofty peaks of the Glärnisch and of the Oberland, watching over the valley of the Vorder Rhine, which here increases notably in breadth. Before us shine

the brightly-colored roofs of Reichenau; to the northeast
Chur peeps out of the lateral valley of the Plessur, towered
over by the distant Scesaplana; rich fields and woods cover
the delta formed by the two branches of the Rhine, up to
the grayish-white heights from which the walls of the old
castle of Rhäzüns (*Rhaetia ima*) look down into the waters
of the Hinter Rhine; and beyond Rhäzüns the eye goes on
up the castle-decked Domleschg valley, which narrows
toward Thusis, until it reaches the defiles of the Via Mala
leading further to the Splügen between closely-crowding
walls of rock. The wild heights around, the rich vegetation of the banks of both Rhines, villages and castles in
the distance, in the foreground the majestic Hohentrins —
all these compose a landscape worthy of the most skilful
painter.

The road falls steeply by Tamins to Reichenau. In the
beautiful garden of M. de Planta, Reichenau offers another
view of the confluence of the two Rhines, which are both
spanned here by old wooden bridges.

The story of Louis Philippe's first exile — under the name
of M. Chabaud he taught mathematics here in 1793; the
wide military road leading to Chur by the village of Fels-
berg, menaced by inundations from the Calanda; Chur
itself, and its recently-discovered mosaic pavements — all
these we may leave to others to describe, as we regretfully take leave of Joseph Antony and set off toward the
Engadine.

To the southwest from Chur the road goes in the direction of Malix, leading through cool fir and larch woods into
the territory of the Ten Jurisdictions. To this belongs,—
at the foot of the Rhaetian chain and next to the Monta-
fonerthal of the Vorarlberg,— the Prättigau in the valley
of the Landquart as far as its junction with the Rhine,
where in the Mayenfeld and Malans districts the golden-
yellow Rhaetian Rhine wine —

et quo te carmine dicam,
Rhaetica vitis? —

is ripened to greater perfection by the sun; and also the Schanfiggthal along the Plessur, and Davos, nestling in the clefts of the Scaletta and the heights which slope down to the Engadine.

Here the partly Teutonic inhabitants had built up for themselves, on the same principles as the people of the Oberland, an organization of village, commune, and wider district, the units of which became confederate as the Ten Jurisdictions; once they were under the lordship of Frederick of Toggenburg, after whose death, in the confusion of the strife over the succession, they contrived cleverly to withdraw themselves from this domination (1436). At the summit of the mountains which rise to the right over Malix, the territory of the Ten Jurisdictions marches with those of the Gray League and the League of God's House. Green Alps and pasture-grounds, on which graze goats and cattle, stretch up toward the rocky snow-covered peaks.

Near Churwalden, where beside the old church a fortress-like building with battlements and dungeons makes a fine foreground to the picture, the eye sweeps up for the last time through the Schanfiggthal to the great Rhaetian masses and the crowning height of all, the Scesaplana, lifting itself proudly above the other crests and snow-fields.

He who takes pleasure in romantic piety may say a prayer in the church at the tomb of Baron Donatus of Vatz, surnamed the Cruel. A great part of the Grisons was subject to him in the fourteenth century, and stories are still told of him. The popular legends, wholly neglecting the statement that he was " learned in both canon and civil law," recount with horror how he told some captive men-at-arms of Montfort who begged mercy of him when they were perishing with hunger, that " the voice of such song-birds was music in his ears," and how, in the course of his physiological studies, he had the bodies of three of his drunken subjects cut open, that he might observe the effects of wine taken to excess.

On a lofty plateau lies the clean Alpine village of Parpan,

not at all unlike Partenkirchen in Bavaria. Crossing the
stony tract known as the Lenzer Heide, in whose peaty
soil pale green lakes reflect the mountain-tops, we soon
reach the summit of the pass, five thousand feet high; and
we enter once more an exclusively Romansch region, whose
speech differs widely from that of the Oberland, and is
more like the " Ladin " of the Engadine.

A little before you descend into Lenz, you get a wide
view down into the Oberhalbstein valley.   To the left rise
the snowy summits of the Tiefenkasten range and the
chain of the Piz d'Err, which stretches as far as the Julier
Pass and the spring of St. Moritz in the Engadine; on the
right is the high Suntail, forming the boundary between
the Oberhalbstein valley and the Schams valley traversed
by the Via Mala.   Warm, rich evening light lay on the
peaks and cut their snowy outlines sharply out of the blue
of the sky; from midway of the height down to the depths
of the valley, there was an autumnal, noticeably darker
atmosphere.

Below, in this Oberhalbstein valley, which is approxi-
mately the centre of all the Rhaetian valleys, rises among
green meadows and hills the church-tower of Vazerol.
Hither came in 1471 the deputies of the communes and
" high courts " of all three leagues, and here was formed
the Confederation of the Lia Cadé or League of God's
House, the Lia Grischa or Gray League, and the Lia dellas
Desch Dretturas or League of the Ten Jurisdictions.   In
the Vazerol letters of union the three federations were
firmly bound together, and their union confirmed for all
time by hand-clasp and oath.

By this act the federal system, which had found in the
Grisons an organic development not reached elsewhere,
was built up to its highest point.   The later wars, the battle
on the Malser Heide, where twenty thousand Grisons
men stormed the strong camp of the Tyrolese and drove
Emperor Maximilian's men-at-arms permanently from their

borders, showed what power such a union possessed from its foundation.

We marched along the path which leads off to one side from Lenz, by the Davos Landwasser, passing the cliff which upbears the ruins of Belfort, to reach at evening the village of Alveneu. The name of this, from *Alba nova*, reminds us that we have reached the region where Etruscan fugitives from the Gauls or from Hannibal's armies found a new home in the Alpine wilderness.

Associated with such recollections, besides what the Engadine, the classic Etruscan valley, offers, are the ancient picture of Rhaetus embracing a lime-tree in Scharans not far away, and the names of certain families, such as that of Catilina living at Stalla, the dividing-point of the Julier and Septimer passes.

Below, in the valley of the Albula, shone the lights of the baths of Alveneu, whose hospitable chambers afforded shelter and refreshment for the night.

Alveneu belongs, with Fideris in the Prättigau and the chalybeate springs of St. Moritz in the Engadine, to the most important baths of the Grisons. From an abundant sulphur spring, in which whitish sulphurous deposits stretch out their quivering arms like the tentacles of polypi, the water is drawn off for bathing and drinking. In the great world outside of this little corner, these baths, which indeed have apparently remained undiscovered by many Swiss travelers on account of the lofty loneliness of their situation, seem to be comparatively unknown. The list of visitors is made up of people from the Engadine and patients from the neighboring valleys. Lack of chemical knowledge prevents us from alluring sufferers to Alveneu by an analysis of the waters; and there is no very strong invitation for the ordinary person in what the " Beschreibung der berühmten Bäder in der Schweiz " adduces among the blessings of this particular " cure " — besides " general well-being " and other symptoms, a " marked eruption on the skin as a result of bathing," " the opening of concealed wounds, reappearance of coughs which have disappeared, and pain in certain parts.''

The comfort of some other watering-places will be sought in vain at Alveneu. No Casino shines in the manifold rays of brilliant chandeliers; the roulette-wheel does not spin, nor are there any sounds of '' *Le jeu est fait — rien ne va plus!* '' Small cells afford the barest necessary room for the guests, and a simple table, for which the Albula provides many plump trout, offers sufficient nourishment. But all other defects are compensated by the invigorating Alpine air and (for any one who has eyes to see) the view of the surrounding mountain-world, where rise majestically the Rothorn and the Arosastock, Züge and Silberberg, Tinzenhorn and Surava.

Following the wild torrent of the Albula, and passing the Romanic Filisur, we soon came to the iron-mines of Bellaluna. Shaft and foundry are now deserted; the greeting of the miners is no longer heard; and only a few blocks of ore in front of the windows of the manager's house speak of the former industry. At present, after the Silesian Count Renard has attempted at great expense but in vain to revive it, nothing but a small quantity of iron is produced.

Narrower and wilder, the rocky walls draw together on each side of the Albula; the mighty gorge known as the Bergünerstein, which reminds one of the Devil's Bridge on the St. Gothard route, begins. A daring road, hewn out of the rock years ago, leads through the ravine; the rock-walls fall sheer away from it, and the Albula brawls six hundred feet below.

In this grim place it is fitting to think once more of Donatus of Vatz, who, with the help of the forest cantons, once smote here the ecclesiastical powers of Chur and Montfort and threw the vanquished into the depths of the Albula, so that, as the admirable chronicler Guler of Wynegg relates, even in his day battle-axes, clubs with iron spikes, helmets and spears were found there.

Beyond the Bergünerstein it grows lighter again. A green hill rises in the midst of the broadening valley, bear-

ing two stone pillars which, as perhaps is the case also
with the two on the Julier, are neither Roman milestones
nor Celtic monuments dedicated to the sun-god Jul, but
simply the attributes of the High Court of Bergün — the
gallows. How magnificently the snow-peaks glisten in the
sunlight all around! The landscape almost seems to need
as its completion a procession of the officials of the old
criminal court, bringing up from the Bergüner Turm, to
the sound of a bell, some poor devil — either a vagrant
gipsy caught setting fire to a house, or a broken-down old
soldier of the Suabian war who has been marauding after
the accustomed manner, such as enriched the speech of
these valleys with the fine words *mordriar and plündriar—*
to his last journey. Many a man who on the way looked
up at the blue sky and thought how fair the world was
must have found it a bitter thing to die on the Bergün
gallows.

These wandering thoughts came to an end in the gloomy
inn at Bergün. In the paneled chamber sat two women,
the grandmother of the house and her sister, dressed in
black, whom our entrance disturbed at their devotions. Up
there in the cupboard stood, as in most houses of the Engadine, the heavily-bound folios of the Bible in the speech of
the valleys, as well as the whole ecclesiastical literature
of prayer-books, spiritual canticles and psalms, created by
the zealous pastors of the Lower Engadine in the sixteenth
and seventeenth centuries. The two aged sibyls had taken
down a pious book in German, a collection of old Protestant
hymns made by Pastor Schmidli of Wetzikon, and, medi-
tating on their approaching death, had picked out a hymn
of preparation which begins thus:

> Come, children, up and onward,
>   The evening draweth near:
> It is not safe to linger
>   Where lurk the shapes of fear.
> Come — for the last long journey
>   Fresh courage swells each breast,
> From strength to strength progressing
>   Toward the end so blest!

These were, the grandmother said, her favorite meditations, and all her life but a preparation for death.

The whole bearing of the two women had something
unquestionably impressive about it. They sat there, simple, unbending, austere, by their Romansch Bibles and
prayer-books. It was a picture of the old Huguenot life;
one was involuntarily reminded by these ancient dames
with their sharply-cut features and their black clothes of
the days when the disciples of Calvin, despite all oppression
and persecution, met by night in the caves of the Cevennes
to listen to the preachers of the new religion and look forward joyfully to martyrdom.

In these valleys lives an uncorrupted, genuine Protestantism. Since 1525, when in the rugged vale of St. Anthony
in the Prättigau the mass was first abolished, the followers
of Calvin in the Upper and Lower Engadine and even in
the territory of the League of God's House were unwearied
in their endeavors to spread the new gospel; and after
stiff disputations, which at times ended in the manner of
the Robber Synod, the surrounding population decided for
the Reformed faith, and held to it in the days that came
after with all the stiff-necked obstinacy of a mountain folk.

The conspiracy of Abbot Schlegel of St. Luzien and the
Bishop of Chur with the Medici for the extermination of
the evangelical doctrine cost the abbot his life under the
executioner's ax; but even the repetition of the massacre
of St. Bartholomew which about 1620 was organized from
Milan in the Valtellina, Poschiavo, and as far as the Engadine, did not bring the Grisons Protestants back to the old
faith. And so they are today the only people of Romance
blood who have remained since the beginning of the Refor-
mation constant to its teachings.

Whoever wanders on a Sunday through one of these
valleys will be surprised to see in what a strict Puritanical
fashion the day is observed. There are no groups in the
streets, no carriages pass along the roads unless to bring
the dwellers in distant valleys to church, and a foreigner

has difficulty in procuring a conveyance. When the bell rings to call them to the bare church, the whole community turns out, the women mostly in black Sunday dresses. We recall with pleasure the impression of peaceful simplicity made upon us one Sunday in the little church of Samaden in the Engadine.

The men and women were separated. First they sang one of the solemn and severe melodies of the old Protestant hymns, the men still keeping their heads covered; then the pastor appeared in his black gown in the pulpit, and after the customary prayers preached on a text from the Psalms, " *Saigniur Diu, ti ess nos rifuggi saimpre e saimpre* " ("Lord, Thou hast been our refuge from one generation to another "). In the measured, sonorous pulpit tone, the gist of his words was intelligible even to one who was not deeply versed in the Romansch tongue — simple praises of the Lord of heaven and earth, who leads the children of men through all the perils of this life and out of the turbulent waves of the torrent of earthly things to a safe haven. A chorale brought the service to a close, and the foreign visitor left the place with the congregation, deeply edified.

Here Protestantism is not formalism, but a living thing that has grown into the flesh and blood of the people. It is to be wished that some historical student may discover a deeper foundation for this phenomenon among a people of Latin descent than has been done by the amateur theorist who explained it by " the cold and inhospitable climate of the district."

In the long winter evenings, when the people read from the heavy, silver-clasped volumes psalms and spiritual exhortations in the vernacular, they tell tales also of the old days when their ancestors sealed their testimony to the new religion with their blood. In more than one ancient Bible is written on a faded leaf the " List of the Protestants murdered in the Valtellina, July and August, 1620 " — a bald list of names numbering several hundred, more impressive than any commentary could be.

The old Huguenot grandmother at Bergün kindly allowed us to inspect her library, which contained almost the whole literature of the sort in the Romansch tongue — for outside of the Bible versions and prayer-books, a few calendars, and today, of course, the inevitable newspaper, there is little in print.

Here at Bergün the Engadine dialect is spoken; but besides a Bible in the "*lingua rumanscha d'Engadina bassa*" there was another in the speech of the Oberland, "*languaig rumonsch de la ligia grischa,*" printed at Chur in 1718, for the use and edification of the Oberland servants of the house.

How extensive the difference is between these two idioms may be seen by a comparison, for example, of the first few verses of Genesis. In the speech of the Oberland they read:

1. Enten l'antschetta ha Deus scaffien ilg Tschiel a la Terra.
2. Mo la terra fora senza furma a vida, ad ei fora scür sin la bassezia. Ad ilg spirt da Deus schaschera sin l'aura.
3. Lura schet Deus: "Ei daventig lgisch!" ad ei fò lgisch.

In the "Ladin" of the Engadine, it reads as follows:

1. In il principi creet Deis il Tschel e la Terra.
2. Mo la terra eira una chiaussa sainza fuorma e vocda. E scurezas eiran sur la fatscha dal abiss, e il spirt da Deis s'muveiva sur la fatscha dallas aquas.
3. E Deis diss: "Saia la lgüm!" e la lgüm fuo.

It is sufficiently obvious from this brief comparison that the Lower Engadine dialect is more distinctive and more closely allied with the other Romance languages than the Oberland idiom with its German elements (like *scaffir*, *schaffen*, instead of the natural *creare*). To this day there is discussion in the Grisons as to which of the dialects has the primacy, and on both sides of the mountains every valley claims the possession of the most beautiful, euphonious and pleasing Romansch.

After a friendly parting from our aged hostesses, we went on through wild gorges and lonely oak-woods, across rush-

ing mountain-brooks, for the most part following the course
of the Albula up toward its source. Two hours' climb
from Bergün, over six thousand feet high, lies a small pale-
green lake from which the Albula issues, and near it the
little Weissenstein Inn, taking its name from a bare, light-
colored wall of rock.

In this dreary corner of the mountains, where the human
race is at most represented by a dejected shepherd-boy on
the scanty grass between the rocks, the German temperament can appreciate the blessing of an inn.

With feelings very similar to those of Columbus when
he first set foot on the shore of San Salvador, we crossed
its threshold. It is inhabited by a homely son of Trins in
the Grisons Oberland, who seemed not at all enchanted by
the charms of his dwelling-place. He told us how, in the
first days of his sojourn, he could scarcely make his Trins
Romansch understood by his Engadine neighbors; how up
there the year was divided into "nine months winter and
three months cold;" how his humble abode was often buried
for weeks together in snow, and the chamois came down to
the lake to nibble a few blades of grass, so that he could
shoot them from his windows.

We listened with sympathy to his unadorned complaints,
and assured him that if ever a publisher, down in the world,
conceived the notion of getting out a new and enlarged
edition of Zimmermann's book on Solitude, he would certainly have a claim from his studies here to be recom-
mended as its editor. The jewels of the lake by the Weissenstein are the splendid trout, of which our host set before
us two specimens that could hardly be surpassed. In this
lake, fed as it is immediately from the glaciers, they acquire
a flavor which is really incomparable, and which compelled
us to express a heartfelt respect.

To the right of the lake rise three similar pyramidal
peaks, deeply cleft, the summits of the Albulastock. Below
them, between the bare parallel walls of rock, the Albula
Pass winds at a height of 7595 feet above sea-level, where

a shapeless cabin of stone offers shelter against avalanches and rock-slides. The last trace of vegetation has ceased by this time; the marshy plateau is covered with chaotic fragments of granite and limestone. With good right the defile is known as the Devil's Gorge. The sprightly tourist Schultze, whose witty remark "A thriving business done here in ruins" adorns many a visitors' book along the St. Gothard route, might with perfect justice have carved it upon a stone tablet here.

Lowering gray snow-clouds veiled the heavens, huge piles of new-fallen snow lay by the roadside. The whole landscape was thoroughly forbidding; and if witches or lemures had suddenly appeared out of a cleft in the rocks, one could only have saluted them as the appropriate personages for such a scene. The weather-beaten cliffs around had lost all color, the distant snow-covered peaks which beckoned from the Engadine, and which beyond the Piz d'Err appeared no longer in the misty violet of evening, raised their heads now in gloomy darkness above the fields of snow. Between black and white, gray was the only medium; with the vegetation the cheerful world of colors had disappeared, and the wanderer unused to such impressions could only look out over the bare waste with the most uncanny feelings, as if a total eclipse of the sun had spread its ashen-gray glimmer over the scene.

Through such a charming landscape, against which in decisive protest we took from time to time a mighty pull at our traveling-flask, the Albula still stretches for a certain distance toward the valley, until a few scattered larches begin to dot the heights. After that it is a swift descent toward the admired Engadine; and we descried with satisfaction the white line of the Inn, which issues here from the Lake of Sils, and the friendly white stone houses of Madulein and Ponte.

We took up our quarters in the well-appointed hostelry of Ponte, near the bridge over the Inn. A foreign guest was prepared to match our praises of the Albula Pass with similar encomiums of the Julier and Septimer, which he had crossed. Above the Romansch sounds of the men of Upper Engadine wrangling in the common-room, rose like a greeting from home the dreamy song,

> When by the window-panes I stand
> And see the night on every hand,.
> My silent tears resistless flow,

with which the hostess was singing her child to sleep in its cradle. Hail to thee, ancient Etruscan valley, mysterious Engadine!

Any one who wishes to grow to feel at home in the Upper Engadine will be well advised to make his headquarters in the " Krone " at Samaden. With a certain dignity this old house, formerly a residence of the Salis family, rose, at the entrance of the large village, with its clean whitewashed walls and deep iron-bound windows; and in the well-kept old-fashioned guest-chambers a specially characteristic breath of the Engadine seems to reach the stranger. Since the days of John de Salis, who took up his abode here just two hundred years ago, nothing has been changed. The heavy ironwork of the door, the clumsy locks whose manifold complications are yet artistically contrived by Lombard masters; the walls paneled with dark-brown walnut; the ceiling bedecked with fine carvings, in which under a double crest the Salis willow and a crossed arrow are still in good preservation; the arms of the old master and his wife; the heavy cupboard against the wall, rich in columns and arabesques, in which are sure to be found the old folio Bibles and vernacular psalms and prayer-books, the hereditary library of the house,—everything, in a word, tells us that here in the peaceful Alpine valleys the changeable fashions of the gay world have not been able to find a following, and that the descendants are still content with what their ancestors built so solidly. Over the dark shield-adorned family bed a voice seems to breathe of love in the old Engadine in the days "when grandfather married grandmother." In this venerable place a contemplative German spirit will do well to rest for awhile, to be fed on chamois and marmoset, to drink Valtellina from an ancient goblet, and to scribble off extracts from the faded records of Guler of Wynegg, the worthy captain and chronicler of the Grisons, or of Ulrich Campbell, the learned pastor of Süss, concerning the forgotten history of the Rhaetian Alps from the days of King Noah, who, after the Flood had subsided, is said to have spent some time in the Engadine.

But today a blue autumn sky was stretched over the valley, and an invigorating, frosty September air allured us out of doors to make the acquaintance of the king of the Engadine Alps, the mighty Piz Bernina, who with all his retinue holds court on the border-line between the Engadine and the Valtellina.

By the colony of old Etruscan cavalry at Celerina, where long ago the Celeres found room enough for horse and man on the Engadine plateau to perpetuate their Italian race, the road goes off to Pontresina.

Huge mountains guard to right and left the entrance of this lateral valley, through which a mule-track — destined in the next few years to be turned into a great military road and important line of communication — leads past the Bernina in the direction of Tirano and Sondrio and the Lombard vines, mulberries and fig-trees.

Standing by the old walls of a church close up against the mountain-side, built in the simple round-arched Romanesque style, it is worth while to look back once more into the Engadine. There rise the bright, clean houses of Celerina and its slender church-tower against a dark background of firs that cover the hill from which flows the chalybeate spring of St. Moritz by its green mountain-lake. Towering above is the Piz Ursina, in the clefts of which dazzling white snow-fields streak the blue of the sky. To the north rise out of the green meadows of the plateau the

villages of Samaden, Bevers, Ponte, Madulein, and (on the
other side of the Inn) Camogasc, offering a friendly contrast to the bare, yellowish-gray rock-walls that come down
from the Albula and Scaletta.

Leaving the valley of the Inn, we approach the little
village of Pontresina. Already, from the distance, between
the fir and larch woods which surround the Roseg valley
as it bends to the right from the Bernina, one or another
dazzling white peak had looked out like a ghost; but near
Pontresina the woods draw back to each side, and before
us stands in unveiled majesty the ice-field of the Roseg
glacier, whose last deposits stretch their gray arms far
down into the valley, while its sunlit heights blind the eye
with their silvery brilliance. The goal of today's excursion was this mighty river of ice, whose frozen streams
unite, on the backbone of the ridge that divides the Roseg
valley from the Berninastock proper, with the masses of
the Bernina glacier that reaches from near the road up to
the summit (13,294 feet), and fill league upon league with
their desolation.

Before starting, however, it is advisable to rest for
awhile in the "Adler" at Pontresina, where guides and
provisions may be secured. From the visitors' book there
one may observe how seldom travelers give proper attention to the wonders of these heights and valleys. Here
and there a casual tourist is visible, or a Heidelberg student, unwearied wanderer over hill and dale. Englishmen
appear but rarely; the book bears witness that now and
then a German collector of butterflies or botanical specimens has penetrated thus far, in order to carry off the
Leiziton areticum from its home between rock and ice.

These peaceful records, however, are interrupted by the
passionate trumpet-tones and drum-beats of "*Evviva
l'Italia libera! Morte al traditor Carlo Alberto! Morte ai
barbari Tedeschi!*" and declamations covering whole pages
in prose or verse, which tell us that in August, 1848, a host
of *crociati* and Lombard *bersaglieri*, less attracted by the

charms of the glaciers than repelled by the news of the
reconquest of Milan, saw fit to turn their backs on the
fatherland and the barbarians, and in the quiet valley of
Pontresina to fire their last shots — in the visitors' book.
At the same time there came down into the Engadine
from the heights of the Splügen and the Stelvio, by the
Bernina road and the rough track which leads over the
Buffalora to Zernetz, more than eight thousand Italians —
and, as malicious tongues relate, before a single Austrian
soldier was on their trail.

Be that as it may, it is not apparent to a single mind
why after a successfully accomplished retreat so much
heroism and martial rage should be displayed in the visitors' book, and why, well behind the firing-line, so loud a
" Dulce et decorum pro patria mori! " should be sounded
in the Alpine stillness.   In many other Swiss visitors'
books a great deal of ink has been spilled to blot out the
records of Custozza and Somma Campagna — in apparent
forgetfulness of the fact that under the circumstances
speech was silver and silence would have been golden.

As a guide for the glacier there presented himself Jan
Colani of Pontresina, son of the mighty Nimrod Jan
Marchiett Colani, who departed this life in 1837 after having killed between his twentieth and his sixty-fifth years,
besides many bears, wild goats, and stags, over two thousand chamois.   Jan Marchiett the elder suffered at the
hands of German literature the worst that can happen to
a man of the Grisons since the days of Sebastian Münster's
" Cosmography "— he was put into print in German
papers while he was yet alive.   In the year 1830 a German
traveler visited the Engadine mountains, and clung to him
persistently until he took him with him to hunt chamois.
But, with the superior humor of an old sportsman, he
always posted the tourist so that he never got a shot, while
he himself, as became Jan Marchiett the elder, picked the
chamois off one by one under his nose.   To show his gratitude, the amateur chamois-slayer immortalized him in the

Morgenblatt, and, apparently believing that in these mountain gorges the laws of historic truth might without reproach be set aside in favor of the growth of legend, threw old Jan Marchiett into such romantic relief as to present him in the light of a person who, by the conceptions of ordinary life (which are more sensible in the Engadine than elsewhere), was indeed distinctly interesting but equally ripe for the penitentiary. In this history it is related how he had already shot a Tyrol man and hung up his equipment as a trophy; how he was a bigamist, though his attempt to instal both wives under one roof had been less successful than it was with the pious Count von Gleichen; how, like a new "Freischütz," he had sold himself to the devil, and in general had accomplished a large number of shameful deeds.

A year and a day passed — and this story reached the Pontresina valley, where it aroused much excitement. It is known that one day the editor of the paper in Stuttgart received a letter with the unfamiliar postmark of Samaden, in which old Colani protested energetically against having his head encircled with such a nimbus, and characterized the tourist's story, in so far as it could not be proved, as wanton calumny. At the foot of the Piz Bernina also the unhappy article had its consequences; it brought about an action for slander on the part of Colani against the other innkeeper on the Bernina, who was accused of having out of envy stuffed the literary German sportsman with these preposterous tales. After hearing many witnesses, the defendant was found guilty by the village tribunal of Samaden, and had to pay more than three hundred francs in costs.

But Colani the elder was never entirely pacified; and it is quite likely that his last thought when he came to die was a silent curse on the invention of printing and on Stuttgart newspapers in particular. Accordingly we recommend to all journalists who write about the Engadine and its chamois-hunters to strive for the most painstaking accuracy.

Our guide (who, with his sister, had from childhood up accompanied his father on his sporting expeditions) was zealous in his endeavors to distinguish between truth and fiction as to his father's history, spoke with marked disrespect of the German author, and dropped dark hints that if he should ever return for the purpose of shooting chamois at Pontresina, a very peculiar reception would await him. In general, Colani showed himself an excellent guide, acquainted with all the dangers of mountain-climbing. He had looked with a keen woodman's eye into all the processes of nature among the mountains, and had made many independent observations of the glaciers, their progress, their diminution, and their many forms, which would be very useful even to a devoted expert in the science of glaciers.

Since the Pontresina valley itself lies at an altitude of nearly six thousand feet, the ascent to the glacier was not difficult. We walked tranquilly toward it through the lonely Roseg valley. Only a few herdsmen's huts appeared here and there by the brook whose strange leaden-colored water flows from the glacier. Bergamasque shepherds, wild-looking Italian figures with yellow faces, their long black hair twisted into large hanging coils, their clothing in picturesque decay, lead their flocks hereabouts in summer, as throughout the whole Engadine, and take them down again plump and well-nourished from the Alps into Lombardy. One of them, who was preparing absentmindedly to depart with his flock without paying the pasturage-fee, had just been notified of an order of arrest from the village magistrate of Samaden; with lively gesticulations he was putting his mule at the gallop, to charge down into the valley and enter a protest.

Colani the younger told us many interesting tales — some from the old legends, according to which the valley was once inhabited by " wild men," whose settlement was completely destroyed by a landslide and the advance of the glacier. In memory of this, in the old Catholic times, long before the "Riforma" came to Pontresina, a requiem mass was said once a year for the victims, "*la messa di Rossedi.*" Colani discussed the name of the glacier, which he derived from *ros*, "dew;" and he could give with accuracy the names of all the heights and peaks that surrounded us. The story of the "wild men" who had once lived here led our historical sense back to the Celtic aborigines of the Etruscan and later immigrations. This was notably confirmed by the name of the great peak which began gradually to lift its snowy summit from the ice-fields of the Roseg glacier behind the Bernina, to be hidden later by the nearer Piz Tschierva. The guide named it "Mittelhorn," but said that its real title was Agaglocks; and when we asked him if this word had any significance in the Romansch of the Engadine, he said no, and added that the peak was known in Romansch as "piz da mezz," but that commonly people called it Agaglocks, without knowing why.

Since, however, as may be seen in Mone's Celtic Dictionary, *clock, clocks* was a widespread Celtic term for "rock," and *aga, ago,* signified "strong, mighty," we were able at once to salute the venerable Agaglocks as a memorial of the long-forgotten Celtic age — as a fellow to our tall friends with Celtic names in the Oberland, Badüs and Sixmadun in the Tavetsch valley. Any one who chooses to look about with care in these lateral valleys and collect place-names from the shepherds and hunters will be able to get together a remarkable list that does not appear in maps and guide-books, but will give great satisfaction to the ear of a lover of the Celtic speech.

After the last herdsman's hut, which we passed at the end of more than two hours' march, the fir-woods and all the larger vegetation ceased; and, framed by the rocky barriers of the Piz Tschierva on the left and the Piz Mortel on the right, the broad, interminable ice-world of the Roseg appears.

A difficult footpath now leads over piles of stones, in whose cavities the "mountanella," or marmot, whiles away the time by producing the peculiar music of his shrill, monotonous whistle. On the sunny slopes there spring from the moist ground various hardy Alpine flowers — bright-colored gentians, luxuriant Alpine roses, the Edelweiss which looks as if it were made out of soft felt, and the gray *Achillea moschuta*, something like a camellia, which the Engadine people call *yva* and from which they brew a heart-warming liqueur. The graceful Apollo butterfly flutters gaily in the breeze.

Soon we were standing at the foot of the glacier. The masses of ice which had pushed down into the valley, swelling out in dome-like shapes, are covered with rocky detritus on the upper surface; but the crevasses were open and not masked by treacherous snow, so that we could climb upon it as confidently as if we were walking on a postroad.

A further march of three-quarters of an hour, without having to cut any steps in the ice and without the need of the rope about the waist which is elsewhere obligatory, relying only on the aid of an alpenstock, brought us nearly to the centre of the glacier world. It is scarcely possible for any one who visits the mountains on the 8th of September to gain with less exertion a more wildly beautiful view.

Immediately before us rose like rocky islands out of a sea of ice the snow-covered summits of the Celtic Agaglocks and the finely chiseled peaks of the Piz Roseg and Piz Mortel. Between Agaglocks and the heights of the Bernina, now for the first time visible on the left (said, according to the most recent measurements, to fall short of Mount Blanc by little more than a thousand feet), broke out the frozen stream of the Vadret da Tschierva. Here the ice is not a compact mass, but an agitated sea of single blocks and fragments, resembling the Rhine when the ice breaks up in the spring and the tossing blocks are piled one upon another by the current. The icy chaos glimmers in the most delicate bluish and greenish tones. From the right of the water-shed come the frozen columns of the Vadret da Mortel, shining in like splendor, and join the Tschierva to form a motionless lake that fills the whole valley and stretches out to meet the offshoots of the Bernina glacier thrust over the side of the mountain like outposts of an invading army.

Far behind us now stretches the vaulted back of the glacier, tending always downward, gray in color and cleft many fathoms deep down to the surface of the ground. Two large moraines, thrown up by the ice which tolerates no foreign substance in its midst for long, also run downward, marked off by dark lines from the glacier itself. Further off, through the dark fir-woods, the houses of Pontresina, just visible, send a greeting to us in this desolate place.

Our stout guide carefully arranged some blocks of stone for table and seats on the spot we chose for our rest, where the solid ice began. Then he placed in a wonderful green cleft of the ice the wine-bottles we had brought, and prepared the simple meal.

The sun shone down on us warmly and as though delighted with the air of the glacier which it was able only to gild, not to melt; in fact, it would tempt even foreign tourists to return for another excursion among these heights. A little honey-bee and a humble-bee flew shyly past us. Colani himself, knowing every aspect of this corner of the mountains, pronounced the day unsurpassed, and by way of contrast described the peculiar effect of a glacier-climb amid clouds and snow-storms, when a man is forced to strive hard against the temptation to lie down on the ice and freeze peacefully into the sleep of death.

With the powerful glass that a chamois-hunter always carries he showed us on the distant slope of the Piz Mortel the tracks of a herd of chamois that had recently passed, and as a spice to our meal recounted a couple of breakneck experiences in his sporting career. Their mad daring showed us once more that the people of the Engadine have

long since forgotten in these mountains the delicate arts
of their Etruscan ancestors and turned to rougher work.

A good German, however, even when he drinks his wine
at eight thousand feet above sea-level, must not be false
to his character of profound subjectivity. Even the author
of the *Sketches of a Pilgrimage in the Orient*, perched
high on King Khufu's pyramid, forgot the hieroglyphs and
ancient legends, and emptied his bottle of Marsala with
self-centred devotion, singing a merry song in the midst of
the desert. So we too felt called upon to enter into closer
relations with the majestic mountain-summits about us,
and drank a deep draught of Valtellina to Bernina and
Agaglocks, as well as to the Piz Mortel, in recognition of
their high claims to our respect. Deep down in the
crevasses of the glacier was heard a cracking and a
murmur, as if the ice-world testified its pleasure that two
German wanderers from the Rhine bore it in mind with
true Engadine piety. It may be some time before another
such health will be drunk up there, before the incense-
clouds of a fine Havana will float gratefully up to the
nostrils of the old snow-giants.

Blue shadows settled down, as the sun gradually disappeared, on the snow-walls that but now were rose-tinted.
The glacier began to take on a grim and ghostly aspect,
until from all the folds and clefts of the rocks the light
mist of evening rose, and veiled the Agaglocks and all its
mysterious charm.

The visitor who wishes to pursue further his studies in
glacier-lore will find, half an hour above Pontresina, another valley in which from the crest of the Piz Bernina
down almost to the road the Bernina glacier rolls down
even greater masses of ice than the Roseg.

Its ascent is attended with greater difficulty, and never
affords so wide and wonderful a view as the latter. We
leave it, therefore, unattempted, and turn back to Samaden,
to add to our collection one more lovely picture of the
Rhaetian Alps.

MARGARETHA* (1854)

In the waves the sun declining,
Heaven's last wild splendor shining;
Slow from earth the day is stealing,
Evening bells afar are pealing:
    Thou'rt my vision, Margaretha!

Leaned against the cliff I stand,
Stranger in a stranger land;
At my feet the waves are foaming,
Through my soul a dream comes roaming:
    Thou'rt my vision, Margaretha!

PARTING* (1854)

'Tis strangely planned in this strange life of ours,
That with the roses ever thorns must grow,
And after all our hearts have longed and fancied
Must come at last the bitter parting woe.
In thy dear eyes I once could read my story,
A dream of happiness and love for me:
    God keep thee, love! It was too fair a vision.
    God keep thee, love! Alas! 'Twas not to be!

Pain, hate and envy, all I too have suffered,
A weary wanderer tossed by storm and sea;
I dared to dream of peace and happy hours,
There led my way from wandering up to thee.
Within thine arms I sought my perfect healing,
And vowed my life in gratitude to thee:
    God keep thee, love! It was too fair a vision.
    God keep thee, love! Alas! 'Twas not to be!

* Translator: Ephraim Emerton.

The dark clouds fly, the wind moans through the forest,
A dreary rain sweeps over wood and plain,
For farewell taking just the fitting weather,
Gray like the storm-cloud looms my world again.
But let it turn to good or turn to evil,
Thou lily maid, in faith I'll think of thee!
    God keep thee, love! It was too fair a vision.
    God keep thee, love! Alas! 'Twas not to be!

OLD HEIDELBERG* (1854)

OLD Heidelberg-beloved!
With honors richly crowned;
In Neckarland or Rhineland
Thine equal is not found.

City of gay companions!
Weighty with lore and wine;
Bright flows thy gleaming river,
And blue eyes brightly shine.

And when, with soft, warm breezes,
Spring breathes upon the town,
She weaves thee, all of blossoms,
A shimmering bridal gown.

Ay! in my heart forever
Thou dwellest like a bride;
Thy name to me is teeming
With lovers' joy and pride.

And if life prove too weary,
And all its charms shall fail,
I'll spur my steed and gallop back
To thee, sweet Neckar Vale!

* Translator: Ephraim Emerton.

THE LIFE OF MARIE VON EBNER-ESCHENBACH

By JOHN PRESTON HOSKINS, Ph.D.

Professor of the Germanic Languages and Literatures, Princeton University

ARIE, FREIFRAU VON EBNER-ESCHEN-BACH, one of the foremost novelists in the German tongue, and one of the best short-story writers in the world, was born at Zdislavic in Moravia on September 13, 1830. Her father, Count Franz von Dubsky, sprang from an ancient Bohemian family that had been settled in Moravia for about two centuries. Her mother, Countess Marie Vockel, a woman of very superior character, was of Saxon Protestant descent. German and Slavic blood is thus mingled in the novelist's veins in about equal proportions and to her lineage is probably due the fact that, in an epoch of race propaganda and race wars, she has risen above the din of contention and conflict to a cosmopolitan view of the world.

Little Marie Dubsky lost her mother in early infancy, but received a careful training from the third and particularly the fourth wife of her father. In accordance with the custom of the Austrian aristocracy she was taught at home by governesses, spending the winters at the town-house in Vienna and the summers at the Moravian family-seat. French, English, music, with a little drawing and modeling, were the chief subjects in which she received instruction.

Her literary proclivities manifested themselves early. Anastasius Grün's romantic epic *The Last Knight* * was the first work that made a deep impression upon her and she began in girlish fashion to improvise herself. Later the Burg Theatre in Vienna became her school. It was the last scions of the old classical drama, Friedrich Halm and

---

* *Der letzte Ritter.*

Otto Prechtler, to whom she owed her inspiration. "On many such a consecrated evening," she tells us in her memoirs, "I sat on a little bench in the back of our box, my head burned, my cheek glowed, one cold shudder after another ran down my back, and I thought, 'sooner or later your productions will be performed here.' Those were hours! Each of them only strengthened my conviction that I was intended to be the Shakespeare of the nineteenth century." On the eve of her fourteenth birthday she writes with unsophisticated frankness to a former governess: "I am determined either not to live or to become the greatest poet of all peoples and times."

With youthful exuberance Marie Dubsky now devoted herself to poetry and produced an epic from Roman history, comedies, tragedies, short stories and miscellaneous poems, none of which have ever been printed. In 1847 some of her work was submitted by her stepmother to Franz Grillparzer. The Austrian dramatist was quick to recognize that she possessed genuine poetic talent and predicted: "To neglect the cultivation of this talent will hardly lie in the caprice of the possessor herself." Unfortunately he was not able to point out the right path for her development to follow. And the cloud of glory which played around the classics of the Burg Theatre proved a mirage alluring her for fifteen years into a course destined to end in bitter disappointment.

On her eighteenth birthday Marie Dubsky was married to a cousin, Moritz Freiherr von Ebner-Eschenbach, a man fifteen years her senior and a captain in the Engineering Corps of the Austrian army. Baron Moritz was a highly educated man whose scientific attainments had already won him a professorship at the Vienna Military Academy. As an engineer, he made several inventions and furnished the plan for the demolition of the ancient city walls. In 1874 he was retired with the rank of Lieutenant Field-Marshal and traveled as far as Iceland and Persia. In his old age he wrote two stories based on reminiscences of

Old Vienna, which artistically do not stand high but bear witness to an interesting personality.

Shortly after the popular uprisings of 1848 the Military Academy was removed to Klosterbruck, a former abbey, in the vicinity of Znaim. In this retired nook Frau von Ebner spent the next ten years of her life. Encouraged by her husband she devoted her mornings to comprehensive studies in history and literature and even took lessons from a German professor in logic and esthetics. Her enthusiasm for the drama was further stimulated by her intercourse with the playwright Joseph Weilen, at that time a teacher in the Military Academy. How many poems and plays she began and finished in this decade we may never know. They are all either lost or buried in the family archives. The only production that saw the light of publicity was a little volume: *From Franzensbad,* six epistles published anonymously in 1858 in which the follies of a fashionable watering-place are lashed with fiery indignation. The book is of no literary significance, but bears witness to the moral interpretation which the author has been ever wont to put on life.

In 1863 the Ebners returned to Vienna, which ever since has been the author's winter home. Here she soon lost sympathy with exclusive society and found her chief satisfaction in a small circle of chosen friends, particularly Ida von Fleischl and Betty Paoli, the lyric poet. As long as they lived, these two friends were the critics and counselors of all her literary plans and in their company she was accustomed weekly to enjoy her cup of tea and game of taroc. Her summers have usually been spent in industrious retirement at the beloved family-seat in Zdislavic with occasional sojourns in St. Gilgen and short trips to Germany to visit her most candid critic and correspondent, Louise von François, the novelist. After the death of her husband in 1898 she spent the two following winters in Italy.

In the year 1900 her birthday was celebrated all over

Austria and Germany. Thousands of congratulations were received from her admirers everywhere. An address with ten thousand signatures was presented to her and a medal struck in her honor. As a crowning distinction, in this same year the University of Vienna conferred upon her the degree of Ph.D. *honoris causâ*. She is the only woman who has ever received this honorary title from the University. "To Marie von Ebner-Eschenbach, the incomparable story-teller, the greatest woman writer in the German tongue, the first among the living writers of Austria, the wise and charitable judge of life,"—thus begins her patent of academic nobility.

Marie Ebner's work is divided by the year 1875. Previous to that date she devoted herself to the drama, after it almost exclusively to fiction. The year 1885 is also of significance in her fiction. As an artistic nature that matured slowly she was over fifty before she attained her full powers and produced her profound studies of life in forms of almost flawless excellence.

A satisfactory account of Frau von Ebner's dramas has still to be written. None of them have ever been included in her published works, pretty good evidence that her own mature judgment regards none of them of lasting value. Why she failed as a playwright is not easy to answer. The accounts of her plays that were actually performed are very conflicting. That she possessed a certain rhetorical virtuosity, even Otto Ludwig, the champion of the realistic drama, acknowledged. That she possessed also a certain power of characterization, as well as a decided vein of comedy, a gift rare in women, seems equally certain. But her enthusiastic admiration for the old classical tragedy seems to have blinded her to the fact that this type was no longer a productive species. A new realistic movement was setting in upon the stage. For this she seems to have had no understanding. The fact, too, that she did not acquire skill in developing a plot until late in life, even in her fiction, warrants the inference that there must have been serious structural defects in her dramas. In comedy, with all her facility in dialogue, she had nothing new to offer in her characters and situations, while her satiric and didactic tendencies were too pronounced to meet the favor of the public.

Her best known dramas are: *Mary Stuart in Scotland,* a tragedy accepted by Eduard Devrient in 1860 for the Karlsruhe theatre; *Marie Roland,* a tragedy of the French Revolution, written in 1867, but never performed; *The Violets* (1863), a satire on polite lies, which later enjoyed a short run in Berlin; *Dr. Ritter,* a one-act dramatization of Schiller's well known sojourn in Bauerbach, written for the Schiller festival in 1869, and *A Forest Nymph,* a very sharp satire on aristocratic society, which was received by the Vienna press with a blast of censure when performed in 1873.

Down to the present day Marie Ebner feels keenly the disappointment that she did not attain the success in the drama of which she had so fondly dreamt. But she was not a spirit to be utterly dismayed. She wrestled with her sorrow until it blessed her. Slowly she came to a knowledge of her own limitations and recognized that her true mission lay in a different field. For over twenty years the short-story had been successfully cultivated in Germany by such writers as Gotthelf, Auerbach, Storm, Reuter, Keller, and Paul Heyse. Turgueniev, in French translations, was gaining a European reputation. Influenced chiefly by Heyse and Turgueniev, Frau von Ebner now abandoned the tragic stage of history to confine herself to the depiction of that with which she had been familiar from her childhood, the life of the Austrian aristocracy in town and country.

Even in the field of fiction Marie Ebner had to struggle for almost a decade before she won a place in the public esteem. Her first fairy-tale, *The Princess of Banalia* (1872), a vague satire, her first book of *Tales* (1875), and her first novel *Božena* (1876), were scarcely noticed by the public press. After the appearance of *Božena,* Baron Cotta is said to have vowed never again to publish anything written by a woman. The five stories included in her volume of *Tales* are now chiefly of biographical interest, but *Božena* is a very noteworthy performance. This Moravian maid-servant that serves three generations in the same family, that has the courage openly to confess her sin and to break with a snap from her seducer, that travels on foot with her foster child from Hungary to Moravia and by sheer force of character compels the designing stepmother to grant the child her rightful inheritance, is a figure worthy of Gotthelf or of Keller. In spite, however, of the vivid characterization and the accurate pictures of Moravian life, the style is prolix, the motives tangled and the work as a whole very faulty in structure.

The next story published by Marie Ebner marks the turning point in her popularity. *Lotti, the Watchmaker* (1880), was accepted by the *Deutsche Rundschau,* the leading literary monthly, and with a bound the author at fifty took her place among the foremost story-writers. In *Lotti,* one of the author's few stories dealing exclusively with bourgeois life, the unpretentious watchmakers who carry on their craft as an art are glorified in contrast to the life of notoriety and sensation led by a fashionable writer who follows his art as a business. In spite of a surer sense of detail and an artistic conscience which shrinks at no effort, this story shows some of the looseness and prolixity of her earlier tales. The action moves slowly and in the character of the heroine there is an excess of goodness, as there is in Claire, the heroine of *Again the Same Old Self* (1885), a better story on a somewhat similar theme.

Marie Ebner's reputation was now established and in the hostility to everything sensational, everything false, everything base, manifested in *Lotti,* lay, as it were, the whole future program of the novelist. During the next two decades tales and novels follow in rapid succession.

The author grouped her stories in seven volumes under the titles: *Tales* and *Stories of Village and Manor-House*. The second title aptly describes almost everything she wrote after 1880. The Austrian aristocracy with their Slavo-German dependents in the Moravian villages constitute the world of her fiction. Country and city are her theatres, noble and peasant keep the balance. Her time is usually the immediate present, seldom — as in *He Kisses Your Hand* * (1885) — does she turn to the brutal customs and smug gallows' humor of the past. All forms of the short-story are at her command; letters, diaries, dialogues, and that most difficult of all forms, the story within a story. In them all there is goodness without effeminacy, sympathy without sentimentality, benignity without cant, and that ever sparkling humor which banishes every trace of monotony.

Who can ever forget *The Barons of Gemperlein* (1881), her first great triumph in humor, these quixotic barons, the one feudal, the other radical, both shipwrecked matrimonial candidates, both obstinate and hot-headed, but both nobly good? Or that most soul-breathing of all her stories, *After Death* (1882), told with a refinement and delicacy of feeling that recalls the tone and technique of Storm? Where can be found a more concrete and genial characterization of the leading political lords and ladies, more lifelike portraits of officialdom and of the much abused peasantry than in her two historic tales: *The District Doctor* and *Jacob Szela* (1883), which have as their background the bloody peasant uprisings in ·Galicia in 1846? Where do we find human sympathy ethically and artistically more refined than in her little masterpiece *Krambambuli* (1887), the story of a dog with spotless pedigree who, like Rüdiger in the *Nibelungen,* perishes in the vain attempt to serve two masters? What humane social tolerance pervades her account of the sporting *Comtesse*

---

*A conventional Polish term of politeness.

Muschi, superficial, but jauntily frank and sincere, who tells her story in breezy letters; and of the more studious *Comtesse Paula* (1884), who dares to be inelegant and devotes herself seriously to the production of memoirs. Everything in these self-confessions is so natural, so full of life and truth and freshness that we easily overlook the art by which they are produced.

In the year 1886 Frau von Ebner published her second novel: *The Child of the Parish*, a tale of Moravian village life. This book depicts the struggles of a waif who, under the most adverse conditions both of temperament and environment, gradually fights his way to a position of thrift and respectability. The story begins with the sober narrative of a murder trial and ends, as it were, with the transfiguration of a saint. This novel is more than an interesting study in child psychology. It is more than a protest against the hereditary curse of sin. It does more than brilliantly formulate a social problem. It is a call to a firmer belief in the goodness of human nature, in the power of education, and especially in the possibilities of self-reliance and self-help. The pupil of Gotthelf and Auerbach here unites the characteristics of the realistic and idealistic village-novel in a higher synthesis. We shudder when we think what a pupil of Zola would have made of such materials.

This novel also marks the vast strides which the author had made during the last ten years in all that concerned her art. She had become more realistic, avoided more and more everything improbable and affected, everything sentimental and prudish. She saw life more steadily, she observed more sharply and chose the essential and the significant with greater accuracy. The structural defects of her earlier works were eliminated. Here we find that clarity, harmony and unity of presentation, that concentration and condensation of the action that marks the great artist. She is still of the conviction that it is not the business of art to give a photographic reproduction of life, but that the divine fire of the artist must purify the materials and transmute them into a work of beauty.

In striking contrast to the happy atonement in *The Child of the Parish* stands *Beyond Atonement* (1889),* a gloomy picture of remorse in the soul of a high-born aristocrat. The heroine, the young Countess Maria Wolfsberg, has married the model cavalier Count Dornach after her father had rejected another suitor for whom she had a deep affection. She becomes a model wife and mother, but in an unguarded moment this former suitor succeeds in entrapping her and she yields to his passion. Now the guilt rests upon her. The book is the history of her remorse. She tries to stifle her feelings by acts of benevolence, by social distraction; naught avails. She seeks the consolations of religion without finding peace. In a sudden accident she loses both her husband and her eldest son. Only the youngest is left, the testimony of her guilt. She openly confesses her transgression. A mortal illness ends her suffering. "All is lost—faith in Providence—faith in my own free will—and yet only one wish—O! that I had never done wrong!" are her dying words.

The question how the guilt of a woman could be atoned had already occupied Marie Ebner in her dramatic period. With riper experience and more consummate art she takes up the question again. Her answer in this case has been the subject of much discussion. Few American readers will be entirely reconciled to Maria's fall, fewer are likely to agree with her own final conclusion that her sin is beyond atonement. Nevertheless, on none of her works has the author expended more love and effort. Artistically it is her finest production and deserves to rank with the great novels of the century. Louise von François called it a German *Anna Karenina*. Structurally this novel is superior to Tolstoy's masterpiece; as a searching study of human life hardly so convincing.

---

* In the *Deutsche Rundschau*.

In 1892 the author dedicated to her dear friend Ida
Fleischl a little volume of *Aphorisms, Parables, Fairy-
tales and Poems*. Of her poetry it may be said that it is
chiefly of biographical interest, it lacks fire and it has no
wings. Her parables and fairy-tales are only the elabora-
tion of her aphorisms with severer ethics and more biting
criticism. In her aphorisms Marie Ebner has concentrated the very quintessence of her philosophy of life and
art. They are not brilliant paradoxes, the witty play of
the understanding in a spirit of egotistical aloofness and
abstraction. But they represent the fruits of a rich experience, of deep self-study, of intellectual battles joyfully
undertaken, and of a searching of conscience victoriously
carried through. They are written with a pen dipped in
her own heart's blood.

During the last ten years of her literary activity the
works of Frau von Ebner grow more profound. For the
problem-novel which charged the literary atmosphere with
" burning " questions during this decade, she has little
sympathy. With that largeness, freedom, insight, and
benignity which characterizes the older idealism of Goethe
and Schiller, she is deeply concerned only with those more
fundamental and universal problems of the human soul
which lie at the very foundation of all education, art, and
religion. She believes that the millennium will come, not
as the result of agitation and social upheaval, but as the
result of a thousand toilsome years of inconspicuous work
on the part of individuals.

The deepest and most significant of the tales that were
written in what has been called her *terzia maniera* is the
novelette *Without Faith?* (1893), another story of village
life, this time in the Austrian Alps. A young country priest
on the verge of losing his faith in God, not as the result
of scientific investigation, nor of the higher criticism, but
in consequence of the terrible human depravity which he
finds in his parish, finally substitutes for his ecclesiastical
creed a faith in humanity and decides to remain in his
parish, content with a modest activity in a narrow circle.

Dr. Székely

MARIE von EBNER-ESCHENBACH

Artistically this novelet is one of the author's best, but as is usual in the case of most novels dealing with religious problems, the question is not settled. The hero's conflict ends in an interrogation point, and his future course is determined solely by temperamental considerations. Perhaps a more heroic outcome was not to be expected on Austrian soil. But in any case, the tale is significant of the vast change that has come over religious thinking even in Roman Catholic countries.

That the author, however, could think through such questions to a conclusion is proved by the modern tragedy in *The Baleful** (1894). A father placed before the difficult choice of saving his only daughter's life by a single word, or of sacrificing her to the bullet of an avenging murderer, lets fate take its course in order that "the Baleful" may be rooted out of the world. With similar indignation the author in *Missing* (1895), and in *Bertram Vogelweid* (1896), turns on the harmful in art. "An artist — a priest" is the author's creed. In the first, an old painter outraged by the hue and cry of the naturalists, retires from the world only to be sought out by one of his former colleagues, a boastful pretender of the modern school. In the second, with far greater whim and humor the author makes short shrift of Nietzscheanism, the young Czech movement, the erotic mania and all other types of *fin de siècle* poetry, often in terms more expressive than elegant. Other stories of this decade are *The Favored Pupil* (1892), which pictures the woes of a poor gymnasium student; *Oversberg* (1893), a flawless example of the author's skill in telling a story within a story; the tragic *Death Watch* (1893), in which the whole fate of a man — past, present, and future — is condensed into a single scene; and that charming idyll *Miss Susanna's Christmas Eve* (1902), in which the author embodies a picture of her own generosity.

Marie von Ebner-Eschenbach belongs to no school. She has been called a realist, but she is a realist only in her

---

*A term applied by hunters to destructive animals.

wonderfully sharp power of observation and in the fact
that she does not avoid the commonplace and the ugly. She
is at heart an idealist who is always seeking the eternal
and universal significance of these every-day common-
places. Her literary significance lies in the fact that in an
age whose art is permeated with a spirit hostile to religious
faith and morality, she, without pedantry, without sentimentality, without cant, has lifted up the banner of idealism
in life and art and once more united the German literature
of the last quarter of the nineteenth century with the literature of the classic period.

Of the qualities that make up a great writer she has the
deep and high truth of substance. She does not view the
world in the rosy light of the idyll. She never seeks to
avoid the ugly. She goes after guilt great and small. But
more, she puts a high moral interpretation on human life.
Her ethics is proof against all egotism and will bear comparison with that of the great moralists, ancient and modern.
To her the soul is everything, externals nothing. She does
not describe persons, but through small characteristic
actions almost imperceptibly conjures up the personality
like a vision. In this method she is without a peer since
Goethe. It is her style which is not free from shortcomings.
Her diction is plain and almost colorless. Her expression
often suffers from a certain harshness and uncertainty disturbing the narrative. To settings she pays little attention
and her work is lacking in lyric appeal.

Marie Ebner has often been compared to George Sand
and George Eliot. She has neither their imaginative power
nor their proselytic zeal. But she is a truer interpreter of
life than the former, and has a finer feeling for structure
than the latter. Her closest kinship is with Turgueniev,
without his sympathy for weak-willed men of feeling and
without his fatalism. She is not so prolific as any of these
three, but it is not improbable that a larger fraction of her
works will live.

THE DISTRICT DOCTOR* (1883)

By Marie von Ebner-Eschenbach

TRANSLATED BY JULIA FRANKLIN

I

OCTOR NATHANIEL ROSENZWEIG had had a youth full of privations. What enjoyment means was unknown to him in the brightest period of life. To suffer from hunger today and earn just enough to be enabled to go on suffering from hunger tomorrow; at two o'clock in the morning to curl himself up like a hedgehog in a corner of the underground room to sleep the dreamless sleep of exhaustion; to be roused by the whining of his old grandmother, who excused herself for being still on earth and for having to be a burden to him; to hurry away to teach in order to attain the possibility of learning himself — this was the course of his life year in, year out. To acquire was the essence of all his thoughts and dreams; to acquire money, knowledge, favor, particularly that of his professors (Nathaniel studied medicine at the University of Cracow); to acquire at any cost save only at the cost of honesty; to acquire and be sure to expend nothing without return, not even the least bit of his own strength; to be unmoved by any sympathetic impulse, any considerations that would retard his progress.

His grandmother and himself, himself and his grandmother, constituted his world, and as his world was small, so were his aims narrow. The first and most difficult achievement was to save enough money to keep himself and the old woman from starving, should some unforeseen stroke of fate incapacitate him for a time. When he had

---

* Permission Gebrüder Paetel, Berlin.

accomplished that he felt as if he was a capitalist, and consoled his grandmother when uttering her daily morning lamentation, with:

"Just go on living in peace; it is not likely that anything bad can happen to us now."

His indefatigable diligence was not lessened after his first success; it increased, on the contrary, with his added strength.

Nathaniel grew up to be a strong man; his spider-like extremities developed into muscular arms and legs, his chest expanded, his figure, despite its spareness, acquired a certain sturdiness. His bearing was so confident, his glance so calm and clear, his speech so decided, that even his first patients — people of very low degree — would say:

"What a clever gentleman our doctor is!"

No one realized how young he was: he had consorted too long with care, and even though he had mastered and conquered it he could not prevent its continuing to gnaw at him secretly.

Gradually he acquired a reputation, modest but favorable, and it was owing to it that he was at the early age of thirty appointed to the position of district physician in the western part of the province. A sure means of livelihood henceforth — ample, too, according to Nathaniel's notions. He need not have been so painfully close in fitting up his dwelling, in the market place of the district-capital, but he was afraid he might become puffed up with pride as most poor people do who rise to sudden wealth, and he threw but little work in the workingmen's way. Always bearing the saying in mind: "An ax in the house saves the carpenter," he provided himself with all sorts of tools, and was pleased to save the cabinet-maker and locksmith as well. And although his household furnishings were dreadful to look upon, that did not disconcert the doctor; he either lacked the esthetic sense or it was not developed.

When the grandmother, aged and unable to move about, could no longer leave her room, yet yearned for the sight of

a green shrub, a flower in bloom, then the doctor became a
gardener, and before long the windows of his house resembled those of a conservatory.

The old woman suffered at times from a recurrence of
her former faint-heartedness, only it manifested itself now
in a different form.

"If I only do not die too soon," said the nonagenarian.
"A funeral costs so much!"

Nathaniel comforted her lovingly.

"Don't die, grandmother, you would defraud me of the
reward for all the pains which I have taken for your sake."

Nathaniel's fortune increased apace, his joy in possession continued to grow and grow. Plans to realize which
would have appeared to the prudent man in his youth a
sheer impossibility, he now pondered with the confidence of
impending fulfilment. His practice was extensive and
remunerative. He was called to all the castles in the neighborhood. The dry, reticent Doctor Rosenzweig, who
brooked no contradiction, who never allowed a flattery to
pass his lips, became the confidant of noblemen, and, what
was far more remarkable, the oracle of their charming,
elegant wives, and the friend of their children.

"The child is very ill, but — Doctor Rosenzweig is treating him." — "I spent the whole day in mortal anxiety
about my little girl — but Rosenzweig is here now."

If only Rosenzweig was there, succor was there, and
should it for once not be forthcoming, why then God did
not wish it to be brought by the hand of man, that was all.

Under no circumstances did his patients show themselves
niggardly toward him — nobody would have dared.—
Doctor Rosenzweig is building himself a house, a house of
burnt brick — that takes money. He has leased a building-
site outside of the city, and a square, one-story box of a
house has been put up on it under his own direction. It
rests upon a solidly built cellar, is provided with stone steps
and a weather-proof tiled roof. The window-frames are
painted a snowy white, the walls whitewashed snow-white

too. The only ornament that graces the façade is the little tablet of the life-insurance company by the side of the door-bell.

The windows of the front — it faces the east and the first story is occupied by the doctor and his grandmother — command a wide prospect — sky and fields. The eye roams unconfined into the endless distance. No hill obstructs it, no wood marks a dark spot upon the smooth surface of the plain, gleaming golden in summer, silvery in winter. Every foot of soil can be saturated by the life-giving rays of the blessed sun. If there is a shadow, it is a shadow that passes and does not chill, that robs not the tiniest blade of the warmth which it requires for its wondrously mysterious growth — the shadow of the fleeting clouds. How often does Nathaniel follow it with attentive gaze, watch it glide over the ripening, swelling abundance, which will be gar-nered in the autumn, shipped on the Vistula to Germany and Russia, and sold at a high price. Could one but have a share in this magnificent profit, have a hundredth, nay, only a thousandth part of the returns flow into one's own pocket! The doctor begins to build air-castles upon the boundless plain, so iridescent and fabulously beautiful that he cannot help smiling as he builds them: Dost thou call to me, too, thou unclaimed heritage of my ancestors — Oriental imag-ination?

He turns from the sight of others' affluence and wishes to draw a line between it and his own modest property. A neat picket fence surrounds the house at a distance of ten yards on every side; after every twenty pickets there is a strong, pointed post. In the space between house and fence a little garden will gradually come into existence; the division into flower and vegetable beds is already outlined. No chessboard can be more exactly divided.

"Next year, grandmother dear, you will see roses and mignonette blooming under your window," Nathaniel prom-ised the old woman, and she replied:

"If I only live to see it, my child. I shall be ninety-five my next birthday."

"Way over a hundred must you live to be!" he cried
eagerly. "You owe it to me, think of that! How people's
confidence would increase still more if everybody were saying, 'He has succeeded in making his grandmother live to
be over a hundred years old.' For people are stupid,
granny, they attribute to my skill what is due to your good
constitution. Just keep up your courage and make up
your mind firmly that you will not die yet. You will continue to live on cheerfully just as long as you can make up
your mind to do so."

The old woman did decide to live on, but as for any real
cheerfulness, that was out of the question.

"I often feel now," she would say, "as if your grandfather stepped before me and spoke to me as he did in his
dying hour: 'Come soon! We shall live as peacefully in
the garden of Eden as we did on earth. Follow me soon,
Rebecca.' * * * Then I could not obey the call of my
loved one, because you kept me back, you helpless little
creature, left so entirely alone. First your father and
mother went and soon after your grandfather. Yes, it was
a fearful pestilence which God visited upon his people in
Kazimirz, and I knew not to whom to turn and say: 'Be
kind to my grandchild if I, too, should lie down and die.'
So I dared not then fulfil the wish of my loved one. But
now, Nathaniel my child, I feel as if I ought not to keep him
waiting any longer."

Such speeches cut the doctor to the heart. Never had the
reserved, silent grandmother spoken in that way before.
A suspicious sign when old people depart from their habits!
The little changes are often succeeded but too soon by the
irrevocable, the final one. And yet another symptom disturbed the doctor. The old woman, who formerly could
never have enough solitude, now no longer liked to remain
alone. Every time Nathaniel bade her good-by she would
say:

"Go, in God's name, but send me the 'Goi'* to keep me

* Gentile.

company, so that I can look at a human face and not only and always at the fields and the sky."

The "Goi" was a youth of eighteen, the doctor's famulus, his servant, his slave. He could not remember a time when his "benefactor" had vouchsafed him a kind word or presented him with a good article of clothing. When Rosenzweig's coats and boots could no longer be used, they would be given to the tall young fellow, with the admonition that they should be treated with the care due to other people's property. The doctor steadily expanded in breadth, and it almost seemed as if he diminished in height. His famulus grew more and more "attenuated," as Doctor Rosenzweig expressed it, every day, and shot up, asparagus like, into the air. The way the benefactor's clothes sat upon him struck the former himself as either pitiful or ridiculous — both with an admixture of contempt.

He simply could not bear the youth, his antipathy was insurmountable and sprang from the thought that the foundling was eating his master's bread gratuitously or nearly so.

Four years since Rosenzweig had picked him up from the street, upon an icy, splendid winter night. With the pride of a triumphant hero, the doctor was spinning along swift as an arrow in the sledge of Count W. At his departure the Count himself had wrapped him carefully in the fur cover which felt so comfortable, had thanked him again and again, and sought over and over for new words to express the inexpressible — the bliss of a loving heart to whom what is dearest, what he had considered as lost, has been restored. Saved was the young Countess, saved from almost certain death by the genius, the resourceful care of the incomparable physician, who stood at her bedside like a hero on the field of battle, almost vanquished, yet with victory in his eye, ready for combat even while succumbing; who had not budged until he could say:

"We have won the day, she will live!"

He had watched so many nights that he looked forward

to the refreshing sleep on his journey home in the comfortable sledge. But his fatigue must have been too great, it banished the longed-for refreshment instead of inducing it. As often as Nathaniel would close his eyes they would open involuntarily and revel in the sight of the star-gemmed moon-lit heavens and the snow-covered plain, which glistened with a wonderful brilliance, like some huge fresh-minted silver coin. * * * How much gold could be had for such a coin? The vaults of his quadrangular dwelling would not have room to contain them, the precious, the adorable ingots! Harborer and bearer of all-conquering forces, latent witchery, garnered power. What cannot be got in exchange for gold? Treasures beyond price are purchased with it — that the man knows who restores the health of those who pay him.

The doctor's flight of thought was suddenly interrupted. The vehicle stopped close to the ditch, and the driver cried:

"Doctor! doctor!"

"What is it, my son?"

"Doctor, two drunken people are lying out there."

"Get down and give them a drubbing so that they won't freeze."

While the driver was dismounting and fastening the reins to his seat, Nathaniel had risen and bent forward, and was gazing with strained attention at the face, brightly illumined by the moon, of one of the figures lying on the ground. No drunkard's face, surely! but one that gave evidence of downright want, and suffering to the limit of human endurance.

The poor devil had, at least at the moment, no consciousness of misery; he seemed to be sound asleep. But when the driver took hold of him and dragged him up, he fell back at once, stiff as a block of ice, into the snow. The driver said:

"Doctor, one of them is already frozen."

Rozenzweig jumped from the carriage and soon convinced himself that the driver's assertion was correct. He was filled with rage. Here again he had been forestalled by death, the kind of death he hated most — not death caused by sickness or old age, but death brought about by chance, a death which gets its prey gratuitously, gaining possession foolishly, absurdly, without any sound reason.

"Let us look after the other one," muttered the doctor between his teeth.

The other was sleeping, too, but not so profoundly.

It was a boy of about fourteen years, evidently closely related to the deceased — his brother, younger by many years, or his son.

With professional ardor the doctor essayed various means of restoration, and after long effort they were crowned with moderate success. A scarcely perceptible trickling coursed through the boy's rigid arteries, and though it ceased almost immediately, the doctor nevertheless declared with victorious assurance:

"I have him now!"

And wrapping the boy in his fur, he lifted him into the sledge, took him home and laid him in his own bed, where he watched over the child of misfortune with the same devotion that he had shown to the Countess in the castle. Next morning the patient was out of danger, and Rosenzweig could not refrain from remarking to himself: "This one, also, saved — two between two risings of the sun!"

He stroked his long, patriarchal beard complacently and rejoiced in his wonderful ability.

But he said to his patient that very day:

"Get up and go."

"Where, doctor, where? Who will take me without my brother," the boy rejoined despairingly; and now the question arose: What to do with him?

The papers found on the person of the deceased showed him to have been a machinist, Julian Mierski by name, who had for many years served as foreman in a factory in Lemberg. In his certificate of character it was stated that his employer was, to his regret, compelled to discharge this excellent workman on account of a severe illness. Since that time he had been unable to make any money, and only very little could be earned by his brother, whom he had taken care of upon the death of their parents — poor cottagers — in a village near Lemberg. Thus, the boy related, the savings of years were used up in a few months, with the exception of some florins, whose exact amount he indicated, and which had actually been found in the dead man's wallet.

The grandmother listened attentively to the lad's tearful account.

"Listen, Nathaniel, my child," said she. "It was not right of that Goi in Lemberg to forsake in his sickness the man who had served him in health so many years."

"A factory is not a charitable institution," rejoined Rosenzweig, and he bade the lad proceed.

The boy continued:

"A week ago an acquaintance of my brother called and told us that there was a factory in Cracow like ours, and that we would surely find work there. My brother was very glad: ' Come, Joseph, let us set out,' he said; and on the journey he would keep saying that it was his long idleness that had prevented him from getting well, that walking was doing him good. But all of a sudden he could go no further and lay down in the snow in order to sleep a while."

"And you allowed that?" the doctor shouted at him. "Don't you know what happens to a person in such bitter cold weather if he lies down in the snow?"

The boy lowered his big eyes, which were still streaming with tears, and remained silent.

"What can one do with such a *chamer?* "* asked Rosenzweig addressing his grandmother.

The old woman replied:

"Let him rest yet another day under your roof. Be merciful to him. He is an orphan like you."

The following day her advice was:

---

* Jackass.

"Keep him. Our maid is growing old and feeble and could make use of some help. Keep him and train him to your service. Who will blame a great man like you for having an assistant?"

Thus the foundling became an inmate of the doctor's home, and although Doctor Rosenzweig would not admit it, an exceedingly useful one. In the eyes of his master Joseph remained a "chamer," who did not gain any knowledge from books, and never could. At eighteen years of age he still found it difficult to read the simplest children's stories. After the first months, the doctor had abandoned the idea of compelling him to go to school, because it was only by corporal punishment that he could get him to attend, and his benefactor did not always find time to administer it. His mechanical aptitude, on the other hand, was great, and great his assiduity in applying it. He, too, dabbled in all trades but with better success than the doctor had done.

In everything that he undertook he displayed a skill, a facility, nay, even a taste, which proved as serviceable to the doctor's pill-boxes as they were to the flower-beds in the little garden before the house. It was always with displeasure that Nathaniel heard him praised, "the idler who knows nothing and never will know anything but how to play."

Once when he gave vent to his usual reproach, Joseph remarked:

"If you could make up your mind to take your fields under your own management, I would prove to you that I am no idler."

The doctor, flying into a passion, cried:

"My fields—what are you talking about? Don't you know that I am a Jew, and as such may not own any landed property? Don't you know that even my house is built on other people's land?"

Joseph flushed crimson with embarrassment, yet he gazed confidingly and openly into the doctor's face as he replied:

"You bought the fields in the name of Theophil von Kamatzki, but they are yours anyway."

"Tell me, boy, where did you get that information?" asked Rosenzweig, and the gesture with which he began to flourish his cane was most threatening.

Calmly Joseph returned:

"It is no secret. All the people know it and they do not begrudge you the fields."

During this colloquy they were standing in the middle of the path which, leading from the street-door to the little garden-gate, ran straight down between two beds of roses neatly bordered by mignonette. On the gooseberry hedges which Joseph had trained along the wooden paling, the first fruits were ripening. All that could be seen of delicately unfolded lettuce plants, turnips with their showy tufts, cauliflowers gleaming yellow among their curly leaves, fresh onion-shoots with their martial-looking helmets, graceful marjoram, and — *dulci cum utile* — as a boundary to every vegetable square, the sweet-scented lavender, whose tiny buds were beginning to swell — all was so exuberant with strength and health that the sight made one's heart, particularly a physician's heart, leap for joy in one's bosom. With a secret satisfaction Rosenzweig contemplated the pleasant gifts of Heaven, and said:

"Because you are a passable gardener you imagine you could be a farmer, too." He wanted to stop there but changed his mind and added, while he dug the end of his cane with great persistence into the ground and apparently followed the operation with great attention:

"I should not have obtained possession of the fields — somewhat wrongfully, I admit — had I not had reason to hope that I should soon be able to own them with good right. I suppose you know that a change is about to be made in the laws of the land, and that the Jews are also to share in the greater degree of freedom which will be given the people of Galicia."

Joseph was aware of that and hoped that the doctor, after the fields were his property before God and man, would no longer lease them but cultivate them himself.

"Then you will have to build stables and barns," the boy concluded. "I learned something by watching the architects in the city and have the plans ready."

"You are a young fool," returned the doctor — yet a few days later he asked to see the plans.

Well, practicable they certainly were not; still it must be conceded that it was remarkable that a foundling whose handwriting was like that of a child of seven should have been able to draft a plan so neat and exact, and correct, too, it may be, in its measurements. He was just one of those who can dance before they have learned to walk. There are such odd fish. They do, to be sure, strike us at times with astonishment; but as a rule they do not turn out to be anything.

Nathaniel, who never pursued a thought which concerned his weal or woe any length of time without making a confidante of his grandmother, questioned her soon after as to what she thought about his managing his estate himself. Then it appeared that that subject had already been discussed between the old woman and the foundling.

"You will grow rich like Laban," she prophesied. "The visible blessing of the Lord is upon you."

This was proved that spring, the spring of 1845, so disastrous to thousands, when the Vistula, overflowing its banks, converted the luxuriant, promisingly ripening crops into a slimy sea. Irresistible as a judgment of God, the tide had surged in, washed away the nurturing soil and with it the property and the hopes of those who cultivated it.

Close up to the boundary of Nathaniel's fields did the devastation extend — before them the waves retreated. Before them the waters had gone back and had divided, as did the waters of the Red Sea when Moses lifted his rod and stretched out his hand at God's command.

And when autumn came, famine reigned round about. Hundreds forsook their homes with their wives and children and wandered about as beggars, as day-laborers, seeking bread and work.

But the grandmother would ask every day:

"When does the harvest begin? This year wheat is worth a hundred times its usual value. When are the reapers coming?"

"Soon, very soon. They are already sharpening their scythes," Nathaniel answered smiling.

The old woman did not, however, live to see the harvest-time. She herself fell back, like overripe grain, into the lap of mother earth before her grandson could say to her:

"The reapers are coming!"

Very late and yet too soon had her life been suddenly extinguished.

There she lay, then, in her narrow coffin, old Rebecca — a strangely poignant picture. Death had straightened her bent form, and, weeping and astonished, Joseph asked:

"Was she as tall as that?"

But he likewise asked:

"Was she as beautiful as that?"

Released from all infirmities, freed from the helplessness of age, how majestic she appeared now in her everlasting rest, in a peace that naught could disturb! The smile seen on the countenances of so many who have conquered, did not hover on her lips. A stony coldness spoke from her features, which had been illumined even in her dying hour by the inspired love and admiration which the presence of her grandson had always called up.

"It is no longer you!" meditated Nathaniel, and the consciousness of his loss seized him with a terrible force.

He motioned to Joseph to leave, he wished to be alone with his dead. Standing at the foot of the bier, he strove to see in his grandmother's strange, altered countenance the one that had so long been familiar and dear to him, and he found it not. The only ideal good that he had possessed, the affection of that old woman, was gone forever, and there he was, a man getting on in years — alone. With a sudden shock the thought flashed upon him: Between you and this old woman there lies a generation. You should now be able to go and weep for her upon your's wife's breast and gather consolation from the sight of your children.

The restlessly striving man who had only looked forward, never backward toward aims which grew with his successes, paused for once in his course, faced about and traversed in spirit the whole of his life's pathway. I have achieved much, he might have said to himself, but never the slightest bit without a thought of you, grandmother. She had been the source of all the brightness and happiness of his life and the void that her death had created yawned all the more painfully before him.

She should not have forsaken him, she whose presence had deceived him as to the flight of time — the sense of which is lost by the very old.

"Do not follow the custom of our people," the old woman would often say. "Do not marry too young and bring beggars into the world. You can wait, my child, you are young."

He had always remained silent at this admonition; today he answered her who could no longer hear him:

"You kept on thinking me too young to be a lover, until at last I got too old to be one."

The reproach which he had addressed to her in her coffin he felt immediately, however, to be a sacrilege. Stepping up to her, he bent over her and, what had never happened while she was alive, he kissed her hand, kissed her brow and the lips forever silent, the only ones on earth from which he had ever heard the words "my child."

II

Joseph took part in the activities of the harvest of his own accord, and one afternoon Rosenzweig, sauntering past indifferently, as if the thing did not concern him, saw him standing aloft on a pretty well-filled harvest wagon. Nimbly and energetically he was stacking the sheaves, and it struck the doctor that the lad in the queer, wide jacket

which had served his benefactor as a coat, and the trousers
so much too short for him, was nevertheless a remarkably
handsome fellow. Tall, slim and vigorous, his countenance
white and red, his well-shaped head crowned with fair, wavy
hair, his whole being breathing joy in his work, in labor —
he looked uncommonly well on his proud eminence.

Among the women and girls engaged in the field was the
daughter of the farmer to whom Rosenzweig had leased
Squire Theophil von Kamatzki's land. A pretty, lively
creature — a genuine daughter of Masovia. Rosenzweig
observed that the brown, sparkling eyes of the girl and the
blue eyes of the lad exchanged glances quite often, and if
then the brown ones were lowered in confusion they were
obstinately pursued by the blue ones — so obstinately, so
boldly, that they were finally compelled to be lifted, whether
she wished it or not.

The disdain with which Rosenzweig regarded Joseph
received new nourishment from this little incident. A fellow condemned to lasting servitude by the miserable nature
of his brain, undertakes to turn that of a girl? And at
what age? A mere boy, of the age which the doctor's son
would be had the doctor married at the proper time. What
he in heroic self-denial had delayed to achieve until he had
missed the chance of achieving it, the happiness of love,
this a crude, penniless fellow, dependent upon others'
favors, aspired to with thoughtless levity!

That evening Rosenzweig summoned Joseph to his room.
It was such a bare, cheerless-looking apartment that every
one shivered who entered it — even in the dog-days. The
furniture consisted of a number of chairs ranged along the
wall, a huge writing-desk painted white, and a long, low
bookcase, likewise painted white, which, like a counter in a
shop, divided the room into two parts. The smaller one,
near the windows, was appropriated by the doctor, the
larger one was where the patients waited until he stepped up
to them through a narrow space which had been left open
between the wall and the bookcase. Upon its topmost shelf

lay or stood all sorts of objects, in gruesome contemplation
of which the people beguiled the time while waiting.
Peculiar looking instruments, knives and forceps and tightly
closed glasses filled with a transparent liquid, which the
Galician instinct at once suspected to be spirits. Only,
unfortunately, the good beverage was spoiled by the highly
unappetizing formations swimming in it.

Across all these things Rosenzweig now called to Joseph,
who had just entered:

"Now tell me what is going on between you and the
farmer's daughter, Lubienka?"

As usual when his benefactor addressed him sharply, the
lad turned fiery red, nor did he at once find a reply. It was
only after Rosenzweig had repeated his question that he
summoned up courage and answered in a low but firm tone:

"I love her."

"And she?"

"She loves me, too."

The doctor broke into a bitter, mocking laugh.

"You imagine so?"

"I know it, sir—"

"And where is this love-making to lead?"

Now, Joseph thought the doctor was making sport of
him, that he just wished to twit him a little, and he answered
quite cheerfully:

"To marriage, sir."

"Marriage! You are thinking of marriage?"

"Yes, sir! And Lubienka is thinking of it, too."

"She, too. * * * What does her father say to that?"

"He finds it all right, Panie Kochanku!"* cried Joseph
with an outburst of overflowing emotion, and he looked as
if he were about to rush into his benefactor's domain, forbidden to all save the doctor.

The latter, however, rose commandingly from his seat and
calling to the lad sternly, "Stay where you are!" fixed him
to the spot.

---

* Dear sir.

In cruel words he laid before him his poverty and his hopeless future. He was indignant at the thought that this fellow had perhaps reckoned upon him, or upon his purse, and he made up his mind to show the interested rascal the door when the work of the harvest should be completed. Meanwhile, he ordered him from the room and retired to rest with the resolve to admonish the farmer the following day to put an end to the love-making between his daughter and Joseph.

Precisely upon that day, however, something occurred which once for all drove every unessential and secondary consideration out of his mind.

Summoned early in the morning by the proprietress of a neighboring estate to the bedside of her son, who had suddenly been taken ill, he was able to reassure the anxious mother regarding the condition of the patient, and would have been glad to go home at once. The hospitable custom of the country forbade that, however. Willingly or unwillingly, he had to partake of an ample breakfast which was served in the drawing-room. A large number of guests stopping at the castle had gathered there — a company well known to the doctor, and as repellant to him as if it had consisted entirely of quacks. Adherents, of both sexes, of " King " Adam Czartoryski, conspirators against the existing order, fanatics for the restoration of the old Polish régime. The lady of the house, still young, handsome, enthusiastic, and since the death of her husband, absolute mistress of the great estate which had been her dowry, was the soul of the party and its powerful support. She kept up a lively correspondence with the national Government in Paris, received and harbored its emissaries, and expended great sums annually upon revolutionary objects.

This fanatical agitation displeased the doctor and distorted the image of the woman so estimable in every other respect — as a good mother, a clever manager of her property, a humane mistress of her subordinates.

With an expression of annoyance he took his seat at the tea-table, ate and drank, and did not utter a word, while the ladies and gentlemen were eagerly discussing politics. It seemed to him as if he were surrounded by children who, instead of playing soldiers, were, for a change, playing conspirators.

Suddenly a fair hand was laid on the arm of his chair.

" Why so dejected, dear doctor, in face of the most beautiful miracle? " said Countess Aniela W. to the man who had saved her life.

Rosenzweig arose and bowed:

" What miracle does your ladyship mean? "

" That of the revival of the Polish Kingdom! " replied the charming woman, and her dove-like eyes flashed an eagle glance, while she raised her graceful figure proudly to its full height.

The doctor suppressed a smile, and a number of patriotic ladies exclaimed in pained disappointment:

" You doubt? Oh, doctor—is it possible? A man so clever! "

" I do not doubt, ladies. Who says that I doubt? "

" Your smile—entirely groundless, since we are in earnest—says so," rejoined the Countess, and folded her arms like Napoleon.

" The moment to shake off the foreign yoke is here. You may be informed of it because you are a good Pole and our confidential friend. The signal for the outbreak of the revolution will be given in Lemberg at the archduke's opening ball! "

A general silence followed this open declaration. The conspirators were dismayed at the arbitrariness with which Aniela disposed of the common property—the plan of the party. Yet she was far too lovable and, besides, looked far too charming to permit of any feeling of resentment against her. She wore a little Parisian cap with a cascade of patriotic red and white ribbons. The rich material of her morning gown had been brought to her from Nijni-

ST. STEPHEN'S CATHEDRAL, VIENNA

Novgorod by her husband at the time of his last mission to Russia — a feat attended with great danger.

Oh, there was quite a history connected with it. * * * But it was not to be related today; surely not at this moment where the main thing was to efface the unfavorable impression which the Countess, in her rôle as a politician, had produced upon the company.

"You people of little faith!" she exclaimed, "do you doubt the loyalty and trustworthiness of a man who has saved my life for my country?"

Several young men hastened to protest, and an old man, of the petty nobility, with a long, drooping mustache, raised his glass of Maderia, emptied it in one draught, and cried:

"Vivat Doctor Rosenzweig!"

The hostess repeated:

"Vivat Doctor Rosenzweig, to whom so many of us are indebted for our own health and that of our children!"

After this toast she gulped down the remainder of her sixth cup of tea. Instead of showing himself grateful, the doctor muttered:

"How often have I told your ladyship not to drink so much tea? You ruin your nerves."

The beautiful hostess answered with a superior smile:

"Good Heavens, my nerves! Quite different demands will soon be made upon them!"

"I understand — at that revolutionary ball!"

"Yes, doctor! Yes!" interrupted Countess Aniela — "the ball where we shall inaugurate an event of world-historic significance!"

"At the mazurka or the française?"

"The cotillion. The ladies choose, simultaneously, all the officers present. The officers divest themselves of their sabers for the dance. The sabers are removed. No sooner is that done than the Poles rush at the defenseless foe and cut them down!"

"Vivat!" cried the old nobleman, who had spoken before, "down with them all, no quarter!"

Some of the ladies protested, and suggested giving quarter to those officers who should ask for it. They withdrew their proposal, however, upon noticing that it excited doubts as to the genuineness of their patriotism.

"Ladies and gentlemen," said Rosenzweig, "this plan is wonderfully conceived, but as to carrying it out, you will not do it."

"Why?" was heard from all sides, "what is to hinder us?"

"Your own nobility of soul, your own loyal nature. Noble women and noble men like you may hate, may fight, but they do not betray and they do not murder."

"Monsieur," said a youth of nineteen who had just returned from a Paris educational institute, "your argument would be valid in war, but it does not apply in a conspiracy."

"Quite right—because * * *" It suddenly occurred to the old noble that it was in order now for him to make a speech; jumping up and clicking his heels together, he cried, after some deliberation:

"Vivat Polonia! Vivat King Adam!"

And now a trembling, hollow voice was heard issuing from a corner of the room. It seemed as if it proceeded from the depths of a mountain—a mountain of silk, soft draperies, laces, ruffles, and ribbons. The voice belonged to Sulpicia, wife of the Starost,* great-aunt of the hostess, in whose house the old lady lived, enjoying a most bounteous charity.

"Olga, Duschenka moja,"† said she, "think above all of your eternal salvation."

The hostess had noticed with consternation the gradual decline of the enthusiasm of her guests, while she herself, after her seventh cup of tea, had attained the highest summit of inspiration. The old lady had with her admonition

---

* A nobleman, owner of a castle or domain called a Starosty.

† My darling.

poured oil upon the fire. It blazed forth at once, too, in the resounding, solemn cry:

"All for Poland! My earthly and my eternal salvation!"

Countess Aniela, quite transported by this loftiness of spirit, threw herself into her friend's arms, the gentlemen kissed the hands of the fair patriots. One of them requested the honor of drinking from the hostess' slipper. She would not permit it, however, out of regard for the exalted earnestness of the hour, and the one whose plea had been rejected seated himself at the piano and struck up a plaintive national melody.

All remained silent, all listened with emotion, many eyes were dim with tears.

The irresistible power of the song affected even one who up to that time had stood impassive in the embrasure of a window and taken no part in the conversation.

Rosenzweig did not know him and, with his innate distrust, was inclined to take him, on account of his striking pallor, for one of those diffident patients who are so glad to put themselves in the way of famous physicians on neutral ground, in order, incidentally, to get their advice, for which they omit to pay a fee.

However, Rosenzweig was mistaken. The stranger made no attempt to approach him, while on the contrary the doctor could not disengage his attention from the stranger.

He was a man of medium height, slender, with a fair, scant beard, with blue and evidently very near-sighted eyes. The impression of great spiritual activity produced by his features was heightened by the pallor which had at first misled the doctor into thinking him an invalid. But he soon changed his mind on that point, too. Ill health does not spiritualize, as the poets often assert; it marks the children of the earth rather with distinct tokens of their origin.

In the appearance of this man, however, no signs of bodily distress were visible. The traces of suffering on his marble-like brow had been stamped there by restless working thoughts, and the lines round the youthful lips by early and strenuous spiritual conflicts. The disdain with which the doings of the company seemed to inspire him had been gradually overcome. The strains of the beautiful national air touched and thrilled him too. One emotion bound him to his brethren — longing, a passionately fervent longing for his lost fatherland.

Of this fount of suffering no people has drunk so deep as the one from whose heart this song has gushed. It sings of the prodigal son who returns to his parental home filled with repentance and glowing love. Halting he stands at the closed door and hears the voice of his father, who calls to him, and hears the weeping of his mother. * * * " Father! Mother! " he groans. They answer: " Come, deliver us, we are lying in chains." * * * He rattles at the iron gate, wounds his hands with knocking, bruises his brow, the blood begins to flow. In vain. Never will that gate yield, never will he be able to unhinge it. He will perish on the threshold.

The song ceased, and the silence that followed it was only broken after a space by the hostess, who rose, went up to the stranger and conferred with him in a low voice.

The stately lady seemed literally to make herself small before her guest, her whole attitude attesting veneration, all her gestures, homage.

Folding her hands, she exclaimed imploringly:

" Speak, oh speak to the assembly! "

The appeal of the hostess received enthusiastic support.

" Oh yes, speak! " cried many voices in unison.—" It would give us new courage."—" We have only been waiting to get the courage to ask you."—" Modesty forbade."

All of them approached, with friendliest mien, with punctilious courtesy — none without a certain awe. Even the triumphant Countess Aniela was constrained, and her lovely lips were tremulous as she said:

" Give us a proof of your marvelous eloquence, of which
we have heard so much. It is said that you are capable of
moving hearts of stone and rousing the morally dead to the
noblest deeds! ''

The stranger laughed, and his laugh was as clear and
fresh as that of a child. Involuntarily Rosenzweig was
forced to think: You have an innocent soul.

" What is his name? " he asked his hostess.

She blushed and replied with a rather unsuccessfully
assumed indifference:

" It is my cousin Roswadowski, from the Kingdom.''*

The doctor had never heard of any famous orator named
Roswadowski; but what did that signify? In times of
national revolt national notabilities spring up over night.

Roswadowski returned the look which the doctor fixed
upon him with one equally searching, and, with a slight
inclination of his head toward him, said:

" Why not ask Doctor Rosenzweig to speak? He might
tell you what he expects from the revolution.''

" We know that in advance,'' rejoined Aniela, " like
every good Pole, the restoration of the kingdom, the general
welfare.''

" Olga, Duschenka moja,'' again the great-aunt let herself be heard, " tell your friend Aniela that no one is a
good Pole who is not a good Catholic.''

Without taking heed of the interruption, Roswadowsky
pursued:

" The general welfare should embrace every individual
interest, consequently that of this man and his co-religion-
ists as well. Why do I not hear any of you who are so
full of his praise say that you purpose to pay the debt
which we all owe to him and his people? ''

" *Ce cher Éduard!* '' exclaimed Count W., and, swaying
his body and smiling suavely, he added, in a voice audible
only to his wife and to Rosenzweig, who was standing near
her: " He is growing madder every day.''

---

* Part of Russian Poland.

The hostess, too, was dissatisfied with her cousin's unexpected outburst, and declared very sharply that she on her part, at least, did not feel as if she owed a debt of gratitude and reverence to the excellent physician.

"And as regards the equal rights of all creeds in the Polish Kingdom," observed Aniela, " it is already established in principle. The modes of procedure will be considered later. Up to this time, however, time has been lacking to enter into details."

" I prostrate myself at your feet! " exclaimed Rosenzweig. " I no longer feel any concern now for the cause of the Jews."

" Your promise arouses his mirth, so great is his confidence " — Roswadowske put in. " He whose whole life consists in the devoted performance of his duty toward us expects from us — nothing."

" Sir, if I did not do my duty, I should forfeit my position," the doctor interposed, in the tone of a man who wishes to put an end to a disagreeable discussion.

His unbidden advocate rejoined, however:

" When I spoke of duty I had a higher one in mind than the one imposed on you by your office. Officially you are an able district-physician — it is your own heart that makes you a Samaritan."

" A Samaritan! * * * I? "

" Yes, you! The one in the Gospel cared for the dying man on the highway and then gave him over to the care of others. The dying man whom *you* found on your path you received in your house, which has become a home for the orphaned Christian boy."

The doctor replied disparagingly:

" Just as one chooses to look at it," and thought to himself grimly: " You are well informed, you flatterer! My house a home for such a *chamer!* "

And at that moment he obtained the answer to a question which he had often pondered — whether a person can think of two things at once; for, in good truth, he was thinking at the same time: Before sending away the *chamer* I shall have a new suit made for him.

" Thus acted a Jew," said the orator, turning to the company, " of his own free will, toward one of a different faith, and what have we of a different faith ever voluntarily done for one of his race? Read your history and ask yourselves whether a Jew *can* wish for the day when Poles shall again govern Poland."

Olga and Aniela remonstrated; as for the gentlemen, most of them had followed Count W. into the adjoining room and seated themselves at the card-table. The venerable noble and the new arrival from Paris alone remained chivalrously with the ladies, the former declaring that he, too, had in his youth occupied himself with the history of his country, but had never read of aught but glorious deeds.

Now the door was flung open, and a servant rushed in and cried:

" The prefect of the district. He will soon drive into the courtyard."

The brave women uttered a cry of horror:

" Great Heavens! The prefect! "

In mortal anxiety the hostess grasped her cousin's hand. "Away, away, hide yourself! "

" I am not thinking of it," returned he quite calmly, " I am very glad to make the acquaintance of so amiable a gentleman."

" You shall not stay! You must go — because your presence compromises us," exclaimed Count W., who, with consternation in his face, had returned to the salon.

An altercation ensued.

" Doctor, I beseech you, hasten to meet the prefect, try to detain him as long as possible on the steps," implored the mistress of the mansion, and hurried Rosenzweig to the door.

" I shall do what I can; I bid you good-by, ladies and gentlemen! " he answered, and left the salon, highly delighted in the bottom of his heart at the turn which the gathering of the conspirators had taken.

From the hall he saw the prefect just entering the house. A portly, elegant-looking man, dressed with the utmost care. The top of his silk hat glistened, in the glimpse which the doctor first had of it, like the moon's disk. No less shone the patent-leather boot on the little foot which he set on the lowest step as Rosenzweig reached him.

"I have the pleasure of welcoming your Honor," said the doctor, flourishing his hat ceremoniously.

"My dear doctor? Is it really you? What?" the official responded, with a most gracious smile, you, too, in the nest of the conspirators?"

"Dropped out like a little unfledged bird! — How fares your Honor?"

"Well. Thanks to your directions."

"And the exactness with which your Honor follows them. You are such an excellent patient that you deserve to be sick all the time."

"Greatly obliged for the Christian wish * * * Pardon me — it was a slip of the tongue." And now came the question which the prefect never spared the doctor even at a most cursory meeting. "But, my dear doctor, when will you at last be baptized?"

The standing question received the standing answer:

"I don't yet know exactly."

"Make up your mind! You are anyway only half a Jew."

"I should presumably be likewise only half a Christian."

"Oh! that is a different matter!" rejoined the official, severely. "We are not talking of that; now tell me — " his expression remained unchanged, but his small, shrewd eyes cast a penetrating glance at the physician: "Is he upstairs, the emissary? Have you seen him?"

"What emissary?"

"In this house he is introduced as Herr von Roswadowski."

An expression of such honest astonishment was pictured on the doctor's countenance, that the official explained:

" You are not initiated! — Well, I shall not rob you of your political innocence. * * * Quite charming, those conspirators! particularly the ladies. For that matter, there is less reason for us to beware of them than for them to beware — of others. There is a storm brewing over their heads of which they haven't the faintest suspicion. These harmless malcontents, who consider themselves dangerous, are themselves threatened by persons discontented from quite different causes and dangerous in quite a different way."

Rosenzweig had no time to ask for an explanation, for the mistress of the mansion, beaming with friendliness, appeared at the head of the stairway, and the prefect advanced to meet her with graceful, rapid steps.

III

Rosenzweig sent word to his coachman to harness up and follow him. He himself started ahead on foot and soon struck a narrow path, which, crossing the field obliquely, led close to a stone cross on the highway. He intended to wait there for his carriage.

He longed to take good long strides, breathe the fresh, free air, inhale the wholesome odor which rose from the ploughed-up earth. But he wondered why he did not experience a keener sense of joy and satisfaction at having escaped from the perfumed atmosphere of the salon.

A feeling of profound discomfort took possession of him, a vague emotion which he could not account for but which troubled him greatly.

Suddenly he cried out loud and repeatedly: " Fool! Fool! "

The apostrophe was intended for the person whom the prefect had termed an emissary, and it was the recollection of the unmerited praise which the fellow had bestowed on him that put the doctor out of humor. Every word that the " fool " had uttered, every trait of his spiritual apostle's face, the expression of rapturous veneration with which his deep-blue eyes had rested upon him — he heard all, he saw all again, and it filled him with wrathful shame.

He, the dry Nathaniel Rosenzweig, intent upon his own advantage, a philanthropist and Samaritan? Alone as he was here in the field, the blood surged to his cheeks in a fiery glow. He recalled the hands which in the course of his long life had been stretched out to him in supplication, and said to himself: " Never have you given help except professionally. And what we do in that way, we do for our own sake." His duty he had done fully; but duty — the word itself implies it — is only an exchange. More than this he had never done — he had given his energy, his talent, the fruits of his steadily increasing knowledge, in exchange for the prosperity and the esteem which he gained through them. Thus had he hitherto acted and — he threw back his head on his stout shoulders — thus he meant to act in the future. Let every one first follow his example; let this degree of morality, though essentially a low one, first be attained by the majority of mankind, then may the idealists, the dreamers of a golden age of universal brotherhood have their say — not before!

Now he was himself again, and strode on firmly and cheerfully, in his usual calm spirit.

Long before his carriage, of which he could not catch a glimpse, though he looked hard, he reached the stone cross. At its foot there cowered a pitiful figure. An old man, his knees drawn up to his chin, a high sheepskin cap on his head, about his shoulders the remnants of a blue dress-coat which the late land-owner had presumably worn in the days of slumbering patriotism. Frayed linen trousers hung about his thin legs, which, like the rest of his body, were trembling incessantly.

When the doctor approached and addressed him, he lifted his bronzed and furrowed countenance slowly and with an effort, and looked at him with his dim, red-rimmed eyes with the humble, suffering expression of an old staghound.

" What are you doing here? " demanded Rosenzweig.

" I am waiting, your Honor, I am waiting and praying," answered the old man, streching out a bony right hand, upon which hung a much used rosary; " I am always waiting for a letter from our good Lord."

" What do you expect our good Lord to write to you? "

" That I may go to Him; it is high time, very high time."

" How old are you? "

" Seventy, no more. But see how I look, and if your Honor knew how I feel. Here " — and he tapped upon his hollow, wheezy chest — " no breath. Every day I think I shall die on the way, that I shall not reach the cross."

" Why don't you stay at home? "

The old man stretched out his arms with an indescribably forlorn gesture. " They drive me out, my daughter, my son-in-law, the children. Well, yes — they have no room themselves in the little hovel."

" To whom does the hovel belong? "

" To my daughter. Yes, my daughter. I made her a present of it for her dowry."

" A petticoat-property, then! " scoffed the doctor. "And now she drives you out of the house that you gave her? "

" Great Heaven, what shall she do? My son-in-law beats her because I live so long. He tells the children: ' Children, pray that your grandfather may die soon ' — Yes."

" You have a fine son-in-law."

" Good Lord, sir, people are that way. Gentlemen like you don't know how people are. There are others in the village who are much worse. Particularly at this time." He lowered his wheezy voice. " Woe to all the *panowies* and *panies** who live to see the coming year! "

" And why? What do you mean by that? "

" Oh the poor gentry! The poor, poor things! " whined the old man, and began to cry bitterly. " Everything will be taken from them, and they will be murdered, too."

---

* Masters and mistresses.

The doctor burst out: "You are not in your right mind!"

And now the old man, wringing his hands, cried:

"You answer me like that, too? That is a misfortune! * * * The priest answered me like that when I told what I knew in the confessional; the agent answered me like that, and the bailiff even threatened to have me flogged for saying such things. * * *" And turning his shifting glance upon the doctor he added: "Are you agreed with them, too?"

"Agreed — I? With whom? * * * Tell me everything," commanded Rosenzweig. "What will happen the coming year?"

"People from beyond the sea will come and will divide all the property of the nobility among the peasants."

"That of Pan Theophilus Kamatzki, too. Just wait, canaille!" mused the doctor, and said: "And what will the Government say to that?"

"The Government? Oh Jesus! The Government had all the land surveyed last spring so that the foreigners may know how it should be divided."

Rosenzweig burst into a loud laugh: "Oh this people * * * I have had dealings with this people for fifty years, but the ways of their folly I have not yet fathomed. * * * Old man! The Emperor had the surveys made because he wants to know how large his Galicia is and how much taxes it can pay him."

The old man shook his head incredulously:

"We know better, pardon me. The Emperor takes away the land from the gentry who are against him and gives it to the peasants who are for him. Then all will be well, most people think. * * * I think it will be bad. Every day will be Sunday, and what do the peasants do on Sunday but fight and get drunk? * * * Oh gracious sir, if it could only be prevented!"

"Set your mind at rest, it will certainly be prevented," returned Rosenzweig, laughing again.

At that the old man's ire was suddenly roused:

"If you had been at the tavern last night and had heard the commissary preach, you wouldn't laugh."

"The commissary? The emissary, I suppose you mean to say. An emissary, such as wander about now by the dozen."

"No, no, not such a one. One who was a master once and says now that there should no longer be any masters. He knows so well what is coming that he preferred to become a peasant at once of his own free will, and has given everything away."

These words aroused Nathaniel's keenest attention and convinced him that the old man was speaking of the same man whom the prefect had termed an emissary and with whom he himself had just stood face to face.

The same! it was he — he, beyond doubt, the enigmatical being the story of whose life was discussed by the sensible with scorn and derision, by the timid with hatred, by the visionary with enthusiasm; it was — *Edward Dembowski.*

Often had he heard that this man exercised a witchery which none could resist, and he had regarded this mysterious influence with the greatest incredulity; and now he admitted to himself that in reality he was experiencing a kindred sensation.

Yes, the pallid enthusiast stalked like a spectre by his side. His image pursued him with intolerable persistence. In vain did he strive to turn his thoughts from it, it emerged ever anew and defied his will to banish it.

The doctor's carriage had been standing for some time on the road. A comfortable *britzschka* with a pair of well-fed, cream-colored mares in graceful harness and collars hung with bells. The driver was a slim fellow, clad in a neat, simply braided coat; the whole formed a handsome turn-out which aroused the envy of many a nobleman.

The doctor patted the horses' stout necks and straightened the little plaits of their black manes. He was just on the point of stepping into the carriage when he turned and called to the old man at the foot of the cross:

"What is your name?"

"Semen Plachta, sir."

"Listen to me, Semen! Crawl home and tell your son-in-law that Doctor Rosenzweig is coming to visit you tomorrow. He should leave you at home. Do you understand me? If I do not find you at home when I come, I shall see to it that your son-in-law shall, even before the general distribution, receive a thrashing as the first advance payment." Rosenzweig had pulled out his purse and taken out a five-gulden note. His face grew very serious as he contemplated it. A brief hesitation—then he handed it to the old man.

"Now, this belongs to you. I want to hear tomorrow whether this money has been expended for you."

Semen stretched out his hand for the fabulous wealth—speak, think, he could not.

The driver, too, was stunned, opened his eyes wide, and almost dropped the reins from astonishment. What in Heaven's name could it mean? His master give away five gulden to a street-beggar!

"Master," said he as the doctor stepped into the carriage, "you gave him five gulden. Didn't you make a mistake?"

"Hold your tongue and drive on!" commanded Rosenzweig, and the whip cracked and the roans started up.

Soon the physician's house came into view on the broad plain. It no longer stood there quite alone like a landmark; neat-looking stables and sheds, ranged in the form of a horse-shoe, were to be seen in the background, and a carefully cultivated nursery filled the space between the dwelling and the outhouses.

The latter had, indeed, been built according to a plan of the *chamer*, which had been approved by the architect, and, it had to be admitted, had turned out well.

Whether Rosenzweig returned to his home from the farm

of a petty noble, from the dwelling of the lord of a manor, or from the castle of a magnate, he always greeted his beloved possession with the same feeling of satisfaction. "Let others have what they may but give me my own!" And in reality he would not have changed with anybody, no matter how profitable the exchange. For he had never loved a living being, his grandmother excepted, as he loved his little estate. And as it lay there so trim before him, the possession so slowly and arduously acquired, an embodiment of his strength and ability, a property founded, as few are, in right and justice, he clenched his fists and dealt an imaginary murderous blow at the imaginary person who should dare to touch it.

That very evening he called on the prefect and reported to him word for word his conversation with Semen Plachta.

The official entered into a detailed discussion of the communistic plots in the country, but the real object of their originator, or the nature of that singular being, he was unable to explain, close as was his knowledge of the whole course of the man's life.

The emissary, who wandered indefatigably through the country and preached in palace and cabin the gospel of the equal rights of all mankind and of the equal division of all landed property, belonged, as a son of the Senator-castellan of Poland and lord of the manorial estate of Rody in the government of Warsaw, to the high nobility. He, too, like the others of his class, had grown up and been trained in the consciousness of transmitted rights and inherited power, and the duty of maintaining and exercising them.

Scarcely had he obtained possession of them, however, when he voluntarily relinquished them. The revenue from his estates found its way into the poor man's wallet or was expended upon revolutionary objects. He himself wandered about recruiting disciples for his doctrines, finding them in the ranks of his own class. He appealed to the impressionable hearts of youth, and the purer and more

innocent they were, the more ardent was their adoration
of him, their longing to follow his self-sacrificing example.
Apostles of the emissary made their appearance in the
Kingdom of Poland, in western Russia, in Posen, in Galicia.
With the words of their idol on their lips, they cried to the
aristocracy: " Cast from you the riches and the privileges
you have too long enjoyed. Privilege is injustice." And to
the people: " Come, ye poor ones! Take your share of
the soil which for hundreds of years you have enriched with
the sweat of your brow, and—oh how often!—with your
blood as well."—But to all they said: "Arise, shake off
the yoke of the foreigner. We want to found a kingdom
where there shall be neither superfluity nor poverty, do-
minion nor servitude, a kingdom such as Christ preached."

The spiritual leader of this missionary campaign had
meanwhile participated in the revolt of 1843 against Russia, frustrated almost at the moment of its outbreak. He
escaped to Posen as a fugitive, was called to account before
long for spreading communistic principles, imprisoned, and
finally banished. He repaired to Brussels, where Lelewel
was paying the penalty for the aberrations of his all too
ardent love of liberty and country in the torments of the
bitterest homesickness. Intercourse with that " Grand
Master of Revolutionaries " heightened Dembowski's enthusiasm to fanaticism. What thenceforth filled his soul
was not alone sympathy with the wretched and the needy,
but a hatred of the powerful and the rich, whether they
were the rulers of the Powers that had partitioned Poland,
or the masters of the Polish junta in Paris, usurpers of the
kingdom which they wished to restore.

The apostle of brotherly love returned to his country as
a political agitator. He who hitherto had followed only his
own impulses undertook to carry out the plans of others,
and the task of preparing the soil of Galicia for revolt. He
was working now to that end. Did those who intrusted
him with that mission know what they were doing? Did
they look upon him and his teaching simply as a leaven

which was to start the dull masses fermenting and set them moving, assuming that they themselves had the power to dictate in what direction?

The sympathy and admiration which every genuine Pole feels for one who has suffered in the struggle against foreign rule was once again attested. The aristocracy shielded the outlaw, although they recognized in him an enemy to their interests. No matter what party he belonged to, the liberation of Poland was one of his aims — they met on the way and grasped each other's hands.

"And see here," concluded the prefect, "the man in me has not been so completely merged in the official that I should not love these Poles for their patriotism, often heedless, blind, but always high-souled — yes, and envy them for it."

"Your Excellency!" exclaimed Nathaniel in a disapproving tone, and both men remained silent. It was only after a long pause that the doctor resumed:

"I believe, your Excellency, that it is, above all, the duty of the Government to protect itself and the nobility from the pernicious influence of the communistic aristocrat." Here he interjected the Ruthenian adage: "It is an evil bird that fouls its own nest." "I cannot understand why they look on so long without taking any action; why he is not prevented from disseminating his deadly poison under the very eyes, as it were, of legal authority."

Disagreeably impressed by Rosenzweig's determined manner, the prefect replied with a cool air of superiority:

"It is hardly done without a reason. Moreover — between ourselves! — we have directions to keep track of him — in an inconspicuous manner."

"Oh — if that is the case!" cried Nathaniel with an excess of zeal, "then I implore your Excellency to make use of my services. Nothing would be more inconspicuous than to intrust a sick man to the care of a physician. And that your 'emissary' is sick — here," and he pointed to his forehand, "and that his proper place is the district-physician's examining room, I can take my oath."

The expression of the official's countenance grew steadily colder; suddenly addressing an indifferent question to the doctor, he dismissed him, warningly citing to him at the same time Talleyrand's famous saying: "*Surtout pas trop de zèle.*"

The warning was fruitless. The doctor's ardor in the cause of law and order once unchained could not be held within bounds. He was anxious to communicate to others the disquiet which constantly possessed him, displayed a supreme disgust against the persistent patience that prevailed among the ruling classes, terming it criminal levity and unpardonable indifference.

His political creed might, up to this time, have been summed up in one sentence: "Our Government will be the best conceivable as soon as it condescends to grant the Jews the right to own land." Now, however, his faith in the wisdom of that Government was shaken, and he began to comport himself as its instructor and adviser. He gave the prefecture no peace; daily he would bring new and increasingly ominous reports regarding the spread of the communistic propaganda, counseling ever more urgently the adoption of energetic precautionary measures.

He had made the close acquaintance of Semen Plachta's son-in-law, and this furnished him much food for thought. He had never before occupied himself with the study of a peasant's soul. A peasant had, in his eyes, been one of the most uninteresting of bipeds covered with a human skin. Now he took one under observation, studied him carefully, even accompanied him to the tavern, entered into discussions with him, and on the third day he knew, what he had really known from the first moment, that the man was lazy, addicted to drink, and stupid. How stupid, appeared only when brandy loosened his heavy tongue; and it needed but a few questions to arrive at the conclusion that he lacked even the cardinal knowledge of the distinction between mine and thine.

The doctor drove over to see the Countess Aniela and delivered a discourse to her on the condition of the rural population. "Yes," he concluded, the peasant is stupid, but how should he become clever, unless he is accidentally so by nature? Yes, the peasant is lazy, but what would industry avail him, it would never lead him to prosperity. His industry would benefit the master rather than himself. Yes, the peasant still takes the penny he earns today to the tavern, but this wastefulness proceeds from his misery. Misery is not frugal, misery cannot even grasp a thought so sane and fruitful as that of frugality."

Countess Aniela raised her graceful head and her lovely lips assumed a mocking expression.

"Honored saviour of my life, you talk exactly like the emissary," she observed, "it seems like hearing him speak."

The doctor remained silent; the playful reproach struck home.

An hour later he was standing in his nursery in front of a sapling which, no thicker than one's finger, yet bore under its crown of leaves three beautiful apples, almost fully ripe, with yellow, glistening skins. Any other time he would have taken pleasure in the sight; today it only heightened his ill-humor. Joseph came out of the house, his implements on his shoulder, and wanted to show his benefactor some saplings just as ambitious to become sturdy trees as the one that had aroused the doctor's admiration.

The doctor remained unresponsive. Turning his eyes, glowing with grim severity under their bushy brows, upon the youth, he said abruptly:

"Tell me, have you never heard anything about a champion of freedom, a sort of fool, who is staying in the neighborhood, and, they say, is preaching revolution to the peasants?"

Joseph was evidently startled, and remained silent.

"Confess! Confess!" commanded Rosenzweig, and he bent his threatening countenance, flaming with anger, close to that of the youth.

"I don't know," stammered the latter, "whether you mean the one who is called the emissary."

"He is the very one I mean!"

"But he does not preach revolution, he preaches diligence and sobriety."

"Diligence in stealing, sobriety in killing — eh?" scoffed the doctor.

Contrary to his wont, Joseph was not to be disconcerted. He went still further — he actually presumed to contradict the doctor.

"You are mistaken. I know him."

Rosenzweig started back with an inarticulate cry, and Joseph continued:

"I had a long talk with him."

"Where? and when? and about what?"

"In the field last week; and the talk was about you."

"—About me?"

He obtained his information about me from the *chamer's* lips?" reflected the doctor.—"Well, that is the way they are!"

"I have never heard him preach," resumed Joseph.

"But you should like to?"

"Oh yes! — I should like to. No preacher can equal him, they say. They say, too, that he will speak tonight for the last time in our neighborhood, in Abraham Dornenkron's tavern, a mile from here, on the road to Dolego."

A long silence followed, which was broken by the doctor, who ordered Joseph to proceed with his work; he himself repaired to the prefect, reported what he had just learned regarding the emissary, and asked whether it would not be advisable to send a detachment of hussars to the tavern and have the agitator arrested.

"All will be done that is necessary, my dear Rosenzweig," answered the official. "We have exact information of

INNSBRUCK

everything that is going on, and find no occasion for anxiety. What are you afraid of? You are one of us. I wish I could instill some of your caution into those who stand more in need of it than you and I."

Rosenzweig then paid a few professional visits and only returned home late in the evening. In front of the garden-gate he met Joseph, who was awaiting him.

"What are you standing there for? Go to bed," he called to him harshly.

He would gladly have found rest himself, but it fled from him on this night as it had on the preceding ones.

Suddenly the thought struck him that Joseph might possibly be stealing away from the house to hasten to the tavern in order to hear the agitator's farewell address. The distance, it is true, is great, and the evening far advanced, but the fellow has young limbs. * * * For that matter — who knows? If he is afraid of being late, he may even take a horse from the stable. * * *

Well, at least *that* doubt should not trouble him long. Quickly seizing a candle from the table, he hurried down the steps and along the hall toward the room that Joseph occupied.

It was years since he had entered it; it was the only poor room in the house and irritated him every time he saw it. A narrow oblong chamber with a brick floor, lighted by a single window. Had Rosenzweig been Joseph's doctor instead of his "benefactor," he would have forbidden him to sleep on that straw-bed in the corner between the turning-lathe and the wall, which fairly dripped with dampness.

He said this to himself when he found the youth who he presumed was on his way to Dolego, stretched out in deep, blessed slumber upon his more than modest couch.

As Rosenzweig bent over him and turned the light upon his face, his eyelids quivered, his fresh, rosy mouth contracted defiantly, but only for an instant, then with lips lightly closed, he continued his peaceful breathing. Had he possessed a thousand tongues, they could not have pleaded more eloquently for his purity of heart than did the expression of unconscious, silent peace on his countenance.

Depositing the candle on the turning-lathe, the doctor looked round the room. The pieces of work he saw there, begun, half-finished, or nearly completed, all were the fruits of the industry of busy, skilful hands. And it must, after all, not have been such a poor brain that directed their execution, for nowhere was there any trace of wasted materials or childish trifling. And the young fellow's every thought was bent upon the prosperity and improvement of the doctor's home; that object absorbed all his efforts, commanded his best strength and insight. One example among a hundred struck the doctor particularly and — almost touched him.

The doctor had lately had the little wooden garden-gate replaced by an iron one and had been satisfied with the work of the local locksmith, but Joseph thought: "It is not pretty enough, I want to add some decoration." Rosenzweig laughed at him at the time, but now the work was under way, the ornament had with infinite pains been cut and filed out of heavy sheet-iron, and the doctor's monogram, quite artistically intertwined, stood out among graceful arabesques.

Rosenzweig smiled, crossed his arms, and, for the first time, sank into a kindly, sympathetic contemplation of this modest Jack of all trades. At the head of his bed he noticed a Saint Joseph, fastened to the wall by four nails, and below the picture in clumsy writing:

" From my Lubienka."

Yours, you poor fellow who own nothing on the broad earth? Have some solid soil under your own feet first before you dare call to a weaker mortal: Come to me! You have as yet acquired nothing, earned nothing in spite of your zealous industry and loyalty, nothing — no wages, no thanks, no rights. What you do for me, the use you are to me, serve only as payment for the involuntary debt you once incurred.

When will that debt be finally canceled, poor fellow?
* * * Has it in reality not been canceled long since? If
you were clever enough to calculate and balance accounts,
you would have said years ago: We are quits! From now
on pay me, master! I, too, want to earn for myself. I am
a hard man, they say, but no one dare call me unjust. If
you had asked I should have given. I should have allowed
you a place in the world, had you asserted yourself. But
you did not; you kept on silent under your yoke and you
will continue to go on the same way until you break down.
You will be in as helpless a condition at the close of your
life as you were at its beginning. * * * Whose the fault?
Why do you not reflect? Why do you not speak? Why
do you waste the precious powers of your youth? * * *
But so it is, and I exploit them — and as I do, so do thousands, hundreds of thousands of others. * * *

One more glance at the peacefully sleeping lad, and
Nathaniel closed his eyes and pressed his hands against his
brow. A light, sharp and blinding as a sudden flash in the
darkness, pierced his mind. He was filled with horror and
dismay as the thought struck him: Here he lies still,
calm and innocent, and hundreds of thousands like him are
sleeping as he is. Yet they will awake — they are already
being aroused. To what deeds? How will they act, these
suddenly unshackled serfs?

A dizziness seized him; he felt as if his house were
tottering.

" Not yet! " he cried, and he stamped the floor in passion.

Joseph awoke and sprang up: " What do you command,
master? " His consciousness was no sooner restored than
this question leaped to his lips.

" I want to know what is going on, what is being preached
to you folks. I want to hear the emissary. Hitch up the
horses; you will drive to the Dornenkron tavern. Hitch
up! "

IV

The night was dark. A fine, close rain was falling steadily, and a liberal splashing was the result of the energetic tramping of the sturdy animals. "Poland's fifth element" enveloped and besprinkled the vehicle that Joseph was driving between a double row of giant poplars on the Kaiserstrasse.

The doctor, wrapped in his cloak, sat silent a long time. He was consumed with impatience.

"We shall be too late," he said finally. "Whip up the horses."

"They are running as fast as they can," answered Joseph. "We have gone a good way." He pointed to a great whitish spot on the leaden-gray horizon: "the Vistula and the Dujanec are hanging their flags out already."

A quarter of an hour later they reached their destination — a low, straggling building. All sorts of vehicles were standing in front of it, preventing Joseph from approaching.

Rosenzweig ordered him to stop, alighted and endeavored to make his way through the tangle of wagons and horses. It was no easy task for one who wanted to enter the house as unnoticed as possible.

Most of the drivers had left their vehicles, the others were, or pretended to be, asleep on the box, and paid no attention to the doctor's orders to allow him room to pass. He had just raised his stick to make his meaning clearer, when Abraham Dornenkron, with a burning torch in his hand, made his appearance in the doorway.

"Get them to make room, Abraham," said the doctor, "it is I, Doctor Rosenzweig."

"Great Heavens!" ejaculated the host in alarm; quickly collecting himself, however, he plunged obligingly into the swamp which formed the driveway to the inn. He made a breach into the stronghold composed of vehicles, calling at the same time with superfluous lung-power:

"It is Doctor Rosenzweig!—Is anybody sick? Where are you going, Doctor?"

As soon as there was a possibility of approaching him the doctor flew at him and caught him by the ear.

"Be still, you rogue. You need not announce me to your guests. I shall attend to that myself."

And as the little man continued in spite of this to proclaim aloud his astonishment at the doctor's advent, the latter jammed him against the doorpost until he could not breathe, and then passed by him into the hall.

"A gibbor!* Shema Israel,† a gibbor, that powerful doctor," whispered Abraham to a misshapen creature, bowlegged like a goblin, who turned up suddenly in the darkness silently as a lizard.

He moved his ill-shapen head to and fro, his intensely black eyes sparkling with cleverness and fire.

"He has come here to play the spy, daddy dear. We'll steal a march on him, so that no misfortune can befall us," whispered the little man.

"Misery upon misery! How steal a march on him?"

"I'll take a horse, daddy dear, and ride to Tarnow swift as the wind to notify the police that the rebellious *Goim* are holding a meeting here, and that the Imperial Government should send the military against them, if the Imperial Government is so disposed."

Abraham contemplated his offspring with a glance of admiring love.

"Ride like the wind, my dearie, so that you may, God willing, soon reach your destination. Ride," he repeated, and added with naïve concern: "But take care that nothing happens to your straight limbs."

Rosenzweig had meanwhile entered, or rather forced his way, into the inn-parlor. A heavy, musty atmosphere pervaded the room, produced by the crowding together of more than a hundred people in wet furs, clothes, and boots. The fumes of liquor and the smoke of a night-lamp suspended

---

* A giant. † Equivalent to "Great Lord!"

from the ceiling contributed their share toward rendering breathing more difficult. Those present, however, experienced unconsciously the oppressive influences which made some faces glow and others turn pale as death. There were men of all ages and stations, in poor garb, in the rich national costume, in the priest's robe, the student's coat, in the shabby black raiment of the petty scribe. Those who had come too late to find a seat stood on benches and, jammed between the crowd and the wall, they paid, at every new onrush, for the advantage of their elevated position, by the danger of getting crushed.

In the front row, towering above those about him, stood a gray-haired, broad-shouldered man in the rich costume of a grandee. As he turned his head, Nathaniel perceived the expressive Asiatic profile of one of the powerful princes of the country.

"You, too, Starosta, *princeps nobilitatis?*" thought Rosenzweig. But a still greater surprise awaited him.

The only space left free in the room was that which led into the adjoining apartment, the open door of which was guarded by a number of young people with a fiery zeal against the importunity of curiosity or fanaticism. And there Dembowski was walking up and down, engaged in conversation with a Polish gentleman in whom Rosenzweig, to his infinite astonishment, recognized the intimate friend of the prefect. Happy in his domestic life, and comfortably circumstanced financially, he was an inoffensive, upright man who prized peace above all things. He had never even succeeded in following a political debate of his neighboring land-owners to its close, for he regularly dropped asleep. And here, walking by the side of the agitator, was this most peaceful and calmest of citizens, burning, glowing in a spiritual conflict whose agony was depicted on his quivering countenance.

Dembowski, his figure slightly inclined, his hand lightly resting on the neophyte's arm, was speaking in a low, insistent tone, uttering thoughts to which his companion ap-

peared unable to say anything in reply. A final word —
then he turned from the man he had thrilled and stepped
in front of his followers, who greeted him with boundless
enthusiasm.

The emissary was dressed like a peasant. He wore a
long white caftan fastened at the throat by two large metal
buttons, high boots, a shirt of coarse linen, and wide
breeches of the same material. A leather belt, from which
there hung a small ebony crucifix, encircled his waist. His
thick, dark-yellow hair was cropped close; it came to a
sharp point over his forehead and was finely arched about
the dull whiteness of his somewhat hollow temples.

He waited calmly till the welcoming outburst should
cease, his arms dropped at his side, his fingers lightly
crossed, and he gazed carelessly, superficially into the
throng, as near-sighted people are apt to do, who, in looking, renounce in advance the idea of seeing.

" Friends, brothers," he began, without raising his voice,
and at once there was a hush of perfect silence — " I greet
you for the last time before the struggle, perhaps the last
time before death."

" Hail to you! " responded a dark-looking fellow with
a martial air, " in struggle, in death, in victory! "

" In victory! " The cry ran through the throng as a sigh
of longing, a cry of hope, an ejaculation of confidence.

" Victory? " repeated the orator, " you have already
achieved it. A struggle such as yours is a victory, and
each one of you a victor, whether he plant his foot upon
his foes or lie trampled by their chargers on the battlefield.
Brethren! whatever fate may be in store for us, the thought
that inspires us cannot perish. It will live on, even on the
lips of those who persecute and kill us on its account. They
themselves will live to spread the sacred doctrine, in recounting the martyrdom that we have suffered."

Gradually the paralyzing fatigue left him; his supple
form rose to its full height:

" Perhaps the memory of our death will be the only

thing we can bequeath to those for whom we should so gladly have lived. We must see to it that that heritage shall be a glorious one. It will be no glorious one unless each one who has sworn allegiance to our league feels himself a priest whose ambition is renunciation, and his glory unstinted devotion to the cause of God.''

Sounds of approval were to be heard here and there, but disappointment was written on many countenances.

'' The cause of God, my brethren! '' repeated the orator. '' I would I had the power to rouse the fiery zeal in your hearts which it has roused in mine, and make you realize the abhorrence and shame with which I look back upon the worldly pleasures I once enjoyed. In the plenitude of their enjoyment the Master found me. I was roused from the dizzy whirl by His call. And the voice with which the All-merciful summoned me was the voice of compassion, and compassion gave birth to doubt, and doubt to knowledge.''

As he spoke his countenance became transfigured, the light of loving, generous thoughts shone upon his brow.

'' I lived the life of a spoiled child of fortune. Because chance had lavished too much upon me, I never knew satisfaction, gold melted in my immaculate white hands.

'' There was one among my servitors — his name was Jelek — a peasant's son, who, alert and efficient, had risen to the position of steward of my estate. He alone dared upon one occasion to give me a warning and he incurred my disfavor in consequence.

'' One summer morning, after a night of gayety, I was riding home with my followers from a fête at the house of my beloved. Her kisses were still burning on my lips, the tones of the music still rang in my ears, alluring visions floated before my eyes, I was filled with a rapturous joy of life. The remembrance of past pleasures was blended in my mind with the expectation of those to come, and in my arrogance I cried to my companions: 'As today so tomorrow and always!'

'' We had reached the edge of the forest; before us lay

the meadows fresh with dew, in the shimmering vapor of the young day, the waving fields of grain, and my castle with its sturdy towers, decked with streamers, beckoning us in the distance. Its windows were glistening; its walls, hoary with age, were illumined by the brilliance of the rising sun as a smile illumines the face of an old man. My venerable, hospitable dwelling presented a fine sight, and my companions galloped toward it with exultant shouts.

" I, however, reined in my impatient horse.

" I had seen a man hurrying along the edge of the wood, and recognized him as Jelek, my steward.

" ' Whence and whither?' I questioned him. He named a distant farm to which the superintendent had sent him on an errand.—'Was there no one in a lower position to attend to it? Since when do you go on errands?'—'Since I incurred your displeasure your superintendent has dismissed me from my office and gives me all kinds of tasks in place of it.'—He was panting and wiping the perspiration from his brow, and I could see that the ground was burning under his feet. I saw also that a long procession was marching from the village toward the highroad, and that it was this he was striving to join. I started to walk my horse and Jelek followed me. Thus we reached the highway along which the people were tramping. There were a couple of hundred men, youths and old men, their scythes on their shoulders, sacks upon their backs. They strode on in silence, with heads bowed, most of them barefoot and ragged — my peasants! * * * And as they, bowing to the earth, trailed past me, joyless as a herd driven to strange pastures, this fact was borne in upon me: These people are hired out for the harvest-time, far away perhaps, and will not behold the soil upon which their own poor crop is ripening until it is covered with snow.

" Jelek had pulled out a small kerchief in which he had tied a few coins, and pressed it into the hands of an old man who was dragging painfully along in the rear of the procession:—' So that you may not be in want on the way, father. May God comfort you. It is on my account that you have to leave.'

" The old man hid the kerchief in his breast, and the Haiduk who directed the troop shoved him forward.

" Tears of sorrow and rage filled Jelek's eyes.

" ' Why did you say,' I questioned him, ' that your father had to leave on your account? '

" ' Because it is the truth. The superintendent would not have dared to hire him out if I still enjoyed your favor as I used to.'

" A few days later I met Jelek as he was berating a field-hand, an aged man, for idleness, and beating him cruelly.

" ' Don't you see that the man is exhausted and is unable to work any longer? ' I said, and he answered:

" ' That's the way my father will be treated away from home. Why should the one be better off than the other? '

" I knew not what to reply, but to the old man I said:

" ' Don't the blows hurt you, that you stand there and do not even complain? '

" ' Oh gracious sir,' he rejoined, ' what would complaining help me? '

" And to that, too, I could say nothing. * * *

" In the evening my house was adorned for the reception of my beloved, and all who courted my favor were assembled to pay her homage. She appeared in all her regal beauty, and the sight of her and the sight of the magnificence that surrounded me and of the cringing complaisance of my followers — abhorrence, my brethren. They aroused abhorrence within me. * * * A demon had, I thought, maliciously sharpened my eye to a terrible clearsightedness. All the brilliance, all the pomp and splendor, and the love of woman and the loyalty of friends — they had a price, and it was paid by misery. Those had paid it who, hired out to compulsory service, had gone off to strange places. * * * The crowd around me, the walls of the hall, became transparent. As through a gleaming veil I beheld a tramping host, beheld clearly the various ranks, every lineament of the faces upon which that morning I had cast but a fleeting glance. Resignation written upon them all! Not fine, manly resignation — no! The disconsolate, hopeless resignation of dull despair. What that victim of the unjust retribution inflicted by my servitor had said, they likewise expressed by their silence: what would complaint avail us?

" Brethren! In that hour I cursed my power and passed sentence upon my happiness. * * * My power had been exercised to the detriment of others, my happiness grew not like a flower from the healthy womb of earth; it was a rank growth, the fruit of its decay, and parasitically nourished by the precious sap of human life."

The speaker threw back his head; his eyelids dropped, he drew in his breath like a soul in torment.

" Then a stream of sorrows flooded my breast. * * * The sorrows of every one who had suffered on my account poured into my heart! * * * And every shortcoming, every wrong committed by those in my service, I felt to be my fault, and heard with shuddering how their cry rose against me to heaven.

" The air in the hall hung heavy as lead, sin looked forth from the eyes of my beloved, the music warbled bewildering melodies, and — I felt I must away, away from the dispelled delusion into the cool, clear night. I wandered under its glistening stars as far as my feet would bear me, and though my heart wrestled and bled, I felt as if I had been restored to life. In the bitter agony through which I was passing, I felt the hand of my Master, comprehended the warning which He had vouchsafed me. And while they were searching for me in the castle and the gardens, I was lying prone in the depths of the forest before my God, and prayed that strength might be given me for repentance and expiation, offered myself to Him as an instrument of His will, a promulgator of His teachings, and besought the primal source of light to illumine my path.

"And it was vouchsafed me. As the old, familiar, though unseen, world was disclosed to the eyes of the man born blind, when the Saviour touched them with His hand, so was disclosed to me the revelation in whose light I had been wandering from my youth on — a blind man. And the deeper I penetrated into the spirit of the divine word, the more clearly did it appear to me that the essence of its wisdom is love. For us mortals — brotherly love."

The swelling waves of enthusiasm with which the emissary had been greeted had gradually subsided. A murmur of disapproval, mingled only with a few scattering cheers, now ran through the assembly. From the group that crowded about the prince a rude voice cried:

"Let the preacher speak of brotherly love, speak you of the liberation of our fatherland."

"They are one and the same!" rejoined the orator. "No liberation without brotherly love. It is the inestimably precious treasure which will redeem us the moment we decide to unearth it. Only you must understand the law that governs it. For you, the powerful and the rich, its first words are: renunciation, privation, atonement!"

A smile played about the lips of the prince, but, with a voice growing ever stronger as he proceeded, the speaker continued:

"There is but one Master, the King of heaven and of earth, and but one people, born equals. He who arrogates a mastery over his brethren sows and reaps evil, the souls of the enslaver and of the enslaved become corrupted."

With rapid steps he approached the prince:

"Save your soul, humble yourself! Remember the sins of your fathers, remember the curses that lie heavy upon your head. What! You demand deliverance from foreign tyranny? What have you ever practiced upon your wretched people but tyranny? You, the nobility, were the State. Never in Poland did any class but yours have any

say, and to what did you reduce the country? * * *
Your selfishness exploited, your dissension disrupted, your
treachery delivered it to the enemy!"

"You lie! Keep quiet! We don't want to hear any
more!" was shouted back at him.

A wild tumult arose.

"Room there! Room for the prince!" cried the attendants of the magnate, who had turned around silently
and contemptuously, and for whom the attendants were
attempting to open a way out by pushing and crowding.

Nathaniel, who was standing near by, proved himself
helpful. The throng was wedged in, as it were, in the doorway, but his iron arm divided it so as to make a passage
for those pushing forward, and there was a general sigh
of relief when the prince with his train had succeeded in
reaching the open.

From outside came the sound of their cries, curses, laughter. The gentlemen whistled for their drivers and their
dogs, whips cracked, vehicles were started up.

The emissary's glance swept sorrowfully over the thinned
ranks of his followers.

"I did not count upon the great of the earth; well for
us had we no other antagonists," said he calmly. "The
oppressors are few, the oppressed many. Were the oppressed to rise and demand, in the name of the All-just,
their share in the possession of the earth, the might of the
mighty would be as chaff. But the colossus that would only
need to stir to burst his bonds — he does not stir. He en-
dures and serves, and will ever endure and serve. Through
the life of indignity which he has led for centuries, the consciousness of his manhood, of his free will, has been stifled
in him. But those who have robbed him of this consciousness have sinned not only against the wretched populace,
upon whom they look with disdain, but — and they do not
bear this in mind — against God, in that they have in-
capacitated thousands of his creatures from reflecting His
image."

He paused and the younger people burst into vociferous cheers. The older men remained silent. Several ecclesiastics had retreated to the door. The disloyal friend of the prefect had disappeared along with the noblemen, after he had, with astonished dismay, beheld Rosenzweig's huge head looming up among the throng. The doctor, however, pressing against the man in front of him with the force of a pillar, gradually succeeded in making the latter give way, and was now standing on the spot previously occupied by the prince, directly in front of the emissary.

A flush of pleasure suffused the latter's countenance on perceiving Nathaniel.

" God will judge the guilty! " he resumed. " Our part is the deliverance of the poor, whose misery we are better able to gauge than they themselves. What I demand of you, masters, you know well; we have discussed it over and over again in long sessions. But you, students and men of science, who stand as close to the people as you do to your fathers, take care of them as if they were your children. Teach them to confide in and to love you; apply your knowledge, your skill, your experience, your strength and your time in their behalf. Forget yourselves in their service. None of you should henceforth cultivate his mind in cold seclusion. * * * By what right do you plunge into the investigation of the most difficult problems of the universe, of existence, while around you there are still people, endowed with claims to knowledge equal to your own, who are incapable of formulating the simplest train of thought? * * * You are seeking ends in your sciences but you will always find only boundaries. I will name an end to you which can be reached: the diminution of error, of delusion, of superstition, among our brethren. * * * The pilgrimage of the human race over the earth is like the march of a vast army that breaks camp at night to hasten to the field of battle. Those to whom strength has been given to outstrip the others have put themselves at the head. They are already advancing in the rosy morning light, the

shadows flee, a land of wonders is opening before them.
Irresistibly they are speeding toward it on their radiant
course, regardless of the rear guard which is groping about
and going astray behind them, unable to find the path that
leads to the happy ones by whose side they too were summoned to fight the battle of life.   *   *   *   Therefore, ye
leaders, halt! Open your ranks, let the rearguard come up.
A broad path for the rearguard! For their salvation, my
brethren! But also for yours, for Heaven will greet you
from eyes hitherto dim, which, thanks to your thoughtful
love, shall have been opened to admit a ray of the truth.''

Some pedagogues close to Rosenzweig exchanged significant glances: '' I am greatly disappointed,'' whispered
a lawyer's clerk to the learned gentlemen; '' it really
amounts to nothing.''

By and by the doctor was standing very comfortably;
there was no question of crowding any longer. The audience left the room slowly and quietly. One vehicle after
another drove off, the horses trotted away.

Those who remained finally tried to stop the exodus. The
imprecations which followed the deserters began to turn
into violence.

The orator raised his arm with a commanding gesture.
'' Let every one go his way unmolested,'' he bade them.
'' Which of you can tell whether the little seed of truth
which seemed now to rebound from the breasts of these
men, has not, unconsciously to themselves, taken root there?
Many a one, perhaps, of those who are leaving us now, may
yet join our ranks some future day. As for me, my brethren, I feel it a blessing that in this hour of parting I am
surrounded by fidelity, heard with understanding. The
deepest significance of my precepts may I pour into your
hearts as into precious vessels which will keep them pure
and unsullied and impart them thus to other hearts.

'' Brothers, we are always being told that without conflict among men the world could not exist; in a universal
peace our energies would rust and our mind become ener-

vated. That is false. Peace among men does not, indeed, mean the end of all conflict; it means, on the contrary, the beginning of a new, a glorious conflict. While hatred has been the author of all conflicts thus far, love will be the mother of those of the future. The combatants whom she summons will have by no means an easy task, for the enemies that confront them grant their conquerors no peace, no rest; conquered every day, they arise every day anew. *Suffering* and *passion* are their names. Fix your eyes upon them well, and you will be obliged to ponder and ask yourselves: Is it possible that we ever engaged in any other warfare but the one against the sufferings of others and against the passions in our own breasts? What — these terrible forces exist in the world, and we have concluded a hollow peace with them? We have accepted them as necessary and inevitable, we have drowsily allowed the vampire to feed upon our vitals and have not indulged our fighting propensity upon *them,* no, but upon our brothers, our fellow-sufferers! We have piled new burdens on the heavy-laden, we have struck the wounded.

" Oh the madness of it! Or the crime — or rather both! Crime is madness, folly is the source of every injustice."

Yes, a thousand times yes, reflected Rosenzweig, with tears in his eyes, shaken in every fibre of his being. He was penetrated by a boundless happiness, experienced the loftiest of all joys — the joy of rising from the narrowing limits of egotism as from a grave. What he had prized most hitherto appeared worthless to him now, wasted the labor that he had expended upon the acquisition of his wealth, despicable the narrow-hearted pleasure he had taken in what had lain, dead, like so much dust, in his hands. His soul was filled with shame, but he surrendered himself to this feeling with ecstasy since it was the token of his transformation, of the beginning of his inner growth and purification. One thought alone clouded the serene beatitude of the moment; it concerned the apostle of compassion and love, and grew more painful and anxious, when the latter began to picture the future of which he dreamed as attainable.—'' Do not deceive yourself!'' the doctor would have liked to cry. '' Your Land of Promise has no place on earth. Be content to have awakened our longing for it. That in itself is deliverance.''

But the emissary continued. The sound of his voice filled the room as with a bodily substance, the fiery stream of his eloquence attained its boldest, most magnificent flights, and finally he concluded:

'' The end and aim of our league is the welfare of the people, the welfare of every dweller on Polish soil; swear fidelity to our league!'' Then all called out, the tone of a common inspiration ringing in the cry which burst from young and old, the experienced and the inexperienced, the prudent as well as the fanatical:

'' We swear!''

They prostrated themselves before him and kissed his hands, his knees, his feet. '' We swear obedience to you unto death!'' one man's voice cried above all the rest. The emissary demurred:

'' Not obedience to me — swear to the cause, to love the poor and oppressed as yourselves, and the Fatherland more than yourselves.''

The protestations were renewed.

''And now go your way. Recruit among the people, raise recruits to do likewise. Send out no one who has not sworn upon the cross. I bring you the form of the oath and the catechism,'' said the agitator, and silence reigned while the tracts were being distributed.

Suddenly it was broken by a shriek of distress that startled all. Abraham Dornenkron rushed in, deathly pale, with disheveled hair:

'' Let everybody save himself who can! My sonnie has been in Tarnow; he saw the hussars mount; they will be here soon, my sonnie rode ahead of them.''

Abraham's warning aroused derision, defiance, consternation. Some stammered a low word of parting and hurried out. Those that carried arms gathered round Dembowski, prepared to defend him. He, however, motioned his faithful followers from him.

"Away! You, I, all of us. The time for battle has not yet struck. An arch-traitor every one who begins the battle too soon. Away! All away!"

The room was soon emptied. The last to leave was the emissary, Nathaniel stepping close before him. In profound silence the conspirators mounted their vehicles and vanished like shadows. The orator's horse was brought forward, he swung himself up and dug in his spurs. The animal reared, fell heavily on one of its forefeet and drew the other up with a quiver of pain.

Rosenzweig rushed to the spot. "Your horse is lame," he said, "you will make but little headway with it."

The inn-keeper came up, carrying a bottle containing a dripping tallow-candle, squatted down on the ground and confirmed with moans the doctor's opinion. A suspicion flashed across the latter's mind, he raised his clenched fist in the Jew's face:

"Wait, fellow, if you have done this!"

Abraham promptly burst forth into lamentations and protestations of innocence. The emissary had alighted from his horse, and stood motionless and listened.

The approach of the riders at full gallop could already be distinctly heard. They were accompanied by the keenly-whistling wind. A yellow-grayish shimmer began to appear on the horizon. The pale glow of opening dawn was spreading over the plain. Nathaniel grew hot and cold by turns. Cold perspiration covered his brow, his throat seemed caught in an iron clutch. *It was fear,* whose symptoms he had so often observed in others, and which he himself had never experienced.

"Conceal yourself in the house," he said to the emissary.

"What would that help me if the inn-keeper is false — and he is," answered the latter. "I will trust to my legs. As much cleverness as the hunted deer I too possess. Somewhere I shall find a cavern, a tree, a pitying bush, that will hide me.''

He was about to start on his flight.

But the doctor seized him with overpowering strength and pushed him to his carriage.

'' Down, Joseph,'' he commanded, '' and see that you get home. But you, take his place. Quick!''

The reluctant emissary was lifted to the box before he was aware of it. The doctor threw the cloak which he had left in the carriage about Dembowski's shoulders, Joseph gave the reins into his hands and started homeward at once with rapid strides.

'' You!'' called Nathaniel, and Abraham bent almost to the ground under the doctor's lightning glance, '' you will find out what I am if you continue to play the traitor!'' Some imprecations followed which flowed readily from his lips. More difficult was it for him to add: '' But if you hold your tongue — then you will get for your silence double what your tale-bearing would yield you.''

He turned about rapidly toward the closely approaching riders.

'' Ho, hollo!'' he cried, putting his hands up to his mouth in the shape of a speaking-trumpet, '' too late, too late.''

A picket of hussars with a very youthful cadet at their head came galloping up. The cadet reined up his horse directly in front of Nathaniel:

'' God's thunder! The doctor! What brings you here?''

'' Curiosity, by Jove! my little count. But you — why just you? A hot ride in the early morning hours will give you, as sure as I know you, a sore throat.''

'' God's thunder! Don't jest! Am I really too late? Is the nest empty? Was the emissary really here? Did you see him?'' questioned the young fellow with headlong haste.

'' Saw, heard, and diagnosed him as a harmless enthusiast.''

'' Harmless? Then it was not he.''

'' It was.''

"It was him," Abraham interposed glibly. "You can still see his horse, sir, which I lamed in shoeing it, so that he can't ride away."

"Which compelled him," Rosenzweig remarked, "to drive away in a friend's coach."

The youth inspected the horse, had the horseshoe removed, and ordered a soldier to take the horse along led by the bridle.

"I take it along as a pledge," he said. "And now — in what direction did he ride, doctor?"

"I would not betray that to you for any price."

"In what direction? The matter is grave. I am a made man if I capture him. We received more rigorous orders yesterday afternoon. — In what direction, doctor? * * * God's thunder! Speak!"

Rosenzweig answered sullenly: "I know nothing. Perhaps you met him yourself on the road."

"I met nobody except some people whom I know well. * * * For that matter"— he paused and pressed his hand to his brow. "They too are suspicious. * * * Right about face!" he commanded his followers, and the hussars wheeled round. "Adieu, doctor. And you, Jew, mind this! A reward has been set on the emissary's head, a reward of a thousand gulden. It would have been yours, had I caught the fellow here."

Abraham started, wriggled like a worm, and uttered a loud shriek. The doctor's foot rested upon his and crushed it unmercifully.

"What is the matter?" cried the hussar.

"He is weeping for the thousand gulden which flew past his nose," returned Rosenzweig.

The cadet resumed his place at the head of his troop: "I shall ride back. The carriages we shall still overtake. * * * God's thunder! We'll keep a sharp eye on them now. * * * Gallop, march!" and the picket clattered off.

Abraham hopped on one foot and held the other, bent back, in his hand as if in a sling.

BOZEN WITH ROSENGARTEN

"Two thousand gulden!" he whimpered. "Doctor, you have mashed, you gibor, two of my toes. * * * But I'll let that go, I won't ask for any damages if you pay me tomorrow my two thousand gulden, which you owe me as true as there is a God in heaven!"

Rosenzweig answered in a hollow voice: "Come now, you scoundrel. When I make a promise I keep it—even to a scoundrel."

He went up to the carriage and, pointing to the rear seat, said to his fellow passenger:

"Climb over there, and give me your seat. I shall bring you to a place of safety." The emissary with one bound stood by his side and grasped his hand warmly:

"I thank you. Do not concern yourself about me any further; I find friends everywhere."

In vain did the doctor seek to detain him; he disengaged himself, and was soon lost to the sight of his rescuer in the enshrouding half light of the dawn.

V

Rosenzweig drove home at a slow, easy pace—just as the horse pleased. He was in no hurry. Had the way been twice as long it would not have seemed too long to him. To one reflecting upon a miracle worked upon himself time passes swiftly.

Lied, duped, bribed a rascal—had he actually done these things, he, the upright Rosenzweig? Done them for the sake of a man whom he had regarded only a short time ago as an enemy of society, as his own enemy?

The most conflicting emotions were battling within his usually placid breast. But remorse, the worst of all, was not among them.

In the afternoon Abraham came to get his money. Yes, the rascal called it his, the precious money that was intended for the purchase of a new field. The doctor gave it to him with a sullen mien.

Then he betook himself to the prefecture.

He had meant to give his chief an exact account of the happenings at the tavern, but found him so busy and so unwontedly excited that he preferred to remain silent. The following days it was no better.

A constant agitation, an unusual activity pervaded the office. It was with difficulty that the prefect maintained his air of cheerful self-confidence. The assurance was forced with which he asserted that he held in his hands all the threads of the net in which Tyssowski in Cracow, Skarzynski in the Bochnian, Julian Goslar in the Sandec, Wolanski in the Jaslo, and Mazurkiewicz in the Sanoc districts, were entangled. The perfidy of his best friend, who had openly gone over to the revolutionary party, made a deep impression upon him. He and the doctor gradually changed parts. The anxious one became unconcerned, the unconcerned one anxious.

One morning Joseph handed his master a letter which had been brought to the house by a messenger. It contained two one-thousand gulden notes folded in a paper upon which were written these words:

"My debt to you can never be wiped out."

Nathaniel hid the sheet of paper in his breast and placed the notes in front of him on the table.

"Joseph," he called.

"What do you wish, master?"

"Look well at these pictures. Do you know what they represent?"

"Much money, I think."

"Money! Money! Well, yes — but something besides."

"What, master?"

"The reward of your long years of labor. * * * No, not reward — the honestly earned proceeds."

Joseph cast an inquiring glance at his master.

"Look at *them*, at the pictures, not at me. They represent still a third thing."

"What, master?" repeated Joseph.

"What? Shall I call Lubienka? She would know at once that it can be nothing but — your marriage-portion."

Then Joseph exclaimed with a cry of ecstasy:

" My benefactor, my master, the kindest of men! " and wanted to prostrate himself before him.

" Stand up! " bade Nathaniel, laying both hands on his shoulders and gazing earnestly into his face, which was lifted to him as to a god.

" You have had a hard youth, my lad."

" I? — What are you saying, master? — Have you not always been like a father to me? "

" No, no, my boy, indeed not. But you have always been like a son to me," answered the doctor, and added what was incomprehensible to Joseph: " If there were many like you then the heavenly emissary would be no fool."

Thenceforth Joseph passed happy days, and they would have been still happier had not the great change which had taken place in his master caused him anxiety. It struck every one, and aroused the astonishment of all the doctor's friends. He, the eager economizer, was often seized by generous impulses. He who had always regarded a beggar and a thief as belonging to the same category, began to discover a great difference between them. He upon whom the rich and riches had hitherto exercised a strong fascination, visited the castles only when summoned, but entered the hovels of the poor unbidden. The restlessness which formerly had left him no peace had disappeared. With calm, persistent zeal he attended to his professional duties. When the revolution broke out and claimed its first bloody victims, he always managed to be where he was most needed. Never, not even in the darkest days, did the calm assurance leave him that there was nothing to be apprehended from the revolution.

The prefect was of a different opinion. While all courageous spirits were coming to the conclusion that the revolt must soon be ended, he still spoke of the province being lost unless an army were despatched in hot haste to fight the thousand-headed hydra of " devastating insurrection." He thought that Rosenzweig had lost his mind when he rejoined one day:

" The insurrection is no thousand-headed hydra, but a helpless child. It approaches with flowers in its hands, with a heart full of love, and words of deliverance on its lips. Thus does it come to us. But we are wolves, bears, tigers; we are ravenous beasts. We do not understand the language of this child. It preaches mercy, justice, and goodness, and we want to know nothing of all that, we want to have mercy upon no one but ourselves, we want to remain what we are, keep what we have, even take, if possible, something from others in order to enrich ourselves. And it will always be so, and he is a fool that doubts it! And we ravenous beasts will rend and devour the child and lie down to sleep satisfied after the heroic deed."

" Pure fantasies! Nothing but fantasies! " cried the official in consternation. " What has happened to you? What demon has confounded your sober senses? "

" Do you know," he resumed after a brief pause, " that it was reported to me that you had attended a meeting where the most dangerous of the communist leaders delivered one of his notorious speeches? Do you know that malicious scoffers assert that his eloquence made a fanatic of you? "

Nathaniel did not allow this accusation to disconcert him.

" I should be a fanatic," he rejoined, " if I believed in the possibility of realizing the Utopias for which this ' communist leader,' as you call him, lives and for which he will die. Well, not even under the influence of his presence, the music of his voice, the lightning-glance of his eyes, did the thought so much as flash across my mind: Who knows? Perhaps after all — * * * Perhaps an example such as yours, may be able to teach us unselfishness and a general performance of the simplest duties. Oh, no, no! I know men too well for that. But what I did think was this: you will be knocked down, trampled upon, called a fool, and — forgotten. Ten years from now there will scarcely be one whom you loved who will mention your name. In spite of that, the powerful prince whom curiosity or the desire of making himself popular, impelled to attend your assembly, is a beggar compared with you.   Only he who gives remains enduringly rich, and the greatness of a man is measured by the greatness of his thought and the sacrifices which he makes for it.   Yours transcended the measure of what may be realized in our petty world.   Its greatness turns it into error, and you into a visionary.   Thus thought I; and I, the physician, the inveterate enemy and persecutor of everything morbid, eccentric, visionary, I sent up a prayer for him to my God:

"Let him die encircled by all the creations of his folly, let him die unhealed, oh Lord!"

———————

This prayer seemed to be answered before long in fullest measure.

The insurrection was frustrated by the resistance of the rural population; the body of men raised by the insurgents was beaten at Gdow by three hundred imperial troops and ten times that number of peasants who had joined them, under Benedek's energetic leadership.

Of this defeat the revolutionary Government at Cracow received distorted reports.

The champions of liberty, so ran the news, had been overpowered not by regular troops, but by fanaticized peasant hordes, which, having pushed on to Wieliczka, were now marching upon the city.

A cry of rage arose.   It was silenced by the eloquence of a man who demanded forbearance for the misguided people, and asked to be sent to meet them as a missionary. That man was Edward Dembowski, and his wish was granted.

Relying upon the power of religion and of his eloquence he left Cracow, accompanied by priests in rich vestments, by monks bearing banners and crosses.   A great mass of people followed, thirty sharpshooters bringing up the rear.

The procession crossed the bridge spanning the Vistula, and marched through the suburb Podgorze on the road leading to Wieliczka.

It lay still and deserted; as far as the eye could see, not a sign of any approaching peasant gangs. From Podgorze, however, came terrifying news, communicated to the rearguard by hasty messengers; it ran through the procession like lightning:

"Austrian troops are marching upon Podgorze."

A rapid command of the leader, and the procession started to retreat, in the hope of reaching the city before the imperial troops and of still being able to gain the bridge.

Arrived at the heights to the right of Podgorze, the emissary could already behold the storming of the town and the victorious advance of the soldiery.

The barracks were captured, the church occupied; the Polish riflemen, driven from their houses, were rushing in disordered flight toward the bridge.

Rage and grief filled the emissary's soul at this sight.

" Forward! Forward with the Lord, we'll fight our way through, we'll gain the bridge yet. Courage! " he cried to the hesitating priests. " You have nothing to fear. Those who are driven to attack put no heart into it. These men are Galicians, they will not shoot at their countrymen, they will not shoot at consecrated priests! "

He bade his followers strike up a hymn, and in stately order the procession descended the height. The emissary, clad in peasant costume, led the way, his light caftan glistening in the gathering twilight, a small black cross in his hand.

The procession marched unmolested through the still unoccupied part of the town to the church. But a company of soldiers had already pushed on to that point, barring their way to the bridge.

The emissary halted.

" Behold your brethren! " he addressed the soldiers and pointed to the bands that followed him. " You, too, are Poles. Don't fight, brothers — make way! "

He was answered by silence. He began once more to adjure the soldiers when the command rang out:

" Charge bayonets! "

With an expression of desperation Dembowski looked around him.

The priests and monks had fallen back. But his faithful adherents and the riflemen crowded about him.

" There is no way out of it. * * * Shoot — and forward! " he cried suddenly, and fell upon the soldiers.

Two discharges answered the unexpected attack.

After the first, Dembowski was still seen standing upright, swinging the cross high above his head.

After the second he fell, shot in the head.

Rosenzweig heard of the emissary's death through the prefect, who wound up his report with the words: "A madman was bound to end like that."

Nathaniel's prophecy was fulfilled; the most idealistic representative of the revolution was unanimously censured and derided by all parties and his memory was soon forgotten among the people, too.

His body was not found among those who had fallen at Podgorze, and for a time it was maintained that he was not dead, that he lived in concealment as a peasant and would appear on the scene of new battles for freedom.

When the storms of 1848, however, broke out and subsided without having lured him from his supposed concealment, the hope of his return was extinguished even among those who had cherished it longest.

It was a mild September evening, at the close of the fifties, in a village a short distance from the Silesian border. In front of the tavern a covered britschka was standing, to which a pair of lusty bays were harnessed. Comfortably, leisurely, as befits hearty eaters, they were enjoying the contents of the feeding-trough set before them. The driver, an elderly man, as well-fed as his horses, had seated himself on a bench in front of the house, was sending out thick clouds of smoke from a short pipe, and took pleasure in answering the questions of the pretty barmaid with a roguish hesitancy, aimed at heightening the curiosity she already felt at the arrival of guests who were total strangers.

"You are traveling a long way, I suppose," she remarked.

"Further than you can imagine," he replied.

"Perhaps way into Hungary?"

"Pooh! That would be only a cat's leap!"

The girl put her arm to her hip and laughed:

"I should like to see a cat that could jump like that!"

"In our place at home there are plenty such. You just come there and you'll see them."

"Oh what stuff! * * * But where is your home?"

"Where?" He pointed with his hand in three different directions: "There — and there, and there."

"Go along, you are joking."

"Ask my master, if you don't believe me."

"Yes, exactly," she rallied, "ask — such a gentleman!"

"Are you afraid?" — he winked at her slyly. "Have you already found out that he is a magician?"

Rapidly and furtively she made the sign of the cross:

"Is that so? I shouldn't have thought it to look at him."

"Yes, a very great magician. Makes the sick well and brings the dead to life."

"The dead?" * * * The girl shuddered.

"The half-dead, then. We are just on our way to one like that."

"Then you'll get there too late, if you have a long way to go yet."

"We never come too late. The master only says: Wait! — and death waits."

"Is that so? Has your master a wife?"

"He has no wife, but he has more than a hundred children."

" Listen to that! " and again she burst into a ringing laugh.

The subject of this colloquy was an old man of sturdy appearance. He wore a traveling-cap and a long coat, loosely fastened at the breast. The lower part of his strong, swarthy face was covered by a beard, which, white and thick as his hair, was divided into two strands and descended almost to his waist. The old man, his hands behind his back, was standing on the further side of the pond, which, situated a stone's throw from the inn, formed a long-drawn oval, at whose narrow extremity gnarled and crooked willows bent their branches to the murky mirror, while the other end grew gradually shallow toward the mounting village street.

The pond was all things in one — bathing-place for the young, washing establishment for the housewife, a lake for aquatic fowl, a watering-place for horses. In the evenings on week-days the place presented a lively sight. Big boys and small, barefooted, their trousers pulled up over their knees, rode their horses into the water, admired and envied by the children standing or sitting on the shore — mostly rather negligent guardians of their younger brothers or sisters. Men and women were returning home from the field, and, announced in advance by the tones of a resounding song, a troop of girls, carrying rakes and sickles, came marching to the village.

Among the children disporting themselves around the pond there was one that aroused the stranger's special attention — a little fellow of about six years, with a most winning but pallid face. His smooth, blond hair, long in the back and cut straight across his brow, escaped abundantly from beneath his little cap. He had deep-set blue eyes, a slim, slightly arched nose, and a sensitive, expressive mouth. Judging by the quality of his caftan and his boots, he belonged to well-to-do parents.

In the open doorway of one of the houses near by

appeared a young and pretty woman with a child in her
arms, and called to the boy:

" Jasin, father is coming."

Thereupon the little fellow turned a somersault and ran
from his companions to meet his parent. The latter stood
still, leaned forward and laughed as his little son ran full
tilt against him. Straightening the boy's cap and taking
him by the hand, he continued on his way.

It was delightful to see them coming along, the peasant
and his child, the little fellow the miniature counterpart,
in bearing, gait, and dress, of his father.

They came nearer, and the stranger noticed on the peasant's face the disfiguring traces of a serious wound. The
right cheek was sunken and seamed with scars, the right eye
closed.

Another veteran of the last uprising, reflected the old
man, and fixed his gaze more and more attentively upon the
approaching figure. A conjecture, strange and wonderful,
flashed across his mind. Suddenly advancing a few steps,
he stood still directly in front of the peasant, stared at him
and cried:

" Is it possible? "

The peasant stepped back in astonishment but only to
rush toward him the next moment.

' " You! Good heavens! you — Doctor Rosenzweig! "
exclaimed he, with a voice whose music had lived unfor-
gotten in the old man's mind. Sooner than the doctor he
regained his composure: " It was not in vain, then, that I
have been expecting you, not in vain that I hoped you would
take your way through our village on one of your Samaritan journeys, in order— " he added on account of the
people around them— " to visit your servant Hawryl."

" Hawryl— " stammered Rosenzweig. " Hawryl, then
* * * How goes it with you, Hawryl? "

" You must see for yourself. Do me the honor of entering my home, rest awhile under my roof."

Silent, still quite stunned, the doctor accepted the invitation, and followed his host to the house, where upon the threshold the young woman had remained standing, and was striving to retain in her arms the lusty child, which was stretching its little hands to its father with shouts of joy.

"My dear wife, doctor," said Hawryl, and turning to her: "Bid him welcome, Magdusia, a worthier guest Heaven cannot send us."

Her countenance reflected, cordially and sincerely, the joy pictured on her husband's face. "A warm welcome to you, sir," she said, turning her smiling, true-hearted glance upon him.

Nathaniel felt as if in a dream. It was only when he found himself alone in the room with Hawryl that he began to recover from his amazement:

"You are alive! — Man, you are alive! Is it true that you are alive? But if it is true, then don't stand there so indifferent — "

"Indifferent!" exclaimed Hawryl.

"Well, give me your hand, then!"

For the second time he held it in his own — one different from before, a rough hand, whose owner did not merely *play* the peasant.

They seated themselves at the table, which occupied the centre of the cheerful room, and it was long ere Hawryl, interrupted again and again by the doctor's exclamations of astonishment, could conclude the singular, and yet simple, story of his deliverance.

He attributed it in the first place to the garb he wore when he was wounded at the church in Podgorze and left for dead. On discovering that he still had life in him, he, along with other country-people, was removed to the hospital at Cracow. There he regained consciousness and soon became convinced that the physician who treated him by no means took him for a peasant. Later, some words that the physician let fall, apparently without any object, betrayed to him that he was recognized.

On the day when he was declared cured, the director, a Pole, — the hospital management had not yet been changed — visited the convalescent room.

The agitator beheld this man for the first and last time in his life.

"Your name is Hawryl Koska," he said to him, "you come from the Kingdom and are a dependent of Count Bronski, who has transferred you to his Galician estate, to a peasant holding. That is what I read in your passport. Is that right?"

And without waiting for a reply he handed him a pass made out in the name, and bearing the personal description, of Hawryl Koska, and, turning to his neighbor, left the newly christened man standing there.

"In the most confused state of mind possible for a man to be in, I had positively expected to be summoned before a court upon my recovery and to be shot as one of the inciters to rebellion, and had prepared myself for death like a true Christian. And now I was to live. My first sensation was one of disappointment, my first thought an arrogant one: God is preserving you for a purpose. He does not want your death, He wants your service. The work which you were chosen to begin, you are also to complete.

"Filled with this proud belief, I mingled with the people and became their comrade; apparently an equal among equals, I was in my own vain sight a prophet in disguise. Oh my friend! a single year of that life, and the pretended prophet had become a humble man. The end that seemed within reach withdrew to immeasurable distances. The temple which I wished to crown with a splendid dome had not even had its corner-stone laid, nay, the ground had not yet been dug for its foundation. What was needed was not the work of the artist but that of the modest day-laborer.

"I realized that.

" And now — should I not have been a miserable blusterer had I disdained to take part in that work, that most important work? * * * So I took hold of shovel and spade, not merely in a figurative sense. The crucifix, in the name of which I once went forth to battle, hangs there above my children's bed. Oh look at the outstretched arms of love, the wounded breast, the bowed, most noble head. * * * Who dares presume to summon to strife and battle in the name of that intercessor? "

He heaved a sigh, but his countenance retained its expression of profoundest, serenest peace, and with a cheerful smile he continued:

" And it is thus that you find the dangerous agitator. Oh when I think of how I started out, of all that I hoped and believed myself capable of doing — and now! I retire to rest contented, and call that day happy when I have succeeded in keeping Jan from beating his wife, Martin from going to the tavern, and in persuading Basil to throw his old plow into the corner and drive to the field in the new one."

" But your secret," asked Nathaniel, interrupting the course of the narrative, " was there never any danger of its being betrayed? "

" The former owner of the land took it with him into the grave. To his successor I am a peasant like any other."

— " A peasant! A peasant! * * * And you mean to continue thus to the end? "

— " To the end; and I do not feel as if I were doing something great, or giving my neighbors more than I receive from them. I am by no means always their instructor; they are likewise mine. Their pleasures I cannot share, but in trouble and sorrow we have often been true companions. I have seen peasants standing before their fields covered with hail, I have seen mothers standing at the bier of their children, and have been awed. Rarely has one of them appeared contemptible to me, but a hundred, innumerable times, deserving of pity."

His eyes shone with the old passionate fire, his swarthy cheeks turned pale with the depth of his emotion.

"There is a treasure-house of patience, perseverance, heroic submission to a higher will, in this people, which all the ill-usage they have experienced has been unable to exhaust. But, unconscious of their wealth, they scatter it around and add nothing to it. Insight is lacking and with it the exercise of active moral forces. Enough! Enough! you know all this as well as I, and likewise that there is plenty of work, not insignificant, to be done in my insignificant post. My capacity just suffices to fill it. Hawryl Koska will not have lived in vain. The *emissary* died without leaving a disciple."

"Yes, one!" cried Nathaniel. "One whom you drew from the ranks of your most zealous opponents. A man whose aims were of the earth, earthy, whose heart hung upon perishable possessions, and whom you taught the value of imperishable ones. Emissary! you see before yourself your white-haired disciple."

Both sprang to their feet at the same instant, and throwing themselves into each other's arms, held each other in a close embrace.

KRAMBAMBULI* (1887)

By Marie von Ebner-Eschenbach

TRANSLATED BY A. I. DU P. COLEMAN, A.M.

Professor of English Literature, College of the City of New York.

MAN may have a kind of liking for all sorts of things and all manner of creatures; but love — the real thing that does not pass away — he learns to know, if at all, only once in his life. This, at least, is the conviction of Ranger Hopp. How many dogs has he had in his time, and liked them too! But to love — what you can really call to love — and never to forget, only one: Krambambuli. He bought him, or more strictly speaking traded him, in the "Lion" tavern at Wischau, from an under-forester out of a job. The very first time he looked at the dog, he was taken with a liking for him that was to last as long as he lived. The master of the handsome beast, sitting at the table by an empty brandy-glass and grumbling at the landlord because he would not give him another, looked like a thorough rascal. He was a little fellow, still young and yet as dried up and weather-beaten as' a dead tree, with yellow hair and a scanty yellow beard. His forester's coat, probably a relic of the departed splendors of his previous service, bore traces of a night spent in wet ditches by the roadside. Although Hopp was not fond of bad company, he took a seat near the fellow and began at once to talk with him. He soon found out that the good-for-nothing drunkard had already pledged his gun and his game-bag to the landlord, and was now inclined to let the dog go the same way; but the landlord, wretched usurer! refused to hear of a pledge that would need to be fed every day.

---

* Permission Gebrüder Paetel, Berlin.

At first Herr Hopp said no word of the liking he had taken to the dog, but called for a bottle of the good Danzig cherry brandy which the landlord had, and made haste to pour some out for the vagabond. In an hour all was settled. The ranger handed over twelve bottles of the liquor on which the bargain had been struck—the other gave up the dog. To his credit be it said, it was not easy for him. His hands trembled so as he fastened the cord about the animal's neck that it seemed as if he would never finish the operation. Hopp waited patiently, admiring the wonderful quality of the dog, in spite of his bad condition. He was not more than two years old; his coloring corresponded to that of the wretch who was abandoning him, though perhaps a couple of shades darker. On his forehead he had a mark, a white streak that ran off in slender lines to right and left, like pine-needles. His eyes were big and black and lustrous, ringed about with clear amber; his ears sat high, long and perfect. In fact, there was not a flaw in the whole dog, from the tips of his paws to the end of his fine, sensitive nose. The whole supple and yet powerful frame was beyond praise, borne on four living columns that might have supported the body of a deer and were not much thicker than a hare's legs. By St. Hubert! the creature must have had a pedigree as long and as pure as that of a knight of the Teutonic Order.

The ranger's heart exulted over the splendid bargain he had made. He stood up, took the cord which the vagabond had at last succeeded in tying, and asked "What's his name?"

"His name—? Why, you can call him the same as what you've bought him for—Krambambuli!"

"Well, Krambambuli it shall be. Come on, then! Are you ready? Off we go!"

But no matter how he called and whistled and pulled, the dog refused to obey. He turned his head toward the man whom he still regarded as his master, only whined when the latter shouted "March!" and accompanied the order with a vigorous kick, and still tried to huddle close to him. Only after a hard struggle did Herr Hopp succeed in taking possession of the dog. Finally he had to be tied up, put in a bag, and carried off on his new master's shoulder to the hunting-lodge which lay several miles away.

It took two full months before Krambambuli, beaten half to death, and chained with a spiked collar after each attempt at flight, at last came to understand to whom he belonged. But then, when his subjection was completed, what a dog he was! No tongue can describe, no word can measure the height of perfection that he reached — not merely in the exercise of his appointed functions but in his daily life as a zealous servant, a good comrade, a true friend and guardian. It is often said of intelligent dogs that nothing is lacking to them but the power of speech; to Krambambuli not even this was lacking — his master, at least, was able to hold long conversations with him. The ranger's wife became actually jealous of "Buli," as she called him scornfully. Sometimes she reproached her husband. She had spent the whole day in silence at her monotonous knitting, when she was not sweeping, washing, or cooking. At night, after supper, when she picked up her knitting again, she would have been glad of a bit of a chat.

"You've always got something to say to Buli, Hopp, and never anything to me! Talking to a dumb brute the way you do, you'll forget how to talk to humans!"

The ranger admitted that there was something in what she said, but he saw no remedy. What was he to talk to his old woman about? They had never had any children; they were not allowed to keep a cow; and a gamekeeper finds no interest in domestic fowls when they are alive, and not much when they are cooked. The breeding or shooting of game, on the other hand, she knew nothing about. Finally Hopp found a way out of the difficulty. Instead of talking *to* Krambambuli, he talked *of* Krambambuli — of the triumphs that he won everywhere, of the

envy that the possession of him excited, of the absurdly
high sums that had been offered for him and contemptuously rejected.

Two years passed by in this manner. Then, one day,
the Countess, his master's wife, appeared at the ranger's
door. He knew at once what the visit must mean; and
when the kind and beautiful lady began "Tomorrow, my
good Hopp, is the Count's birthday — " he took up the sentence quietly with a smile: "And your gracious ladyship
wishes to make him a present — and you have come to the
conclusion that you couldn't give him anything else as good
as — Krambambuli!"

"Yes, yes, my dear Hopp — you've guessed it!" The
Countess flushed with pleasure at finding him meet her
half-way, spoke of her gratitude, and begged him to name
the price that should be paid for the dog. The wily old
ranger chuckled, put on an exceedingly deferential air, and
presently came out with a decisive declaration.

"Please your ladyship, if the dog stays at the Castle,
if he doesn't bite through every cord and break every chain,
or strangle himself trying, then your ladyship may have
him for nothing — for that is just what he would be worth
to *me*."

The test was made; but it did not go as far as strangling,
for the Count, before that point was reached, lost all pleasure in the obstinate creature. It was useless to try to win
him by kindness or to conquer him by force. He snapped
at every one who came near him, refused to eat, and (for
a hunting-dog has not much reserve flesh) wasted away to
a skeleton. In a few weeks Hopp got word to come and
take away his worthless cur. When he speedily responded
to the summons and sought the dog in his kennel, there
was a meeting full of indescribable joy. Krambambuli
uttered a feeble bark, jumped on his master, put his fore-
paws against his breast, and licked away the tears of joy
that were running down the old man's cheeks.

On the evening of this blissful day, the pair paid a visit

to the tavern. The ranger played cards with the doctor and the steward; Krambambuli lay in the corner by his master's chair. Now and then Hopp looked round at him, and the dog, no matter how sound asleep he seemed to be, instantly began to thump with his tail on the floor, as if he would say " Here I am! " And when Hopp, carried away by joy, shouted out as if it were a song of triumph, " How goes it with my Krambambuli? " the dog rose with respectful dignity, stood at attention, and answered with his clear eyes, " It goes well! "

About this time, not only in the Count's preserves, but in the whole surrounding district, a band of poachers carried on their operations in the boldest fashion. The leader was a dissolute rascal. He was called " Yellow " by the wood-cutters who met him drinking his brandy in some tavern of ill-repute, the game-keepers who now and then got on his track, though they could never come up with him, and the customers whom he had for his ill-gotten booty among the lowest class in every village.

He was the most daring rogue that ever set a problem for honest game-keepers. He must have been at one time in the profession himself, or he would never have known how to track out the game with such accuracy or so cleverly to avoid every trap that was set for him.

His depredations reached an unheard-of height, and all the men employed on the estate were grimly bent on catching him. Thus it happened only too often that those who were caught in some small breach of the game-laws were more roughly treated than at another time they would have been or than could quite be justified. This caused a great deal of bitterness in various places. The head game-keeper, against whom the feeling was strongest, received not a few well-meant warnings. The poachers, it was said, had taken their oath to make an example of him the first good chance they got. The bold, high-spirited man, however, tossed these warnings to the winds, and took all the more care to let it be known that he had enjoined the greatest strictness on his subordinates, and was prepared to take the entire responsibility for any unpleasant consequences. Most frequently he reminded Ranger Hopp of the need for strict execution of his duties, and sometimes reproached him for lack of sharpness — at which, however, the old man only smiled. But Krambambuli, at whom on such ocasions he looked down with a wink, yawned loudly and contemptuously. He and his master bore no grudge against the head game-keeper, who was the son of the memorable hero that had taught Hopp all the noble lore of the chase, as Hopp in turn had initiated the game-keeper when a boy into the same calling. The ranger still thought with pleasure of the trouble he had taken with his education, was proud of his former pupil, and loved him in spite of the rough handling which he, as well as the others, got from him.

One June morning he met him again in the act of administering justice.

It was in the circular clearing among the lime-trees, at the end of the park on the border of " the Count's Wood," and in the neighborhood of the breeding-places, which the head game-keeper would have liked to protect with murderous mines. The trees were at their best just then, and a dozen small boys had climbed into their branches. Nimble as squirrels they swarmed over the limbs of the splendid trees, broke off all the smaller branches within their reach, and threw them on the ground. Two women quickly picked them up and stuffed them into baskets, which were already more than half full of the fragrant spoils. The head game-keeper flew into a terrible rage, and ordered his subordinates to shake the boys out of the trees, regardless of the height from which they fell. While they crawled to his feet with cries and lamentations, one with the skin scratched off his face, another with a dislocated shoulder, a third with a broken leg, he gave the two women a sound drubbing with his own hands. In one of them Hopp recognized the light hussy whom rumor pointed out as the mis-

8. Praha, Staré město (1893)

tress of "Yellow." And when the women's baskets and shawls and the boys' hats had been seized and Hopp was charged to produce them before the court, he could not get rid of an unpleasant foreboding.

The order which the head keeper, wild as a devil in hell and surrounded by wailing and tortured sinners, shouted to him then, was the last he ever had from him. One week later he came face to face with him again in the circular clearing among the beech-trees — dead. From the appearance of the body it was plain that it had been dragged here, through mud and underbrush, that it might lie in state on this very spot. It had been placed upon a pile of broken boughs, the forehead encircled with a chaplet of blossoms, and another wreath of the same sort laid across his breast. His hat was by his side, also filled with blossoms. The murderers had left him his game-bag too — only they had removed the cartridges and replaced them with more blossoms. His fine breech-loader was missing; in its stead was a worthless old musket. When, later, they found the bullet that caused his death, buried in his breast, it fitted exactly the barrel of this weapon which had been laid in mockery across his shoulder. Hopp stood petrified with horror, gazing down at the disfigured corpse. He was unable to lift a finger, and even his brain seemed paralyzed; he could do nothing but stare and stare, and it was only some moments later that he regained his power of observation and asked himself a silent question — "What's the matter with the dog?"

Krambambuli was sniffing at the corpse, and running about distractedly, his nose on the ground. Once he whimpered, once he uttered a shrill yelp of joy; then he gave tongue and made a few quick leaps, just as if a long slumbering memory had awaked in him.

"Down!" cried Hopp, "Down with you!" And Krambambuli obeyed; but he gazed at his master with intense excitement, and (as Hopp would have expressed it) *said* to him, "For goodness' sake, don't you see anything?

Don't you smell anything? Oh, master dear, do look — do smell! Master, come — come this way!" And he thumped with his tail against the ranger's knee, stole back to the corpse, often looking round as if to say, "Do you follow me?" and began to take the heavy gun in his mouth, plainly trying to lift it.

A shudder ran down the ranger's spine, and all kinds of conjectures began to dawn in his mind. But because it was his business, not to see millstones, not to give instruction to the authorities, but rather to leave untouched the ghastly thing he had found and go his way, which in this case led straight to the ministers of justice — well, he did just what it was his business to do.

After all the formalities prescribed by the law in the case of such a catastrophe had been fulfilled, which took the whole day and part of the night, Hopp found time before he slept for another conversation with his dog.

"Old dog," he said, "now the police are at work, and they'll be skirmishing about all over the place. Are we going to leave it to others to rid the world of the blackguard that killed the chief? My old dog knows the low-lived villain — yes, yes, he knows him! But nobody needs to know that — I haven't told 'em. Ha! ha! I think I'll bring my dog into the job — there may be some sport!" He stooped over the dog, who sat between his outspread legs, and pressed his cheek against the animal's head, taking his grateful caresses in return. Then he went on murmuring, "How goes it with my Krambambuli?" until sleep overtook him.

Psychologists have attempted to explain the mysterious impulse that drives many criminals to return again and again to the scene of his crime. Hopp knew nothing of their learned disquisitions; but none the less he scouted incessantly, with his dog, in the neighborhood of the circular clearing.

On the tenth day after the head keeper's murder he had for the first time given a few hours' thought to something

else than his vengeance, and had been busy in "the
Count's Wood" marking the trees which were to be taken
down at the next cutting.

When he had finished his task, however, he threw his
gun over his shoulder once more and took the shortest way
through the woods to the breeding-places near the circle.
At the particular moment when he set foot on the path
that runs along the side of the beech-wood, he fancied he
heard something rustle in the underbrush. A moment later
silence reigned again — a deep, continuing silence. He
would almost have thought there had been nothing to take
note of, if the dog had not looked with such special keen-
ness into the thicket. His hair bristling, his neck outstretched, his tail stiff, he glared at one particular spot
in the undergrowth. "Oho!" thought Hopp, "if that's
you, my fine fellow — just wait!" He slipped behind a
tree and cocked his gun. His heart beat wildly in his
bosom, and his naturally short breath came near failing
him entirely — when suddenly, wonderful to relate, "Yellow" came through the hedge on to the footpath. Two
young hares were hanging from his bag, and on his
shoulder the headkeeper's breechloader with its Russia-
leather straps. It was a strong temptation to shoot down
the villain from the safe concealment.

But Hopp was not the man to fire upon even the worst
offender without first warning him. With one bound he
sprang out from behind the tree and on to the path, crying,
"Give yourself up, you cursed rascal!" As the poacher,
for his only answer, snatched the gun from his shoulder,
the ranger pulled the trigger. Good heavens! a flash in
the pan! a harmless crack instead of a heavy detonation!
The loaded gun had been left too long leaning against a
tree in the damp woods.

"Good-by — so this is death!" thought the old man.
But no — he is still unwounded; only his hat flies off, rid-
dled with shot. The other, too, has no luck today — that
is the last cartridge in his gun, and he must pull another
out of his pocket.

"At him!" cries Hopp hoarsely to his dog—"Seize him!"

"Here, Krambambuli—here to me!" calls the other with a soft and coaxing voice—ah, a well-known voice!

And the dog. * * * * What happened next took less time to happen than to relate.

Krambambuli had recognized his first master, and ran toward him—half the way. Then Hopp whistled, and he turned; "Yellow" whistled, he turned again—quivering in desperate uncertainty on a spot equally distant from the two men, attracted at once and repelled.

Finally the poor beast gave up the hopeless conflict, and put an end to his doubts, but not to his suffering. Baying, howling, his belly on the ground, his body taut as a sinew, his head raised as though he were calling on heaven to witness his torture, he crawled—to his first master.

At the sight a thirst for blood seized Hopp. With trembling fingers he had put in a fresh cartridge; with calm sureness he took aim. But the poacher had once more raised his barrel to point it at him. This time it would be decisive! Both of them knew this—and, whatever thoughts were going through their minds, they faced each other as calmly as if they had been painted on canvas.

Two shots rang out. The keeper hit, the poacher missed.

And why? Because, as the dog leaped upon him with excited caresses, he started at the moment of pulling the trigger. "Beast!" he hissed between his teeth, then fell backward, motionless.

The executioner came slowly toward him. "You've had enough," he was thinking; "'twere a pity to waste another bullet on you." Nevertheless, he set his gun on the ground and loaded it anew. The dog sat up straight in front of him, his tongue hanging out, panting quickly and loudly, and gazing at the ranger. And when he had finished his loading and picked up his gun once more, they held a colloquy of which no witness could have understood a word, had a living man been there instead of the dead.

" You know for whom *this* bullet is meant? "

" I can guess."

" Deserter — traitor — vile scum, forgetful of all faith and duty! "

" Yes, master — that I am."

" You were my joy once. But now it is all over. You are no more to me."

" I know, master," and Krambambuli lay down, his head pressed close to his outstretched paws, and looked at the ranger.

Yes — if the wretched brute had not looked at him! He might have made a quick end of it all, and saved himself and the dog further pain. But he could not. Who could shoot a creature that looked at him like that? Hopp muttered a few curses between his clenched teeth, each one more lurid than the last — bent over the poacher's body, took the hares, and went on his way.

The dog followed him with his eyes until he had disappeared among the trees; then he rose to his feet, and a blood-curdling howl rang through the woods. He went round a few times in an aimless circle, and then sat down again by the dead man. In that position the officers of justice found him, when, led by Hopp, at nightfall they came to view the body and provide for its removal. Krambambuli drew back a few paces when the men approached. " There's your dog," said one of them to the ranger.

" I left him here to watch," answered Hopp, ashamed to confess the truth. But it was no use — the truth came out just the same; for when the corpse was put on the cart and carried away, Krambambuli trotted after it, head and tail drooping.

Next day a court attendant saw him slinking about near the room where the body of " Yellow " lay. The man gave him a kick and called out " Go home! " Krambambuli snarled at him and ran away, as the man thought, in the direction of the ranger's house. He did not go there, though, but began to lead a miserable vagabond life.

Wild, and worn to a skeleton, he wandered about the poor dwellings of the cottagers at the end of the village. Suddenly he darted on a child that was standing in front of the last house, and snatched greedily from him the crust of bread that he was munching. The child was speechless with fright, but a small Spitz dog ran out of the house and barked at the robber. Krambambuli dropped his booty and fled.

That same evening Hopp was standing at his window before going to bed, looking out into the bright summer night. In fancy he saw the dog sitting on the other side of the heath by the edge of the wood, gazing at the scene of his former happiness with unchanged longing — the truest of the true, masterless!

The ranger closed the shutters and went to bed. But after a while he got up again, went once more to the window and looked out — but the dog was not there. Again he tried to sleep, and a second time it was in vain.

He could bear it no longer. Whatever had passed, he could not get on without the dog. "I'll take him back!" he thought to himself, and felt himself a new man after the decision.

At the first peep of day he dressed himself, told his wife not to wait dinner for him, and hastened away. But as he left the house, he stumbled over the wanderer whom he had gone to seek afar off. Krambambuli lay dead at his feet, his head touching the threshold that he had not dared to cross.

The ranger never got over it. Those were his best hours in which he forgot that he had lost him. Deep in affectionate thought, he would murmur as of old, "How goes it with my Krambam—." But in the middle of the name he would stop suddenly, remembering, shake his head, and say with a heavy sigh — "Too bad about the old dog!"

APHORISMS * (1892)

By Marie von Ebner-Eschenbach

TRANSLATED BY MRS. ANNIS LEE WISTER

BE the first to say what is self-evident, and you are immortal.

What delights us in visible beauty is the invisible.

They understand but little who understand only what can be explained.

An opinion may be controverted; a prejudice, never.

Confidence is courage; fidelity is force.

The men of today are born to criticise; of Achilles they see only the heel.

How happy are the pessimists! What joy is theirs when they have proved that there is no joy!

No one ever accomplished the ordinary who did not attempt the extraordinary.

Conquer, but never triumph.

Accident is veiled necessity.

To see, without envy, others acquire what we ourselves are striving for, is greatness of mind.

Arrogance is a plebeian vice.

Have patience with the quarrelsomeness of the stupid. It is not easy to comprehend that one does not comprehend.

Our greatest indulgence toward a man springs from our despair of him.

---

* Permission J. B. Lippincott & Co., Philadelphia.

To grow old is to receive sight.

Grace is the outcome of inward harmony.

How wise must one be to be always kind.

The simplest and most familiar truth seems new and wonderful the instant we ourselves experience it for the first time.

The man of cold nature and superior intellect sneers at nothing so bitterly as at a magnanimity of which he feels himself incapable.

We often demand virtues from others only that we may give free play to our own faults.

" The wiser yields! "—an immortal phrase. It establishes the universal supremacy of folly.

Never strive, O artist, to create what you are not irresistibly impelled to create!

The character of the artist fosters his talent, or destroys it.

Iron endurance and uncomplaining renunciation are the two poles of human force.

Nothing is so often irrevocably neglected as an opportunity of daily occurrence.

We usually learn to wait only when we have no longer anything to wait for.

Passion is always suffering—even when gratified.

Shrinking stupidity and bashful poverty the gods hold sacred.

If there be a faith that can remove mountains, it is faith in one's own power.

The consequences of our good actions persecute us inexorably, and are often harder to bear than those of our evil actions.

The good humor of commonplace people is like the will-o'-the-wisp: trust to its delusive brilliancy and it will surely lead you into a slough.

There are women who love their husbands as blindly, as enthusiastically, and as enigmatically, as nuns their cloister.

A burnt child either fears the fire, or falls in love with it.

Pity is love in undress.

Matches are made in heaven, where, however, no care is taken that they turn out well.

Whoso believes in the freedom of the will has never loved, and never hated.

Most men need more love than they deserve.

The poet who knows one human being can portray a hundred.

One of the rarest pieces of luck is an opportunity for merited beneficence.

Most imitators attempt the inimitable.

To have and not to give is often worse than to steal.

The poor never estimate as a virtue the generosity of the rich.

The people whom we never contradict are those whom we either love most, or respect least.

Those who need forbearance least exercise it most.

His power over us is boundless who inspires at once pity and respect.

No one can appreciate reason who does not possess some himself.

When any one shows himself able where ordinary men are unable, they console themselves with the reflection that he is certainly unable where they are able.

Beware of the virtue which a man boasts is his.

If one reads the ancients only, one is sure of always remaining modern.

The sympathy of a fool is a flame without warmth.

He is a poor instructor of the young who does not distinctly remember his own youth.

The incurable ills are the imaginary ills.

Even the most modest of men rates himself more highly than he is rated by his best friend.

When art finds no temple open, it takes refuge in the workshop.

We must do the right that there may be some in the world.

Hatred is a prolific vice; envy, a barren vice.

We should always forgive; the penitent for his sake, the impenitent for our own.

The motive for a good action is sometimes nothing save timely repentance.

There is something so beautiful in trust that even the most hardened liar must needs feel a certain respect for those who confide in him.

What you wish to do you are apt to think you ought to do.

Even virtue is an art, and even its devotees are divided into those who practise it and those who are merely amateurs.

Age transfigures, or petrifies.

Kindness which is not inexhaustible does not deserve the name.

The few who practise goodness are the only ones who believe in it.

It is unfortunate that superior talent and a superior man are so seldom united.

There are more truths in a good book than its author meant to put into it.

We excuse nothing so easily as follies committed for our sake.

Undeserved reproof is often a delicate form of flattery.

Be lord of your Will and slave of your Conscience.

Nature is truth. Art is the highest truth.

A desire fulfilled too late brings no refreshment; the thirsty soul consumes it as does hot iron a drop of water.

Fools usually know best that which the wise despair of ever comprehending.

When curiosity is felt about serious things we call it thirst for knowledge.

One thing we should always try to learn from our very good friends — their keen perception of our faults.

Love not only has rights, but is always right.

Only what is too good for the present is good enough for the future.

Those to be feared are not those who dispute, but those who concede.

The mountain which brings forth a mouse has quite as severe a labor as has Vesuvius when it sends flames heaven-high.

Unattainable wishes are often called "pious." This seems to intimate that only profane desires are fulfilled.

Wit is an intermittent fountain; kindness is a perennial spring.

One can buy many things that are beyond price.

When two good men contend about principles, both are always right.

Nothing is less promising than precocity. A young thistle is more like a future tree than is a young oak.

When envy can no longer deny merit, it begins to ignore it.

The sympathy of most people consists of a mixture of good humor, curiosity, and self-importance.

Power is duty; freedom is responsibility.

Since the well-known victory over the hare by the tortoise, the descendants of the tortoise think themselves miracles of speed.

There are times when to be reasonable is to be cowardly.

To be content with little is difficult; to be content with much, impossible.

The modesty which loses its unconsciousness loses its life.

There is only one proof of ability — action.

If you pursue a well-trodden pathway for a long while, you will finally pursue it alone.

The understanding of some men is clear, that of others is brilliant. The former illumines its surroundings, the latter obscures them.

Never expect women to be sincere so long as they are educated to think that their first aim in life is — to please.

In youth we learn, in age we understand.

He who has trusted where he ought not will surely mistrust where he ought not.

But little evil would be done in the world if evil never could be done in the name of good.

All that is due to us will be paid, although not perhaps by those to whom we have lent.

Those who need us give us a hold upon life.

There is a beautiful form of dissimulation: self-conquest — and a beautiful form of egotism: love.

It often discourages the most ardent philanthropist to find so many in need of help whom it is impossible to help.

A weak readiness to admit that two and two make five is the caricature of resignation.

The believer who has never doubted will hardly convert a doubter.

The world would be much better off if the pains taken to analyze the subtlest moral laws were given to the practice of the simplest.

" It is impossible to help all," says the miser, and — helps none.

Whoso knows nothing should believe everything.

Parents are least ready to forgive in their children faults which result from their own training.

When a high-minded man takes pains to atone for his injustice, his kindness of heart shows in the best and purest light.

The cavils of envy have often helped merit to a recognition.

What does a fool care for a sensible man? The object of his admiration is some other fool, who rates him highly.

A sense of beauty and an enthusiasm for the beautiful are one.

Desire is the father of hope.

We are not always even what we are most.

In fashionable society one must wear a dress-coat, a uniform, or — a livery.

He who says Patience, says Courage, Endurance, Strength.

Consider existence as a task, and you will be able always to endure it.

Intelligence often goes much farther than intellect.

Many think they have good hearts who have only weak nerves.

Two very different virtues may be long at war with each other, but the time will come when they will perceive that they are sisters.

Upon the death of one dear to us we find a kind of consolation in the belief that the pain of our loss will never abate.

The strength of a man's mind is shown alike by what he believes and by what he doubts.

It is easy to bear the severest blame if we feel that he who blames would rather praise.

Old servants are petty despots, to whom we are bound by the great despot — custom.

Pity despised may turn to cruelty, as love despised may turn to hate.

From a desire for the superfluous art was born.

How much less a wise man troubles himself about the faults of others than about his own.

We cannot right every wrong, but we can, indeed, wrong every right.

Dulness will as surely be the result of prolonged abstinence as of luxurious excess.

The thought of the transitory nature of earthly things is a source of endless misery — and of endless consolation.

Where would the power of women be were it not for the vanity of men?

Men who are perpetually engaged in accumulating wealth, without ever allowing themselves time to enjoy it, are like hungry folk who are always cooking without ever sitting down to dine.

To pursue a thought — how graphic the phrase! We hurry after it, clutch at it, it eludes us, and the chase begins afresh. The final victory is to the stronger. Should this prove to be the thought, it never lets us rest; it starts up perpetually, teasing, vexing, twitting our incapacity to grasp it. But if by force of intellect we succeed in mastering it, the eager contest is followed by a blissful indissoluble union for life and death, and the children springing thence take the world by storm.

Morals refine manners, as manners refine morals.

Nothing is more pitiable than resignation too soon displayed.

The poor love to bestow.

One must learn to accommodate one's self even to good fortune when it is new.

The vain weak man sees a judge in every one, the proud strong man owns no judge but himself.

Authors from whom others steal should not complain, but rejoice. Where there is no game there are no poachers.

When silly folk take pains to conceal a secret from us, we shall certainly learn what it is, strive as we may to escape the knowledge.

The poor man wishes to conceal his poverty, and the rich man his wealth; the former fears lest he be despised, the latter lest he be plundered.

Intellectual sloth, superficiality, and obstinacy are feminine failings; greed of pleasure, selfishness, and harshness are masculine failings; waywardness, vanity, and inquisitiveness are childish failings.

Whoso sneers or lies in the presence of children is guilty of a capital crime.

Vanity refuses all wholesome food, and lives entirely upon the poison of flattery, upon which it thrives luxuriantly.

Pain is the great teacher of mankind. Beneath its breath souls develop.

Man is the master of the house, but woman should alone rule the home.

Genuine love may exist between persons of very unequal deserts; lasting friendship only between those alike deserving. Therefore the latter is far rarer than the former.

A clever woman has millions of born foes,—all stupid men.

The old saying, "All beginning is difficult," is true only of accomplishments. In art nothing is more difficult than finishing which means a finish.

A blockhead, in judging of others, may possibly transport himself into their place, but never into their manner of thought and feeling.

There is no wrong, and scarcely any right, that has not been at some time the work of vanity.

Master of his passions, kindhearted, intelligent, gracious, easy in manner, reverent toward sincerity, appreciative of a jest—*summa summarum:*—a charming man.

We must accept blame from any one, but we should know something of him from whom we would have praise.

To listen only to reason in contracting a marriage means, in most cases, to summon all one's reasoning power to assist in the most insane transaction of which a human being is capable.

He who understands how to inform others gracefully and interestingly of what they knew beforehand, soonest acquires a reputation for cleverness.

Nothing comforts us for the arrival of certain guests save — the hope of their departure.

In all ages there are some great truths abroad in the air; they constitute the intellectual atmosphere of the century.

What are men the readiest to dub stupid? The cleverness which they cannot understand.

With our parents we bury our past, with our children our future.

One thought cannot awake without awakening others.

They are the most insufferable of hypocrites who baptize by the name of duties all the pleasures that are born to them.

Disputes between true friends and true lovers are of no consequence. The only dangerous quarrels are those between people who do not quite understand each other.

There are many little impertinences and indiscretions, in themselves of very slight consequence, which are terrible as symptoms of the condition of mind that they betray.

Generosity, to be perfect, should always be accompanied by a dash of humor.

A certain amount of good will is necessary for the apprehending of what is simplest, for the comprehending of what is clearest.

" Plain to the common understanding " means: comprehensible by common people, and often means besides: quite uninteresting to uncommon people.

To be young is delightful; to be old is convenient.

More honorable names have been ruined by thoughtlessness than by malice.

If you must choose between a falsehood and a rudeness, choose the rudeness; if the choice lies between a falsehood and cruelty, choose the falsehood.

Taciturn people always inspire respect. It is difficult to believe that one has no secret to keep but that of his own insignificance.

The sense of loneliness is painful when it comes over us in the bustle of the world, but intolerable when it overcomes us in the bosom of our family.

Spoilt children are the most unfortunate; in their earliest years they know what tyrants suffer.

" He is a good man," people say thoughtlessly. They would be more chary of such praise if they reflected that they could bestow none higher.

We are valued either too highly or not highly enough. We are never taken at our real worth.

Would you know what your acquaintances say of you? Listen to what they say of those who are worth more than you.

In the course of life everything loses its charm as well as its terrors. One thing only we never cease to fear: the unknown.

Sterility hates all creators, most of all those who create before its very eyes.

The husband who finds himself confuted in argument by his wife instantly begins to outroar her. He can — he must

— he will — prove that, even although he sings false, the first part in the duet always is his of right.

A capacity for calm deliberation: — the beginning of all wisdom, the source of all excellence.

Exceptions do not always prove the rule; they may be even the first germs of a new rule.

Many would be free if they could but arrive at the consciousness of their freedom.

Courage of the weak, gentleness of the strong — both worthy of adoration!

We ask the poet: "What subject have you chosen?" instead of: "What subject has chosen you?"

A wife loses the sense of her own value in her love for a distinguished husband; a husband truly appreciates himself first when he loves a noble wife.

The weakling is always ready to repudiate even his virtues, if he thinks they give offense.

The philosopher draws his conclusions; for the poet they must be born.

Many a truth is the result of an error.

A literary thief who takes great pains with his stealing may all his life long be thought honest and original.

In choosing between two duties, decide for the hardest.

One true friend adds more to our happiness than a thousand enemies add to our unhappiness.

Great men create what is great; good men, what is lasting.

An interesting book is food that makes us hungry.

The understanding and the heart are upon excellent terms. The one often takes the place of the other so perfectly that it is hard to decide which is at work.

Manuscripts either molder in your drawer, on mature there.

Whoso appears before the public should expect no consideration and demand none.

A man of lofty ideas is an uncomfortable neighbor.

Even more than for the happiness of our youth do we long in old age for the desires of our youth to return.

To conquer is better than to sue.

It is the tittle of truth which many a lie contains that makes it formidable.

With regard to our bad qualities there can be only perpetual warfare or disgraceful peace.

Whatever thou really possessest has been bestowed upon thee.

Happy they who love only what they may and hate only what they should.

They who sin least do the greatest penance.

It is well to exchange thoughts with the grandly-endowed; it is well to live with the delicately-endowed.

A merited victory comes almost always too late.

Respect the commonplace! It is the garnered wisdom of centuries.

The lazy and the industrious can never live happily together; the lazy despise the industrious too much.

If you would not cease to love mankind you must not cease to do them good.

The noble "I will!" has no worse enemy than the cowardly, self-deceiving "Yes, if I choose!"

Everything depends upon surroundings. The sun in the clear sky has a far more humble opinion of itself than has a tallow candle burning in a cellar.

Let the artist hasten to efface all trace of the pains his work has cost. If his pains are evident, he has taken too little.

The mastery of the moment is the mastery of life.

We may seduce fancy, but must not seek to do it violence.

Not the mortal, but the incurable, diseases are the worst.

No man stands so high that he can afford to be only just toward others.

When the time comes in which one could, the time has passed in which one can.

Association with an egotist is ruinous, because self-defense forces us to fall gradually into his fault.

"It will pass away," weak parents say of some fault of their children. Oh, no, it will not pass away, it will develop.

The right of the strongest is the strongest wrong.

The greatest enemy of the law of right is the law of prerogative.

Between what you can and what you do lies a sea, and in its depths lies buried the wrecked will.

A proud man demands of himself extraordinary ability; an arrogant man ascribes it to himself.

Admiration for virtue is a talent for virtue.

Many think that when they have confessed a fault there is not need of correcting it.

They are most to be pitied who possess a sense of duty, but not force sufficient to obey it.

In meeting again after a separation, acquaintances ask after our outward life, friends after our inner life.

Obstinacy — lack of cultivation. Jealousy — avarice.

Those who are elated with a little fame do not deserve much.

To say what one thinks may be the greatest folly, and may be the greatest art.

People who talk much of themselves produce, however clever they may be, the impression of immaturity.

There are more naïve men than naïve women.

The wise man is seldom prudent.

We ought to speak not of the art of being happy, but of the art of feeling happy.

True prophets sometimes, false prophets always, have fanatical adherents.

As far as earth can be heaven, it is so in a happy marriage.

Humility is invulnerability.

A good joke should seem unintentional. It does not proclaim itself, but in a flash the acuteness of the hearer detects the witty thought under the mask of a simple phrase. A good joke travels incognito.

Some virtues can be attained by feigning them for a long while. Others are all the more impossible of attainment the more we try to feign them. Among the first belongs courage; among the last, modesty.

Well-bred people talk in society neither of the weather nor of religion.

That government is most degraded which is obliged to listen silently while notorious roguery preaches morality to it.

Widely as the possession of like faults separates us, the possession of like weaknesses unites us as closely.

Hobbies protect us from passions. *One* hobby becomes a passion.

What a difference there is between how we do it and how it should be done!

The line which genius dashes off at one stroke, talent may, in lucky hours, construct by minute dots.

A nothing may suffice to shake our confidence in ourselves, but only a miracle can again confirm it.

To have experienced much does not mean that experience is gained.

In every exalted joy there mingles a sensation of gratitude.

Those people in whom heart and understanding balance each other develop late.

A book cannot easily be too bad for the general public, but may easily be too good.

Where are there two things so opposite and yet so nearly related, so unlike and yet often so hard to be distinguished from each other as humility and pride?

It is not what life brings us, but the manner in which we receive it, that shapes our destiny.

There would be no social life, every family tie would be loosened, were our thoughts written upon our foreheads.

" If my heart does not speak, my reason also is silent," says the woman. " Be silent heart, that my reason may speak," says the man.

Love all mankind, but let the sufferer be your child.

The tedium of many a book is its salvation: the critic, after raising his javelin, falls asleep before he hurls it.

In rheumatism and in true love we believe only when attacked by them.

Physicians are hated either from conviction or from economy.

The ambrosia of earlier ages is the daily bread of later ages.

A really good and amiable man may have as many friends as he chooses, but not always those whom he chooses.

None pride themselves upon inborn virtues.

A whole book — a whole life.

The worth of men and of things can be estimated only when they are old.

The benevolent do not fear malevolence.

We should take far too little pains if we never took needless pains.

Not only does every Ulysses find his Homer, but every Mahomet his Khadijah.

Every man of the world would rather consort with a well-bred rogue than with an ill-bred saint.

When we remember the joys of the past, or hope for those of the future, we always picture them as unalloyed.

Not every great man is a grand human being.

The love lavished upon us, which we cannot regard as a joy and a blessing, we regard as a burden.

We learn nothing so late, and forget nothing so soon, as to admit that we are wrong.

Deeds speak, but even they fail to convince the doubter.

All poets and all honest poetasters write with their hearts' blood; the quality of the fluid makes all the difference.

If we wish to enjoy an unalloyed pleasure, it must fall to the lot of one whom we love.

Genius points the way; talent pursues it.

Those whom we spoil most are not always those whom we love most.

One must forgive a large self-consciousness to a great poet. We cannot deny a certain Godlikeness to one who creates men from his brain.

Consider once before you give, twice before you receive, and a thousand times before you ask.

The scale which we apply to things is the scale of our own minds.

The artist should care, not to have his work receive recognition, but to have it deserve it.

A single word sometimes betrays to us the depths of a soul, the power of a mind.

So soon as a fashion is universal it is out of date.

Nature may well be lavish; even what is thrown aside as apparently useless falls at last into her lap.

The smallest fault that a man commits for our sake, lends him more value in our eyes than the greatest virtues that he practises without regard to us.

It is bad when a married pair bore each other, but far worse when only one of them bores the other.

The greatest power is exercised over a man by a woman who, while rejecting him, contrives to convince him that she returns his love.

Bear in mind every service that you can render; forget every service that you have rendered.

He who prefers the material delights of life to its intellectual pleasures is like the possessor of a palace who takes up his abode in the kitchen and leaves the drawing-room empty.

In the course of life our vices grow threadbare, like our virtues.

The world belongs to those who long for it, and is despised by those to whom it should belong.

"If I did not have to preach, I should not chastise myself," said a priest who loved the truth.

An artist — a priest.

There is never a moment when a blockhead does not deem a wise man capable of uttering nonsense or of committing folly.

Indifference — spiritual death — is sometimes a sign of exhaustion, most frequently a sign of intellectual impotence, and always — good style.

Of what value is fame, when one cannot enjoy posthumous fame?

For nothing are we so grateful as for gratitude.

Many a man without talent can say of the work of a man with talent: — "If I could do that, I would do it better."

Dilettanti have done no lasting service in even second-rate art, but have done well in the first of all sciences, philosophy: witness Montaigne, La Rochefoucauld, Vauvenargues.

Although we have no faith in the flattery, the flatterer after all attracts us. We cannot but feel some gratitude toward one who takes the trouble to lie to please us.

From pity for others springs ardent, courageous benevolence; from pity for ourselves, feeble, cowardly sentimentality.

The smaller the grain of sand, the more certain is it to consider itself the axis of the world.

Only the cleverest of men make use of their acuteness in judging not only of others but of themselves.

THE LIFE OF HEINRICH SEIDEL

By Arnold Werner-Spanhoofd, Ph.D.

Head of the Modern Language Department in the Washington, D. C., High Schools

EINRICH SEIDEL has been justly called "The Poet of Happiness," and it would be difficult indeed to find another more deserving of the title. While other modern poets are inclined to give expression to deep philosophical thought, and not infrequently seem to find satisfaction in presenting the dark and melancholy phases of human experience, Seidel on the contrary revels in depicting the quiet everyday life of the normal middle-class. His characters are no psychological problems, but simple, unpretentious people who pass through life without "storm and stress," without tragic conflicts or heart-breaking sorrow. Seidel kept entirely aloof from the great social questions of the day; it was not for him to war against the besetting sins of mankind, but rather to give pleasure to himself and others. For all that, he was sufficiently realistic to be true to life; he did not paint all sunshine where there should be shadows, but by the alchemy of his genial humor, his joyous optimism, he so transformed discordant elements that their painful attributes become insignificant. Thus Seidel's writings are always the direct expression of his own attractive personality, and what he says of his famous character Leberecht Hühnchen, is equally true of himself: "He was one of those fortunate mortals in whose cradle a good fairy had placed that best of gifts — the art of being happy." In his poetic fancy the realistic and fantastic are most happily blended; in his soul the simplest things were transmuted into pure gold; "he possessed the faculty of drawing honey from every flower, even from the poisonous ones."

It was Seidel's happy fortune to have been reared amid the simple and healthy influences of country life. The son

of a village parson, himself a man of poetic instincts and
an author of some repute, Heinrich Seidel was born June 25,
1842, in the little hamlet of Perlin, in the Grand Duchy of
Mecklenburg-Schwerin. Here he passed an ideal childhood. His home and its surroundings, we are told, constituted '' a veritable child's paradise.'' An old-fashioned
garden with many large fruit trees, shaded nooks, bowers,
and dense shrubbery was a potent influence which inspired
him to impersonate Robinson Crusoe, Uncas, the Last of
the Mohicans, and similar boyhood heroes. Adjoining the
garden was the village graveyard where in a fragrant,
whispering grove of overshadowing lindens nestled a
romantic chapel in which rested the remains of a beautiful
young countess of whom he had often heard his mother
speak. An ancient bell-tower with chimes, which always
seemed so human to him, was another object of inspiration
and affection. An environment such as this, to a child
retiring and dreamy by nature, was most favorable to the
development of latent seeds of poetry and creative fancy.
These pleasing recollections of his youthful days always
remained vivid in his mind and heart. Garden, wood,
meadow, bell-tower—every spot of his beloved home is
familiar to us through some exquisite and tender touch
which greets us everywhere throughout his writings.

This happy life, however, came to an abrupt end in his
ninth year, when his father was called as court chaplain
to Schwerin, the capital of the State. He now entered the
gymnasium, but having neither talent nor inclination for
the classics, became the despair of his teachers. He ex-
celled only in German composition, geography, and the
natural sciences — subjects that in a classical school were
considered of no account whatever. Meanwhile his interest
in nature never flagged. With some favorite book as his
sole companion he roamed through field and forest in the
charming region round about Schwerin, gathering flowers
and collecting butterflies, birds' eggs, and various minerals.
No wonder that his progress at the gymnasium was not

HEINRICH SEIDEL

remarkable; at sixteen he had not advanced beyond the Tertia and, despairing of ever being able to finish the course satisfactorily, he left the school to prepare for a technical profession.

After a short apprenticeship in one of the machine-shops of the Schwerin Railroad he entered the Polytechnic Institute in Hanover, where, however, because of his youth and insufficient preparation, he did not make much progress in his chosen profession. He took more interest in a gay student life than in the prosecution of his studies. He became a prominent member of one of the student societies, fought his duels, and soon frequented the fencing halls more than the lecture room. At the death of his father, Seidel returned to his native state and took a position in a machine-shop in Güstrow, where under the direction of a skilful chief he prepared himself thoroughly in theory and practice for the higher branches of his profession. The earnestness with which he now attended to his work gained for him the esteem and admiration of his superiors, who did everything in their power to assist him in his endeavors. It was a hard struggle, but in his leisure hours he still found time eagerly to peruse the works of Jean Paul, E. T. A. Hoffmann, Gottfried Keller, Mörike, and, above all, Fritz Reuter, Stifter, and Theodor Storm. Among English writers Dickens, Sterne, and Swift were favorites of his. A duo-decimo edition of Uhland's poems was always in his pocket, and he carried them with him on his rambles and even enjoyed them at odd moments in the factory. But the future poet's education was gained more from nature than from books. The impressions received in the solitude of field and woodland were ever present with him even amid the din and confusion of the machine-shop, inspiring him to compose many of his own verses while hammering and filing away at vise or lathe. "I introduced one of these verses, 'The White Rose,' into my collection of poems," he tells us; "the connoisseur will observe at once that the rhythm of screw-cutting has impressed itself upon the little verse."

In 1866 Seidel entered the Berlin Institute of Technology, where he was graduated with high honors in 1870. He then accepted a position in Wöhler's machine-shop in Berlin, and later became construction engineer for the Berlin-Potsdam-Magdeburg Railroad. In this capacity he distinguished himself by the construction both of a huge crane for lifting locomotives and of the immense iron roof of the Anhalt Station, at that time the largest on the continent.

The severe application of the engineer's profession was relieved by a sympathetic friendship with Friedrich Eggers, the talented professor of history in the Institute of Technology. It was Eggers who discovered Seidel's unusual poetic gifts. He introduced him to the "Tunnel über der Spree," an authors' club, where he came in personal contact with the prominent writers of the day. The inspiration received here aroused his love of story telling, and soon one after another of his finest lyric verses and some of his most artistic prose works made their appearance and won the sympathies of his countrymen. In May, 1878, Seidel retired from his profession as engineer, and since then until his death, November 7, 1906, in Gross-Lichterfelde, a charming suburb of Berlin, devoted his time entirely to literature.

Seidel wrote in both poetry and prose; in his delicate fancy the real world is never separated from the fairy realm of the imagination. His fine lyric verses are an overflowing heart's spontaneous expression clothed in exquisite form. His stories are full of poetic imagination. There is nothing artificial, nothing forced; a perfect style charms with its natural grace, its refreshing humor, and genuine love of nature. In fact nature is the background for all his writings. It is true there is nothing grand or imposing in the North German landscape, and Seidel's scenery is therefore quiet, romantic, full of sweet repose alike to mind and eye; he charms more by means of its detail than through its general effect, more through the perfect harmony with which he combines the setting with the characters he introduces; nature always seems to be in perfect sympathy with all the common interests of human life. To Seidel nature was more than a pastime — it was a necessity. From the busy life of the metropolis with its dust and noise he always lures one to some idyllic, secluded nook, such as a tiny garden in the suburbs where happy people are feasting on the simple offerings of the season. And when the longing for those happy days of his youth overcame him he wrote the charming stories, *The Golden Time*, and *Reinhard Flemming's Adventures* — the latter a delightful picture of German boy life, into which the poet emptied all the accumulated treasures of pleasing recollections of his own youthful days.

Foremost perhaps among Seidel's qualities is the exquisite delineation of his characters — men and women of ordinary life, who are happy and content in themselves and, though circumstances are not always fortuitous, make an honest attempt at least to rise above them — ordinary characters to be sure, but intensely interesting through his truthful and sympathetic portrayal. Among these his inimitable Leberecht Hühnchen, with his delightfully optimistic views of life, is beyond question the best, and has long since become a general favorite of the German people.

Seidel's works embrace eighteen small volumes, published by J. C. Cotta's successors, Stuttgart. Principal among his prose writings are: *Leberecht Hühnchen, Jorinde and Other Stories, Suburban Stories, The Golden Time, Reinhard Flemming's Adventures by Water and Land.* Under the titles *Chimes* and *Windblown Leaves* are published many of his choicest lyric verses.

HEINRICH SEIDEL

LEBERECHT HÜHNCHEN* (1882)

TRANSLATED BY ARNOLD WERNER-SPANHOOFD, PH.D.

Head of the Modern Language Department in the Washington, D. C., High Schools

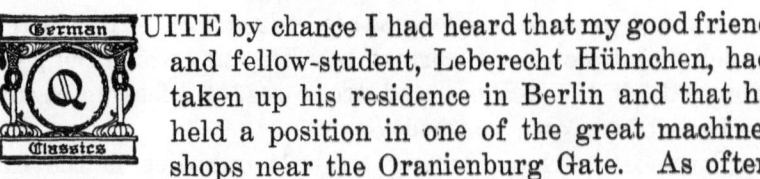

UITE by chance I had heard that my good friend and fellow-student, Leberecht Hühnchen, had taken up his residence in Berlin and that he held a position in one of the great machine-shops near the Oranienburg Gate. As often happens, a correspondence brisk in the beginning had gradually dwindled, and finally we had lost sight of each other completely; the last sign of life had been the announcement of his marriage, which had occurred some seven years before in a small Westphalian town. Closely associated with the name of this friend was the memory of a joyous student-life, and I instantly determined to look him up in order to see the admirable fellow again and to brush up the recollections of those good old times.

Leberecht Hühnchen was one of those fortunate mortals in whose cradle a good fairy had laid that best of gifts — the art of being happy; he possessed the faculty of drawing honey from every flower, even from the poisonous ones. I do not remember ever having seen him depressed for more than five minutes at a time; then the perennial sunshine of his nature would assert itself triumphantly, and he could so twist and turn even the most disheartening circumstance that it would actually become rose-color.

In Hanover, where we had been classmates at the Polytechnic Institute, he received the least possible assistance from home and earned the necessaries of life by poorly paid private tutoring. He did not, however, exclude himself on

---

* Permission J. G. Cotta, Berlin.

this account from any of the social gatherings of his fellow-students and, what to me was the greatest mystery of all, he was almost never without money and could even lend some to others. One winter evening I found myself in the not unusual position—I must confess it—of having exhausted all my resources, while my regular allowance was not due for several days. After a careful turning inside-out of all my pockets and a thorough investigation of every bureau drawer, I managed to scrape together just thirty pfennigs, and with this capital, which jingled forlornly in my pocket, I sauntered through the streets in deep reflection as to its best possible investment. From these meditations Hühnchen suddenly interrupted me and with the cheeriest face in the world asked me to lend him three thalers. As I had just about made up my own mind to ask a similar favor of him, I could not help laughing, and then explained how matters stood. "Bully!" he cried; "so you still have thirty pfennigs? Now, if we combine our resources we shall be no better off. I have just this minute given my last pfennig to our townsman Braun, who has to take part in a great anniversary banquet, and, of course, needs the money. So you still have thirty pfennigs? With that we will have a jolly evening!"

I looked at him in astonishment.

"You just give me the cash and I'll do the marketing," said he; "I have, besides, some odds and ends at home. We will live like Lucullus tonight—like Lucullus, say I!"

We passed through several narrow streets of the suburb of St. Ægidii to his rooms. On the way he disappeared into a miserable little shop which advertised itself to the public by means of a couple of crossed clay pipes, several dusty packages of chicory and tobacco, blacking boxes and mustard pots, shortly reappearing with two paper bags.

Leberecht Hühnchen roomed in the gable of an absurdly small and insignificant cottage which stood in an equally diminutive garden. There was just enough space in his sitting room for two unassuming persons to stretch their legs, while adjoining this was an attic-chamber so completely filled by the bed that whenever Hühnchen wished to take off his boots it was first necessary to open the door. This little bird-cage, however, had a characteristic air of comfort; something of the sunny nature of its occupant pervaded the place.

"Now, first of all, let's fire up," said Hühnchen. "You sit down on the sofa there, but take care that you find a hollow. The sofa is somewhat hilly; one must see to it that he selects a valley."

The fire in the little cannon-shaped iron stove, which in size resembled a dachshund as compared to a Newfoundland dog, was soon kindled by the vigorous blowing of my friend, who regarded the flickering blaze with satisfaction. This stove was to him a constant source of enjoyment.

"I cannot understand what people have against iron stoves," he said. "In a quarter of an hour the room will be warm, and that the fire requires watching and poking is to me no objection whatever, for that is the most agreeable pastime I know of. And then, when out of doors bone and marrow freeze, it is just fine as it stands there in the corner, glowing red and defiant against the cold."

Herewith he fetched a small rusty tin pot, filled it with water, and set it on the stove; then he prepared the table for supper. In a little wooden cupboard were his housekeeping utensils. There were two cups — one narrow and tall with blue forget-me-nots and a saucer that did not match, the other quite broad and flat, which had lost its handle. Then appeared a small irregular butter dish, a tin can with tea, and a round pasteboard box which formerly had harbored shirt-collars but was now promoted to the rank of sugar bowl. The choice piece, however, was a little round teapot of brown clay, which Hühnchen always handled with especial care and respect; for it was a family heirloom and a cherished relic. Three plates, two knives as unlike each other as it is possible for table knives to be, and a fork with only two remaining tines and an annoying incli-

MARKET SCENE, HILDESHEIM

nation to lose its handle—these and two bent German silver teaspoons completed the outfit.

When with a certain deftness he had arranged all these things, Hühnchen glanced over the collection with an expression of satisfaction and exclaimed: "All my own! It is, indeed, the beginnings of a home."

Meanwhile the water was boiling, and Hühnchen produced five eggs from the largest package; these he now skilfully proceeded to boil with the assistance of his watch. After he had put fresh water on the stove for the tea and had produced a huge loaf of bread, he placed himself beside me in a neighboring valley of the sofa with a look of perfect contentment, and the evening meal began.

As my friend finished the first egg, he took a second and regarded it thoughtfully. " See," said he, " an egg like this contains a whole chicken; it needs but to be hatched. And when this chicken is grown it in turn lays eggs from which still other chickens come, and so on, generation after generation. I see them before me, numberless hordes which populate the earth. Now I take this egg and with one swallow destroy them all. Now, see—that's what I call genuine feasting."

And thus we feasted and drank our tea. One rather small, peculiar yellow egg remained, for five cannot be divided equally by two, and this we decided to share between us. " It happens," said my friend, carefully tapping around the shell with his knife in order to halve it equally, " it happens occasionally that a very unusual specimen is found among ordinary eggs. Pheasants lay just such little yellow ones as this; I firmly believe that this is a pheasant's egg. I had one formerly in my collection, that looked just like this one." Separating his half carefully from the shell he swallowed it with deliberation. Then leaning back with half-closed eyes he whispered with gastronomic grimaces: " Pheasant! just like Lucullus!"

After supper a problem presented itself. There was indeed tobacco at hand, for the pointed blue paper bag

which Hühnchen had previously purchased contained five
pfennigs' worth of this choice weed, but my good friend happened to possess but one decrepit pipe, whose mouthpiece
had been worn off to the last ring, and whose bowl, with
evidently too small a sponge-holder, had the annoying trick
of suddenly inverting itself, thus scattering the sparks
over one's trousers.

"This difficulty is easily solved," asserted Hühnchen.
"I have *Don Quixote* here"—which, by the way, together
with a Bible and some professional works composed his
entire library, and which he read indefatigably—"let one
of us smoke, while the other reads aloud, alternating with
each chapter. You, as guest, take the pipe first; well, that
is settled."

As I filled the pipe and he thoughtfully sipped his tea,
a new idea came to him. "It is wonderful," he mused,
"when one thinks of it, how while I sip my tea here in perfect comfort and while you smoke your pipe, the industrious Chinaman in that far-away land is planting for us,
and the negro under a tropical sun is toiling for us. Yes,
and not only that, the great steamships plough their courses
over the mighty ocean, battling through storm and turbulent wave, and the trailing caravans plod over the burning
sands of the desert. The proud multimillionaire merchant-
prince who lives in a palace in Hamburg and who on the
banks of the Elbe can call a princely country-seat his own,
must devote some portion of his energy and forethought
to producing these luxuries for us, and when business complications and anxieties cause him sleepless nights we can
stretch ourselves comfortably and dream pleasant dreams,
leaving him to work and worry in order that we may obtain
our tea and our tobacco. When I think of it, it makes them
taste all the better!"

Alas, he did not take into account the fact that doubtless
the larger part of this tea had been gathered from native
willow-trees growing on the banks of some sluggish German creek, and that this tobacco at best could call the

district Ukraine its fatherland, if it did not indeed owe its origin to that same tuber from Magdeburg's fruitful fields which was the mother of the sugar with which we had just sweetened our tea.

We then became absorbed in the old immortal *Don Quixote,* and thus the evening came to a cheerful and happy conclusion.

These, and similar trivial incidents of that joyous time were recalled while on my way to the present home of my friend, and a longing for those days which never would return took possession of me. Where had it vanished — that golden lustre which had so glorified the world? And how was it with my friend? Had the real problem of life perhaps also destroyed the sunny essence of his spirit, leaving nothing but a speculating, calculating automaton, as was the case with so many others I had known?

He was said to live in Garden Street, but I was not sure about the number. I had just decided to enter a house which I surmised to be the right one in which to make inquiry, when I became aware of two attractive, neatly dressed children, about five and six years of age, who were enjoying themselves in apparently happy fashion before the door of the neighboring house. It had been a cloudy summer day, and now, toward evening, a gentle rain was beginning to fall. Then it was that the boy, the older of the two, had discovered the delightful game of turning his face toward the sky, letting the raindrops fall into his open mouth. With that enthusiasm which children usually bring to a new discovery the little girl had immediately followed her brother's example, and there they stood, their happy childish voices breaking out from time to time into ringing shouts of joy over this new and simple pleasure. The spirit of their game was so characteristic of my friend that it flashed through me like lightning: These are Hühnchen's children.

I asked the lad, "What is your father's name?"—"My father's name is Hühnchen," was the reply.—"Where does he live?"—"He lives here in this house, three flights up."—"I should like to see him," said I, stroking the boy's blond head.—"Yes, sir, he is at home," he answered, and then they both ran ahead of me, clambering hastily up the stairs on their short legs to herald my coming. I followed slowly, and when I reached the upper landing I found the door already open and Hühnchen awaiting me. It was dark in the hall and he did not recognize me. "Please step inside," said he, as he pushed open another door;—"with whom have I the honor to speak?"

I made no reply, but stepped into the room and looked at him. He was the same as ever, only his beard had grown heavier, and the hair on his forehead had retreated somewhat. As of old the imperishable sunshine still glowed in his eyes. In the brighter light he recognized me instantly. His joy was unbounded. We embraced each other; then, holding me at arm's length, he scrutinized me closely.

"Do you know what I should like to do?" he exclaimed at last—"what we used to do formerly when we could not contain ourselves for joy. I want to dance an Indian dance like the one you invented, you recollect, from sheer delight, when your sister became the fiancée of your favorite teacher. You remember, how I hopped about with you then out of sympathy," and he shook his legs and made a few leaps in a manner not discreditable to his younger days. Embracing me again he suddenly became serious.

"My wife will be so glad," he said; "she knows and loves you through the stories I have told her. But there is one thing I wish to tell you; I believe you do not know it. My wife is"—here he tapped himself on the left shoulder—"she is not quite straight. I never notice it any more—in fact I never did really see it, for I fell in love with her eyes, with her heart, with her kindness, and with her gentleness; in short, I love her because she is an

angel. And why do I speak of this to you now? Well, you
see, if you did not know it you might look surprised when
you meet her, and she might read it in your face. So you
will not observe anything, will you?" I pressed his hand
sympathetically, and he ran to another door, opened it and
called: "Lore, here is a welcome visitor, my old friend
from Hanover whom you already know."

In she came and behind her the two friendly children
with their rosy faces. My friend's warning had not been
in vain, for I do not know whether in the surprise of the
first moment I should have been able to hide my sentiments.
But there was a glow of inexhaustible love and tenderness
in the depths of this woman's dark eyes, and wavy hair of
unusual thickness surrounded her pale face, which, while
not beautiful, was illumined by the sweet reflection of her
innate kindness.

After the first greetings Hühnchen announced: "You
are to remain with us this evening—that goes without
saying! Lore, you must provide a princely repast; everything on the table that the larder can supply!" Then
turning to me, he said: "In fact, the larder supplies nothing. Housekeeping in Berlin requires no provisions. We
have, nevertheless, a wonderful arrangement. The wife
puts on a shawl, takes a basket and runs across the street;
there behind plate-glass windows lives a florid, portly man
who, in a white apron, presides over a marble counter. And
near him you will find a florid, portly woman, and a florid,
portly shop-girl, also in white aprons. The wife steps into
the store and in her hand she carries a magic bag—
ordinary people call it a pocket-book. Under the charm
of this magic bag the busy knives are set in motion and
cut from the choice viands lying upon the counter whatever the heart desires and the purse can pay for. The little
wife again runs across the street and in ten minutes the
table is prepared and set with everything that one can
wish for—as if by magic."

Meanwhile his wife and children had gone out, and

as Hühnchen noticed that I was examining the simple yet
tasteful furnishings of the room, he continued, " Purple
and fine linen you will not find in my home, and the treasures of India still keep out of my way, but this I say to
you: He who has health "—and here he stretched his
arms after the manner of a circus-athlete—" he who has
health, and such a splendid wife as I and two such fine
children—I am proud to say this although I am their
father—he who possesses all these and still is not happy,
it were better for him that a millstone were hanged about
his neck, and that he were drowned in the depths of the
sea." He was silent for a time and then, looking at me
with shining eyes, went on: " During the time before our
boy was born my wife was often troubled with unhappy
thoughts, for the fear never left her—not being straight
herself, you know—that the child might inherit the deform-
ity, and many times when she thought I slept I heard
her weeping silently. And when the boy was born her
eyes swept over him with anxious haste, and a sudden
gleam of joy spread over her face as she cried: ' He is
straight! Is it not so? He is straight! Oh God, I thank
thee! I am so happy!' Then she sank back upon the pillows and closed her eyes, but her expression was quiet and
peaceful. Well, and what did I do? I went out quietly
into the next room, bolted the door, drew off my boots, so
as to make no noise, and executed such an Indian war-
dance as never before. It was very fortunate that no one
saw me or I should without doubt have been locked up in
the insane asylum at once."

Mrs. Hühnchen had meanwhile returned from her errand
and with housewifely efficiency prepared the table, while
the two children assisted her with evident importance.
Suddenly Hühnchen looked meaningly at his wife, raised
a finger, and said, " Lore, I believe *this* to be the occasion."
The little wife smiled comprehendingly and promptly
fetched a bottle of wine and glasses which she placed upon
the table. Hühnchen nodded to me: " It is Tokay," said he;

" recently I secured some money for some private work, and it made me feel so prosperous to have it jingling in my pocket that I was seized with the desire to be extravagant, and so I went and bought a bottle of Tokay, of the very best brand too. But when I was about to open it that evening I changed my mind, and said: ' Lore, put it away; some more suitable occasion may soon present itself.' I firmly believe in presentiments, for a sudden thought of you passed through my mind at the time."

How happily and cheerfully this little supper passed off! It was as if the sunshine which in the mountains of Hungary had ripened this glowing wine, once again became potent and flooded the room with its cheerful rays. The Hungarian sunshine painted with rosy hue the pale cheeks of the little wife. Presently she seated herself at a small, thin-toned, wheezy piano and sang with pleasing expression a number of folk-songs — among them: " Stealthily the Moon Rises," and " Were I a Wild Falcon." Later we sat comfortably beside the table and chatted over our cigars. I questioned Hühnchen about his business affairs, and discovered that his salary was remarkably small and that he had to work as remarkably hard to earn it. " It was much better formerly," he assured me, " in the so-called time of the stock-companies, for then there were all sorts of outside jobs to be had. We always go twice every year to the opera, and to a right good one too; in those better days we even aspired to the balcony, where we proudly sat and, assuming an aristocratic mien, anticipated the day that perhaps might come when we should still further descend, even to the parquet whence the glistening bald heads of the prosperous, rotund capitalists shone in our faces. However, the so-called hard times came, and finally it happened that our chief had to dismiss a number of the clerks and considerably reduce the salaries of those who were retained. Well, then we clambered up to the upper balcony again. On the whole it does not matter, for I even find that the illusion is enhanced by a greater distance from the stage. And do not imagine that one does not discover a good class of people up there; indeed, I have seen professors and fine artists there. You will often find people in the upper balcony who understand more about music than all the rest of the audience put together — people who have scores in hand and follow the conductor note for note, and who pardon no mistakes either.''

It was eleven o'clock when I finally took my leave. But first I was conducted to the bedroom to see the children, who in the healthy, rosy slumber of childhood lay in their little cot. Hühnchen stroked the edge of the bed tenderly. '' This,'' he whispered with shining eyes, '' is my treasure chest. Here I guard my most precious belongings; all the wealth of the Indies could not buy these.''

As I turned slowly homeward through the warm summer night my heart was touched and there welled up in me innumerable good wishes for the future of these estimable, contented people. But what should I wish for them? Would riches increase their happiness? Would fame and honor for which they care nothing be of any benefit to them? '' Kind Providence,'' I finally concluded, '' give them bread and give them health to the end; for the rest they can easily look out for themselves. For he who carries happiness in his own contented breast, wanders with a light heart through this world and is not deceived by the shimmering, golden mirage which others eagerly pursue; for the greatest of all possessions is already his.''

A VINTAGE FESTIVAL AT LEBERECHT HÜHNCHEN'S

As time passed things had gone well with Leberecht Hühnchen. He had exchanged his position in the factory near the Oranienburg Gate for a similar one with the railroad, and had thereby gained a slight increase in salary. Added to this, a totally unexpected small inheritance had fallen to him, and he availed himself at once of this circumstance to carry out his favorite wish of many years — that is, to secure a house of his own with a little garden. One day last March he came to me and, after the first greetings, without saying anything further, he began to strut up and down the room, thumbs thrust into the armholes of his vest, evidently trying to give himself a pompous and imposing appearance. After I had regarded this procedure for some time with astonishment, he planted himself before me, legs spread haughtily apart, and inquired with shining eyes and triumphant manner: "Do you not observe anything about me?"

"It appears to me that you have breakfasted well," said I.

"Not in the least;" he replied, "but do you not notice something prosperous, almost ostentatious in my appearance? Can one not see, a hundred paces away, that I am a land-owner and a householder?"

I was thoroughly astonished at the unexpected news.

"Yes, wonderful things happen," said he, placing himself before the mirror and nodding well-pleased at his reflection. "So that's the way one looks!" he commented.

"Above all else, satisfy my curiosity," I begged. "What does it all mean?"

"Nothing less than that yesterday I bought myself a house with a garden in Steglitz — a charming cottage! It is indeed very small, but very attractive. Don't imagine that it is a so-called Villa; pillars and caryatids and vegetable ornamentations are lacking. I bought it from a shoemaker who is going to America. It smells of leather and tan at present, but that will disappear when it is once papered. The garden is charming — that is, it will be, when I have planted it as I intend to do; at present there is absolutely nothing in it but a little walnut-tree and a pear-tree. The shoemaker swears that it is a Bergamot-pear. A young grape-vine is growing on the house, and last year, as this same man assures me, it bore seven bunches of grapes of a ' good, sweet variety.' Just think — all these things will grow and increase! Imagine what I shall add to these in the way of fruit-trees! I shall naturally have only the choicest, for the ground is valuable.

What would you say to a hotbed? Would you consider it
an unwarranted luxury if I were to raise melons?

"On the shady side of the house, ivy is to be planted,
and on the west side, climbing roses. Finally it is to be
entirely covered and festooned with vines, just as it always
is in stories when a poet wishes to depict an idyllic romance.
Upstairs there is a gable-room which overlooks the garden,
wonderfully suited to an elderly lady who paints flowers,
or to a bachelor who makes verses. This room we wish to
rent. It will be a not inconsiderable contribution toward
paying the interest on the invested capital. We move in
on the first of April. Lore and the children are almost
beside themselves with delight. Now, you see, this is the
great piece of news!"

I endeavored, as well as I could, to share in the pleasure
of my good friend and promised to visit this glorified idyl
as soon as they were comfortably settled. One Sunday
toward the end of April, with this object in view, I jour-
neyed to Steglitz and was welcomed with much rejoicing
by the Hühnchen family. As I had already supposed, it
was an insignificant little cottage, but what these people
had made out of it was surprising. On the first floor,
besides a little entry, there were a tiny kitchen and three
rooms, one of which was as narrow as a bird-cage and
reminded me vividly of Hühnchen's bedroom in Hanover
where he could not draw off his boots without first opening
the door of the adjoining room. Into this apartment Hühnchen led me first and, indeed, with especial satisfaction.

"See, good friend," said he, "all fruits ripen gradually
upon the Tree of Fulfilment, and fall gently into one's lap.
My wish of years, ever since I was married, to have a
corner all to myself is now also gratified."

I glanced about the little space. Before the window
stood a table taking up the entire width of the room, covered with some green stuff that hung to the floor. Two
chairs and a book-shelf were all that there was of furniture—more could not very well have been crowded in.

A CANAL AT HAMBURG

On the wall opposite the book-shelf ('' gracefully grouped,''
as Hühnchen expressed it) hung the photograph of a
locomotive, portraits of his parents and of many friends;
the Technical Museum, the Ancestral Hall, and the Temple
of Friendship, as he described it.

With a sly shrewdness of look and manner he now pointed
to the green-covered table on which were writing-materials
and old books, and asked, '' Is there not something very
impressive and really imposing about that piece of furniture? It expresses a certain august grandeur, does it
not?''

I admitted this, smiling.

'' Infernal delusion!'' ejaculated Hühnchen; he raised
the cover and regarded me triumphantly. The table proved
to be nothing more than a huge packing box, placed on its
side with the opening toward the front.

We then inspected the other rooms of the dwelling and I
found everything as cozy and attractive and neat as was
possible for the simple furnishings to make it. Then we
went into the garden. It was unbelievable — the things that
were sown and planted in this limited area! There was a
potato patch four yards square, besides all kinds of imag-
inable kitchen truck in beds of diminutive dimensions.

''Above all things,'' said Hühnchen, '' I have endeavored
to have a great variety of cultivation; in this respect this
garden shall become the crowning achievement of this
estate.''

He drew a paper from his pocket and spread it out before
me. '' The plan for the cultivation of the soil,'' he said
impressively. '' Every year it will be reconstructed in
order to observe a scientific rotation of crops.''

All the beds were, on this paper, indicated in varying
light colors, and in a neat, round hand-writing the plantings
were noted down. Beside the walnut-tree, which was represented by a little green circle, I saw a black square with
the inscription, '' Little Hans.''

'' What is this? '' I asked.

"There lies buried our good little canary-bird," Hühnchen replied. "He must have taken cold during the moving, for directly afterward he puffed up his feathers and
became ill. Lore asserts that he coughed, but this may be
a mistake; he had at best very delicate health. Just
before his death, he twittered and sang very softly, as
if in a dream; then suddenly he fell from his perch and
was dead. It must have been heart-failure or something
similar. We buried him with much ceremony. First he lay
in state upon rose-colored cotton in a box with snowdrops.
Afterward, as the children carried him out, Lore played a
dirge. Here is his monument."

We had reached the nut-tree by this time, where a flat
stone, marked "Little Hans," was in evidence. A sprig of
ivy was planted beside it.

We explored the garden further. The part allotted to
fruit showed an increase of six gooseberry-bushes of as
many different varieties. There were the same number of
currant-bushes, while the specimens of raspberries reached
the imposing figure of twelve.

"Observe with reverence these two newly-planted trees,"
said Hühnchen—"a Gravenstein apple and a Napoleon
Butter-pear." He pronounced the last word with epi-
curean unction as though the juicy fruit were already melting on his tongue.

In conclusion, after I had admired the mountain range—
a creation of six boulders—and the pond—a buried water-
butt for catching rain-water—I noticed a tin vessel on the
top of the summer-house which as yet consisted only of
bare lattice-work. I inquired about it.

"Reservoir for the waterworks," Hühnchen informed
me. "The apparatus is still in course of construction.
When you come again to see us we will celebrate by letting
the great fountain play. That will give the whole a special
and festive touch.

*   *   *   *   *   *   *   *   *   *

During the course of the spring and summer I did not

come in contact with Hühnchen again. But in the latter
part of September I received a note from him whose contents were as follows:

STEGLITZ, *September* 28, 1881
Villa Hühnchen

Mr. and Mrs. Hühnchen request the honor of your presence at a
Vintage Festival, Sunday, the 2d of October, at 5 P. M.

PROGRAMME.

1. Reception of Guests.
2. Inspection of Garden and Menagerie.
3. Ushering in of Vintage by Salute of Cannon.
4. Gathering of Grapes and Nuts.
5. Procession of the Vintagers.
6. Fireworks.
7. Banquet.
8. Musicale and Dance.

R. S. V. P.

Needless to say, I accepted. But one other guest besides
myself had been invited, a dignified, elderly lady who
rented the gable-room and who there subsisted upon the
income from a modest property as well as upon the recollection of a brilliant past. She was a formal, pretentious
personage who, if one failed to pay her sufficient attention,
conveyed an impression of being neglected and aggrieved.

" She has seen better days," whispered Hühnchen to me.
" She comes of a wealthy family which was later, however,
much reduced in fortune. In her early days she dined off
silver-plate. She had five different opportunities to marry
profitably, once even a Count, but she did not choose to do
so. Hers has been a hard fate, and she has therefore become somewhat morbid and embittered — but, of course, we
treat her with indulgence, as you may well imagine."

Hühnchen, with much pride, showed me the garden. The
waterworks had been completed and proved to be a thread-
like fountain about a yard high, whose waters fell into a
basin lined with many-colored pebbles.

" Unfortunately it is a little asthmatic," said Hühnchen,

"for the reservoir is small and must be re-filled every half hour. However, it looks imposing and festive."

The grape-vine had yielded fifteen bunches of grapes this year and the walnut-tree bore twenty-one nuts.

"There were really twenty-five," explained Hühnchen, "but three fell prematurely and one disappeared in an incomprehensible manner. That same evening, however, as Lore was about to say good-night to the children, already in bed, they both began to sob unrestrainedly and confessed with many tears what had become of the missing nut. Hans, driven by the Demon of Desire, had appropriated it and had then enticed Frieda to share in his misdeed. They had gone to the attic with their plunder, and there consumed it together."

By this time we had reached the pear-tree. "Here is recorded a shameful deception," said Hühnchen. "The shoemaker has proved to be an arch liar, for instead of Bergamots, the tree has produced nothing but ordinary cooking pears. The children, however, derive much satisfaction from the fact, for they are especially fond of this common fruit."

After inspecting the menagerie in which the mammals were represented by a black rabbit, the feathered tribe by a tailless young starling, and the amphibians by a mournful tree-toad, Hühnchen led me to a shady corner of the little garden, where a pile of earth, weeds, decaying brush-wood, leaves, and refuse caught my eye.

"This creation here I beg of you to regard with respect," said he, "for here slumbers the future. This is, namely, the compost-heap. Strength and mildness, spice and sweetness, all lie buried here in order that they may, in the coming years, rise in all their glory and, as choice vegetable or luscious fruit, nourish and refresh us."

Just then the children came from the house, each provided with a little basket and scissors, and we betook ourselves to the summer-house where a small brass toy cannon, ready loaded, awaited us on the table. Hühnchen solemnly

lighted a piece of German tinder carefully fastened to a
stick, and then with great deftness fired the festive salute.
The cannon produced a feeble and muffled report, and the
vintage began. By reason of the excessive zeal of the young
vintagers it was finished in half a minute; the formal
gathering of the nuts did not require any more time.
Hühnchen now took a small tin fife out of his pocket, placed
himself in the lead of his descendants, and held a triumphal
procession through the garden while piping an animated
march to a pathetic melody distorted by a false tempo.
When this promenade was ended and the collected fruit
duly surrendered, Hühnchen made the preparations for the
fireworks, as darkness was already falling. After an ex-
pectant interval they were ushered in by the already
familiar cannon salute. The first part consisted of a grand
coruscating fire, on which at least twenty-five-pfennigs'
worth of powder had been squandered. The second part,
however, produced the greatest effect, the illumination of
the fountain with colored lights — a number which was
encored unanimously. This complimentary demand, however, could not be satisfied, for the powder was exhausted.
" The celebration is only half complete without a rocket,"
asserted Hühnchen; " but that is impossible on account of
the neighborhood; however, I can make a perfectly harmless kind of rocket."

Thereupon he stuck a finger in his mouth and imitated
so cleverly the noise of a rushing and exploding rocket that
we clapped our hands and admiringly exclaimed "Ah," as
the onlookers are apt to do when the shower of many-
colored stars brilliantly bursts forth — of course, always
excepting the formal old Spinster with the Aristocratic
Past. Solemnly she sat there like an ancient mummy and
looked inscrutable.

The supper was entirely in keeping with the other festivi-
ties. At each place lay a little card beautifully inscribed as
follows:

Menu

1. EATABLES

Potatoes boiled in their Jackets, and Pickled Herrings. Onion and Bacon sauce.

(N. B.   Potatoes and Onions grown in our own garden.)

Potato Pancakes with Currant Jam.
(N. B.   Specialty of Mrs. Hühnchen's.)

Bread and Butter.   Rare old Berlin Cheese.

Grapes and Walnuts.   (Own growing.)

2. DRINKABLES

Caraway Cordial, Gilka brand, and Beer from the world-renowned Brewery of Mr. Patzenhofer of Berlin.

This delicious meal was seasoned by the very entertaining speeches of Hühnchen, and by the general singing before the second course of Matthias Claudius' pretty song:

> " Pastry here, and Pastry there,
>   What do we care about Pastry? "

With special emphasis the last verse was vigorously sung by Hühnchen:

> " Right rosy the potatoes are,
>   And white as alabaster.
>   Assimilated quite with ease,
>   And man and wife and child appease —
>   In truth, a stomach-plaster."

We gradually reached the fruit, and here was recorded a sentiment of extravagance which one would not have expected in this household.   As the last bunch of grapes disappeared from the dish Hühnchen expressed himself in this wise: " How long and painstakingly has Mother Nature striven with spring rains and summer sunshine to ripen this bunch of grapes.   Months have been necessary to produce this lusciousness which now in a few moments' time is dissipated. This but gratifies me — my soul is uplifted and my heart is filled with satisfaction. The Earth is mine and I command it. What She with arduous labor has matured just serves to give a fleeting relish to my palate."

The dance followed. Mrs. Lore sat at the piano and played an ancient waltz, the Brümmer Waltz it was called, which for many years had been handed down in the family. It was the only dance-music that she could play. The elderly lady accepted my invitation with a tremendous curtesy and solemnly danced like an animated yard-stick, while Hühnchen hopped about merrily with his little daughter. As I sat beside the Spinster after the dance she became talkative and was moved to various confidences.

" The Hühnchens are good people," she said, " but when one has lived all one's life in the best society, as I have, one must say they are lacking in manners. I have given myself much trouble with the children to inculcate correct behavior, decorum, and grace; but are they not hopping about there like the children of peasants? And how loud they laugh! Yes, that is in the blood; that must be inborn. My sister, the wife of Councillor Ritzebügel of the Department of the Interior, has a daughter of the same age; but what a difference! Such tact, and such exquisite manners the girl has; no court-lady conducts herself better. When the child still lay in the cradle she already used her little hands in the most graceful manner. You will never see her running, or doing any other improper thing."

At this moment Hühnchen called me to see his diagram for the next year's planting of the garden.

" Pardon me for interrupting your conversation," said he, " but that about the garden-plan was only a pretext. You see, the old lady is troubled constantly with toothache. I have noticed several times today that she has put her hand to her cheek with an expression of suffering. Now I know that a little wine is an excellent remedy for this pain. Between you and me, she has several large bottles upstairs in a little cupboard from which she now and then takes a table-spoonful for this horrid pain. I wanted to fill the little glass for her which stands behind her. As I know she would not care to have you see this — you understand how it is with elderly ladies — I called you away. That's why, you see.''

Then he slipped quietly behind her and re-filled the little glass. After a while, as I came in sight of it again, it was empty. The bottle was near-by, however, and I noticed that Hühnchen now and then made occasion to go over there.

At last the old lady became quite genial, placed herself at the piano after much urging, and sang in a thin voice to the sympathetic whining of the little wheezy instrument: '' I'll not complain.'' The singing of this song, however, appeared to touch the chords of her inmost soul all too ruthlessly, for she was very much depressed afterward and sobbed audibly. She declared that she should never have sung this song, for such sad memories were associated with it. Then sighing regretfully, '' Oh, my youth,'' she was assisted upstairs by Mrs. Hühnchen.

'' She has had much sorrow,'' said Hühnchen, adding sympathetically: '' Poor, old, lonely creature!''

As the generous programme was now exhausted and the time for the Berlin train had arrived, I took my leave likewise, and thus ended the Vintage Festival at Leberecht Hühnchen's.

A CHRISTMAS EVE WITH LEBERECHT HÜHNCHEN

The Invitation

I had not seen my friend Leberecht Hühnchen for a long time, when one day, shortly before Christmas, I met him in Leipzig Street. He had been shopping, and was quite loaded down with bundles and packages which dangled from his buttons and fingers and which were stowed away over his person wherever a place could be found, so that he presented in his overcoat a greatly enlarged and irregular appearance which brought a smile to the lips of almost every passer-by. His pleasure at seeing me was unbounded, and he exclaimed: "If you have the time, do accompany me to the Potsdam Station, so that we can have a little chat together." I assented, and on the way, as usual, he opened the confidential flood-gates.

"Something very unusual happened last summer," he began, "I made some alterations to my house, adding two rooms, one upstairs and one downstairs. The elderly lady with her toothache and her Aristocratic Past was on this account obliged to move out, but in her place we have introduced something quite dazzling into our enlarged quarters, namely, a genuine Major, retired from service. He has a small position with the railroad and is equipped with various talents. He is especially fond of recounting little incidents from his past military career which possess a unique charm from the fact that they never have a point. Now imagine, just when one becomes interested and thinks, here's the point—snap, the story breaks off! This is an entirely new effect of very unusual power. On this account among ourselves we call him 'the Pointless Major.' He paints pretty pictures for the children, representing elegant young ladies with honey-sweet charms, and brave soldiers in absolutely regulation uniforms, while from the blue eyes of these warriors there flashes the heroic courage of a past Prussia, and victory perches upon the points of their mustachios.

"The gift of poetry was also bestowed upon him. Once upon a time he sent a comedy to Intendant Hülsen, who, however, returned it 'with a most friendly letter.' Since then he has kept it locked up in his desk, for with a pride worthy of imitation he declares, 'Upon no other than the imperial stage will I allow my work to be presented.'

"If you imagine that this exhausts his list of accomplishments, you are mistaken; no indeed; whenever the recollection of old times takes possession of him he sits down at the piano and in a light but quite agreeable little tenor voice sings all sorts of arias from operas no longer in existence. Yes, an agreeable, companionable gentleman, and not at all proud; he will celebrate Christmas Eve with us, for he is quite alone in this part of the world. As a companion-piece to the Major we have also invited the lady with the Aristocratic Past. They supplement each other admirably, and his indescribable gallantry lures an unwonted glow to her features. Indeed, there is no telling how it will end; she has a nice little property, and the Major, for one of his age, is still quite energetic. * * * '' Hühnchen waved first his left hand, then his right, as if he were introducing two people, then clasping his hands together, with an exceedingly sly expression said: '' Yes,— yes!''

'' By the way,'' he continued, '' it just occurs to me! Where are you going to be on that evening?''

I replied that I should probably sit at home and drown my melancholy thoughts in a lonesome punch. Hühnchen's eyes brightened. '' Of course you must come to us,'' he cried. '' Lore and the children will be more than delighted. It goes without saying that we shall have carp and you will also have punch at my house, made indeed from a very famous recipe. Now, no objections!'' I saw that there was no getting out of it, so accepted. Meanwhile we had reached the Potsdam Station; Hühnchen arrived just in time to clamber with his numberless packages into the train, and as he waved to me from the window and called '' Good-by, till next time!'' he was off for Steglitz.

On the Way

On the 24th of December the snow lay foot deep everywhere and it was bitterly cold. Hühnchen had begged me to come early, and so after a one o'clock luncheon I found myself on my way to the station. A peaceful unrest, if one may so call it, prevailed in the city at this time, and scarcely a person was seen who was not carrying something. Even the most hardened bachelor and the most conscienceless parent, as well as that pitiable class of human

MARKET PLACE AT GOSLAR

beings which considers the distribution of gifts a burdensome farce, had at last been caught in the stream, and to fulfil their Christmas duty had secured some trifles from toy and other shops, where at this season " confusion worse confounded " reigned.

The Christmas-tree venders stood shivering but contented among their diminished stock, and worked off their left-overs upon belated purchasers. Rocking-horses, which some time before had been in a sad state of disrepair, had in some mysterious manner vanished from their accustomed haunts, and in St. Nicholas' wonderful heavenly pastures had eaten themselves fat and sleek. Their scars were healed, and now from the shoulders of their bearers they looked contentedly with great glassy eyes into the cold winter day. Doll-houses of fabulous grandeur and great, wrapped objects of fantastic shapes staggered past; the delivery-wagons of the big stores hurried everywhere, halting now here, now there; the so-called " Kremser " vans, which the postal service is accustomed to hire at Christmas-time, rumbled heavily from house to house, well laden with treasures; drays thundered along the streets already swept clean or, where this was not the case, whistled and squeaked over the hard-frozen snow — in short, it was the contrary of the otherwise familiar saying, it was " the storm before the quiet."

This festive disquiet extended even to the train which went to Steglitz. The cars were filled with belated shoppers who anxiously guarded bundles of every description and immense paper-bags from which emanated odors of sweet pastries; in truth, one could safely have offered a prize to the one who was not thus provided with something to carry. I surely should not have won it, for besides a little box of sweetmeats from Thieles in Leipzig Street for Frau Lore, I had with me a cigar-holder for Hühnchen the bowl of which was made from the skull of a goose which, by means of clever painting, a pair of glass eyes, and a tongue of red cloth, had the appearance of a hideous, jagged devil's mask. I knew that this work of art would arouse in Hühnchen the greatest enthusiasm. For the children, Hans and Frieda, I had bought Robert Reinick's *Fairy-tales, Stories, and Songs,*— a book that I should like to give to every child who does not already possess it— and a doll which in the opinion of competent feminine authority was "simply sweet." So I suppose I can say that my Christmas conscience was as spotless as the freshly-fallen snow outside, and, with that peace of mind which the conviction of duty fulfilled accords one, I anticipated the immediate future.

A JOURNEY TO THE SOUTH POLE

Villa Hühnchen, as its owner, not without a slight touch of irony, was wont to call the little cottage, was, in spite of its enlargement, still a decidedly small dwelling, but it had a neat and pretty appearance; for Hühnchen, taking advantage of this opportunity, had had it freshly plastered and painted. On one of the frosted windows was a peep-hole the size of a silver dollar, which children love to make with a heated coin, and as I came in sight an eye disappeared from the spot and immediately another took its place and twinkled pleasantly at me. In the entry where an agreeable odor of coffee was noticeable, Hühnchen came cordially to meet me, calling out: " Welcome, dear Christmas guest; step into our not overheated, but nevertheless comfortable, festive halls. No amount of heat can overcome the cold of this winter, although the stoves have fairly roared the entire day. The children were so eager to keep a watch for you, they begged me to give them a mark to melt a hole on the frosted window-pane. But I said, Christmas comes but once a year, and so I loaned them a silver dollar for the purpose."

The Spinster with the Aristocratic Past was already there and did me the honor to remember me. The good lady appeared to be dressed today " fit to kill;" all sorts of ornaments jingled and sparkled everywhere and her whole person was enveloped in a fantastic haze of artificial youth. She looked like a newly bound edition of Matthison's Poems.

When Frau Lore and the children had been duly greeted, Hühnchen said: " Before we sit down to our coffee, dear friend, I must acquaint you with a peculiarity of this extraordinary house which has been realized through the alterations. As your skilled architect's eye has doubtless remarked, the new staircase leading upstairs has been built in what was formerly our large north room, and thus it happens that where you see that sofa, we now have a passageway which leads into the south room. We have not yet aspired to storm windows — single ones, by the way, have the advantage that they ventilate more thoroughly — and thus on such cold winter days as today the wonderful fact asserts itself that we in the microcosm of these two rooms can enjoy all zones and climates. Let us begin our travels here at the north end. Close to the window we find ourselves in the frigid zone, and can lay a finger on polar ice. This peep-hole shall represent the North Pole. Now we move toward the south, and near this grandfather's chair we reach the temperate zone. A tropical breeze is wafted to us from the stove at the entrance of the broad passageway. This stove indicates the tropic of Cancer. We pass it and arrive in the passageway, the torrid zone. This sofa which invites to repose is Kamerun. Here in a congenial climate I sometimes indulge in a postprandial nap, if pressing business of the Society of Contemporaries has detained me until the small hours of the night in the circle of my friends." Here he looked roguishly at his wife who, smiling, shook her finger at him reprovingly. Then he continued: " What you consider cracks in the wooden floor are the parallels of latitude, and this one here, which is larger than the rest, marks the equator. We are now, accordingly, in the southern hemisphere, and stepping through this open door into the next room we find another stove, the tropic of Capricorn. Slowly we pass through the south temperate and frigid zones till we are again confronted by polar ice. And, mark you, all this within the space of a few seconds and without the help of seven-league-boots like Peter Schlemihl who, meeting a polar bear in the North when botanizing, stumbled through all climes in his mad flight, now hot, now cold, and thus contracted that fatal pneumonia. We can do the same thing more comfortably in slippers. But now, let's have some coffee!"

Enter the Major

As we sat at coffee twilight fell, and gradually it became dark, much to the delight of the children who knew that soon now the distribution of gifts would take place. When Mrs. Hühnchen had lighted the lamp the creaking of boots was heard on the steps; some one knocked, and in walked a short, stocky gentleman who in his movements displayed dignified deliberation. "Major Puschel," said Hühnchen, introducing him. The Major greeted the ladies with wonderful gallantry and as, with a charming bow, he kissed the Spinster's hand and complimented her upon her appearance, a reflection of her former grandeur spread over her features, visibly beautifying them. From established military custom he brought his heels sharply together, made me a slight bow and while twisting the left point of his mustard-colored mustache upward, as was his habit, he said to me in the rasping voice which old soldiers so often affect: "When I was still engineer officer in charge of fortifications at Pillau, I had a comrade of your name. Only yesterday I was reminded of him. That is to say, in the evening I was not at all well as I had taken a bad cold and feared that I should not be able to join in this little fête here tonight. Then it occurred to me to make myself a big glass of grog; a voice within said that grog was just suited to my case. And, astonishing to say, this morning it was as if everything had been swept away, and I felt extremely well. Yes!"

At this he seated himself and looked about the circle with his round, water-blue eyes to note the effect of this marvelous cure.

Hühnchen chimed in at once. "Yes indeed, at times some of the most curious things will help sick people. In Hanover, when my friend Knövenagel was deathly sick and the doctors had given him up, he was seized with a consuming desire for loppered milk. His landlady was weak enough to bring him a large bowl of it, for she thought if he were going to die anyway he might as well have his wish gratified. Knövenagel ladled the whole bowlful down, turned on his side, fell asleep, sweat like a fire-hose, and by next morning the disease was conquered. It was not prepared for loppered milk."

"This is just why my comrade of Pillau came to my mind yesterday," said the Major. "He was suffering from typhoid fever, and the case was so critical that the doctor shook his head as to the outcome. It was on a Thursday, and the woman with whom he boarded had prepared peas, sauerkraut, and corned-beef. His door was left open for a moment and a wave of odors from the kitchen filled the room. My comrade thereupon insisted upon having some of that dish, and nothing would do but she must bring him some. And now this is the strangest part of it all; as he caught sight of the food he turned his face to the wall and would not touch it. No, he would not look at it nor touch it. Yes!"

Hühnchen gave me an amused glance at this unexpected conclusion, and I could not refrain from asking: "Did he recover?"

"Dear me, no," replied the Major, "he died that same night."

Meanwhile the children had become very restless and finally Hans brought a large shining mother-of-pearl shell on which lay the end of a small wax candle. This he handed to his father with a pleading look, while his sister supported the silent appeal.

"Very well, children," said Hühnchen, "the time and the hour have arrived." Then taking the candle-end, he showed it to me, and as he held it with a tender reverence between his finger-tips, he said: "You are aware, my dear friend, that in many places it is still the custom on Christmas Eve to burn the mighty Yule-log in the open fireplace, and the unconsumed portions are kept in order to kindle next year's log. We have, alas, no fireplace; they are not economical and heat the open air more than they do the rooms. I have, therefore, introduced another custom which I consider none the less ingenious. I carefully preserve all the candle-ends from the Christmas-tree in this mother-of-pearl shell and during the year they serve many purposes which require a brief flame, such as sealing letters, etc. Some pine-needles adhere to almost every one of them, and so a fragrant chain of sweet incense accompanies us through the entire year from one festival to another, and every time one of these ends is extinguished the children cry delightedly: 'Oh! how that smells like Christmas!' The last one of all—here it is—is under no circumstances whatever permitted to be used, for with that one are lighted the candles of next year's Christmas-tree. And upon this solemn business I now betake myself to the Place of Mysteries." Herewith he left the room, while the children from excitement and joyous expectation hopped about on tiptoe.

The Distribution of Gifts

"A very entertaining man, your husband," said the Major to Mrs. Hühnchen; "he always reminds me of a former acquaintance of mine, named Hirsewenzel, and, what is quite remarkable, he was very fond of Hamburg eel-soup. It must be admitted that he was of a more melancholy disposition than your husband, and when he was a bit tipsy and happened to hear music, he would sob and cry bitterly. Later he drifted to America, and it is said that he established a nice little new religion there. Yes!" I must confess that I was not always able to follow the Major's erratic leaps of thought. His fancy appeared to double on its tracks as does the hare when fleeing to cover.

Presently the house was suddenly filled with the shrill clamor of a table-bell and the children rushed to the hall beyond which the Christmas-room disclosed itself. We followed at more moderate pace and stepped into the Sanctuary, through whose door streamed the brilliant light of many candles. I must admit that the splendor was great, and the two children stood as if spellbound and dared not approach this gorgeous Sesame-cave so full of glistening and bedazzling treasures. But finally our eyes became accustomed to all this brightness, and soon we began to examine and to admire.

Hühnchen next claimed my attention on behalf of the fir-tree. "My dear fellow," said he, "it is a well-known fact that every one considers his own tree the finest and scorns all others just a trifle, but you surely must allow that my pride in this one is not without justification. Do you not feel that a certain harmony of color emanates from it, like delicate music? And this is not mere accident; no, it is the result of wise calculation and careful reflection. All these various papers and colored decorations are chosen by lamp-light in order that they may be effective by candle-light, and are combined according to the principle of complementary colors. What appears to you as natural and only charming is the result of severe meditation and sympathetic study of the matter, my boy. We also have a novelty this time, namely, gilded pine-cones. The poet Theodor Storm, whose works you also treasure so highly, likewise decorates his tree with them. The little fir-tree is indeed a bit crooked, and in many places where a branch should be, curiously enough there is none; but does this not

add a new charm? It is only a Philistine who raves over
absolute symmetry.''

Then assuming the attitude of one absorbed in the beauty
of the Sistine Madonna, he stood awhile regarding with
enthusiastic eyes the little crooked tree which, with its
variegated decorations, looked very much as they all do.

For their little daughter the parents had prepared a
doll-house which was truly fascinating and served as a
dwelling for a second Hühnchen family reduced to one-
tenth their natural size. Words cannot describe this masterpiece; suffice it to say that there was nothing lacking,
absolutely nothing, that belonged to the real Hühnchen
household, and that everything was of great elegance and
taste. The wardrobes were filled with the tiniest clothes
and house-linen; and the kitchen with the prettiest dishes;
even toys, picture-books, and copy-books were there of
Lilliputian size, and portraits of the Hühnchen ancestors
hung in neat gold frames on the walls.

The Major had also displayed his art in making for Hans
from pasteboard, an Hussar riding upon a steed in whose
veins there evidently flowed the blood of Arabia, while
the rider, accoutred according to regulation, was of such
valorous, heroic beauty that no one ventured to doubt his
power over all feminine hearts. For Frieda he had pasted
and illuminated a work of art of a more tender nature,
namely, The Sleeping Beauty in a rose bower, whose pale-
pink loveliness was full of charm and sweetness beyond
all human conception. And the sky-blue knight who had
just appeared and was bending over her had such dainty
little hands and feet, such large moon-eyes, and such a
fascinating mustache that one could see, a hundred paces
off, that he was a genuine prince. This work of art was
at the same time mechanical, for when one pulled a little
string the handsome knight bent down and kissed the
Sleeping Beauty, while she raised her arm, according to
Uhland's instructions:

"The Prince sought to discover
　If life the image blessed,
And bending down beside her
　His lips to hers he pressed.
Responded soon the maiden,
　Her breath came sweet and warm,
And, slumbering still, she circled
　His neck with clinging arm."

It would take entirely too long were I to attempt to describe and relate here all of the many surprises — for instance, the wonderful fortress with waterworks which Hühnchen had created for his boy, and all the trifles with which the parents gave one another pleasure. It was, as Hühnchen expressed it, "simply great!"

Over the Punch-bowl

The candles on the Christmas-tree gradually burned low and with cracklings and sputterings scorched the pine-needles and twigs, so that finally a general blowing-out contest began and the whole room was filled with Christmas fragrance. Then while we sat about conversing comfortably, and the children busied themselves with their new possessions, the time for supper drew nigh, and Hühnchen disappeared in a mysterious manner for a half hour. When he reappeared a delicious odor of punch followed him; we betook ourselves to the next room for the supper, where we paid due honor to the excellent carp as well as to the no less good liquid refreshment.

"The recipe for this wine-punch was given me by my friend Bornemann," said Hühnchen. "He used to give three punch-evenings every winter to his good comrades, because he himself loved it so inordinately. I was usually the first to arrive and regularly found him at the table, which was already set and laden with all kinds of good things, while before him stood an immense punch-bowl. He appeared serious and meditative, and already his face was rather flushed. 'My dear friend,' he would then say, 'I am glad that you have come for I need your judgment. I have been sitting here for an hour, tasting one glass after another without coming to any conclusion other than that the punch is good. In spite of this careful investigation I can reach no other decision; what say you?' Then I would drink a glass and reply: 'Wonderful, as always!'— 'That relieves me greatly,' he would say; 'this confirmation of my own opinion pleases me!' Then he would empty another glass, sipping it thoughtfully and continue: 'Yes, you are right; I have done my share, now see to it that you do yours!' However, it never happened that our united efforts succeeded in reaching the bottom of this enormous bowl, but after we, with heavy heads, had taken ourselves off, friend Bornemann still sat there like an oak-tree, silent and solitary, and smoked and drank until he could see the bottom of the vessel. And then, with a melancholy look into its empty depths, he would sigh a little and go to bed.''

The Major meanwhile had become somewhat restless and had already made several attempts to interrupt the quietly flowing stream of words of his loquacious host; Hühnchen, however, always took possession of the floor again; but when he began to enlarge in enthusiastic terms upon cherished habits and upon the sweet influence of tradition and the established customs of certain days, the Major cleared his throat so raspingly and persistently and made such energetic efforts to enter his wedge into some rift in the conversation that Hühnchen at last was silent and gave him a chance to talk.

"Yes, speaking about the force of habit," said he, "I have had a very unusual experience. When I was still engineer in charge of fortification at Pillau we had there a military convict; the fellow was sentenced to twenty years and had always behaved himself well. Well, one day his term expired and we said to him: 'You are free, you can go now!' The fellow was frightened and implored: 'Oh! do let me stay here; where can I go? I know no one in the whole world.' Yes, we were sorry for him and let

LIMBURG AN DER LAHN

him remain in his old cell to which he had become accustomed, and occupied him as well as we could. So there he sat and cut staves for the reinforcement of the sloping turf-banks and continually cut staves and was entirely satisfied. That lasted quite a time, and I was meanwhile transferred to another garrison. Yes!''

The Major regarded us pleasantly for a while with his colorless eyes, and, when he observed that we appeared to expect something more, continued: '' When after a few years I came again to Pillau and wanted to look the fellow up, he was no longer there. He was no longer there. Yes!''

A story truly of remarkable effect! When one supposes that he still has a considerable mouthful in his glass and then suddenly finds that it is entirely empty, such a discovery would make a similar impression. But the lady with the Aristocratic Past did not seem to feel this lack. She listened with evident attention to the Major's stories and never failed at their close to commend them regularly with a '' very interesting,'' or, '' highly ingenious.'' As the Major probably was seldom accorded such consideration, it pleased him very much and strengthened the favorable opinion he had already formed of the cleverness and unusual intelligence of this lady, and he could not refrain on these occasions from casting admiring glances at her from his clear, round eyes, while fiercely twisting his left mustache. Finally he became quite excited under this unaccustomed approval and began to relate stories of manœuvres and drills which sometimes had neither an end nor a beginning nor a middle, and to lie dreadfully — about a certain Lieutenant Besenried, for instance, who was so immensely tall that, '' when I stood before him, I saw only buttons, and when I wished to look him in the face it was like looking up at the clock in the church steeple. But I can assure you, believe it or not as you please, we had a fellow in our company who was still taller. He was called Kickebusch and came from Dramburg. When he was seated and began to rise, it always took almost five minutes before he was entirely erect.''

This incited Hühnchen again to draw similar yarns from the treasures of his experiences — of the iron stove which he had invented, that only needed to be wound up once in the morning, when it would run about the room in overshoes until it was glowing hot and then would place itself in the corner and throw off heat;— or of the mouse-trap animal of Borneo, to whom Nature had given a breath that smelled enticingly of fried bacon, and by means of which the mice, which constituted its food, were lured into its jaws.

As the lies were bandied back and forth between the two, Mrs. Hühnchen finally became tired of this sort of entertainment and suggested a little music. This was hailed on all sides with pleasure, and the Spinster must, in spite of many objections, take her place at the piano — when it developed that she had brought her music with her! She was indeed not quite sure, but a careful search through her reticule disclosed a number of pieces. The lady was apparently much astonished over it; she must have put them there absent-mindedly, she assured us, as she was often totally preoccupied by her many absorbing ideas.

Romeo and Juliet

While the Spinster was busy at the piano with Mrs. Hühnchen, each rummaging among the sheets of music, the Major said to Hühnchen: ''A very agreeable lady, who gains upon acquaintance! One can see that she has moved in good society. She lives in comfort?'' Hühnchen, knowing very well what the Major was driving at, for on former occasions the latter had endeavored by all sorts of subtle means to satisfy himself on this point, replied innocently: '' Yes, I suppose so, especially since she has been free from the toothache which formerly troubled her constantly.''

'' Toothache is bad,'' said the Major rather disappointed; '' I knew a person who considered himself fortunate when he carried his last tooth on his watch-chain. He was a very amusing fellow, could do very wonderful tricks with cards, and died later of cholera. Yes!'' Then suddenly assuming an easy tone of studied indifference he said carelessly: '' She is a lady of independent means?''

Hühnchen at last took pity on his curiosity and replied: '' She has about twenty-five thousand marks absolutely safely invested in gilt-edged mortgages.''

'' H'm, h'm,'' ejaculated the Major, evidently agreeably surprised; and then he became very reflective. Meantime the Spinster had decided upon a song, and playing the prelude, began:

> "A lonely pine is standing
>   On the crest of a northern height;
> He sleeps, and a snow-wrought mantle
>   Enshrouds him through the night.
>
> He's dreaming of a palm-tree
>   Afar in a tropic land,
> That grieves alone in silence
>   Mid quivering leagues of sand." *

During the singing the Major stared at the lady with his round expressionless eyes and twisted both mustaches with consuming eagerness. Scarcely had she finished when he broke into vigorous applause and betaking himself to the piano with much bringing together of heels and many bows, exhausted his supply of elaborate compliments which the Spinster absorbed with much relish and rewarded with gracious, but careful, smiles. For Nature had bestowed a rather large mouth upon her, and as a rule it pleased her to appear as if about to say '' prunes and prisms.'' The Major accidentally spied a piece of music and his eyes brightened: '' Oh! what do I see, my dear lady!'' he cried. '' Why, here you have the duet from Romeo and Juliet. How often have I sung it in my lieutenant days with Miss Esmeralda von Stintenberg of the noble family of

---

* From Heine's *Book of Songs*. Translated by Charles Wharton Stork, VOL. VI of THE GERMAN CLASSICS.

Käselow! Oh, I remember every note perfectly.'' Here
he began to trill vigorously in his thin little tenor, and the
end of it was that the two good people set to work on this
old-fashioned duet by some obsolete Italian composer whose
name I have forgotten. It was rich to see how the Major
at the tender words of the song looked ardently and triumphantly, as becomes a soldier, upon the lady, while she,
with maiden modesty, lowered her eyes and even succeeded
in bringing a fairly successful blush to her cheek. The
couple were so absorbed in their music that they never
noticed when Mrs. Hühnchen quietly slipped out to listen at
the door of the room where the children were, to see if the
healthy sleep of youth were proof against the vigor of these
tones. Then, after a while, Hühnchen under the pretext
of showing me something, I know not what, in his little
study, mysteriously led me away and I gladly followed, for
music of this sort is improved by distance. When we returned after some time there was no sound to be heard, and
as Hühnchen silently opened the door a wonderful scene
presented itself. Pine and Palm had found one another
and no longer stood solitary, but were held in a tender
embrace. And as the slender Palm was a trifle higher than
the stocky Pine, she had gently bowed her summit, and,
forsooth, they kissed each other! As they hurriedly separated and the Spinster, embarrassed, hid her face in her
hands, the Major, victorious and triumphant, drew her hand
through his arm, stepped forward heroically and spoke,
while with his free left hand he twirled his mustache:
'' Gentlemen, I have the honor to present my betrothed.
Yes!''

Here at last was a point and a right good one too. And
I do not believe that I can find a better with which to con-
clude this little story of a Christmas-eve festival with
Leberecht Hühnchen. '' Yes!''